A Century of International Adjudication: The Rule of Law and it Limits

Jean Allain

T·M·C·ASSER PRESS
The Hague

Published by T.M.C. ASSER PRESS,
P.O.Box 16163, 2500 BD The Hague, The Netherlands

Sold and distributed in North, Central and South America
by Kluwer Law International,
675 Massachusetts Avenue, Cambridge, MA 02139, U.S.A.

In all other countries, sold and distributed
by Kluwer Law International, Distribution Centre,
P.O.Box 322, 3300 AH Dordrecht, The Netherlands

ISBN 90-6704-125-4

Lay-out and cover: Oasis Productions, Nieuwerkerk a/d IJssel, The Netherlands
Printing and binding: Koninklijke Wöhrmann BV, Zutphen, The Netherlands

PREFACE

This study considers the first century of international adjudication as a permanent fixture of the international society. By using specific international courts to which I was attached, as either a researcher or an employee, I was allowed to consider the various limitations to effective adjudication on the international plane.

I recall the day in January of 1992 when the seeds of this manuscript were first planted. I was on the fourth-floor of the Loeb Building at Carleton University leafing through a copy of Thomas Burgenthal's *International Human Rights Law in a Nutshell* when I came upon a chapter on the Inter-American Court of Human Rights. "How could this be?", I thought. "A little known human rights court in a part of the world fraught with human rights abuses".

That semester, I followed through on a course in international human rights law with Professor Maureen Davies and accepted a University Fellowship to do graduate work at Brock University (Canada) the following year. Supported in my interest by Professor James Patrick Sewell, I sought and received an Organization of American States Fellowship to spend an academic year studying the Inter-American Court of Human Rights, *in situ*, in San José, Costa Rica. It is from this period that I witnessed first-hand how the Inter-American Court, although similar on paper to the European Court of Human Rights, was limited in its effectiveness through the lack of financing and staffing allocated to it by American States. While in San José, I also conducted research on the 1908 Central American Court of Justice, which is published in Chapter Three. The legacy of the Court demonstrates that political machinations can impede and, in this specific instance, ultimately destroy an international court.

Having completed my Fellowship requirements in Central America, personal fortune found me in Germany and soon thereafter enrolled me at the *Institut universitaire de hautes études internationales* (IUHEI) of the University of Geneva. By chance in my first year, Professor Lucius Caflisch was charged with teaching a course on the peaceful settlement of international disputes; and I attached myself to his star. Ultimately, this was a very fruitful relationship for me, because Professor Caflisch, (who is currently a Judge of the European Court of Human Rights) focused on the prose which allowed me to concentrate on the content. Also, this business-like relationship allowed for frank exchanges and the setting of specific expectations with which I felt very comfortable. I would like to take this opportunity to publicly thank him for supervising my work.

Between the years of my D.E.S. degree, I was fortunate enough to land a six-month position as a legal assistant (law clerk) at the International Criminal Tribunal for the Former Yugoslavia (ICTY) located in The Hague. It is from the insights gained then and later as a consultant to the Defense team of Zenjil Delalic (the first accused international war criminal acquitted since Nuremberg) that I considered the role that judges play in the ensuring respect for the rule of law. Various cases before the Yugoslav Tribunal are considered in Chapter Five to demonstrate the extent to which judges have sought to establish an "effective" international criminal law system often at the expense of the rights of the accused, and as a result have limited the effectiveness of international adjudication. Their judgement may well have placed the ICTY on the same slippery slope of 'political trials' which was first trodden upon at Nuremberg and Tokyo.

After my second full year in Geneva, I returned to The Hague and spent the rest of 1997 and a large part of 1998 at the Peace Palace Library conducting research on the 'Hague System' of adjudication. Conducting research in the same building as the Permanent Court of Arbitration and the International Court of Justice allowed me to consider the structural limitation of an international judicial system predicated on volunteer acceptance of adjudication. I would like to thank Francisca Markx-Veldhuijzen and the other staff members for their assistance. I would further like to acknowledge the stackers in the backroom who, due to the nature of the Library's system, were forced to carry literally tons of books to my desk over that period.

During the summer of 1998, I was accepted on an exchange programme known as the Grotius Research Co-operation Network, from IUHEI to conduct research at the T.M.C. Asser Institute for Private and Public International Law and European Law, in The Hague. However, my time there was cut to a few short weeks as I accepted my present position at the American University in Cairo. I would like to thank Professor Enid Hill and Provost Tim Sullivan for having the faith in hiring me at that juncture of my academic career. I believe this book, in part, proves their sound judgment.

I returned to the exchange programme at the Asser Institute during the summer of 1999 with the assistance of a Research Grant from the American University and completed the final chapter there, while having the good fortune of having shared an office with Dr. Andrea Ott who gave me many insights and cut several weeks off a steep learning curve. My time at the Asser Institute was rewarding in two manners: it first allowed me to focus on the European Court of Justice in my attempt to demonstrate that the rule of law can be effective internationally if States so desire. The second was the willingness of Marjolijn Bastiaans of T.M.C. Asser Press to guide my manuscript through its publication.

Finally, the glue that holds this recollection together is no longer in my life and it is to her that this book is dedicated, as it could not have been achieved without her.

Cairo, October 29, 2000

JA

Für Carolin

TABLE OF CONTENTS

TABLE OF CASES

INTRODUCTION

1. Introduction

As Louis Henkin wrote in 1979, "almost all nations observe almost all principles of international law and almost all of their obligations almost all of the time"[1]. Yet, is this not an accurate assessment, by analogy, to municipal systems where laws are respected in most but not all cases? What distinguishes the municipal systems from the international system is the ability, in situations where a law is not observed, to have a third party ensure respect for it. A monopoly on the use of force goes a long way towards insuring respect for the law municipally; yet for the rule of law to exist, more is required. For the rule of law to be given effect municipally – and, for that matter, internationally – there must exist a system of adjudication which will rule on the law, render findings, and make judgments. Where the system breaks down on the international plane, where it fails to place the rule of law over self-interest, is where limitations are found to effective adjudication. It is these limits which are worthy of investigation.

While it has been said that the concept of the rule of law on the international level "is more easily invoked than understood", thus "contributing to the ease with which it may be invoked"[2], the opposite may be more accurate. That States have understood, in quite clear terms, what the 'rule of law' requires, has not precluded them from praising it when they stood to benefit and turning their backs to it when it no longer suited their interests. This is where adjudicative organs come into play. If we are to acknowledge that an international system governed by law rather than politics is why international law exists, and that this is proper, then the recourse to third parties to settle legal disputes is paramount. The legal means of dispute settlement – adjudication – have existed as permanent institutions on the international plane for only one hundred years. Recourse to international law to settle disputes has made significant headway this century, but any progress that has been achieved has been limited by States.

The focus of this manuscript is to highlight the majority of international courts, both past and present, and to establish the limits imposed on such adjudicative organs. By using specific judicial organs to draw out specific issues, this work seek to highlight both the evolution of international adjudication and to pinpoint some of the failings of the State system to allow international courts fully to subscribe to the rule of law. Primary consideration will be given to the voluntary

[1] Louis Henkin, *How Nations Behave*, 1979, p. 47.

[2] Arthur Watts, "The International Rule of Law", *German Yearbook of International Law*, Vol. 36, 1993, p. 15.

nature of international adjudication, which allows States to auto-determine whether they will be bound by an obligation to adjudicate and to respect the judgments of international courts. Over the first two chapters, it will become evident to what extent this voluntarism impedes full respect for international law. At quite specific times, in 1899, 1907, 1920, and again in 1945, jurists put forward schemes for obligatory recourse to binding settlement, yet States balked. As a means of placating those who advocated that law should reign internationally, they built what may be called 'The Hague System' of adjudication. Made up of the Permanent Court of Arbitration and the current International Court of Justice, these institutions lack obligatory jurisdiction and as a result are effectively bit players on the international stage.

Having considered this structural limitation to international adjudication, the book will highlight, over Chapters 3 and 4, further limitations imposed by States to the full respect for the rule of law. The rise and fall of the first full-time international court, the 1907 Central American Court of Justice, will be considered to demonstrate to what extent political machinations can, not only limit the effectiveness of a court, but cause its demise. This example of political impediments to the effectiveness of the rule of law is followed by a display of how financing can effect international adjudication. A comparison of the European and Inter-American human rights systems is undertaken to demonstrate that despite having had analogous constitutive instruments, international courts can vary in their effectiveness. The lack of backing of the Inter-American Court by American States is thus highlighted to demonstrate to what extent an international court can be hobbled by lack of support.

Beyond the limitations to the rule of law which can be attributed to States, international adjudication is only effective to the extent which its guardians – international judges – are prepared to fully integrate the rule of law. Chapter 5 considers the role of judges in upholding full respect for the rule of law and shows where they have failed to do so. Individual cases heard before the International Criminal Tribunal for the former Yugoslavia are brought forward to highlight the fact that judges have been inclined, in certain situations, to play fast and loose with the rights of the accused so as to ensure a *prima facie* 'effective' international criminal law system seen to be placing criminals behind bars. This type of development in international criminal law, as the legacy of Nuremberg attests, demonstrates that if the rule of law is not respected by judges, proceedings will be considered as nothing more than show trials.

Finally, having considered the various limits to the rule of law at the international level, Chapter 6 considers the European Court of Justice. So effective has this Court been in upholding the rule of law that the European Community is seen as being set apart from traditional international law, as being *sui generis*. Yet the European Court is an international court. Its effectiveness lies not in its qualitative nature, but in the quantitative output. The achievements of the Luxembourg Court in the domain of economic integration make it possible to realize to what extent international law can be dynamic. Fundamentally, the limits of the rule of law are not insurmountable. Yet this study points to the various obstacles which have been placed in the path of the rule of law on the international plain. Does the evolution of the European Court point in a new direction away from those impediments? Not entirely, but what the experience of that Court does, is allow us to realize how malleable international law can be. Using this as a basis, the call for respect of the rule of law on the international plain is not impossible, it is within the grasp of those that are willing to reach out and advocate it.

2. The Rule of Law

Before embarking on the study of the various adjudicative organs presented in this piece, consideration should first be given to the notion of the 'rule of law' to establish its parameters. A.V. Dicey, in his 1885 British classic *Introduction to the Study of the Law of the Constitution*, outlined the basis of what is to be understood as the 'rule of law' at the municipal level. He spoke of the rule of law as reflected in three concepts: "the absolute supremacy or predominance of regular law as opposed to the influence of arbitrary power"; "equality before the law" for all citizens including the sovereign; and "the general principles of the constitution [that] are with us the result of judicial decisions determining the rights of private persons in particular cases brought before the courts"[3]. Discounting the common-law predisposition to depend on judge-made law, the rule of law must to be understood as imposing a hierarchy whereby law reigns supreme and every person is subject to the law.

The rule of law may be said to be more effective at the municipal level than at the international level, as a State has a monopoly of wielding power to insure its respect. There the rule of law is strongest, for the State apparatus guarantees that the legal framework that has been established is respected by the effective maintenance of the legal order and through the proper and effective implementations of the "law-making, law-determination and law-enforcement functions" of the State[4].

The picture of the legal framework on the international level is, by comparison, fundamentally alien to that of municipal law. Yet a near-analogy of how international law functions can be found within municipal systems when considering the laws governing the conduct of legislators. Within the very limited field of law governing the privileges and immunities of parliamentarians, we find a regime in which individuals (like States at the international level) enact laws for themselves. Yet this analogy does not go very far, for the laws governing the

[3] A.V. Dicey, *Introduction to the Study of Law of the Constitution*, 1960, pp. 195, 202.
[4] Antonio Cassese, *International Law in a Divided World*, 1986, p. 13.

privileges and immunities of parliamentarians to be fully analogous to international law would require that they be adopted unanimously (and not simply by majority) and that any legislator who voted against such a law would not be bound by it. This is clearly not the case, as parliamentarians are not above the law and thus all fall under the umbrella of the State apparatus ensuring respect for the rule of law.

By way of contrast, internationally, a State will not always respect fully the rule of law[5]. The international community forms a decentralized system where each State auto-interprets the law and, by implication, determines whether it will integrally respect any given rule. It is only where States agree to surrender to a third party the ability to interpret the law that it may be said that the rule of law exist to its full extent on the international level. This is not to say that where States have not surrendered this ability, a lawless society ensues. On the contrary, a simple examination of State action on a daily basis demonstrates that, to a very large degree, States respect and abide by their legal obligations. Furthermore, the regime of State responsibility fills the *lacuna* left by a lack of universal system of obligatory dispute settlement. Thus, in cases where a State is not bound by an obligation to adjudicate, a breach of international law may be considered a wrongful act which entails international responsibility. However, even in cases where responsibility is at issue, a State must be willing, either bilaterally or with the assistance of a third party, to accept responsibility and give satisfaction to an injured State. Such acts are voluntary, however, the rule of law requires more – it requires that the law be respected as binding. States respect international law because it is in their interest to do so; the rule of law, however, mandates that legal obligations be respected at all times, no matter their perceived benefit, value, or outcome.

If commitment to the rule of law is to be taken seriously, it must be understood that this concept is intrinsically linked to third-party dispute settlement and more specifically to obligatory third-party settlement. This line of thought is picked up by Richard Bilder, who expresses the opinion that "[s]ubjecting nations to the rule of law has been equated with subjecting their behavior to the judgment of impartial international tribunals"[6]. This link between the rule of law

---

[5] See generally J. L. Brierly, "The Rule of Law in International Society", in H. Lauterpacht and H. Waldock (eds.), *The Basis of Obligation in International Law and Other Papers*, 1958, pp. 250-264; G. Fitzmaurice, "The United Nations and the Rule of Law", *Transactions of the Grotius Society*, Vol. 38, 1953, pp. 135-151; F. N. Keen, *Crossing the Rubicon: The Passage from the Rule of Force to the Rule of Law among Nations*, 1939; J. Quigley, "Prospects for the International Rule of Law", *Emory International Law Review*, Vol. 5, 1991, pp. 311-320; "The New World Order and the Rule of Law", *Syracuse Journal of International Law and Commerce*, Vol. 18, 1992, pp. 75-110; and A. Watts, *op. cit.* n. 2, pp. 15-45.

[6] Richard B. Bilder, "Some Limitations of Adjudication as a International Settlement Technique", *Virginia Journal of International Law*, Vol. 23, 1983, p. 1. As a basis for this proposition, Bilder cites Herman Mosler and Rudolf Bernhardt, *Judicial Settlement of International Disputes*, 1974.

and its applicability has been further emphasized by Gerald Fitzmaurice who wrote:

> The concept of the denoting of The Rule of Law may now be restated in more specific terms as denoting the considerations and settlements of all issues that arise between States, or in international organisations, by reference to the rules of general international law and to treaty obligations, wherever those rules or obligations are applicable or relevant, and – perhaps even more important – the practice of considering and settling these issues by the use of appropriate legal methods and procedures specifically adapted to that end[7] .

The rule of law is further strengthened through obligatory third-party dispute settlement on account of the fact that if a State knows that at the end of the day it will have to appear before an adjudicative organ, it will be made to focus more sharply on gaining the best diplomatic settlement possible in an attempt to avoid an imposed settlement. It is within these parameters that we may speak of the rule of law.

---

[7] Gerald Fitzmaurice, "The United Nations and the Rule of Law", *Transactions of the Grotius Society*, Vol. 38, 1953, p. 135.

Chapter 1
THE PERMANENT COURT OF ARBITRATION

1. Introduction

The most fundamental limit to the rule of law being applied in its integrity on the international plane is the voluntary nature of adjudication. Without hesitation, it may be said that States understand clearly what the rule of law entails and that they have contested its institutionalization for nearly two hundred years. States have been forced to struggle against the establishment of a system of obligatory adjudication because, time and again, non-governmental groups have assailed them. For most of the nineteenth century, States were under constant pressure to establish treaties and dispute settlement mechanisms geared to obligatory arbitration. It was only at the turn of the century, with the realization that peace movements could not be discounted, that it was understood that States would have to accommodate the wishes of those who advocated the rule of law at the international level. However, accommodation did not mean total surrender; States provided morsel after morsel of an adjudicative system until the pressure from outside governmental corridors had subsided. The outcome of this process was the Permanent Court of Arbitration: not a very impressive legacy for those who advocate obligatory recourse to arbitration as opposed to war. That legacy would prove its futility during the first half of the twentieth century, when European States, discounting the rule of law and their legal obligations, plunged their people into two World Wars.

As much as the Permanent Court of Arbitration (PCA) was futile in preventing the First World War, the establishment of the Permanent Court of International Justice (PCIJ) in 1920 had little effect on the move towards the Second World War. Over the following two chapters, this survey will consider these organs, which together may be referred to as the 'Hague System' of dispute settlement, thus demonstrating that, time and again, States have had the opportunity to establish a system based on the rule of law but have chosen not to. While fine words have been spoken as to the virtue of an international system which mandates that all legal disputes be settled by recourse to adjudication, when the time came to have those words turned into deeds, very few States were prepared to do so. The following two chapters consider the evolution of the current system of dispute settlement in an attempt to demonstrate the dichotomy that has always existed between the assertions of States in favour of obligatory adjudication and a practice which is, in many ways, in dire opposition to such pronouncements. The movement towards the 'Hague System' has its genesis in the peace movements of the nineteenth century, which placed great pressure on States to seek the peaceful resolution of their disputes by way of mandatory arbitration. The aims of such movements, however, were channeled through such organizations as the Inter-Parliamentary Union and the Institute of International Law, which were looking for a common ground between the wishes of States to have an unfettered right to settle disputes through belligerent means and the international peace movement, intent on having States assume the obligation to have all their disputes settled by arbitration.

Time and again, whether at the Hague Peace Conferences of 1899 and 1907, or at the preparatory discussions for the establishment of the Permanent Court of International Justice in 1920 and for the International Court of Justice (ICJ) in 1945, a large majority of States expressed their willingness to support obligatory recourse to adjudication, be it arbitration or judicial settlement. On each occasion, however, their deeds fell short of the pronounced goals. As a result, the 'Hague System' is simply another decentralized international system which allows each State individually to determine the obligations it will undertake. Thus, when examining the fundamental nature of international adjudication, we look at a system predicated on *voluntary* undertakings: Each State may determine, first, whether it will join the system made available by the provisions establishing the PCA or the ICJ; and, second, under what conditions it will join. It is this structural flaw of the international system, allowing for the voluntary nature of international adjudication to persist, that undermines the rule of law and is its most fundamental limit internationally.

1.1. **Voluntary Nature of Adjudication**

The fundamental limitation of the rule of law in international adjudication is its voluntary nature[1]. It cannot be emphasized too strongly that any case brought be-

[1] See generally S. A. Alexandrov, R*eservations in Unilateral Declarations Accepting the Compulsory Jurisdiction of the International Court of Justice*, 1995; N. Becirevic, "Limitations and Expectations of the Compulsory Settlement of Disputes According to the United Nations Convention on the Law of the Sea", *Thesarus Acroasium*, Vol. 17, 1991, pp. 675-686; R. B. Bilder, "Some Limitations of Adjudication as a International Settlement Technique", *Virginia Journal of International Law*, Vol. 23, 1983, pp. 1-12; W. B. Briggs, "Reservations to the Acceptance of Compulsory Jurisdiction of the International Court of Justice, *Collected Courses of The Hague Academy of International Law*, Vol. 93, 1958, pp. 229-363; M.K. Bulterman and M. Kuijer, *Compliance with Judgments of International Courts*, 1996; J.P. Cot and A. Pellet, "Article 94", *La Charte des Nations Unies*, 1989, pp. 1275-1285; R.R. Churchill and J.R. Young, "Compliance with Judgments of the European Court of Human Rights and Decisions of the Committee of Ministers: The Experience of the United Kingdom, 1975-1987", *British Yearbook of International Law*, Vol. 62, 1991, pp. 283-346; J. Elkind, *Non-appearance before the International Court of Justice: A Functional and Comparative Analysis*, 1984; K.O. Kufuor, "Securing Compliance with the Judgements of the ECOWAS Court of Justice", *African Journal of International and Comparative Law*, Vol. 8, 1996, pp. 1-12; S. M. Schwebel, "The Compliance Process and the Future of International Law", *Justice in International Law*, 1994, pp. 598-607; and R. Wägenbaur, "How to Improve Compliance with European Community Legislation and the Judgments of the European Court of Justice", *Fordham International Law Journal*, Vol. 19, 1996, pp. 936-950.

fore an international adjudicative body must have gone through a process of acceptance on the part of both parties, be it by way of an agreement with respect to the case at hand or by an undertaking to future cases[2]. As was noted as early as 1923, in the *Eastern Carelia* case, it:

> is well established in international law that no State can, without its consent, be compelled to submit its disputes with other States whether to mediation or to arbitration, or to any other kind of pacific settlement[3].

While one of the guiding principles of the current international system is that States "shall settle their international disputes by peaceful means"[4], this is to be understood as trying to ensure that dispute settlement is not undertaken through belligerent action. This provision does not amount to an obligation to settle a difference; it is simply an obligation, once a State has committed to settling a dispute, to do so peacefully[5].

While it may be said that all disputes, whatever their nature, could, if containing a legal aspect, be settled by recourse to adjudication, this type of thinking has never been held in high esteem by States. So while Robert Jennings and Hans Kelsen are quick to agree with Hersch Lauterpacht's assessment that

> there is no fixed limit to the possibilities of judicial settlement; that all conflicts in the sphere of international politics can be reduced to contests of a legal nature; and that the only decisive test of the justiciability of the dispute is the willingness of the disputants to submit the conflicts to the arbitrament of the law[6].

States remain obstinately defiant of such advocacy. However, as was determined in the first judgment rendered by the Appeals Chamber of the International Criminal Tribunal for the former Yugoslavia:

> [t]he doctrines of "political questions" and "non-justiciable disputes" are remnants of the reservations of "sovereignty", "national honour", etc. in very old arbitration treaties. They have receded from the horizon of contemporary international law, except for the occasional invocation of the "political question" argument before the International Court of Justice in advisory proceedings and, very rarely, in contentious proceedings as well.

---

[2] An exception to this principle may be made for individuals accused of international crimes who appear before international tribunals almost exclusively without having consented.

[3] *Status of Eastern Carelia* case, Permanent Court of International Justice, 23 July 1923, Series B, No. 5, 1923, p. 27.

[4] See Article 2(3) of the Charter of the United Nations.

[5] Brownlie points out the obvious when he writes that the "absence of a duty to settle disputes constitutes a gap in the international system". Ian Brownlie, *Principles of Public International Law*, 1990, p. 270.

[6] Hersch Lauterpacht, *The Function of Law in the International Community*, 1933, p. 164, as quoted in: Robert Jennings, International Courts and International Politics, 1986, p. 3.

> The Court has consistently rejected this argument as a bar to examining a case. It considered it unfounded in law.[7]

As will be demonstrated, when States have consented beforehand to obligatory adjudication, they have done so only in restricted and limited forms. Such limitations have taken two distinct forms. First, States have excluded from the body of agreements envisioning adjudication certain aspects of the competence of a court or arbitration board. In a general manner, these exceptions have been formulated with respect to overriding categories of disputes such as those involving "national sovereignty"[8], "the principles of the Constitution" of a State[9], "the vital interests, national independence or honour"[10], "the interests of third parties"[11], or "political independence or territorial integrity"[12]. The second method of limiting the field in which States consent to undertake obligatory adjudication is through the use of reservations. While a State may agree to a treaty provision that calls for disputes to be settled via adjudication, it may reserve the right to have only specific items adjudicated[13], or exclude specific items from consideration[14]. Typically, such reservations are made in a separate declaration at the time of accepting the jurisdiction of an international court. Such declarations are also made when ratifying a treaty containing provisions for

---

[7] *Decision of Defence Motion for Interlocutory Appeal on Jurisdiction*, 2 October 1995, IT-94-1-T (*Tadic* case), para. 24.

[8] Article 1, Additional Treaty to the Treaty of Peace Friendship (Spain-Peru), 14 August 1879, *British and Foreign State Papers*, Vol. 89, p. 598.

[9] Article 1, General Treaty of Arbitration (Argentina-Paraguay), 6 November 1899, *British and Foreign State Papers*, Vol. 92, p. 486.

[10] Article 1, Agreement between France and United Kingdom Providing for the Settlement of Arbitration of Certain Classes of Questions Which May Arise between the two Governments, 14 October 1903, *Treaty Series* (U.K.), No. 18.

[11] Article 1, General Arbitration Convention for Settling Disputes before The Hague Court of Arbitration, (Peru-United States of America), 5 December 1908. Christian Lange, *L'arbitrage obligatoire entre nations en 1913*, 1914, p. 20.

[12] Instructions by United States Secretary of State John Hay to the American Delegation to the 1899 Hague Peace Conference. John Brown Scott, *Instructions to the American Delegation to the Hague Conference and their Official Reports*, 1916, p. 9.

[13] Consider the 1989 declarations of Zaire (now the Democratic Republic of the Congo), where Zaire accepted the compulsory jurisdiction of the International Court of Justice, but only in "legal disputes concerning: (a) The interpretation of a treaty; (b) Any question of international law; (c) The existence of any fact which, if established, would constitute a breach of an international obligation; (d) The nature or extent of the reparation to be made for the breach of an international obligation". International Court of Justice, *Yearbook 1994-1995*, 1995, p. 119.

[14] Consider the following limits placed on the 1970 Declaration of the Republic of Botswana when accepting the compulsory jurisdiction of the International Court of Justice: "This Declaration does not extend: (a) to disputes in respect of which the parties have agreed or shall agree to have recourse to another means of peaceful settlement; or (b) to disputes relating to matters which, by international law, are essentially within the domestic jurisdiction of the Republic of Botswana". International Court of Justice, *Yearbook 1994-1995*, 1995, p. 82.

the recourse to obligatory adjudication as a means of settling disputes[15].

Beyond these means by which States accept fragments of obligatory international adjudication while limiting its scope, it should be noted that States have sometimes refused to honour legal undertakings to submit to adjudication. Through non-appearance, they have limited, not the procedure of adjudication – at least with respect to judicial settlement, proceedings do take place – but its effectiveness[16]. The decentralized nature of the international system is such that no State can be compelled to appear before an adjudicative body against its will, no matter what obligations it may have previously undertaken.

Another means by which States may impinge upon the effectiveness of adjudication is by non-compliance with a judgement or award. In cases of non-compliance with arbitration awards, little can be done by an arbitration panel as ordinarily it has no means of forcing compliance. The only recourse to ensuring compliance with an arbitration award is to include specific procedures related to non-compliance in the *compromis*. In the case of judgments rendered by international courts, various means of enforcing the judgment may be utilized depending on the forum; typically enforcement is left to the political organs of the international organization that has established these institutions to deal with the issue.

2. The Peace Movement and the Emerging Call for Obligatory Arbitration

As has been noted, one may say that while States are generally in favour of the concept of obligatory adjudication as a matter of principle, they are quite reluctant to accept it in practice. It should come as little surprise, then, that the original advocates of obligatory arbitration came, not from within the ranks of States or governmental organizations, but from those individuals outside of government who were committed to a religious belief in peace and, as a result, fostered a nascent peace movement. This movement, established towards the end of the Napoleonic Wars, may be considered the longest sustained effort by non-governmental actors to influence international public policy. Such influence was achieved with growing sophistication, as the earliest efforts were undertaken by pockets of individuals in Europe and in the United States of America, content in attempting to sway public opinion through speaking tours and essay-writing competitions. These means were then supplemented by direct pressure on governments in the

[15] Herbert W. Briggs, "The Optional Protocols of Geneva (1958) and Vienna (1961, 1963) Concerning the Compulsory Settlement of Disputes", *Recueil d'études de droit international en hommage à Paul Guggenheim*, 1968, pp. 628-641.

[16] For cases of failure to abide by judgments and examples of non appearance before the International Court of Justice, *op cit.*, n. 1 and 2, p. 67.

form of petitions, letter-writing campaigns, and direct meetings with policy-makers. Ultimately, the results that were achieved with respect to the pacific settlement of international disputes consisting in the adoption of the agenda of the peace movement by parliamentarians of various States as part of the "internationalist" movement of the late nineteenth century.

The pioneers who advocated settling international disputes by peaceful means came, above all, from Christian backgrounds and were "largely Quakers in origin"[17]. Peace societies came into existence almost simultaneously on two continents, but quite independently from each other. In late 1815, in the American States of Massachusetts, New York, and Ohio, peace societies were formed, to be followed in mid-1816 by the British "Society for the Promotion and Permanent and Universal Peace"[18]. These societies were supplemented by other bodies in France in 1821 and in Switzerland in 1830[19]. While the European movement tended to be fragmented, the peace movement in the United States of America was consolidated in 1828, under the leadership of William Ladd, who sought to develop concrete plans to eradicate war. It was the advocacy of Ladd that saw the Legislature of the Commonwealth of Massachusetts adopt a resolution on April 25, 1838, which was then forwarded to the President of the United States of America and called for:

> the institution of a Congress of Nations for the purpose of framing a code of international law and establishing a high court of arbitration for the settlement of controversies between nations is a scheme worthy of the careful attention and consideration of all enlightened governments[20].

While this petition came to naught, there was a realization within the United States peace movement that, while propaganda in the form of speaking tours and congresses was essential in winning support for the crusade against war, effective change could only be sought by attempting to influence the seats of power. However, the peace movements on both sides of the Atlantic had not, as of yet, focused on the means to achieve the ends they sought. However, that focus was sharpened by prize essay competitions which were first introduced by the French "Society of Christian Morals" in 1824. The seeds then planted would finally bear fruit in 1842. In that year, the American Peace Society sponsored its "Prize Es-

---

[17] A.C.F. Beales, *The History of Peace: A Short Account of the Organised Movements for International Peace*, 1931, p. 45. See more generally G. W. Knowles, *The Quakers and Peace*, 1920 and K. Frederic, *Early History of the Peace Movement in the United States (1846-61)*, 1928.

[18] Beales, *Ibid.*, p. 46.

[19] The main advocates during the birth of these peace societies were: David Low Dodge (United States of America), William Allen (United Kingdom), Duc de Rochefoucauld-Liancourt (France), and Comte de Sellon (Switzerland).

[20] W. Ladd, *An Essay on a Congress of Nations for the Adjustment of International Disputes without Resort to Arms (1840)*, 1916, p, 128.

says on a Congress of Nations" competition. William Ladd, as leader of the American Peace Society, took it upon himself to summarize the non-winning essays in a publication entitled: *An Essay on a Congress of Nations for the Adjustment of International Disputes without Resort to Arms*. This work was considered by James Brown Scott, in 1935, as being "responsible in no uncertain way, it may truly be said, for the Hague Peace Conference, the Permanent Court of International Justice and the present League of Nations"[21].

While the above passage by Scott may be somewhat overstated, it remains true that Ladd's essay was found to be so complete in its attempt to provide an all-encompassing programme for the United States peace movement that it "anticipated every essential principle embodied in the Hague conferences and the international court more than half a century later"[22]. William Ladd best summarizes his essay by outlining its two principal elements:

> First — A congress of ambassadors from all those Christian and civilised nations who should choose to send them, for the purpose of settling the principles of international law by compact and agreement, of the nature of a mutual treaty, and also of devising and promoting plans for the preservation of peace, and ameliorating the condition of man.
> Second — A court of nations, composed of the most able civilians in the world, to arbitrate or judge such cases as should be brought before it, by the mutual consent of two or more contending nations[23].

While Ladd's proposals did not go so far as to advocate obligatory adjudication in general, nor obligatory arbitration specifically, the same year saw the publication of a book entitled: *War and Peace: The Evils of the First and a Plan for Preserving the Last,* by the American William Jay. In this book, "a powerful case was made out for the insertion of a "compromissory clause" in future treaties, and for the arbitration of all disputes arising specifically from the interpretation of treaties"[24]. Jay's strongly held belief was that "no plan will be effectual in suppressing war that does not, in time of peace and good will, anticipate future differences, and provide for their accommodation"[25].

---

[21] James Brown Scott, preface to Georg Schwarzenberger, *William Ladd: An Examination of an American Proposal for an International Equity Tribunal*, 1935, p. xi.

[22] E. L. Whitney, *American Peace Society Centennial History*, 1928, pp. 53-54.

[23] Ladd, *op. cit.* n. 20, p. xlix; see also Mark W. Janis, "Protestants, Progress and Peace: Enthusiasm for an International Court in Early Nineteenth-Century America"; M. W. Janis, (ed.), *The Influence of Religion on the Development of International Law*, 1991, p. 230.

[24] Beales, *op. cit.* n. 17, p. 63,

[25] William Jay, *War and Peace: The Evils of the First and a Plan for Preserving the Last, (1842),* J. B. Scott (ed.), 1919. p. 90.

2.1. Specific Obligations as Found in Europe and the United States of America

William Jay's *War and Peace* deals at length with the social and economic costs of war and goes on to propose that the United States of America underwrite with France, a State for which at the time "no rivalry exists in commerce or manufactures", a treaty that would include the following article:

> It is agreed between the contracting parties that if, unhappily, any controversy shall hereafter arise between them in respect to the true meaning and intention of any stipulation in this present treaty, or in respect to any other subject, which controversy cannot be satisfactorily adjusted by negotiation, neither party shall resort to hostilities against the other; but the matter in dispute shall, by a special convention, be submitted to the arbitrament of one or more friendly powers; and the parties hereby agree to abide by the award which may be given in pursuance of such submission[26].

The notion of a compromissory clause, as was first advanced in Jay's book, should be understood in this instance as "a provision for the settlement by arbitration of disputes which may arise in regard to the interpretation or application of the particular treaty in which the clause appears"[27]. The advocacy of inclusion of compromissory clauses was picked up the following year, when the various national peace movements came together for the first time at the London Peace Conference of 1843. The Conference acknowledged its debt to William Jay, who favoured the use of compromissory clauses, and passed a resolution stating that: "treaty stipulations to refer their differences to the "arbitration" of a friendly power" were "the most available means for the prevention of war"[28].

The international peace movement, using the momentum gathered during what would later become yearly international peace congresses, focused its goals through the formation of "arbitration leagues" and increasingly sought to influence public policy directly. Through the presentation of a great number of petitions, the peace movement saw its call for compromissory clauses taken up by parliamentarians. The first concrete result for the peace movement was attained in Italy, where the future Foreign Minister and father of the Italian peace movement, Pasquale Stanislao Mancini, introduced the following draft resolution, which was passed by the Italian Chamber of Deputies in 1874:

---

[26] Jay, *Ibid.*, pp. 81-82. Jay, the son of former U.S. President John 'Jay Treaties' Jay, was at the time the President of the American Peace Society.

[27] Helen May Cory, *Compulsory Arbitration of International Disputes*, 1932, p. xi.

[28] Janis, *op. cit.* n. 23, pp. 235 (quoting the daily newspaper the *London Inquirer*).

> It trusted that the Government would endeavour, in their relations with Foreign Powers, to render arbitration an acceptable and frequent mode of solving, according to the dictates of equity, such international questions as may admit of that mode of arrangement, as well as to introduce opportunely into any treaty with those Powers a clause to the effect that any difference of opinion respecting the interpretation and execution of those treaties is to be referred to arbitration[29].

This Resolution was not only prompted by theoretical calls from the peace movement, but also was based on the positive experience of Italy with the compromissory clauses it had inserted in a handful of treaties, the earliest dating from 1856[30]. From the mid-1870s onward, the use of the compromissory clause became increasingly prevalent, as arbitration became more acceptable to States in theory and was utilized more often in practice. However, up to 1872, one may not speak of any true practice developing either towards a general use of compromissory clauses or a recourse to arbitration.

3. The Growth of Arbitration

The use of arbitration in international relations may be traced back nearly three thousand years to the Greek city-states[31]. While arbitration fell into general disuse during the Roman era, it was picked up again during the middle ages by city and micro-States. The German cities of Hamburg and Lübeck, for instance, agreed to settle their differences stemming from their association of 1210 by arbitration and, in what would later become Switzerland, a permanent arbitration treaty was signed between the cantons of Uri, Schwyz and Nidwald, in 1291, that stated:

---

[29] Leone Levi, *War and Its Consequences: Economical, Commercial, Financial, and Moral; With a Proposals for the Establishment of a Court of International Reference and Arbitration*, 1881, pp. 74-75.

[30] For example, the Treaty of Amity, Commerce and Navigation (Chile-Sardinia), 28 June 1856, *British and Foreign State Papers*, Vol. 46, p. 1051. Article 26 states that in cases of property being seized an indemnity will be determined by two arbitrators and "in case of disagreement about the choice of the umpire or disagreement amongst the arbitrators, the final decision without appeal will be given by Government of a third and friendly country". My translation.

[31] A. Raeder, "Les Messéniens offrent a Sparte l'arbitrage avant la première guerre messénienne. Vers l'an 740", *L'Arbitrage international chez les Hellenes*, 1912, pp. 14-16. Note that there is some doubt as to whether this proposal to arbitrate was ever made; if this claim is false, then the earliest known arbitration in the Western World took place about the year 650 A.D. See also E. Egger, *Étude historique sur les traités publique chez les Grecs et chez les Romains*, 1866.

> If a disagreement has come between the confederates the most prudent will intervene by arbitration to end the dispute by the means which appear the most appropriate, and if one or another of the parties is against the sentence, the other confederates will declare themselves against her[32].

While arbitration was used sparingly during the next five hundred years, it has been said that there was a modern "revival of international arbitration in 1794"[33]. In that year, the United States of America and Great Britain signed what came to be known as the Jay Treaty establishing mixed commissions to settle claims emanating from the American War for Independence[34]. These undertakings have been considered as "the historical landmark from which the trend which was to lead to the establishment of a true international judicial system is usually dated"[35]. Undoubtedly, the Jay Treaty gave an impetus to the utilization of arbitration on the international scene, however, it did not envision obligatory arbitration. The 1794 Treaty set forth the exact issues that were to be adjudicated and did not foresee the possibility of further issues being brought forward unilaterally. While the European States and the United States of America were being urged on by their respective peace movements to include compromissory clauses in future treaties, a quiet revolution had been underway in Latin America where, as early as 1829, general obligatory arbitration treaties were being signed.

3.1. **General Obligation to Arbitrate in Latin America**

Latin American States spurred on by their liberator, Simón Bolivar, and by an Iberian sense of origin, unity, and brotherhood, felt compelled to agree through general instruments to arbitration. Such general arbitration agreements were typically found in compromissory clauses, but they provided that arbitration could apply to *each and any dispute* between the parties, thus going beyond the scope of the treaty in which the clause was inserted. During much of the nineteenth cen-

---

[32] Edouard Langlade, *De la clause compromissoire et des traités d'arbitrage permanent*, 1899, p. 33. My translation.

[33] *Georges Pinson (France) v. United Mexican States*, 19 October 1928, Decision No. 1, (France-Mexico Claims Commission), *Reports of International Arbitral Awards*, Vol. 5, 1953, p. 335.

[34] Treaty of Amity, Commerce and Navigation, (United States of America-United Kingdom), 19 November 1794, *Consolidated Treaty Series*, Vol. 52, pp. 245-272. Hans-Jürgen Schlochauer, "Jay Treaty (1794)", *Encyclopedia of Public International Law*, Vol. 1, 1981, p. 108-111.

[35] Sir Muhammad Zafrulla Khan, "Commemoration of the Fiftieth Anniversary of the Institution of the International Judicial System", International Court of Justice, *Yearbook 1971-1972*, 1995, p. 130.

tury, however, the agreements calling for general arbitration must be seen as little more than paper tigers. For instance, the first treaty including a general provision obliging the parties to submit disputes to adjudication was an agreement between Colombia and Peru of 1829. This Treaty contained a general compromissory clause at Article 19, which provided:

> 2. That, whatever ground of misunderstanding may arise between the two Republics, whether on account of complaints of injuries, insults, or other grievances, it shall not be lawful for either of them to authorizes acts of reprisal, nor to declare war against the other, without previously submitting their differences to the government of a power friendly to both parties.
>
> 3. That, before they apply to a third power, to decide their doubts upon any one or more of the articles contained in the present treaty, or to accommodate their differences, they shall mutually employ every means of conciliation and adjustment which are becoming to two neighbouring nations, united by ties of blood and the most intimate and cordial relations.[36]

However, it is clear that these arbitration provisions cannot be considered as obligatory. Robert Wilson wrote:

> [i]t has long been recognized that unless the part of a general agreement covering the method of referring disputes is adequate, a strict construction of the instrument may leave it little more than the expression of a noble wish. Evasion or frank disregard may easily follow[37].

Furthermore, during the early eighteen hundreds, the States, by their actions, demonstrated that it was unimaginable "that one State might summon another to court"[38]. As there existed no provision calling for the establishment of such an adjudicative body or for rules of procedure, it is not surprising that an arbitration panel would take until 1875 to render an award based on such a general provision[39]. Though approximately fifty treaties contained this type of general obligation – without reservations and including all possible disputes – were concluded between Latin American States between 1820 and 1890, such obligations only gradually evolved from duties in name to agreements having the teeth (or techniques) necessary to induce actual arbitration.

---

[36] Treaty of Peace between Peru and Colombia, 22 September 1829, *British and Foreign State Papers*, Vol. 26, p. 1246.

[37] Robert R. Wilson, "Clauses Relating to Reference of Disputes in Obligatory Arbitration Treaties", *American Journal of International Law*, Vol. 25, 1931, p. 469.

[38] Cory, *op. cit.* n. 27, p. 10.

[39] Affaire de *la liquidation des dépenses navales dans la guerre contre l'Espagne* (Chile-Peru), 7 April 1875, A. de Lapradelle and N. Politis, *Recueil des arbitrages internationaux*, Vol. 3, 1954, pp. 531-563.

At the bilateral level, Central and South American States gradually concluded true general treaties of obligatory arbitration in the sense of providing a framework allowing for the establishment of panels. These treaties, however, increasingly contained provisions seeking to limit their own applicability. In the case of Argentina, for example, its general arbitration treaties excluded questions "which might affect the independence, the sovereignty and the fundamental principles on which the political organization of the two countries rest". As William Manning's study, *Arbitration Treaties among the American Nations*, attests, with the increased use of reservations Latin American States were prepared to make general arbitration treaties a norm[40].

At the First Pan-American Conference of 1889, the participants established that arbitration was a "principle of American international law". It would seem, however, that in the domain of arbitration agreements a more accurate statement of the international law emerging from Latin America was that obligatory arbitration is worthwhile in theory but not in practice. While a clear majority of delegations at the Conference agreed that "all controversies concerning diplomatic and consular privileges, boundaries, territories, indemnities, the right of navigation and the validity, construction, and enforcement of treaties"[41] were susceptible to obligatory arbitration, only half signed a multilateral treaty to that effect and none ratified it.

4. The Consolidation of International Arbitration

The paper tigers established by general arbitration provisions in Latin America, as noted earlier, did not roar until the mid-1870s. The use of arbitration made in Latin America during the last quarter of the nineteenth century was part of a general pattern of acceptance of arbitration that was starting to be felt internationally. With the willingness of the United States of America and Great Britain to have the *Alabama* dispute arbitrated in 1872 came the realization among States that arbitration could indeed be effective and viable as an instrument of international relations[42]. It was hoped by those who advocated obligatory arbitration that "the favour, which this famous case did towards arbitration in general, also assists as a consequence the call for obligatory arbitration"[43]. However States, through their representatives, ensured that calls for obligatory arbitration would develop within an acceptable framework.

---

[40] See W. R. Manning, *Arbitration Treaties among the American Nations to the Close of the Year 1910*, 1924, p. 59.

[41] Cory, *op. cit.* n. 27, pp 18-19.

[42] *The Alabama Claims*, 14 September 1872, A. de Lapradelle and N. Politis, *op. cit.* n. 39, Vol. 2, 1957, pp. 713-983.

[43] N. Politis, *La justice internationale*, 1924, p. 195. My translation.

The willingness of other States to consider arbitration as a real option manifested itself primarily through legislative resolutions passed, not only by Mancini of Italy, but by legislators in Belgium, Britain, Denmark, The Netherlands, Sweden, and the United States of America[44]. These various acts were not adopted in isolation, but were an extension of the international peace movement whose new leadership, drawn from the ranks of government, was both more politically acute and active. In the late nineteenth century, the advocates of the peace movement and obligatory jurisdiction moved from presenting petitions to receiving them, as they were now drawn from the ranks of national parliaments. Further, the internationalist trend that was emerging at this time, and manifesting itself in various forms such as the International Red Cross Society or the Socialist Internationals, was also diversifying within the realm of the peace movements. While the Universal Peace Conference was becoming a yearly event, other organizations were established that were to have great effect on the call for obligatory arbitration. In 1873, the *Institut de droit international* (Institute of International Law) came into existence and was followed, in 1889, by the influential Inter-Parliamentary Union.

4.1. Institute of International Law

The Institute of International Law met for the first time in Ghent in 1873 and was, to some extent, an offshoot of the international peace movement, yet its members, consisting of the likes of Asser, Calvo, and Mancini, were more in tune with the requirements and wishes of States than with an overall concern for peace. The Institute was originally established to allow international lawyers and practitioners to consider international law from a scientific point of view and to discuss the possibility of codifying that law.

That pragmatism was reflected in the Institute's Resolution of 12 September 1877, in which it attempted to provide States with a model arbitration procedure for cases where the parties could not agree or had not agreed upon such a framework. In this manner, the Institute was attempting to ensure that obligations consented by treaty would be translated into reality. It strongly recommended that compromissory clauses be included in future treaties and that arbitration be utilized in cases where there was disagreement as to the application and interpretation of treaty rules. The Institute then called on States to use the following provision as a compromissory clause:

---

[44] C. Lange, *L'Arbitrage obligatoire entre nations en 1913,* 1914; pp. 397-398 and Cory, *op. cit.* n. 27, p. 23.

> If the contracting States have not agreed beforehand to other methods of determining the procedures to be followed before an arbitration tribunal, they will apply the rules developed by the Institute during its session in The Hague on 28 August 1875.[45]

The rules of procedure developed by the Institute were the first of their kind. Before 1877, States which had agreed to arbitrate were forced to draft a *compromis ex nihilo*. As Alexandre André notes in his work on obligatory arbitration, the lack of a pre-established model of procedure was reason enough for some States not to go to arbitration[46].

4.2. **Inter-Parliamentary Union**

With a growing sense of international camaraderie between parliamentarians who were meeting as a result of their ties to national peace movements, came the wish, as early as 1875, to establish an organization of parliamentarians committed to peace. It was left to Randal Cremer[47], an English peace activist, who, for twenty years, had been the secretary of London's International Working Men's Association, later the International Arbitration League, to do so. Having been elected to Westminster, he took the lead by establishing the Inter-Parliamentary Union. The credentials that allowed Cremer to lead this push towards the Union were developed in 1887, when he presented to the President of the United States of America a petition of 232 signatures from Members of the British House of Commons requesting that the United States Congress invite Britain to negotiate a general treaty of obligatory arbitration[48].

With the advent of the Inter-Parliamentary Union came the impetus that would propel the trend toward obligatory adjudication from a non-governmental forum to a governmental one. The Union acted as a halfway house whose members, while part of their respective municipal legislative bodies, acted without the power of governmental legitimacy on the international level. Yet by 1889, a major shift took place which can be seen as the key for the push towards obligatory adjudication. In that year a fundamental shift of emphasis occurred within the international peace movement: no longer was the drive for obligatory adjudication abandoned to representatives of national peace societies and arbitration leagues, who could only address parliamentarians by way of petition. The new leaders of

[45] Institut de droit international, "Arbitrage international — Clause compromissoire — Resolution votée en séance du 12 septembre 1877", *Annuaire de l'Institut de droit international*, Vol. 2, 1878, p. 160. My translation. For the Institute's rules of procedure, see *Annuaire de l'Institut de droit international*, Vol. 1, 1877, pp. 126-133.

[46] Alexandre André, "L'Institut du droit international et l'arbitrage obligatoire", *De l'arbitrage obligatoire dans les rapports internationaux*, 1903, p. 58.

[47] See Howard Evans, *Sir Randal Cremer: His Life Work*, 1909.

[48] Cory, *op. cit.* n. 27, p. 28.

the international peace movement were increasingly being elected to national legislatures, or were drawn from the ranks of members of parliament who had taken up the cause. As such, the Inter-Parliamentary Union was a device allowing the advocates of peace to "assail governments from within"[49].

In Paris, during the summer of 1889, a true passing of the torch took place as, within two days of the end of the Universal Peace Conference, the first Parliamentary Arbitration Conference was held by the Inter-Parliamentary Union. A great interchange occurred between these two bodies, as many of those attending the Universal Peace Conference were legislators and members of the Inter-Parliamentary Union. It has been noted that the fundamental difference between the two bodies was that the former was said to be "idealistic and popular", destined to elaborate "the abstract idea of international justice and recommend it to the world at large". By way of contrast, the Inter-Parliamentary Union was considered to be "positive and practical" and, thus, as avoiding "exaggerations and speculations aiming at a gradual progress from theory to fact"[50]. This difference was made clear during the Universal Peace Conference, where delegates advocated "that arbitration should not only form a fundamental part of the constitutions of every State, but should be embodied in principle in every future treaty as an obligatory and not an optional undertaking"[51].

As a result of the Inter-Parliamentary Union's more State-oriented approach, the work taken up by parliamentarians, which until then had been reserved to "exalted preachers, poets and revolutionaries", was now being viewed by States as the embodiment of their legitimate aim[52]. However, in many respects, the legitimacy of the Union was due to the fact that statesmen were coming to understand that the peace movements and their call for obligatory arbitration could no longer be ignored. By considering the work of the Inter-Parliamentary Union, States could sidestep the issue of obligatory adjudication by accepting the notion of international adjudication, but limit its effectiveness by making it optional or voluntary in nature. Nicolas Politis noted this fundamental shift when he pointed out that:

> the peace writings and propaganda, having started with the aim of obligatory, ended towards [the late of the nineteen century], less ambitions but more practical by contenting itself, within the Inter-Parliamentary Union, to a tribunal that was to be purely voluntary; destined to make arbitration available to all of good will.[53]

---

[49] Beales, *op. cit.* n. 17, p. 193.

[50] *Ibid.*, p. 194.

[51] *Ibid.*, p. 192.

[52] Yefime Zarjevski, *The People Have the Floor: A History of the Inter-Parliamentary Union*, 1989, p. 39.

[53] Politis, *op. cit.* n. 43, p. 96. My translation.

The link that the Inter-Parliamentary Union established between the peace movement and States was made in Hungary at the 1896 Inter-Parliamentary Conference. In attendance at the Budapest Conference was an attaché of the Russian Ministry of Foreign Affairs named Priklonski who, attending in his private capacity, forwarded a report of the proceedings to St. Petersburg. There it lay in a drawer until, having been recalled to the capital, the attaché brought the Union's plans to the attention of Moravieff, the Foreign Minster, who knew of the pressures that increased demand for armaments were placing on Russia and, in turn, made the Czar aware of the work of Inter-Parliamentary Union[54].

4.3. **The First Hague Peace Conference (1899)**

Taken by the idea of convening a general conference on peace, the Czar had a note delivered to the St. Petersburg diplomatic corps stating his belief "that the present moment would be very favourable for seeking, by means of international discussion, the most effective means of ensuring to all peoples the benefit of a real and lasting peace"[55]. As part of the proposed programme to a conference that would be held at The Hague[56], Russia sought to prepare "the way for a discussion of the questions relating to the possibility of preventing armed conflicts by the pacific means at the disposal of international diplomacy"[57]. The proposal established by the Czar was set out in eight precise points, "with all questions which do not directly fall within the programme" being "absolutely excluded from the deliberations of the Conference"[58]. So, to the great dismay of those who advocated obligatory adjudication, that Conference was to deal only with the "acceptance, in principle, of the use of good offices, mediation, and *voluntary arbitration*"[59].

Twenty-six States attended the first Peace Conference in the Dutch capital from 18 May to 29 July 1899[60]. The main absentees at the Peace Conference were some Latin American States, which it will be recalled, were the strongest

---

[54] Lange, *op. cit.* n. 44, pp. 403-404.

[55] Count Moravieff, "Russian Circular Note Proposing the First Peace Conference", 12 August 1898, James Brown Scott (ed.), *The Reports of the Hague Conferences of 1899 and 1907*, 1917, p. 1.

[56] For the Russian reasoning for holding the Peace Conference at The Hague, see M.J.P.A. François, "La Cour permanente d'arbitrage, son origine, sa jurisprudence, son avenir", *Collected Courses of The Hague Academy of International Law*, Vol. 87, 1955, pp. 464-465.

[57] Count Moravieff, "Russian Circular Note Proposing the Programme of the First Conference", 30 December 1898, in James B. Scott, *The Hague Court Reports*, 1916, p. 3.

[58] *Ibid.*, p 3.

[59] *Ibid.*, p 3. Emphasis added.

[60] The States participating were: Austria-Hungary, Belgium, Bulgaria, China, Denmark, Germany, France, Great Britain and Ireland, Greece, Italy, Japan, Luxembourg, Mexico, Montenegro, The Netherlands, Persia, Portugal, Romania, Russia, Serbia, Siam, Spain, Sweden and Norway, Switzerland, Turkey, and the United States of America.

advocates of general arbitration treaties providing for obligatory jurisdiction[61]. Owing to this major omission, the Peace Conference was primarily left with the mechanism of obligatory adjudication to which European States were accustomed – specific compromissory clauses. Having initiated the Conference, the Russian delegation produced a draft convention on the peaceful settlement of disputes which sought to provide an arbitration mechanism with respect to "controversies concerning legal questions, and especially with regard to those concerning the interpretation or application of treaties in force [...]"[62]. The Russians not only advocated arbitration but went beyond the Czar's original programme by calling for obligatory arbitration:

> Upon the ratification of the present document by all the signatory Powers, arbitration will be obligatory in the following cases, so far as they do not concern the vital interests nor national honour of the contracting States:
>
> I. In case of differences or disputes relating to pecuniary damages suffered by a State, or its nationals, as a consequence of illegal actions or negligence on the part of another State or its nationals:
>
> II. In case of disagreement relating to the interpretation or application of the treaties and conventions mentioned below:
>
> 1. Treaties and conventions relating to the posts and telegraphs, railroads, and also those bearing upon the protection of submarine telegraph cables; regulations concerning methods to prevent collisions of vessels on the high seas; conventions relating to the navigation of international rivers and interoceanic canals.
>
> 2. Conventions concerning the protection of literary and artistic property as well as industrial property (patents, trade-marks, and trade-names); conventions relating to money and measures; conventions relating to sanitation and veterinary surgery, and for the prevention of phylloxera.
>
> 3. Conventions relating to inheritance, exchange of prisoners, and reciprocal assistance in the administration of justice.
>
> 4. Conventions for marking boundaries, so far as they concern purely technical and non-political questions[63].

---

[61] While Mexico did attend the Conference, other Latin American States did not maintain legations in St. Petersburg, except for Brazil, whose absence was, according to a Delegate of the United States of America, due to "indifference and carelessness". Andrew D. White, *Autobiography of Andrew D. White*, Vol. 2, 1905, p. 284. Note, however, that neither Siam nor Switzerland maintained representatives in St. Petersburg, yet received invitations to the Conference. See Edgar de Melville, *L'Oeuvre de La Haye (1871-1921)*, 1924, p. 38.

[62] Russian Delegation to the Peace Conference "Outlines for the Preparation of a Draft Convention to be concluded between the Powers Taking Part in the Hague Conference", Article 7, Scott, *op. cit.* n. 57, p. 92.

[63] *Ibid.*, pp. 92-93. Note that items I and II, as well as the added issue of the determination of territorial claims, were advanced beforehand on a bilateral level as the basis of the unperfected "Olney-Pauncefote" Treaty between Great Britain and the United States of America signed 11 Janu-

In an explanatory note regarding the Russian proposal to have the above items fall within the purview of the Conference, it noted that:

> no Government would consent *in advance* to adhere to a decision of an arbitral tribunal which might arise within the international domain, if it concerned the national honour of a State, or its highest interests, or its inalienable possessions. [...] But from another point of view, it cannot be doubted that in international life differences often arise which may absolutely and at all times be submitted to arbitration for solution; these are questions which concern exclusively special points of law and which do not touch upon the vital interests, or national honour of States[64].

The Note goes on to explain that obligatory arbitration should apply to disputes that do not pose "a direct menace to the maintenance of peace", but to lesser disagreements which disrupt the interaction between States, "creating an atmosphere of distrust", which in turn might start a war[65].

Due to the number of issues under consideration during the Peace Conference, working groups were established to consider specific items. The Third Commission, designated to draft a treaty on the pacific settlement of international disputes, considered the Russian proposal for a limited number of domains to which obligatory arbitration could apply. While a majority of the delegates spoke in favour of accepting the proposition that the domains proposed by Russia be governed by obligatory arbitration, these provisions were never to find their way into the final draft convention. As the Conference was run on the basis of consensus among the Parties, it was left to the German delegation, which, in general terms, was antithetic to the Conference, to insist that all traces of obligation be removed from a future treaty[66]. As a result, the Convention for the Pacific Settlement of International Disputes signed at the Peace Conference included a general affirmation, in Article 19, that States should continue to strive for obligatory arbitration:

---

ary 1897. Christian L. Wiktor, *Unperfected Treaties of the United States of America (1776-1976)*, Vol. 3, 1979, pp. 253-261; see also Chapter 4: "The Olney-Pauncefote Treaty", in Cory, *op. cit.* n. 27, pp. 28-38.

64 Russian Delegation to the Peace Conference, "Explanatory Notes Concerning Article 5 and 10 of the above Outlines for the Preparation of a Draft Convention", Scott, *op. cit.* n. 57, pp. 97-98.

65 *Ibid.*, p. 98.

66 Baron Descamps, "Report to the Conference from the Third Commission on Pacific Settlement of International Disputes", *ibid.*, p. 61. While Germany would later accept the establishment of the Permanent Court of Arbitration, the Kaiser wrote to his Chancellor that "to prevent the disgrace of the Tsar in the face of Europe I vote for this nonsense. But in my actions, now and hereafter, I shall trust and invoke only God and my sharp sword". G. L. Dickinson, *International Anarchy (1904-1914)*, 1926,pp. 362-363. While Germany was hostile to obligatory arbitration in general, other States were opposed to specific items enumerated in the Russian proposal; for instance, the United States "demanded the exclusion of those [provisions] relating to international rivers and interoceanic canals, and to monetary systems". W. Hull, *The Two Hague Conferences and their Contributions to International Law*, 1908, p. 329.

> Independently of general or private treaties expressly stipulating recourse to arbitration as obligatory on the signatory Powers, these Powers reserve to themselves the right of concluding, either before the ratification of the present Act or later, new agreements, general or private, with a view to extending arbitration to all cases which they may consider it possible to submit to it[67].

As Nicolas Politis noted, "from a positive standpoint" Article 19 added little: "at first sight it appeared somewhat juvenile, as the parties granted themselves a right which nobody would challenge" as already existing; however, "the provision had a moral value. It stated officially the tendency which States ought to follow"[68]. The reverse of the coin is that States demonstrated their unwillingness to bind themselves in even the most banal of domains to obligatory arbitration. As one of the United States delegates to the Conference would later write, "as to arbitration, we cannot make it compulsory, as so many very good people wish; it is clear that no power here would agree to that"[69] !

5. Consolidation of Voluntary Arbitration

It may be said that, with the coming together of State delegations at The Hague Peace Conference of 1899, the peace movement was effectively sidelined from the domain of the peaceful settlement of disputes. As the objectives of the peace movements, as will be seen, were being implemented during the early years of the twentieth century – in a piecemeal and above all limited manner – the movement's ability to mobilize public opinion in favour of obligatory arbitration quickly diminished. The peace movement's popularity, which peaked towards the end of the nineteenth century, with over two hundred peace societies publishing more than forty newspapers and maintaining over a million active members, would give way, having only achieved the institutionalization of universal voluntary arbitration[70]. The effect of the peace movement, however, was seen elsewhere, as up to the year 1900, seventy-seven treaties had been ratified which included general compromissory clauses calling for obligatory arbitration of all disputes, while 61 treaties including a compromissory clause specific to their interpretation and applications were ratified[71].

---

67 Article 19, Convention for the Pacific Settlement of International Disputes, 29 July 1899.

68 Politis, *op. cit.* n. 43, p. 200. My translation.

69 White, *op. cit.* n. 61, p. 259.

70 Eduard Langlade, *op. cit.* n. 32, p. 39.

71 H. La Fontaine, *Pasicrisie internationale: Histoire documentaire des arbitrages internationaux (1794-1900)*, 1902, pp. x-xiv.

5.1. **The Permanent Court of Arbitration**

The legacy of the 1899 Peace Conference, within the realm of arbitration, was not that it resulted in a treaty provision requiring States to settle their disputes in an obligatory manner, but in that it provided for the establishment of a permanent mechanism to which States, through a compromissory clause, could refer their disputes. Thus, the peace movements gained what they had wanted only in part – a permanent court (if in name only) – yet the States limited its effectiveness by endowing it with only voluntary jurisdiction. Article 20 of the 1899 Treaty on the Pacific Settlement of International Disputes called for the establishment of this first permanent international adjudicative organ:

> With the object of facilitating an immediate recourse to arbitration for international differences, which it has not been possible to settle by diplomacy, the Signatory Powers undertake to organize a permanent Court of Arbitration, accessible at all times and operating, unless otherwise stipulated by the parties, in accordance with the Rules of Procedure inserted in the present Convention.

The Permanent Court of Arbitration[72], as the often-quoted James Brown Scott stated, "is not permanent because it is not composed of permanent judges; it is not accessible because it has to be formed for each individual case; and finally is not a court, because it is not composed of judges"[73]. The Court is made up of a registry in the form of the International Bureau, a Permanent Administrative Council comprised of the diplomatic representatives to the Dutch capital of the States Parties to the Hague Convention, which oversees the functioning of the Bureau, and finally, a list of arbitrators. States, upon agreeing to have a dispute settled *via* the Court, are to choose up to five individuals from the list to arbitrate, using the procedures set out in the Convention. The Permanent Court of Arbitration may be considered a "machinery by which a temporary tribunal can be created"[74] or as "a device for facilitating the creation of tribunals and a machinery for aiding in the conduct of arbitral proceedings"[75].

---

[72] The origins of the Permanent Court of Arbitration can be traced to a report presented by Philip Stanhope at the 1894 Inter-Parliamentary Conference. On the basis of this report, a draft plan for a Permanent Court of International Arbitration was presented at the following year's Conference in Brussels that included the notion of a list of arbitrators, two individuals being drawn from each States Party to the Court. Beales writes that "the plan has historical value in that it formed the basis of the official British plan put forward at the Hague Conference of 1899" which, in turn, was the basis of the Permanent Court of International Arbitration. Beales, *op. cit.* n. 17, pp. 227-228.

[73] J. B. Scott (ed.), *The Proceedings of The Hague Peace Conference; Conference of 1907*, Vol. 2, 1921, p. 319.

[74] Scott, *op. cit.* n. 57, p. xiii.

[75] Manley Hudson, "The Permanent Court of Arbitration", *American Journal of International Law*, Vol. 27, 1933, p. 445.

5.2. The Second Peace Conference (1907)

At the second Hague Peace Conference, held from 14 June to 18 October 1907, 44 States were represented[76]. This increase was due, largely, to the invitation of Latin American States excluded from the first Conference. As Russia was in the midst of a war with Japan, it was left to the Secretary of State of the United States of America, John Hay, to act upon the wishes of the delegates of the 1899 Peace Conference by convening a second Conference. His call was prompted by a request from the Inter-Parliamentary Union made at its annual meeting, at St. Louis, in 1904[77]. Having canvassed States as to their interest in such a Conference, the United States of America left it to the Russian Czar, who, by then, had concluded the peace of Portsmouth, to call once again for a gathering of diplomats at The Hague in the form of a second Hague Peace Conference[78]. Part of the proposed programme for the 1907 Conference was the issue of improvements "to be made in the provisions of the Convention for the pacific settlement of international disputes as regards the Court of Arbitration and international commissions of inquiry"[79]. Again, nothing was said of obligatory arbitration.

However, just as at the First Peace Conference, the discussion of delegates at the second Conference turned to obligatory arbitration. While more than a dozen States provided schemes that would add obligatory arbitration to a revision of the 1899 Convention on the Pacific Settlement of International Disputes, it was left, once again, to the German delegation to ensure that no such stipulations would be included in a future treaty[80]. The intransigence of Germany towards obligatory arbitration was based on the universal character of such obligations; Germany believed that such undertakings should only be taken bilaterally. The exasperation towards the German delegation for once again standing in the way of provisions

[76] The States participating were: Argentina, Austria-Hungary, Belgium, Brazil, Bolivia, Bulgaria, Chile, China, Colombia, Cuba, Denmark, Dominican Republic, Ecuador, El Salvador, France, Germany, Guatemala, Great Britain and Ireland, Greece, Haiti, Italy, Japan, Luxembourg, Mexico, Montenegro, The Netherlands, Nicaragua, Norway, Panama, Paraguay, Persia, Peru, Portugal, Romania, Russia, Serbia, Siam, Spain, Sweden, Switzerland, Turkey, the United States of America, Uruguay, and Venezuela.

[77] John Jay, "The Secretary of State to the Representatives of the United States Accredited to the Governments Signatories to the Acts of the Hague Conference, 1899", 21 October 1904, Scott, *op. cit.* n. 57, pp. 180-182.

[78] Baron Roman Rosan, "The Russian Ambassador to the Secretary of State", *ibid.*, pp. 186-187.

[79] *Ibid.*, p. 186.

[80] For the various proposals by States for obligatory arbitration, see: "Section (C) — Obligatory Arbitration", Annexes 14-30, *ibid.*, pp. 471-488. For the second scuttling of obligatory arbitration by Germany see: Cory, *op. cit.* n. 27, pp. 71-75; N. N. Stoïka, *La Question de l'arbitrage obligatoire aux Conférence de la Paix*, 1909, pp. 109-113 and 148, where the author states: «Ce fut surtout l'opposition de l'Allemange qui, nous l'avons vu, a donné le coup de grâce à l'arbitrage obligatoire aux deux Conférences de La Haye».

dealing with obligatory arbitration, was given voice, during a session of the Conference, by the American representative Joseph Choate:

> Baron Marschall is an ardent admirer of abstract principles of arbitration and even obligatory arbitration, and even of general arbitration between those with whom he chooses to act. But when it comes to putting this idea into concrete form and practical effect he appears as our most formidable adversary. He appears like one who worships a divine image in the sky, but when it touches the earth it loses all charm from him. He sees as in a dream a celestial apparition which excites his ardent devotion, but when he wakes and finds her by his side he turns to the wall, and will have nothing to do with her[81] .

As a result of the German position, delegations could only muster the following watered-down declarations whereby the participants of the Conference were unanimous:

> 1. In admitting the principle of compulsory arbitration.
>
> 2. In declaring that certain disputes, in particular those relating to the interpretation and application of the provisions of international agreements, may be submitted to compulsory arbitration without any restriction.
>
> In proclaiming that, although it has not yet been found feasible to conclude a convention in this sense, nevertheless the divergences of opinion which have come to light have not exceeded the bounds of judicial controversy, and that, working together here during the part four months, the collected Powers not only have learned to understand one another and to draw closer together, but have succeeded in the course of this long collaboration in evolving a very lofty conception of common welfare of humanity[82].

Politis argues that the "inclusion in the Final Act of the Conference of these Declarations is a building block upon which the structure of obligatory arbitration will be built. It constitutes a moral undertaking by civilized States to orient themselves more and more towards the ideal of international justice"[83] . Yet Politis was once again too optimistic, as this argument has failed to withstand the test of time. The Declaration instead bears witness to the intransigence of States, in the wake of the collapse of the popular components of the peace movements; as Dickinson notes:"[p]ublic opinion was either indifferent or unorganized throughout the world, and the diplomats and governments had the game in their hands. The object, as they saw it, was to fend off a tiresome, incipient, but fortunately

[81] C. D. Davis, *The United States and the Second Hague Peace Conference*, 1975, p. 282.

[82] James B. Scott, *The Hague Conventions and Declarations of 1899 and 1907*, 1915, pp. 27-28.

[83] Politis, *op. cit.* n. 43, p. 213. My translation.

dispersed and feeble agitation" of peace advocates[84]. In so doing, States, for the second time, thwarted attempts to insert provisions on obligatory arbitration into a universal instrument.

The Second Peace Conference, however, was not a complete failure with respect to solidifying arbitration as, in two very limited areas, States agreed to include provisions in the 1907 Convention for the Pacific Settlement of International Disputes which would ultimately lead to the settlement of disputes by arbitration[85]. The first area, covered in Article 53(1) of the Convention, allows for the unilateral seizing of the Permanent Court in situations where States have failed to settle a dispute on the basis of a general arbitration treaty. Thus, in circumstances where a State has accepted an obligation to arbitrate under a general treaty, the Court was given the power to ensure that, that obligation was respected. Accordingly, it was left to the Court, upon unilateral seizure by a complainant State, to establish a *compromis* where the States concerned could not agree on the modalities of arbitration. Article 53 provides, *inter alia*:

> The Permanent Court is competent to settle the "Compromis", if the parties are agreed to have recourse to it for the purpose.

The Court was given further competence even if the request was being made by only one party, when all attempts to reach an understanding through diplomatic channels had failed, whenever:

> A dispute covered by a general Treaty of Arbitration concluded or renewed after the present Convention has come into force, and providing for a "Compromis" in all disputes and not either explicitly or implicitly excluding the settlement of the "Compromis" from the competence of the Court. Recourse cannot, however, be had to the Court if the other party declares that in its opinion the dispute does not belong to the category of disputes which can be submitted to compulsory arbitration, unless the Treaty of Arbitration confers upon the Arbitration Tribunal the power of deciding this preliminary question.

The second area where arbitration appears to have been reinforced were disputes of a pecuniary nature. The acceptance of the provision of Article 53(2) is the first indication of a nascent international judicial system. The following clause:

> A dispute arising from contract debts claimed from one Power by another Power as due to its nationals, and for the settlement of which the offer of arbitration has been

---

[84] Dickinson, *op. cit.* n. 66, p. 367. The following private correspondence is illustrative of the disdain that many had towards advocates of peace: the Russian Foreign Minister Isvolski considered the Second Peace Conference but "a dream of Jews, Socialists, and hysterical women". *Ibid.*, p. 364.

[85] Convention for the Pacific Settlement of International Disputes, 18 October 1907. For full text of the Convention, see Appendix 1.

> accepted. This arrangement is not applicable if acceptance is subject to the condition that the "Compromis" should be settled in some other way;

was a direct result the second arbitration award made by the Permanent Court of Arbitration. This award, made in the *Venezuelan Preferential* case[86], related to belligerent reprisals in the form of the bombardment and blockade of Venezuelan ports by Britain, Germany, and Italy in 1902. These actions were taken as a result of the suspension of the repayment of contractual debts owed by Venezuela and its citizens to foreign nationals[87]. Following this instance of European gunboat diplomacy, the Venezuelan President Castro sought the assistance of the Ambassador of the United States of America for proposing that the dispute be settled by arbitration. This proposal was, in due time, accepted by the three States. It was then left to the American President Roosevelt (who had originally been asked to act as arbitrator) to step aside, so that the Court of Arbitration could hear the case[88]. The outcome of the arbitration, which had not included the questions of the legality of the naval operations or of whether all pacific means had been exhausted, was a blow to those who advocated peace, as the award upheld the claims of the plaintiffs who had bombarded the coast of Venezuela.

While discontent was heard in the Americas as a result of the *Venezuela Preferential* case, this feeling was reflected in two very distinct doctrines. The first, in the framework of the Monroe Doctrine, was stated eloquently by Calvin Davis in the following passage:

> No longer did Theodore Roosevelt talk of the right of a European power to spank a misbehaving American state. It was clear to him that if any spanking were to be done the United States would have to do it[89].

The second, a reflection of the view of most Latin American States, is known as the Drago Doctrine and may be stated in the following terms:

> a public debt cannot give rise to the right of armed intervention, and much less to the occupation of the soil of any American nation by any European power[90].

The results of these partly diverging views were reconciled at the Second Peace Conference, where the Drago Doctrine won the day through the signing of the

---

86 The *Venezuelan Preferential* case, 22 February 1904 (Germany, Great Britain and Italy v. Venezuela), Bureau international de la Cour permanente d'Arbitrage, *Recueil des actes et protocoles concernant le litige entre l'Allemange, l'Angleterre et l'Italie et le Vénézuela*, 1904, pp. 123-128.

87 Patrick Daillier and Alain Pellet (eds.): Nguyen Quoc Dinh, *Droit international public*, 1994, p. 857.

88 Davis, *op. cit.* n. 81, p. 83.

89 *Ibid.*, p. 89.

90 Wolfgang Benedek, "Drago-Porter Convention (1907)", *Encyclopedia of Public International Law*, Vol. 1, 1992, p. 1102.

Convention Respecting the Limitation of the Employment of Force for the Recovery of Contract Debts which provided, in its Articles 1 and 2, that:

> *Article 1*
> The contracting Powers agree not to have recourse to armed force for the recovery of contract debts claimed from the Government of one country by the Government of another country as being due to its nationals.
>
> This undertaking is, however, not applicable when the debtor State refuses or neglects to reply to an offer of arbitration, or, after accepting the offer, prevents any *compromis* from being agreed on, or, after the arbitration, fails to submit to the award.
>
> *Article 2*
> It is further agreed that the arbitration mentioned in paragraph 2 of the foregoing article shall be subject to the procedure laid down in Part IV, Chapter III, of the Hague Convention for the pacific settlement of international disputes [...][91].

A reading of the above two Articles makes it clear that debtor States must proceed to arbitration or face military action. Under such circumstances, recourse to the Permanent Court of Arbitration *via* Article 53(2) of the Convention for the Pacific Settlement of International Disputes of 1907 would seem to neutralize the possibility of a claimant States proposing such an outlandish *compromis* that the debtor State would have no alternative but to refuse, thus providing a *casus belli*. The other side of the coin, however, is that an obligation to arbitrate befalls the debtor State, which must seek to arbitrate under the threat of force. Regardless of which side of the coin is considered, the result of Article 53(2) at the time was that disputes over the recovery of debts were to settled in a pacific manner, in the last instance by arbitration. While these provisions were the first to limit war on the international plane, the fundamental underpinnings of the Drago Doctrine and the Convention regarding the recovery of contract debts must today be considered as moot, having been superseded by the general prohibition to the use of force which came into being after the Second World War[92].

---

[91] Article 1, Convention Respecting the Limitation of the Employment of Force for the Recovery of Contract Debts, 18 October 1907.

[92] This outlawry of the use of force is expressed in Article 2(4) of the Charter of the United Nations, with the exceptions that force may be used by the UN Security Council by virtue of Chapter VII, or by States individually or collectively, in self-defence, as outlined in Article 51. Consider also the pronouncement of the International Court of Justice in the *Norwegian Loans* case, where it states that the "aim of the Convention [regarding the recovery of contractual debts] is not to introduce compulsory arbitration in the limited field to which it relates. The only obligation imposed by the Convention is that an intervening Power must not have recourse to force before it has tried arbitration". Case of *Certain Norwegian Loans* (France v. Norway), *I.C.J. Reports*, 1957, p. 24. Note, however, that the Court did not consider the obligation found in Article 53(2) of the 1907 Convention for the Pacific Settlement of International Disputes.

As a result, it may be said that the relevance today of the Second Peace Conference of 1907 and the Permanent Court of Arbitration is that they solidify the notion that arbitration as voluntary. The only relevant provision to have emerged in 1907 is Article 53(1) of the revised Convention, in which States agreed to what, in effect, is the mandatory establishment of a *compromis* – as a device for meeting *their* previous undertakings under general treaties to resort to obligatory arbitration. Hardly the compulsory arbitration which peace advocates sought, but quite in line with the wish of States to maintain as much freedom of action as possible in their international relations.

5.3. **The Practice of the Permanent Court of Arbitration**

By the end of 1999, there were 49 States Parties to both the 1899 and 1907 Convention for the Pacific Settlement of International Disputes; 21 States had ratified the 1899 Convention while 20 the 1907 Convention[93]. All cases brought before the Permanent Court of Arbitration were based on at least one of the parties having ratified either the 1899 or 1907 Conventions. By virtue of the identical provisions of Articles 26 of the 1899 Convention, and 47 of the 1907 Convention, however, the "jurisdiction of the Permanent Court may, within the conditions laid down in the Regulations, be extended to disputes between non-Contracting Powers or between Contracting Powers and non-Contracting Powers, if the parties are agreed on recourse to this Tribunal"[94]. These provisions have lead to eight inter-State arbitration cases having been submitted to the Court.

5.3.1. *Treaties*

As a result of the establishment of the Permanent Court of Arbitration in 1899, France and Great Britain negotiated a general arbitration treaty that would become a model for similar instruments, using the Court of Arbitration as their third-party dispute settlement mechanism. The Articles of the treaty reads:

---

[93] The following States have ratified both Conventions: Australia, Austria, Belgium, Belarus, Bolivia, Brazil, Burkina Faso, Cambodia, Cameroon, Canada, Chile, China, Colombia, Cuba, Denmark, Dominican Republic, El Salvador, France, Germany, Guatemala, Haiti, Honduras, Hungary, Iceland, Iraq, Japan, Kyrgysztan, Laos, Lebanon, Luxembourg, Mexico, The Netherlands, Nicaragua, Norway, Panama, Paraguay, Portugal, Romania, Russia, Senegal, Spain, Sweden, Switzerland, Thailand, Ukraine, United Kingdom, United States, and Zaire.

The following States have only ratified the 1899 Convention: Argentina, Bulgaria, Croatia, Ghana, Ecuador, Fiji, Greece, India, Iran, Italy, Mauritius, New Zealand, Pakistan, Peru, Slovenia, Sri Lanka, Turkey, Venezuela, Yugoslavia, and Zimbabwe.

The following States have only ratified the 1907 Convention: Costa Rica, Cyprus, Czech Republic, Egypt, Finland, Israel, Jordan, Libya, Liechtenstein, Malta, Nigeria, Poland, Singapore, Slovak Republic, South Africa, Sudan, Suriname, Swaziland, Uganda, and Uruguay.

[94] "Cases Submitted to Arbitration before the Permanent Court of Arbitration", Annex 2, *Permanent Court of Arbitration: 96th Annual Report*, 1996, pp. 27-35.

> *Article 1*
> Differences which may arise of a legal nature, or relating to the interpretation of treaties existing between the two Contracting Parties, and which it may not have been possible to settle by diplomacy, shall be referred to the Permanent Court of Arbitration established at The Hague by the Convention of the 29th July, 1899, provided, nevertheless, that they do not affect the vital interests, the independence, or the honour of the two Contracting States, and do not concern the interests of third Parties.
>
> *Article 2*
> In each individual case the High Contracting Parties, before appealing to the Permanent Court of Arbitration, shall concluded a special agreement defining clearly the matter in dispute, the scope of the powers of the arbitrators, and the periods to be fixed for the formation of the arbitral tribunal and the several stages of the procedure.
>
> *Article 3*
> The present Agreement is concluded for a period of five years, dating from the day of signature[95].

The fact that these two European Powers were prepared to have recourse to the Permanent Court of Arbitration led to their Treaty being the basis of approximately 80 similar agreements concluded before 1914. Yet, as a *prima facie* reading of the agreement reveals, whatever pronouncements that were made regarding obligatory arbitration in Article 1 were negated in Article 2, as it was exclusively up to the parties to establish the *compromis*. Thus, arbitration was in effect left to the parties, due to the fact that if no agreement could be reached on the *compromis*, the Court was not empowered to attempt to settle that dispute.

It should be noted that the treaties containing the same provisions, and concluded after 1907 were to take on a new interpretation for States that ratified the second Convention for the Pacific Settlement of International Disputes. As noted earlier, according to Article 53(1) of that Convention, either party could, unilaterally, bring to the attention of the Court any disagreement based on a general arbitration agreement. As a result States Parties to the 1907 Convention undertook a much wider obligation to arbitrate when ratifying a treaty based on the Anglo-French model as concluded after 1907. Such treaties concluded after the Second Peace Conference by State Parties to the settlement treaty were in effect signing general treaties of obligatory arbitration in the truest sense, for the obligation undertaken could be invoked unilaterally by its Parties and could lead to the elaboration of a *compromis* by the Court of Arbitration[96].

---

[95] Agreement between the United Kingdom and France Providing for the Settlement of Arbitration of Certain Classes of Questions Which May Arise between the two Governments. Bureau international de la Cour permanente d'arbitrage, *Traités généraux d'arbitrage*, Vol. 1, pp. 33-35.

[96] See Cory, *op. cit.* n. 27, pp. 52-53, n. 2, for treaties based on the Anglo-French model signed after 1907. The author mentions ten such treaties which were signed between 1907 and 1914.

5.3.2. *Cases*

The Permanent Court of Arbitration has dealt with 33 arbitration cases[97], the bulk of which were heard during the first three decades of its existence. After 1932, the Court has considered only five inter-State cases[98]. Over the same period, the Court kept itself busy in three different areas. First, through an extensive interpretation of Article 47 given by the Administrative Council in 1960, the Court made its services available for disputes between States and non-State entities[99]. Second, since 1982, the Court's premises have been used to serve the Iran-United States Claims Tribunal when the need for a larger courtroom was required. Third and finally, the Court has made its premises available to international commercial arbitrations, for which the rules are agreed to on an *ad hoc* basis[100]. Furthermore the Court, in recent times, has sought to expand its mandate by developing rules which would make arbitration more appealing to States[101] and by introducing various optional rules meant to encourage various international subjects to arbitrate[102].

Of the 32 cases which have been dealt with by the Permanent Court of Arbitration, only one has been heard as a result of a general treaty of arbitration, the type which would have called for arbitration even if the parties could not agree on a *compromis*. The *Muscat Dhows* case was brought as a result of the 1903 Anglo-French Arbitration Treaty, more precisely of a *Compromis* signed on 13 October 1904 in which the parties "agreed that the questions shall be determined by reference to arbitration, in accordance with the provisions of Article 1 of the

97 "Cases Submitted to Arbitration before the Permanent Court of Arbitration", Annex 2, Permanent Court of Arbitration, *op. cit.* n. 78, pp. 27-35.

98 *Radio Orient* case, 1 April 1940 (States of Levant under French mandate - Egypt) *Administration of Lighthouses* case, 24 July 1956 (France - Greece); *Heathrow Airport User Charges* case, 2 May 1994, (United States of America - United Kingdom); *Loan Agreement between Italy and Costa Rica*, 26 June 1998 (Italy – Costa Rica); and *Sovereignty of Various Red Sea Islands* case, 9 October 1998, (Eritrea - Yemen). P. Hamilton *et al.* (eds.), *The Permanent Court of Arbitration: International Arbitration and Dispute Resolution*, 1999.

99 Rules of Arbitration and Conciliation for Settlement of International Disputes between two Parties of which only one is a State, Permanent Court of Arbitration, Annex 3, *The Permanent Court of Arbitration – New Directions*, 1991, pp. 45-55. These Rules were replaced in 1993 by the Permanent Court of Arbitration Optional Rules for Arbitrating Disputes between Two Parties of Which only One Is a State. Since 1966, the year the first case was brought under the above Rules, five cases have been heard as between a State and a non-State entity.

100 Permanent Court of Arbitration, *op. cit.* n. 94, pp. 9-11.

101 Permanent Court of Arbitration, Permanent Court of Arbitration Optional Rules for Arbitrating Disputes between Two States, 20 October 1992, IB/doc/93/1.

102 Permanent Court of Arbitration, *op. cit.* n. 94, p. 15. Consider para. 43, where mention is made of the following rules which have taken effect on 1 July 1996: Permanent Court of Arbitration Optional Rules for Arbitration Involving International Organizations and States; Permanent Court of Arbitration Optional Rules for Arbitration between International Organizations and Private Parties; and Permanent Court of Arbitration Optional Conciliation Rules.

Convention concluded between the two countries on the 14th October last, and that the decision of The Hague Tribunal shall be final"[103]. The questions to be settled were based on a mutual agreement by the parties dating back to 1862, whereby "they engaged reciprocally to respect the independence of the Sultan of Muscat"[104]. It was contended by Britain that the dhows (or vessels) of Muscat that might be carrying slaves and were flying French flags were in breach of the General Anti-Slavery Act of Brussels of 1890. In its award of 8 August 1905, the panel found that while France was empowered to allow whomever to fly its flag, that right was limited by the General Act[105]. As has been noted, as this case came up on the basis of the 1899 Convention rather than that of 1907, the Court did not have the authority to determine the provisions of the *compromis* where agreement could not be reached. In any event, this case cannot be considered as having come before the Court through compulsion, as it formed the object of mutual agreement; as a result, the Permanent Court of Arbitration has never dealt with a case of obligatory arbitration.

6. Conclusion

During the nineteenth century States were no longer impervious, for the first time, in their international relations to the demands of the general public. But, States translated the demands for obligatory arbitration made by national peace movements into the voluntary schemes advocated by their legislators. The move to be more "practical", initiated by the Inter-Parliamentary Union and the Institute of International Law, meant that the aims of these bodies were in line with the aims of governments. This practicality was given substance at the Peace Conferences of 1899 and 1907, where States failed to agree on establishing a system of obligatory arbitration. The establishment of the Permanent Court of Arbitration and the subsequent practice are a testimony to the ineffectiveness of the system. The Permanent Court in reality shows that States may profess to be willing to be bound by the rule of law, but that when it comes to turning professions into deeds, this is all they are willing to produce.

This chapter has sought to demonstrate how attempts at forcing States to respect the rule of law through the avocation of obligatory arbitration failed. The end product of these movements was the establishment of the Permanent Court of Arbitration. That Court's record speaks volumes as it has sat in splendid isolation in a world rife with violations of international law. In the aftermath of the horrors

[103] *Muscat Dhows* case, 13 October 1904, Bureau international de la Cour permanente d'Arbitrage, *Recueil des actes et protocoles concernant le differend entre La France et La Grande Bretagne à propos des boutres de Mascate*, 1905, p. 5.

[104] James B. Scott (ed.), "The Muscat Dhows Case", *op. cit.* n. 57, pp. 93-109, at p. 93.

[105] *Muscat Dhows* case, *op. cit.* n. 103, pp. 69-74.

of the First World War came a renewed impetus to set up an international system governed by the rule of law. The outcome of the process was the creation of what is today called the International Court of Justice. To what extent that Court has been successful in solidifying and institutionalizing the rule of law on the international level will be the focus of the next chapter.

Chapter 2
THE PERMANENT COURT OF INTERNATIONAL JUSTICE AND THE INTERNATIONAL COURT OF JUSTICE

1. Introduction

As a result of the failure to have obligatory arbitration consolidated at the international level, interests turned elsewhere. It may be said that the great expectations regarding obligatory adjudication "shifted from public international arbitration in the nineteenth century to the International Court in the twentieth"[1]. With the establishment of a standing mechanism for arbitration – the Permanent Court of Arbitration – the focus of those advocating obligatory arbitration shifted to a call for the establishment of a court of law with compulsory jurisdiction. Having failed to secure the obligatory nature of recourse to the Permanent Court of Arbitration, advocates turned their attention to what would, in 1920, become the Permanent Court of International Justice.

These two mechanisms, the Permanent Courts of Arbitration and the Permanent Court of International Justice (the latter having been subsequently superseded by the International Court of Justice) are the basis of what may be termed the 'Hague System' of adjudication which remains, to this day, the universal mechanism for the legal means of peaceful settlement of international disputes. The following chapter considers the evolution of the World Court to demonstrate the attempts made to have the two Courts function with obligatory jurisdiction. As States balked at this idea when instituting both the Permanent Court of International Justice in 1920, and again in 1945 with the creation of the International Court of Justice, consideration will be given to what was instituted in its place. The establishment of the voluntary system of adjudication as found in the provisions of Article 36(1) and (2) of the Statute of the International Court will be examined to consider to what extent States have translated into practice their supposed interest in obligatory adjudication.

2. The Permanent Court of International Justice

The utter failure of the dispute settlement mechanism established during the Hague Peace Conferences to impede the march towards the First World War

[1] M. W. Janis, "The International Court", Janis, M. W. (ed.), *International Courts for the Twenty-First Century*, 1992, p. 17.

made it necessary for States to reconsider the means by which the peaceful settlement of international disputes might be achieved. With the defeat of the Central Powers and, in particular, Germany, it was felt by most advocates of obligatory adjudication that the time had come for the establishment of a court that would allow the rule of law to reign at the international level. While no mention of an international court was made in the Fourteen Points proclaimed by the United States President Wilson as a basis of a future peace settlement of the 1914 war, Article 14 of the Covenant of the League of Nations, establishing the first universal international organization, provided as follows:

> The Council [of the League of Nations] shall formulate and submit to the Members of the League for adoption plans for the establishment of a Permanent Court of International Justice. The Court shall be competent to hear and determine any dispute of an international character which the parties thereto submit to it. The Court may also give an advisory opinion upon any dispute or question referred to it by the Council or by the Assembly[2].

This provision was part of the League of Nations' attempt to outlaw war by introducing a general system under which, by virtue of Article 12, States could not resort to war until they had either brought their dispute before an adjudicative body or to the attention of the League's Executive Council. If either party to the dispute did not comply with an award or a recommendation of the Council, the parties, after a three-month cooling period, were entitled to resort to war to settle their dispute.

The League of Nations thus attributed an important role to adjudication in the new international system. But, even thought the States Parties agreed:

> that whenever any dispute or difficulty shall arise between them which they recognize to be suitable for submission to arbitration or judicial settlement, and which cannot be settled satisfactorily by diplomacy, they will submit the entire matter to arbitration or judicial settlement[3],

this undertaking cannot be said to amount to a submission to obligatory adjudication. The fact that it was left to States to "recognize" which disputes were "suitable for submission" to adjudication clearly demonstrated the voluntary nature of this provision; however, this did not mean that the League system as a whole rested on a basis of voluntary adjudication. As Politis notes, "if the League of Na-

[2] The Covenant of the League of Nations, Malcolm D. Evans (ed.), *Blackstone's International Law Documents*, 1991, pp. 1-8.

[3] Article 12, *ibid., p. 3.*

tions did not bless obligatory [adjudication], it did make place for the idea of an obligation within its judicial organization"[4].

2.1. **From the Advisory Committee of Jurists to the Assembly of the League**

At the League Council's second meeting in London, on 14 February 1920, it was decided that an advisory committee of jurists made up of ten eminent scholars and diplomats would draft the "plans for the establishment of a Permanent Court of International Justice", as required by Article 14 of the Covenant. This Advisory Committee met at The Hague from 16 June to 24 July 1920 and prepared a draft which, with some modifications, was accepted by the Council on 5 August 1920 and, on 13 December 1920, by the Assembly of the League of Nations as the Statute of the Permanent Court of International Justice. For those who were true advocates of an international system governed by the rule of law, however, the "modifications" were devastating as they included the removal of a recommendation, made by the Advisory Committee of Jurists, that the Permanent Court be endowed with obligatory jurisdiction.

The Committee had used as a basis of its draft proposal various sources, including the Statute of the defunct Central American Court of Justice, the ill-fated Court of Arbitral Justice proposed at the 1907 Peace Conference but never constituted, the official drafts proposals of various Central Powers and Neutral States[5], as well as proposals from such groups as the Inter-Parliamentary Union[6]. Using these schemes and Statutes as their guide, the Committee sought to bring the new court into the "Hague System" of dispute settlement by determining in Article 1 that:

> A Permanent Court of International Justice is hereby established, in accordance with Article 14 of the Covenant of the League of Nations. This Court shall be in addition to the Court of Arbitration organized by the Hague Conventions of 1899 and 1907, and to the special Tribunals of Arbitration to which States are always at liberty to submit their disputes for settlement"[7].

While this provision remained intact, two draft articles prepared by the Committee, calling for obligatory jurisdiction, did not:

---

[4] N. Politis, *La justice internationale*, 1924, p. 235. My translation.

[5] Draft Convention Relative to the Creation of a Judicial Arbitration Court (Annex to the first "Vœu" of the Second Peace Conference). James B. Scott, *The Hague Conventions and Declarations of 1899 and 1907*, 1915, pp. 31-40. For the Central American Court of Justice, see Jean Eyma, *La Cour de Justice Centre Américane*, 1928 and J. B. Scott, "The Closing of the Central American Court of Justice", *American Journal of International Law*, Vol. 12, 1918, pp. 382-385.

[6] Helen May Cory, *Compulsory Arbitration of International Disputes*, 1932, p. 116.

[7] Article 1, Statute of the Permanent Court of International Justice, Annexed to the Protocol of Signatures of 16 December 1920, Permanent Court of International Justice, *Statute and Rules of Court and Other Constitutional Documents, Rules and Regulations*, Series D, No. 1, 1936, pp. 12-28.

Article 33
When a dispute has arisen between States, and it has been found impossible to settle it by diplomatic means, and no agreement has been made to choose another jurisdiction, the party complaining may bring the case before the Court. The Court shall, first of all, decide whether the preceding conditions have been complied with; if so, it shall hear and determine the dispute according to the terms and within the limits of the next Article.

Article 34
Between States which are members of the League of Nations, the Court shall have jurisdiction (and this without any special convention giving it jurisdiction) to hear and determine cases of a legal nature concerning:

a. The interpretation of a treaty;
b. Any question of international law;
c. The existence of any fact, which if established, would constitute a breach of an international obligation;
d. The nature or extent of reparation to be made for the breach of an international obligation;
e. The interpretation of a sentence passed by the Court.

In the final Report to the Council of the League of Nations, the President of the Committee of Jurists, Baron Descamps, explained why the Committee considered the time ripe for the inclusion of obligatory jurisdiction in the Statute of the proposed Permanent Court of International Justice. He noted that States must move forward in the direction pointed to at the 1907 Peace Conference, where "more than three quarters of the States represented had given their adherence to a draft of a treaty of universal arbitration"[8] and had made a declaration admitting the principle of obligatory arbitration. The Report made it clear that the Committee was going beyond its mandate set out in Article 14 of the Covenant, which would only empowered the Court "to hear and determine any dispute [...] which the parties thereto submit to it". The Descamps Report noted that the proposal of obligatory jurisdiction was perhaps "not strictly in accordance with the letter of the Covenant, [however, it] follows its spirit so exactly that it would seem a great pity, now that the Court is being definitely organized, not to complete the progress made by this last provision"[9]. The political organs of the League of Nations, however, would have none of it.

Over a four-month period, from August to November 1920, the Council of the League of Nations considered the draft prepared by the Committee of Jurists and decided to replace Articles 33 and 34 by a provisions stating that "the jurisdiction of the Court is defined by Articles 12, 13 and 14 of the Covenant"[10]. The Council

[8] Baron Descamps, "Report", Permanent Court of International Justice, Advisory Committee of Jurists, *Procès-verbaux of the Proceedings of the Committee*, 1920, pp. 726-727.
[9] *Ibid.*, p. 728.
[10] Manely O. Hudson, *The World Court (1921-1931)*, 1931, p. 111.

then passed the amended draft on to the Assembly, where it was greeted with dampened spirits as a result of the exclusion of the provisions related to obligatory jurisdiction. The Assembly, having transmitted it on to various sub-committees for further consideration, approved what would become the Statute of the Permanent Court of International Justice on 13 December 1920. That a consensus was reached was due, in large part, to a proposal by the Brazilian delegate Raoul Fernandes, who sought to find some middle ground between obligatory and voluntary jurisdiction. His proposal, "the so-called optional clause, made it possible for any nation to accept the Court without compulsory jurisdiction, while allowing the supporters of compulsory jurisdiction to accept it then and there so far as they were concerned"[11].

2.2. Obligatory Jurisdiction at the Permanent Court of International Justice

Article 36 of the Statute of the Permanent Court of International Justice provided two means by which States could undertake obligations which would mandate their future appearance before the Court. The Article reads:

> 1. The jurisdiction of the Court comprises all cases which the parties refer to it and all matters specially provided for in treaties and conventions in force.
>
> 2. The Members of the League of Nations and the States mentioned in the Annex to the Covenant may, either when signing or ratifying the Protocol to which the present Statute is adjoined, or at a later moment, declare that they recognize as compulsory ipso facto and without special agreement, in relation to any other Member or State accepting the same obligation, the jurisdiction of the Court in all or any of the classes of legal disputes concerning:
>
> a. the interpretation of a treaty;
> b. any question of international law;
> c. the existence of any fact which, if established, would constitute a breach of an international obligation;
> d. the nature or extent of the reparation to be made for the breach of an international obligation.
>
> 3. The declaration referred to above may be made unconditionally or on condition of reciprocity on the part of several or certain Members or States, or for a certain time.

[11] Antonio Bustamante, *The World Court*, 1925, p. 104. It comes as little surprise that the optional clause system should emerge from South America, as it resembles in many respects the Latin American traditions towards reservations to treaties. This decentralized tradition was considered by the International Court of Justice in its 1951 Advisory Opinion *Reservations to the Convention on the Prevention and Punishment of the Crime of Genocide*, and later introduced into general international law by Articles 19 to 23 of the Vienna Convention on the Law of Treaties, 23 May 1969. Eric Suy, *Corpus Iuris Gentium*, 1996, pp. 103-104.

4. In the event of a dispute as to whether the Court has jurisdiction, the matter shall be settled by the decision of the Court.[12]

The first of these means, found in Article 36(1), determines that States may accept the jurisdiction of the Court *via* a *compromis*. The latter part of Article 36(1) may be seen as the end product of the advocacy of the compromissory clause that had been emphasized in Europe and the United States since the late eighteen-hundreds. This provision, "all matters specially provided for in treaties and conventions in force", could be read as including compromissory clauses in bilateral and in multilateral treaties but could also be framed as a general treaty of the type of those concluded in Latin America with respect to arbitration but recast for the Permanent Court[13].

The second means by which States may undertake an obligation to appear before the Court based on a previous undertaking is found at Article 36(2) of its Statute. This Article introduces the "optional clause" system that allows each State to decide unilaterally whether or not to accept the jurisdiction of the Court and to determine the parameters of that undertaking. Some States such as Haiti made unilateral declarations accepting to have any dispute heard by the Permanent Court[14]. Most States, however, accepted the jurisdiction of the Permanent Court under the optional-clause but limited their obligation through reservations. These reservations were based, for the most part, on reciprocity, thus effectively closing the optional-clause system to States unwilling to join it and thus ensuring that only States having undertaken such obligations could find themselves before the Court in a contentious case. The reservations made during the Permanent Court era were quite banal and fall into several common patterns. They included, for instance, reservations limiting the acceptance of the jurisdiction to disputes arising after a given date, to disputes for which a solution had not been reached by diplomatic means, or to cases where the parties had not agreed on another method of dispute settlement.

Beyond these two elements of jurisdiction – treaty provisions referring to the Court and the "optional-clause" system – which States could accept, the Permanent Court was given a further power which is a main ingredient in establishing

---

[12] Article 36, Statute of the Permanent Court of International Justice, *op. cit.* n. 7.

[13] This was the case with the General Act of Geneva of 1928, whereby 24 States agreed to submit all disputes to the Permanent Court of International Justice unless they could come to an agreement to arbitrate, and subject to a number of reservations. See Article 17, General Act for the Pacific Settlement of International Disputes. Permanent Court of International Justice, *Collection of Texts Governing the Jurisdiction of the Court*, Series D, No. 6, 1932, p. 75. The reservations made to Article 17 are stated at Article 39(2) and (3), and include: disputes arising before the accession of one of the Parties, over questions solely within the domestic jurisdiction of a State, over clearly specified subject-matters, and on the basis of reciprocity. *Ibid.*, p. 80.

[14] "Au nom de la République d'Haiti, je déclare reconnaître la compétence obligatoire de la Cour permanente de Justice intenationale". Permanent Court of International Justice, *Collection of Texts Governing the Jurisdiction of the Court*, Series D, No. 6, 1932, p. 37.

obligatory adjudication. Under Article 36(4), the Court was endowed with the ability to determine its own jurisdiction. As was pointed by the Appeals Chamber of the International Criminal Tribunal for the former Yugoslavia:

> This power, known as the principle of "*Kompetenz-Kompetenz*" in German or "*la compétence de la compétence*" in French, is part, and indeed a major part, of the incidental or inherent jurisdiction of any judicial or arbitral tribunal, consisting of its "jurisdiction to determine its own jurisdiction"[15].

With the power to determine the limits of its own jurisdiction, the Permanent Court gained something that was absent from the universal arbitration system established at The Hague Conferences except for the very specific area of general arbitration treaties concluded after 1907. With the absence of jurisdiction to settle a *compromis* in most areas and the Permanent Court of Arbitration permanency existing in name only; it is of little surprise that the practice of Court of Justice should quickly outstrip that of the Court of Arbitration.

2.3. The Practice of the Permanent Court of International Justice

While the Permanent Court of International Justice was in existence, 43 States accepted its jurisdiction under the optional-clause system. By the time the Court had heard its last case, only the following 29 States remained bound by the optional clause: 1) Union of South Africa, 2) Australia, 3) Bolivia, 4) Brazil, 5) United Kingdom of Great Britain and Northern Ireland, 6) Bulgaria, 7) Canada, 8) Colombia, 9) Denmark, 10) Dominican Republic, 11) Estonia, 12) Finland, 13) Haiti, 14) India, 15) Iran, 16) Ireland, 17) Latvia, 18) Luxembourg, 19) Netherlands, 20) New Zealand, 21) Norway, 22) Panama, 23) Paraguay, 24) Portugal, 25) Salvador, 26) Siam, 27) Sweden, 28) Switzerland, and 29) Uruguay. The other 14 States which had accepted the jurisdiction of the Court under Article 36(2) were no longer Parties to the system by 1945: 1) Albania, 2) Belgium, 3) China, 4) Ethiopia, 5) France, 6) Germany, 7) Greece, 8) Hungary, 9) Italy, 10) Lithuania, 11) Peru, 12) Spain, 13) Romania, and 14) Yugoslavia[16].

2.3.1. *Treaties*

During the era of the Permanent Court of International Justice, 585 instruments, mostly bilateral in nature, included provisions granting the Court predominantly

---

[15] *Decision of Defence Motion for Interlocutory Appeal on Jurisdiction*, 2 October 1995, IT-94-1-T (*Tadic* case), para. 18.

[16] See Permanent Court of International Justice, *Collection of Texts Governing the Jurisdiction of the Court*, Series D, No. 6, 1932, p. 50. Note that Nicaragua is not included in this listing, although the International Court of Justice later decided that its declaration of 24 September 1929, accepting the Court's jurisdiction under the optional clause, was valid. *I.C.J. Reports*, 1984, p. 392.

obligatory jurisdiction[17]. The earliest compromissory clauses referring to the Court were inserted in peace treaties ending the First World War and, in fact, preceded the establishment of the Court. Beyond these treaties, many compromissory clauses were included in treaties of commerce and navigation, communication and transit (rivers, railways, ports, telephones, telegraphs, radio, air navigation, etc.), as well as in agreements on a variety of other topics. Helen May Cory noted that the signatories of the treaties containing such clauses were "nearly always European countries"[18]. Taking Cory's statement into consideration and keeping in mind the list of the States which had accepted the "optional clause", it would seem that the ancient dichotomy between European and Latin American States regarding the types of obligations they were prepared to undertake in the field of arbitration persisted with respect to the Permanent Court. Furthermore, while the European States may well have been willing to subscribe to the optional clause, many of them did so hesitantly, including in their declarations of acceptance a set time-period, typically of five years. In stark contrast, the Latin American States, while concluding but a few treaties establishing specific obligations to have recourse to the Permanent Court, joined the optional-clause system with more vigour – some unconditionally – by simply subscribing to Article 36(2) on the basis of reciprocity.

2.3.2. *Cases*

ARTICLE 36 (1)

From its inauguration at the Hague Peace Palace, on 15 February 1922, to its last public sitting on 4 December 1939, the Permanent Court dealt with 66 cases, 38 contentious and 28 advisory opinions, rendering 32 judgments[19]. Of those 38 contentious cases, 12 were brought by unilateral application to the Court, based on its jurisdiction, under Article 36(1) of the Statute, to hear cases "referred to it and all matters specially provided for in treaties and conventions in force". So it was that the following disputes were brought forward, using what truly may be termed obligatory compromissory clauses. The *S/S Wimbledon* case dealt with a French-chartered British steamer carrying munitions and refused use of the Kiel Canal by the Germany authorities on the basis of a German neutrality order. The case was brought as a result of the instituting of proceedings by France, Britain, Italy, and Japan, on the basis of Article 386 of the Treaty of Versailles, which provided:

[17] For references to all 585 treaty provisions, see Permanent Court of International Justice, *Collection of Texts Governing the Jurisdiction of the Court*, Series D, No. 6, 1932 and the *Eighth* through *Sixteenth Report of the Permanent Court of International Justice*, Series E, Nos. 8-16, chapter 10, section 2.

[18] Cory, *op. cit.* n. 6, p. 161.

[19] Shabtai Rosenne, *The Law and Practice of the International Court*, 1985, p. 10

> In the event of violation of any of the conditions of Articles 380 to 386 [provisions relative to the Kiel Canal], of disputes as to the interpretation of these articles, any interested Power can appeal to the jurisdiction instituted for the purpose by the League of Nations[20].

The *Mavrommatis Concessions* case, dealing with the loss of a construction concession granted to a Greek national in Jerusalem, came as a result of Greek intervention under Article 26 of the Mandate for Palestine:

> The Mandatory agrees that, if any dispute whatever should arise between the Mandatory and another Member of the League of Nations relating to the interpretation or the application of the provisions of the Mandate, such disputes, if it cannot be settled by negotiation, shall be submitted to the Permanent Court of Justice provided for by Article 14 of the Covenant of the League of Nations[21].

The compromissory clause under which the *German Interests in Polish Upper Silesia* case and the Case concerning the *Factory at Chorzow* were submitted to the Court is found at Article 23(1) of the Geneva Convention on Upper Silesia.

> Should differences of opinion respecting the construction and application of Articles 6 to 22 arise between the German and Polish Governments, they shall be submitted to the Permanent Court of International Justice[22].

These disputes dealt, *inter alia*, with a Germany factory established in Upper Silesia during the First World War and later liquidated by the Polish Government. Under the same Geneva Convention, but by virtue of its Article 72, two more cases were brought forward. The first, brought by Germany against Poland, was later withdrawn (*Prince von Pless* case[23]); the second, relating to the *Rights of Minorities in Upper Silesia*, was a result of Polish nullification of the admission of several thousand students to German minority schools in divided Upper Silesia. The Permanent Court found that it had jurisdiction under Article 72(3) of the Geneva Convention, which read:

> Germany further agrees that any difference of opinion as to questions of law or fact arising out of these articles between the German Government and any other Power, a Member of the Council of the League of Nations, shall be held to be a dispute of an international character under Article 14 of the Covenant of the League of Nations. The German Government hereby consents that any such dispute shall, if the other Party thereto demands, be referred to the Permanent Court of International Justice. The

---

[20] *S/S Wimbleton* case, 17 August 1923, *C.P.I.J.*, Series A, No. 1, p. 20.

[21] *Mavrommatis Concessions* case, 26 March 1925, *C.P.I.J.*, Series A, No. 10, p. 15.

[22] *German Interests in Polish Upper Silesia* case, *C.P.I.J.*, Series A, No. 7, p. 13; and Case concerning the *Factory at Chorzow*, 13 September 1928, *C.P.I.J.*, Series A, No. 9, p. 12.

[23] Case concerning the *Administration of the Prince of Pless* case, 2 December 1933, *C.P.I.J.*, Series A/B, No. 52, p. 13.

> decision of the Permanent Court shall be final and shall have the same force and effect as an award under Article 13 of the Covenant[24].

The German Government unilaterally submitted two further cases against Poland. In the first, which concerned the *Polish Agrarian Reform and the German Minority*, the Court rejected a German request to grant interim measures further to protect "Polish nationals of German race" whose land had been expropriated under a Polish decree. This case, which was withdrawn by Germany after the interim measures phase, was entertained by the Court as a result of Article 12(3) of the 1919 Convention between the Allied and Associate Powers and Poland which was, in substance, identical to the Geneva Convention regarding Upper Silesia:

> Poland further agrees that any difference of opinion as to questions of law or fact arising out of these Articles between the Polish Government and any one of the Principal Allied and Associated Powers or any other Power, a Member of the Council of the League of Nations, shall be held to be a dispute of an international character under Article 14 of the Covenant of the League of Nations. The Polish Government hereby consents that any such dispute shall, if the other Party thereto demands, be referred to the Permanent Court of International Justice. The decision of the Permanent Court shall be final and shall have the same force and effect as an award under Article 13 of the Covenant[25].

The final case brought by Germany was a request, by virtue of Article 60 of the Statute of the Permanent Court of International Justice, to interpret the judgment on jurisdiction in the Case concerning the *Factory at Chorzow*[26]. Article 60 stated that:

> The judgment is final and without appeal. In the event of dispute as to the meaning or scope of the judgment, the Court shall construe it upon the request of any party.

Beyond these cases, the Court received unilateral applications in five other matters. The case of the *Interpretation of the Treaty of Neuilly* case, came before it, once again, as a result of Article 60 of the Statute of the Permanent Court[27]. The Court was further called upon by Britain, France, Italy, and Japan, in the *Interpretation of the Statute of the Memel Territory* case, to settle a "difference of

---

[24] *Rights of Minorities in Upper Silesia (Minority Schools)* case, *C.P.I.J.*, 26 April 1928, Series A, No. 15, p. 17.

[25] Case concerning the *Polish Agrarian Reform and the German Minority*, *C.P.I.J.*, 2 December 1933, Series A/B, No. 58, p. 175. Article 12, Convention between the Allied and Associate Powers and Poland, *The Consolidated Treaty Series*, 28 June 1919, Vol. 225, 1981, p. 419.

[26] *Interpretation of Judgments Nos. 7 and 8 (The Chorzow Factory* case), *C.P.I.J.*, 16 December 1927, Series A, No. 13, p. 5.

[27] *Interpretation of Judgment No. 3 (*the *Treaty of Neuilly* case), 26 March 1925, *C.P.I.J.*, Series A, No. 4, p. 4.

opinion" that they had with Lithuania over the proper functioning of that State's executive. The four States were endowed with the ability to bring this issue before the Permanent Court by Article 17 of the Convention concerning the Territory of Memel which read, in part:

> In the event of any difference of opinion in regard to questions of law or fact concerning these provisions, between the Lithuanian Government and any of the Principal Allied Powers, Members of the Council of the League of Nations, such differences shall be regarded as a dispute of an international character under the terms of Article 14 of the Covenant of the League of Nations. The Lithuanian Government agrees that all disputes of this kind shall, if the other party so requests, be referred to the Permanent Court of International Justice. There shall be no appeal from the Permanent Court's decision, which shall have the force and value of a decision rendered in virtue of Article 13 of the Covenant[28].

A further case, the *Appeal from a Judgment of the Hungaro-Czechoslovak Mixed Arbitral Tribunal*, was brought forward by Czechoslovakia as an appeal from a decision of an arbitration panel regarding the restoration of property to the Royal Hungarian Peter Pázmány University. Under Article 10 of Agreement No. II concerning the Settlement of Questions relating to the Agrarian Reforms and The Mixed Arbitration Tribunals, either of the parties could appeal to the Permanent Court:

> For all judgments regarding jurisdiction or merits rendered by the Arbitration Tribunals in all cases other than those envisioned under Article 1 of the present Agreement, Romania, Czechoslovakia, Yugoslavia, on the one hand, and Hungary, on the other, agree to recognize the competence of the Permanent Court of International Justice as its appeal Chamber, without special agreement[29].

The final case submitted to the Permanent Court *via* unilateral application was based on a compromissory clause found in a dispute settlement convention. The *Société commerciale de Belgique* case pertained to a request by Belgium to find Greece in violation of its international obligation for not having carried out an arbitral award. The case was brought under the terms of the Treaty of Conciliation, Arbitration and Judicial Settlement of 1929, which stated in particular that:

---

[28] *Interpretation of the Statute of the Memel Territory* case, 24 June 1932, *C.P.I.J.*, Series A/B, No. 49, p. 296. Article 17, Convention concerning the Territory of Memel, 8 May 1924, *League of Nations Treaty Series*, Vol. 29, 1924, p. 93.

[29] *Appeal from a Judgment of the Hungaro-Czechoslovak Mixed Arbitral Tribunal(The Peter Pázmány University v. the State of Czechoslavakia* case), 15 December 1933, *C.P.I.J.*, Series A/B, No. 61, p. 209. Agreement (No. II) concerning the Settlement of Questions Relating to the Agrarian Reforms and the Mixed Arbitration Tribunals between Hungary, Romania, Czechoslovakia, and Yugoslavia, Permanent Court of International Justice, *Collection of Texts Governing the Jurisdiction of the Court*, Series D, No. 6, 1932, p. 620.

> All disputes with regard to which the parties are in conflict as to their respective rights shall be submitted for decision to the Permanent Court of International Justice, unless the Parties agree, in the manner hereinafter provided, to have resort to an arbitral tribunal[30].

ARTICLE 36(2)

Beyond the referrals to the Court based on Article 36(1), the Permanent Court was seized on eight occasions by unilateral applications under the optional-clause system. The first was the *Denunciation of the Sino-Belgian Treaty*, where China sought to put an end to one of its "unequal treaties"[31]. As a result, Belgium brought action under Article 36(2) of the Statute, maintaining that the principle of *rebus sic stantibus* did not justify China's denunciation of the Treaty. As a result of interim measures indicated by the Court, the parties reopened negotiations and settled their dispute without further assistance. In its 1933 judgment in the *Eastern Greenland* case, the Court, having received an application by the Danish Government, found that Denmark in fact, had maintained sovereignty over large areas of Greenland despite the opposition of Norway[32]. The next case to be dealt with by the Permanent Court under the optional-clause system was the unilateral submission of the *Losinger & Co.* case by the Swiss Government against Yugoslavia. At issue in this instance were acts by the Yugoslav legislature to thwart attempts by a Swiss firm to bring a case to arbitration. While the Court upheld the rights of the Swiss Government in the preliminary phase of the hearings, the parties later agreed to discontinue the procedure[33].

In the *Phosphates in Morocco* case, the Italian Government initiated proceedings before the Permanent Court against France over a dispute regarding the ownership of rights to mineral fields[34]. During the preliminary phase, the Court found that it had jurisdiction despite assertions by France that the dispute could not be adjudicated as a result of the declaration made by it under the optional-clause system. In the *Diversion of the Water from the Meuse* case, the Netherlands sought to have the construction of certain Belgian canals and irrigation works declared in violation of international law by the Permanent Court. The submissions of the parties were however rejected by the Court, which confined

---

[30] *Société commerciale de Belgique* case, 15 June 1939, *C.P.I.J.*, Series A/B, No. 78, p. 161. Article 4, Convention of Conciliation, Arbitration and Judicial Settlement between Belgium and Greece, 25 June 1929, *League of Nations Treaty Series*, Vol. 113, 1931, p. 121.

[31] *Denunciation of the Treaty of November 2nd, 1865, between China and Belgium* case, 25 May 1929, *C.P.I.J.*, Series A, No. 8.

[32] *Legal Status of the South-Eastern Territory of Greenland* case, 2 August 1932, *C.P.I.J.*, Series A/B, No. 48. Note that after the Danish Application Norway followed by bringing a counter-Application against Denmark.

[33] *Losinger & Co.* case, 14 December 1936, *C.P.I.J.*, Series A/B, No. 67.

[34] *Phosphates in Morocco* case (Preliminary Objections), 14 May 1938, *C.P.I.J.*, Series A/B, No. 74.

itself to examining provisions of the most recent treaty in force. As a result, the parties were left no closer to settling their dispute[35]. A further action, although of little note, undertaken through the system contemplated by Article 36(2), was the *Panevezys-Saldutiskis Railway* case that saw Estonia, on behalf of its nationals, take action against Lithuania in an attempt to gain compensation for the loss of their investment in a train company[36].

The final two cases brought forward under the optional-clause were the *Electrical Company of Sofia* and the *Gerliczy* cases which were later "discontinued, although no formal orders were issued"[37]. The first, which in fact led the last judgment rendered by the Permanent Court, began with a request, on the part of Belgium, to have Bulgaria pay compensation for acts related to its influence over retail pricing of a Belgium-owned utilities company[38]. During the preliminary phase, the Court rendered a judgment finding that Belgium was entitled to have her contentions dealt with on the merits, as the Court did indeed have jurisdiction over the issue because both parties had previously subscribed to the optional clause. The case, however, was never heard as a result of German occupation of the Netherlands, which forced the Court to go into hibernation. After the Second World War, Belgium withdrew its claim. The *Gerliczy* case came as a result of Liechtenstein's invocation of both its own and Hungary's declaration under Article 36(2) of the Statute of the Permanent Court. In this instance, the Court set time-limits for the filing of documents in a dispute that revolved around the settling of debts as a by-product of the dissolution of the Hapsburg Empire. However, once again, "[o]wing to the war and to the invasion of the Netherlands"[39], the case was not heard and simply faded away.

3. The International Court of Justice

As a result of the Second World War, the Permanent Court of International Justice was moved to Geneva, where it remained dormant[40]. It became clear during the war years, as reflected in texts such as the Atlantic Charter, that a new international system and organization would be the basis of a post-war peace and that the Permanent Court would be superseded by a new body. What was not clear, however, was whether this new international system would be endowed with an international court possessing obligatory jurisdiction.

[35] *Diversion of the Water from the Meuse* case, 28 April 1937, *C.P.I.J.*, Series A/B, No. 70.

[36] *Panevezys-Saldutiskis Railway* case, 28 February 1939, *C.P.I.J.*, Series A/B, No. 76.

[37] Rosenne, *The Law and Practice of the International Court, 1920-1996*, Vol. 1, 1997, p. 17.

[38] *Electrical Company of Sofia and Bulgaria* case, 4 April 1939, *C.P.I.J.*, Series A/B, No. 79.

[39] *Gerliczy* case, Permanent Court of International Justice, *Collection of Texts Governing the Jurisdiction of the Court*, Series D, No. 6, 1932, pp. 154-158, at p. 158.

[40] Rosenne, *op. cit.* n. 37, p. 23.

3.1. Transition from the Permanent Court to the International Court of Justice

The first concrete sign that a new court would be established in the aftermath of the Second World War appeared in the Report of the Informal Inter-Allied Committee on the Future of the Permanent Court of International Justice which met for the first time on 20 May 1943, in London, and delivered its Report to the Allied Governments on 10 February 1944[41]. This Committee, consisting of twelve jurists, with Gerald Fitzmaurice acting as its Secretary, considered that a new court might take on one of two basic forms:

> (a) the existing Permanent Court of International Justice, continued in existence with such modifications in its present Statute as may be necessary, or
>
> (b) a new Court established by means of a new Statute, which, however, would probably contain a number of provisions taken from or based upon present one[42].

This wish for continuity between the Permanent Court and any future court was the main theme running through the Report. The Committee agreed that the optional-clause system appeared "to us to constitute a satisfactory definition of what the Court's jurisdiction should be"[43] and thus rejected, in quite strong terms, endowing the new Court with any obligatory jurisdiction.

As the War appeared to be drawing to a close, the Allied Powers agreed, at Dumbarton Oaks, that a committee of jurists should gather to consider the issue of a new international court. The Washington Committee of Jurists met on 9 April 1945 and dealt, in large part, with drafting a statute which would ensure a true continuity of the work of the Permanent Court. One question, however, remained open, which was "whether acceptance of compulsory jurisdiction was to be a condition of membership in the [United Nations] Organization, and this in turn raised the question of the extent to which the organizational structure for the pacific settlement of international disputes was to contain elements of compulsion"[44]. At the San Francisco Conference establishing the United Nations, it was decided that obligatory adjudication would find no place in the new international organization[45]. Instead, a more general obligation was placed on States, by virtue of Article 2(2) of the United Nations Charter, to settle their differences by peaceful means, in which arbitration and judicial settlement were to be but two of amongst several options made available[46].

---

[41] Report of the Informal Inter-Allied Committee on the Future of the Permanent Court of International Justice, 10 February 1944, Misc. No. 2, 1944, para. 1.

[42] *Ibid.*, para. 3.

[43] *Ibid.*, para. 57.

[44] Rosenne, *op. cit.* n. 37, p. 32.

[45] Documents of the United Nations Conference on International Organizations, Vol. 14, 1945.

[46] See Article 33, Charter of the United Nations.

It was further decided that the new court, to be named the International Court of Justice, would retain as much continuity with the Permanent Court of International Justice as possible. This link between the old and the new Court is made evident by Article 92 of the UN Charter which notes that the latter would function in accordance with the new Statute, "which is based upon the Statue of the Permanent Court of International Justice". From a jurisdictional point of view, it was decided to leave intact the provisions of Article 36(2) of the Permanent Court's Statute. The changes introduced in new Article 36 of the Statute of the International Court of Justice were meant to ensure continuity between the old Court and the new Court's proper functioning within the new United Nations system. Article 36 of the Statute of the International Court of Justice reads:

> 1. The jurisdiction of the Court comprises all cases which the parties refer to it and all matters specially provided for in the Charter of the United Nations or in treaties and conventions in force.
>
> 2. The States Parties to the present Statute may at any time declare that they recognize as compulsory *ipso facto* and without special agreement, in relation to any other state accepting the same obligation, the jurisdiction of the Court in all legal disputes concerning:
>
> a. the interpretation of a treaty;
> b. any question of international law;
> c. the existence of any fact which, if established, would constitute a breach of an international obligation;
> d. the nature or extent of the reparation to be made for the breach of an international obligation.
>
> 3. The declarations referred to above may be made unconditionally or on condition of reciprocity on the part of several or certain states, or for a certain time.
>
> 4. Such declarations shall be deposited with the Secretary-General of the United Nations, who shall transmit copies thereof to the parties to the Statute and to the Registrar of the Court.
>
> 5. Declarations made under Article 36 of the Statute of the Permanent Court of International Justice and which are still in force shall be deemed, as between the Parties to the present Statute, to be acceptances of the compulsory jurisdiction of the International Court of Justice for the period which they still have to run and in accordance with their terms.
>
> 6. In the event of a dispute as to whether the Court has jurisdiction, the matter shall be settled by the decision of the Court[47].

[47] For the full text of the Statute of the International Court of Justice, see Appendix 2.

While Article 36(5) assured the continuation of the "optional-clause" system[48], a new provision, Article 37, was required to ensure the continuity of the second type of obligatory jurisdiction, i.e. that dealt with in Article 36(1) of the Statute of the Permanent Court. Article 37 of the new Statute provides that:

> Whenever a treaty or convention in force provides for reference of a matter to a tribunal to have been instituted by the League of Nations, or to the Permanent Court of International Justice, the matter shall, as between the parties to the present Statute, be referred to the International Court of Justice.

3.2. **The Practice of the International Court of Justice**

At its inauguration on 18 April 1946, the International Court of Justice came out of a seven-year hibernation simply to pick up where it had left off as the Permanent Court of International Justice. As a result, the 'Hague System' of dispute settlement remained intact and continues to this day – from a jurisdictional perspective – in much the same fashion as it functioned in the 1920s. The following 61 States were by the end of the year 1999, bound by the optional clause: 1) Australia, 2) Austria, 3) Barbados, 4) Belgium, 5) Botswana, 6) Bulgaria, 7) Cambodia, 8) Cameroon, 9) Canada, 10) Colombia, 11) Costa Rica, 12) Cyprus, 13) Denmark, 14) Dominican Republic, 15) Egypt, 16) Estonia, 17) Finland, 18) Gambia, 19) Georgia, 20) Greece, 21) Guinea-Bissau, 22) Haiti, 23) Honduras, 24) Hungary, 25) India, 26) Japan, 27) Kenya, 28) Liberia, 29) Liechtenstein, 30) Luxembourg, 31) Madagascar, 32) Malawi, 33) Malta, 34) Mauritius, 35) Mexico, 36) Nauru, 37) The Netherlands, 38) New Zealand, 39) Nicaragua, 40) Nigeria, 41) Norway, 42) Pakistan, 43) Panama, 44) Paraguay, 45) Philippines, 46) Poland, 47) Portugal 48) Senegal, 49) Somalia, 50) Spain, 51) Sudan, 52) Suriname, 53) Swaziland, 54) Sweden, 55) Switzerland, 56) Togo, 57) Uganda, 58) United Kingdom of Great Britain and Northern Ireland, 59) Uruguay, 60) Yugoslavia, 61) Zaire (now the Democratic Republic of Congo)[49]. It should also be noted that beyond this, 12 other States have also made declarations accepting the compulsory jurisdiction of the Court, but their undertakings have either expired, been withdrawn, or been terminated. Those States are: 1) Bolivia, 2) Brazil, 3) China, 4) El Salvador, 5) France, 6)

[48] This continuity exists with respect to seven States that had made declarations with respect to the optional clause during the Permanent Court of International Justice era. As their declarations under Article 36(2), have neither lapsed nor been withdrawn, they remain in force. The States, which maintained their obligations under the optional clause by virtue of Article 36(5) of the ICJ Statute were: 1) Colombia, 2) Dominican Republic, 3) Haiti, 4) Luxembourg, 5) Nicaragua, 6) Panama, and 7) Uruguay.

[49] International Court of Justice, *Annual Report to the General Assembly*, 1 August 1997, 12 July 1998.

Guatemala, 7) Iran, 8) Israel, 9) South Africa, 10) Thailand, 11) Turkey, and 12) United States of America[50].

3.2.1. *Treaties*

Of the 585 treaties[51] conferring jurisdiction on the Permanent Court of International Justice during its existence, only a handful appear in the current Yearbook of the International Court of Justice as being in force. It seems quite clear that many other instruments have remained in force and confer jurisdiction on the International Court *via* Article 37 of its Statute, but have not been brought to the attention of the Court's Registry. By the end of 1999, 264 new treaties which have been concluded since 1945 had been communicated to the Court by the Secretariat of the United Nations[52]. The treaties that are known to the Court are almost evenly split between bilateral and multilateral agreements.

There remains only one universal treaty, however, which envisions referring disputes to the Court in an obligatory manner, by virtue of Article 37 of the Statute, namely, the General Act of Geneva signed in 1928[53]. Beyond this Act, two regional treaties, the 1948 Pact of Bogotá and the 1957 European Convention for the Peaceful Settlement of Disputes, bestow jurisdiction on the International Court as though the parties had agreed, as between themselves, to be bound by Article 36(2). A further way in which multilateral conventions can provide for recourse to the International Court of Justice is through a compromissory clause. During the 1960s, such clauses were typically found, not in the body of conventions, but in optional protocols to which States might subscribe[54]. A noted exceptions to this rule may be found at Article 66 of the Vienna Convention on the Law of Treaties, which allows for unilateral recourse to the International Court in cases of disputes regarding the invalidation of treaties based on violations of *jus cogens*[55]. This use of optional protocols appears, however, to have been a practice resorted to only in a transitional phase. As from the 1970s onward, true

---

[50] *Ibid.*, p. 81, n. 1.

[51] For references to all 585 treaty provisions, see Permanent Court of International Justice, *Collection of Texts Governing the Jurisdiction of the Court*, Series D, No. 6, 1932 and the *Eighth* through *Sixteenth Report of the Permanent Court of International Justice*, Series E, Nos. 8-16, chapter 10, section 2.

[52] International Court of Justice, *Yearbook 1995-1996*, 1996, pp. 122-139.

[53] Consider the reaction of the ICJ with respect to the validity of this Act in Rosenne (1997), *op. cit.* n. 37, Vol. 2, pp. 668-670.

[54] See for example, the 1958 Geneva Law of the Sea Conventions, and the Vienna Conventions on Diplomatic Relations (1961) and Consular Relations (1963). For the history of these protocols, see the work of Paul Guggenheim as related in: H. Briggs, "The Optional Protocols of Geneva (1958) and Vienna (1961, 1963) Concerning the Compulsory Settlement of Disputes", *Recueil d'études de droit international en hommage à Paul Guggenheim*, 1968, pp. 628-641; and P. Ruegger, "Des clauses arbitrales et de juridiction dans les conventions internationales récentes", *ibid.*, pp. 687-701.

[55] Articles 53, 64, and 66, Vienna Convention on the Law of Treaties, 23 May 1969; Eric Suy, *Corpus Iuris Gentium*, 1996, pp. 99-120.

compromissory clauses conferring obligatory jurisdiction on the International Court have been directly included in the multilateral treaties themselves[56].

3.2.2. *Cases*

ARTICLE 36(1)

Since the submission of the first case to the International Court on 22 May 1947, there have been 82 contentious cases examined and 23 advisory opinions delivered[57]. Of the 82 contentious cases, 17 were brought unilaterally on the basis of compromissory clauses bestowing jurisdiction, *via* Article 36(1), on the Court. One case was submitted by way of an attempt to invoke the 1928 General Act of Geneva. This attempt was not successful, however, and as a result the Court found that it could not adjudicate on the delimitation of the continental shelf between Greece and Turkey. The Court came to the conclusion despite the invocation by Greece of Article 17 of the 1928 General Act for the Pacific Settlement of International Disputes, which reads:

> All disputes with regard to which the parties are in conflict as to their respective rights shall, subject to any reservations which may be made under Article 39, be submitted for decisions to the Permanent Court of International Justice, unless the parties agree, in the manner hereinafter provided, to have resort to an arbitral tribunal. It is understood that the dispute referred to above included in particular those mentioned in Article 36 of the Statute of the Permanent Court of International Justice[58].

A reservation made by Greece precluded the Court from examining the merits. While the Court may well have been empowered to hear the case by Articles 37 and 36(1) of its Statute, it was prevented from even considering the validity of the General Act by a Greek reservation under Article 39 which stated, *inter alia*, that questions "relating to the territorial status of Greece" were excluded.

The last case placed on the docket of the International Court in the 1900s was brought forward by Nicaragua against Honduras "with regard to legal issues between the two States concerning maritime delimitation in the Caribbean Sea"[59]. Beyond invoking the optional clause as a ground for establishing jurisdiction, Nicaragua invoked the regional 1948 Pact of Bogotá, which under Article XXXI, vests the Court with general jurisdiction:

---

[56] See, for example, Article 30 of the Convention against Torture and Other Cruel, Inhuman and Degrading Treatment or Punishment, 10 December 1984, *ibid.*, p. 469.

[57] International Court of Justice, *Yearbook 1995-1996*, 1996, p. 3. The case dealt with in May 1947 was the *Corfu Channel* case. Note that of the 82 contentious cases, 13 were pending as of 31 January 1999.

[58] *Aegean Sea Continental Shelf* case, 19 December 1978, *I.C.J. Reports* 1978, p. 14.

[59] International Court of Justice, *Press Communiqué*, 99/52, 8 December 1999.

> In conformity with Article 36, paragraph 2, of the Statute of the International Court of Justice, the High Contracting Parties declare that they recognize, in relation to any other American State, the jurisdiction of the Court as compulsory *ipso facto* without the necessity of any special agreement so long as the present Treaty is in force, in all disputes of a juridical nature that arise among them concerning:
>
> (a) The interpretation of a treaty;
> (b) Any question of international law
> (c) The existence of any fact which, if established, would constitute the breach of an international obligation;
> (d) The nature or extent of the reparation to be made for the breach of an international obligation.

An example of an instance submitted on the basis of a compromissory clause in an optional protocol of a multilateral conventions is the *Hostage* case. When personnel from the Embassy of the United States of America in Tehran were taken hostage, the United States called on the International Court, citing, among possible bases of jurisdiction, the provisions of the Optional Protocols of the Vienna Conventions of 1961 and 1963:

> Disputes arising out of the interpretation or application of the Convention shall lie within the compulsory jurisdiction of the International Court of Justice and may accordingly be brought before the Court by an application made by any party to the dispute being a Party to the present Protocol[60].

Likewise, in the case concerning the *Vienna Convention on Consular Relations* and the *LaGrand* case, Paraguay and Germany sought, and were granted, Provisional Measures calling on the United States of America to prevent the execution of one of their nationals. The disputes centered around the alleged violation of the Convention on Consular Relations by the United States which had neglected to inform the Paraguayan and German authorities that one of their nationals was being detained in America, thus depriving those States of their right to exercise diplomatic protection. The International Court found, in both cases, that it had *prima facie* jurisdiction, based on the Optional Protocol of the 1963 Vienna Convention[61].

Other cases have been submitted under the provisions of multilateral conventions, including the *Genocide* case. In this case, Bosnia–Herzegovina and Yugo-

---

[60] Case concerning *United States Diplomatic and Consular Staff in Tehran*, 24 May 1980, *I.C.J. Reports*, 1980, p. 24, para. 45.

[61] Case concerning the *Vienna Convention on Consular Relations* (Order – Provisional Measures), 9 April 1998, paras. 23 - 34. The case was withdrawn from the Court's docket by Paraguay on 10 November 1998 noting that "it did not wish to go on with the proceedings and requested that the case be removed from the Court's List". See ICJ website: http://www.icj-cij.org/idocket/ipaus/ipausframe.htm. The *LaGrand* case was instituted on 8 March 1999; see ICJ website: http://www.icj.cij.org/icjwww/idocket/igus/igusframe.htm. Note that the American Government failed to stop both executions.

slavia have made claims and counter-claims regarding violations of the 1948 Convention on the Prevention and Punishment of the Crime of Genocide. The proceedings before the Court were originated by Bosnia–Herzegovina, invoking Article IX of that Convention[62]. Based on this application, the Court found that it had jurisdiction[63]. Article IX of the Convention reads:

> Disputes between the Contracting Parties relating to the interpretation, application or fulfillment of the present Convention, including those relating to the responsibility of a State for genocide or for any of the other acts enumerated in Article III, shall be submitted to the International Court of Justice at the request of any of the parties to the dispute[64].

A further series of cases, which found its way onto the docket of the Court but had not been considered by the end of 1999, were the *Armed Activity on the Territory of the Congo* cases. The Congo instituted proceedings claiming that Burundi, Rwanda, and Uganda attempted to "seize Kinshasa through the lower Congo, in order to overthrow the Government of Public Salvation and assassinate President Laurent Désiré Kabila, with the object of installing a Tutsi régime or a régime under Tutsi control"[65]. The cases were brought forward by the Congo as against Uganda by virtue of the optional-clause system, but as against Burundi and Rwanda on the basis, *inter alia*, of a compromissory clause found in the multilateral 1984 Convention against Torture and Other Cruel, Inhuman or Degrading Treatment or Punishment[66]. That clause is found at Article 30 and reads:

> 1. Any dispute between two or more States Parties concerning the interpretation or application of this Convention which cannot be settled through negotiation shall, at the request of one of them, be submitted to arbitration. If within six months from the date of the request for arbitration the Parties are unable to agree on the organization of the arbitration, any one of those Parties may refer the dispute to the International Court of Justice by request in conformity with the Statute of the Court.

---

[62] Note that Croatia also instituted proceeding against Yugoslavia, invoking the same provision of the Genocide Convention. See International Court of Justice, *Press Communiqué*, 99/38, 2 July 1999.

[63] Case concerning the *Application of the Convention on the Prevention and Punishment of the Crime of Genocide* (Preliminary Objections), 11 July 1996. See ICJ website: www.icj-cij.org/idocket/ibhy/ibhyjudgment/ibhyjudgmentframe.htm.

[64] Article IX, Convention on the Prevention and Punishment of the Crime of Genocide, 9 December 1948; Suy, *op. cit.* n. 55, pp. 472-474.

[65] See The Democratic Republic of Congo institutes proceedings against Burundi, Uganda and Rwanda on account of "acts of armed aggression", International Court of Justice, *Press Communiqué*, 99/34, 23 June 1999, at ICJ website: http://www.icj-cij.org/icjwww/idocket/icb/icbframe.htm.

[66] Convention against Torture and Other Cruel, Inhuman or Degrading Treatment or Punishment, G.A. res. 39/46, 1984, entered into force 26 June 1987. Suy, *op. cit.* n. 55.

A further ground on which the Congo claimed jurisdiction was a provision of the Montreal Convention related to Civil Aviation. Libya invoked this same provision in its dispute with the United States and the United Kingdom in the *Lockerbie* cases, which revolved around the downing of a United States airliner over British soil. While the Court had not considered the Congolese case by the end of 1999, it did find that it had jurisdiction in the *Lockerbie* cases and that it could proceed to the merits[67]. The Court's decision revolved around Article 14 of the Montreal Convention for the Suppression of Unlawful Acts against the Safety of Civil Aviation, which reads[68]:

> Any dispute between two or more Contracting States concerning the interpretation or application of this Convention which cannot be settled through negotiation, shall, at the request of one of them, be submitted to arbitration. If within six months from the date of the request for arbitration the parties are unable to agree on the organization of the arbitration, any one of those Parties may refer the dispute to the International Court of Justice by request in conformity with the Statute of the Court[69].

Basing itself in large measure on the above provision, Iran filed an application instituting proceedings against the United States of America as a result of the destruction of an Iranian civil airliner by the United States warship USS "*Vincennes*" over the Persian Gulf in 1988. By mutual agreement the parties settled their dispute out of Court and the case was discontinued[70]. In fact, a large number of cases, brought forward by unilateral applications based on compromissory clauses, have been discontinued. To date, during the era of the International Court of Justice, ten cases submitted in this fashion have been discontinued:

> *Protection of French Nationals and Protected Persons in Egypt* (France v. Egypt), 1950; *Haya de la Torre* (Colombia v. Peru), 1951; *Ambatielos* (Greece v. U.K.), 1953;

[67] A further case concerning the downing of an aircraft, which the Court had not considered by the end of 1999 was one instituted on 22 September 1999 by Pakistan against India for the downing of a Pakistani naval plane. The Court, shortly thereafter, decided to separate the jurisdiction from the merits phase. It would appear, *prima facie*, that the Court does not have jurisdiction in this case as Pakistan cited, as its basis for bring the claim forward, Article 2(4) of the UN Charter, and the provisions of the Agreement of 6 April 1991 between itself and India regarding violations of their mutual airspace, as well as "the obligations under customary international law not to use force and not to violate the sovereignty of another State". International Court of Justice, *Press Communiqué*, 99/43, 22 September 1999.

[68] *Questions of Interpretation and Application of the 1971 Montreal Convention Arising from the Aerial Incident at Lockerbie* case (Preliminary Objections), 27 February 1998 (Libya v. U.S.A. and U.K.). See ICJ Website: www.icj-cij.org/idocket/iluk/ilukjudgment/ilukjudgmentframe.htm.

[69] Convention for the Suppression of Unlawful Acts against the Safety of Civil Aviation, 23 September 1971; Suy, *op. cit.* n. 55, pp. 616-620.

[70] *Aerial Incident of 3 July 1988* case, International Court of Justice, *Yearbook 1995-1996*, 1996, pp. 161-163.

Electricité de Beyrouth Company (France v. Lebanon); *Barcelona Traction, Light and Power Company, Limited* (Belgium v. Spain), 1961[first case]; *Compagnie du Port, des Quais et Entrepôts de Beyrouth and Société Radio-Orient* (France v. Lebanon), 1960; *Trial of Pakistani Prisoners of War* (Pakistan v. India), 1973; *Elettronica Sicula S.p.A.* (United States of America v. Italy), 1989; *Border and Transborder Armed Actions* (Nicaragua v. Costa Rica), 1987 and (Nicaragua v. Honduras), 1992; and *Vienna Convention on Consular Relations* (Paraguay v. United States of America), 1998.

As has been pointed out by Shabtai Rosenne, the fact that so many cases have been discontinued may be due to the proceedings having been instituted to reinforce diplomatic efforts for settling the dispute[71]. As was noted earlier, the obligatory jurisdiction of international tribunals has the secondary effect of focusing the attention of States – with the possibility of being cited before the Court – on seeking negotiated solutions. In the above cases, it was necessary to bring the abstinent State before the Court, to induce the parties to reach a diplomatic solution.

Of the disputes submitted to the International Court of Justice by way of a compromissory clause, the first was the *South-West Africa* case. The Court was found to have jurisdiction on the basis of Article 36(1) of the Statute of the Court, but *via* Article 37, as the treaties invoked by Ethiopia and Liberia against South Africa had been concluded during the League of Nations era and had referred to the Permanent Court of International Justice. The Court relied on Article 7 of the Mandate of 17 December 1920 for South Africa, which reads:

> The Mandatory agrees that, if any dispute whatever should arise between the Mandatory and another Member of the League of Nations relating to the interpretation or the application of the provisions of the Mandate, such dispute, if it cannot be settled by negotiation, shall be submitted to the Permanent Court of International Justice provided for by Article 14 of the Covenant of the League of Nations[72].

In the next instance, the *Northern Cameroons* case, Cameroon claimed that the United Kingdom had failed to respect obligations incumbent upon it by virtue of the Trusteeship Agreement for the Territory of the Cameroons under British Administration. These obligations pertained to plebiscites administered by the United Kingdom, which saw parts of the Northern Cameroons join Nigeria. Cameroon wished its rights to be adjudicated upon the basis of Article 19 of the Trusteeship Agreement; however, this was to no avail, as the Court found that General Assembly Resolution 1608 had effectively terminated the Agreement before the case could be considered. Article 19 of the Trusteeship Agreement mirrors the compromissory clause of the League of Nations mandate era, mentioned above, and reads:

---

[71] Rosenne (1997), *op. cit.* n. 37, Vol. 2, p. 666.
[72] *South-West Africa* case, 12 December 1962, *I.C.J. Reports*, 1962, p. 335.

> If any dispute whatever should arise between the Administrative Authority and another Member of the United Nations relating to the interpretation or application of the provisions of this Agreement, such disputes, if it cannot be settled by negotiation or other means, shall be submitted to the International Court of Justice, provided for in Chapter XIV of the United Nations Charter[73].

In the *Appeal Relating to the Jurisdiction of the ICAO Council*, the Court found that it had jurisdiction to entertain the appeal by India against a decision made by the Council of the International Civil Aviation Organization to the effect that the Council had jurisdiction over a dispute regarding overflight through Indian airspace. While the Court held that it had jurisdiction to hear the matter under the following provisions, it further found that it had jurisdiction to hear the dispute proper:

> *Article 84 of the Convention*
> If any disagreement between two or more contracting States relating to the interpretation or application of this Convention and its Annexes cannot be settled by negotiation, it shall, on the application of any State concerned in the disagreement, be decided by the Council. No member of the Council shall vote in the consideration by the Council of any dispute to which it is a party. Any contracting State may, subject to Article 85, appeal from the decision of the Council to an *ad hoc* arbitral tribunal agreed upon with the other parties to the dispute or to the Permanent Court of International [Justice]. Any such appeal shall be notified to the Council within sixty days of receipt of notification of the decision of the Council.

Section 2 of Article 2 of the Transit Agreement provides that:

> If any disagreement between two or more contracting States relating to the interpretation or application of this Agreement cannot be settled by negotiation, the provisions of Chapter XVIII of the above-mentioned Convention – [*nota*: containing the above quoted Article 84] – shall be applicable in the same manner as provided therein reference to any disagreement relating to the interpretation or application of the above-mentioned Convention[74].

In the *Fisheries Jurisdiction* cases, pitting the United Kingdom and Germany against Iceland, the Court was seized on the basis of a compromissory clause contained in an Exchange of Notes between them and the Respondent dealing with the exclusive fishing rights of Iceland. The 1961 Exchange of Notes indicates, *inter alia*, that Iceland:

---

[73] *Northern Cameroons* case, 2 December 1963 (Preliminary Objections), *I.C.J. Reports*, 1963, p. 25.

[74] *Appeal Relating to the Jurisdiction of the ICAO Council* case, 18 August 1972, *I.C.J. Reports*, 1972, p. 55.

> shall continue to work for the implementation of the Resolution of 5 May 1959, regarding the extension of the fishery jurisdiction of Iceland. However, it shall give the Government of the Federal Republic of Germany [also the United Kingdom Government] six month's notice of any such extension; in case of a dispute relating to such an extension, the matter shall, at the request of either party, be referred to the International Court of Justice[75].

The final case to be heard on the basis of a compromissory clause was one based on a provision of the Treaty of Amity, Economic Relations and Consular Rights between the United States of America and Iran. The *Oil Platforms* case related to the attack and destruction of "three offshore oil production complexes, owned and operated for commercial purposes by the National Iranian Oil Company, by several warships of the United States Navy on 19 October 1987 and 18 April 1988, respectively". Article 21(2) of the Treaty stipulates:

> Any dispute between the High Contracting Parties as to the interpretation or application of the present Treaty, not satisfactorily adjusted by diplomacy, shall be submitted to the International Court of Justice, unless the High Contracting Parties agree to settlement by some other pacific means[76].

ARTICLE 36(2) – SIMPLE INVOCATION

Beyond the cases heard by it under Article 36(1), the International Court of Justice has been seized on 20 occasions on the basis of the optional-clause system. The first of them was the *Fisheries* case, in which the Court found that the Norwegian delimitation of a fishing zone was not contrary to international law, despite the United Kingdom's assertions to the contrary[77]. The judgment in this case was followed by another, one year later, relating to the status of *U.S. Nationals in Morocco*. The case related to various rights of citizens of the United States in the French Zone of Morocco and to the extent of the consular jurisdiction possessed by the United States of America in that zone[78]. In the *Interhandel* case, the Court did not proceed to make a determination on the merits[79]. The Court found that it had jurisdiction by virtue of the optional-clause in this dispute between Switzerland and the Untied States of America concerning the restitution of the assets of a Swiss company; however, it decided that the

---

[75] *Fisheries Jurisdiction* cases, 2 February 1973, *I.C.J. Reports* 1973, p. 12, para. 13 (U.K.), and p. 54, para. 14 (F.R.G.).

[76] Case concerning *Oil Platforms*, 12 December 1996; International Court of Justice, *Press Communiqué*, 96/33, 12 December 1996, at ICJ website: www.icj-cij.org/idocket/iirus/iirusframe.htm.

[77] *Fisheries* case, 18 December 1951, *I.C.J. Reports*, 1951, p. 118.

[78] Case concerning *Rights of Nationals of the United States of America in Morocco*, 27 August 1952, *I.C.J. Reports*, 1952, p. 178.

[79] *Interhandel* case (Preliminary Objection), 21 March 1959, *I.C.J. Reports*, 1959, p. 8.

company in question, Interhandel, had not as yet exhausted local remedies, thus finding the Swiss application inadmissible.

Beyond these cases heard in the early years of the Court's existence, recent instances have seen States invoke Article 36(2) without problem. Consider the *Passage through the Great Belt* case, where Finland sought to halt a Danish project to build a low-level bridge over a sea area that would interfere with the free passage of ships[80]. Finland relied primarily on the optional-clause in bringing the case, and Denmark did not contest the Court's jurisdiction. The same is true of a case instituted by Denmark against Norway over a dispute concerning the maritime delimitation between Greenland and the Norwegian island of Jan Mayen. Here again, the Court's jurisdiction under the optional-clause was not challenged[81]. While Australia contested jurisdiction in the *Nauru* case, the Court rejected the objection almost summarily, finding that it did indeed have jurisdiction over the case, which concerned a claim of Nauru that Australia had failed in its obligations under its Trusteeship Agreement properly to administer Nauru's phosphate resources[82]. A further example of the Court's jurisdiction under the optional-clause being the object of little debate was the case over maritime delimitation initiated by Guinea-Bissau, where Senegal did not contest the Court's jurisdiction[83].

Beyond the recent instances where the Court made determinations as to its jurisdiction under the optional clause, there were a number of cases pending towards the close of the twentieth century in which one of the parties invoked the provisions of Article 36(2) as a jurisdictional basis for its actions. For instance, Cameroon filed an application instituting proceedings against Nigeria in a dispute concerning the question of sovereignty over the Bakassi Peninsula and an area around Lake Chad, and it also requested the Court to determine part of its maritime frontier[84]. While the Court has completed hearings in the preliminary phase, it will not have had a chance, by the end of 1999, to render a judgement.

[80] Case concerning *Passage through the Great Belt* (Request for the Indication of Provisional Measures), 29 July 1991, *I.C.J. Reports*, 1991, p. 13.

[81] Case concerning *Maritime Delimitation in the Area between Greenland and Jan Mayen*, 14 June 1993, *I.C.J. Reports*, 1993, p. 38.

[82] Case concerning *Certain Phosphate Lands in Nauru* (Preliminary Objections), 26 June 1992, *I.C.J. Reports*, 1992, p. 244.

[83] *Arbitral Award of 31 July 1989*, 12 November 1991, *I.C.J. Reports*, 1991, p. 62, para. 24. Note that a second case, the *Maritime Delimitation between Guinea-Bissau and Senegal*, was pending after the 1991 Judgment, however, the case was discontinued after a diplomatic solution to the dispute was found. See International Court of Justice, *Yearbook 1995-1996*, 1996, pp. 163-165.

[84] *Land and Maritime Boundary between Cameroon and Nigeria* case, International Court of Justice, *Press Communiqué*, 98/8, 11 March 1998, at ICJ website: www.icj-cij.org/idocket/icn/icnframe.htm. Note that on 25 March 1999, the Court rejected Nigeria's request to interpret the 1998 Judgment. See *Request for Interpretation of the Judgment of 11 June 1998 in the Case Concerning the Land and Maritime Boundary between Cameroon and Nigeria* (Cameroon v. Nigeria), Preliminary Objections (Nigeria v. Cameroon) on the ICJ website at: http://www.icj-cij.org/icjwww/idocket/inc/INcFRAME.HTM.

Cameroon referred to the declarations made by both States accepting the Court's jurisdiction under Article 36(2) of the Statute, while Nigeria contended that the Court had no jurisdiction. Another case placed on the docket late in the 1990s was the result of proceedings by Spain against Canada resulting from action against two Spanish vessels, the *Estai* and the *Cape Roger*, on the high seas in March 1995. While Spain contended that the Court had jurisdiction under Article 36(2), Canada invoked its declaration of 1994 accepting, *inter alia*, to appear before the Court over all disputes other than those "arising out of or concerning conservation and management measures taken by Canada with respect to vessels fishing in the NAFO Regulatory Area [...] and the enforcement of such measures". The Court upheld Canada's claim, making it clear that it could not proceed with this case as it lacked jurisdiction on account of Canada's reservation[85].

Apart from the Congo's invocation of the optional-clause against Uganda in the *Armed Activity on the Territory of the Congo* case, the Court, in 1999, placed on its docket two further cases submitted under Article 36(2). In the *Ahmadou Sadio Diallo* case, Guinea exercised diplomatic protection on behalf of one of its nationals who claimed to have been jailed and later expelled from the Congo[86]. In the absence of any amicable agreement, Guinea decided to bring the claim before the International Court. The second case, is in fact a series of cases, was brought forward by Yugoslavia in relation to the NATO's bombing of that State. Yugoslavia sought to have the bombing halted by requesting the Court to indicate provisional measures as against ten States. The Court refused to indicate such measures and further ordered that the cases against Spain and the United States of America be dismissed, finding that it "manifestly lacks jurisdiction to entertain Yugoslavia's Application". Despite this setback, Yugoslavia invoked its declaration of 25 April 1999, accepting the optional-clause system to pursue its case against Belgium, Canada, France, Germany, Italy, The Netherlands, Portugal, and the United Kingdom"[87].

ARTICLE 36(2) – SUBSTANTIVE INTERPRETATION

In various cases heard since 1945, much case-law has been developed by the Court regarding the provisions of Article 36. In the following four cases, the Court examined the limitations resulting from reservations to unilateral declarations made under Article 36(2). The *Anglo-Iranian Oil Co.* case ended after its preliminary phase as the Court found that it lacked jurisdiction over British submissions regarding the nationalization of the oil industry in Iran. The Court determined that a reservation made by Iran prevented the United Kingdom

[85] *Fisheries Jurisdiction* case, International Court of Justice, *Press Communiqué*, 97/17, 5 December 1997.

[86] For the *Ahmadou Sadio Diallo* case, International Court of Justice, *Press Communiqué*, 98/46, 30 December 1998.

[87] See Request for the Indication of Provisional Measures, Case concerning *Legality of the Use of Force*, (Yugoslavia v. Spain and Yugoslavia v. United States of America) 2 June 1999 at: http://www.icj-cij.org/icjwww/idecisions.htm.

from invoking treaties entered into prior to its declaration as a basis for litigation[88]. It found that it had jurisdiction in the *Nottebohm* case, where Liechtenstein claimed damages suffered by one of its nationals in Guatemala. On the basis of Article 36(2), the Court rejected the preliminary objection of Guatemala claiming lack of jurisdiction, as the action by the Liechtenstein was prior to the expiration of the Guatemalan declaration[89]. In the *Nicaragua* case, the Court found that a United States declaration deposited just days before Nicaragua filed suit, alleging American involvement in military and paramilitary activities against it, could not prevent the forthcoming proceedings. It noted that the 1946 declaration of the United States contained a six-month notice clause for termination and that this clause could not be overridden by the subsequent 1984 declaration, as the obligation was to be fulfilled in good faith, thus drawing an analogy to the law of treaties[90].

While the Court found that the United States reservation was of no consequence in the *Nicaragua* case, the *Norwegian Loans* case revolved around the French declaration under the optional-clause system which precluded, through a reservation, any dispute "relating to matters which are essentially within the national jurisdiction as understood by the Government of the French Republic"[91]. The Court found that it could not determine the means by which Norway was to repay loans issued on the French market, for, by virtue of reciprocity, Norway could invoke the reservation contained in the French declaration, thus ending the proceedings. The use of a reservation was key in the *Nicaragua* case as well, where the Court determined that it had jurisdiction over the dispute by virtue of the optional clause, but that jurisdiction was limited by an American reservation to its declaration accepting the jurisdiction of the Court[92]. Due to the American "multilateral treaty" reservation, the Court could, first, only consider treaties if all parties to that treaty which would be affected by the Court's decision were parties to the dispute or, second, if the United States agreed to the Court's jurisdiction. As the United States did not so agree and as all parties affected by the treaties invoked by Nicaragua were not parties to the dispute, the Court relied on the customary rules underlying those treaties as a basis for its decision.

The *Nicaragua* case was also relevant to the issue of the continuity of declarations made in the era of the Permanent Court of International Justice. Before the Court accepted that the case could proceed to its merits, it considered whether the Nicaragua declaration of 1929 was still valid (or, for that matter, whether it had ever been valid). The Court found that while Nicaragua had authorized the ratifi-

---

[88] *Anglo-Iranian Oil Co.* case, 27 August 1952, *I.C.J. Reports*, 1952, p. 110.

[89] *Nottebohm* case (Preliminary Objection), 18 November 1953, *I.C.J. Reports*, 1953, p. 122.

[90] *Military and Paramilitary Activities in and against Nicaragua* (Jurisdiction and Admissibility), 26 November 1984, *I.C.J. Reports*, 1984, pp. 417-421, paras. 58-65.

[91] *Case of Certain Norwegian Loans*, 6 July 1957, *I.C.J. Reports*, 1957, p. 25.

[92] *Military and Paramilitary Activities*, *op. cit.* n. 90, p. 424, para. 73.

cation of its 1929 declaration, through the instrument of ratification never reached the League of Nations. This being so, Nicaragua was not a party to the optional-clause system during the Permanent Court era; however, on account of the objectives of the United Nations and the structure of Article 36(5), the Court found Nicaragua to be a party to the clause from 1946 onwards[93]. In the *Aerial Incident* case, the Court was called upon to examine whether the declaration made by Bulgaria, in 1921, at the time of the Permanent Court, was still in force by virtue of Article 36(5) of the Statue of the International Court[94]. The Court rejected an Israeli claim that the destruction of one of its airliners by Bulgaria fell within its jurisdiction under the optional-clause system, acknowledging that the Bulgarian declaration was no longer valid. It held that as Bulgaria was not an original signatory of the United Nations Charter, it was not bound by Article 36(5). The Court's reasoning was based on the fact that the transition from the Permanent Court to the International Court was meant to be seamless. If a State was not an original member of the United Nations, continuity between the two Courts was not possible as, shortly after the establishment of the International Court, the Permanent Court was dissolved. At that point, States outside the United Nations system were neither parties to the new Statute nor to that of the defunct Permanent Court.

On the strength of the *Aerial Incident* case, Thailand sought to have the *Preah Vihear* case dismissed in its preliminary phase[95]. When Cambodia instituted proceedings relating to territorial sovereignty over a temple, the Thai Government sought to have the case dismissed on the ground that its 1950 declaration mentioned the "Permanent Court of International Justice" and not the "International Court of Justice". As Thailand had joined the United Nations much in the same manner as Bulgaria had, after the dissolution of the Permanent Court, it argued that it could not be bound by the optional-clause by virtue of Article 36(5). The Court rejected this assertion by finding that, by 1950, Thailand was aware that the Permanent Court no longer existed and considered that the real intention of the Thai declaration was to bind itself to the International Court.

Another case which adds to the case-law related to Article 36 is the *Right of Passage* case, where the Court examined the provisions of Article 36(4) calling on the United Nations Secretary-General to forward copies of declarations deposited with the United Nations to the Parties. Portugal argued that it had a right to transit through Indian territory to reach its enclaved territories. During the preliminary phase, the Court considered six objections made by India, one of which was that Portugal had instituted proceedings before the Secretary-General had

[93] *Ibid.*, pp. 412-413, para. 47.

[94] Case concerning the *Aerial Incident of 27 July 1955* (Preliminary Objection), 26 May 1959, *I.C.J. Reports*, 1959, pp. 136-138.

[95] Case concerning the *Temple of Preah Vihear* (Preliminary Objection), 26 May 1961, *I.C.J. Reports*, 1961, p. 28.

had time to transmit the copies of the new Portuguese declaration[96]. While the Court rejected the objection resulting therefrom, it joined two other preliminary objections to the merits and proceeded with the case. Finally, one further case was brought before the International Court of Justice by virtue of the provisions of Article 36(2), and once again it was Portugal which brought suit. This case considered a fundamental issue with respect to the Court's jurisdiction – can the Court render a judgment in which it makes a determination as to the rights and obligations of a third party which has not accepted its jurisdiction under the optional-clause system? The case at hand was instituted by Portugal against Australia and concerned a treaty which the latter had concluded with Indonesia over the exploitation of the Timor Gap[97]. In so doing, the Applicant argued, Australia had breached its international obligations towards East Timor, a State invaded and annexed by Indonesia, and, as a consequence, had also breached Portugal's rights as the administering Power of that territory. Australia argued that Portugal's dispute was with Indonesia and therefore should not be heard, as that State was not a party to the dispute. The Court agreed with the Australian contention, finding that it would necessarily have had to rule on the lawfulness of the conduct of Indonesia as a prerequisite for deciding the case.

4 Conclusion

The above survey has attempted to demonstrate how, during the formation of the 'Hague System', States have persistently balked at establishing a universal system of obligatory adjudication. While a vocal international peace movement sought to have compulsory arbitration incorporated into the international system during much of the nineteenth century, States ultimately accepted the Permanent Court of Arbitration with an understanding that if they did not wish to arbitrate, they need not do so. The twentieth century saw the creation of the Permanent Court of International Justice, later the International Court of Justice, which went further towards solidifying the rule of law. However, it also fell short of mandating obligatory adjudication, as it was left to each State individually to determine if and to what extent it would join the "optional clause" system of the World Court.

Throughout the formation of the 'Hague System', the previous two chapters have highlighted failing attempts to turn rhetoric into reality and wishes into deeds. If Germany was properly seen as the cause of the failure to institute obligatory arbitration at the Hague Peace Conferences, this does not excuse an in-

[96] Case concerning *Right of Passage over Indian Territory* (Preliminary Objection), 26 November 1957, *I.C.J. Reports*, 1957, p. 145.

[97] Case concerning *East Timor*, 30 June 1995, *I.C.J. Reports*, 1995, p. 90.

ternational system which allowed a single State to scuttle a move to strengthen the universal nature of the rule of law. Further, after the Treaty of Versailles, States were given the opportunity to incorporate obligatory adjudication into a universal system by the work of the Advisory Committee of Jurists which drafted the Statute of the Permanent Court of International Justice. Yet the Jurists' work was rejected in favour of the optional-clause system and the further provisions of Article 36 of the Court's Statute.

Having considered the formation of the 'Hague System', the present chapter turned to the functioning of that system in an attempt to highlight the occasions where there had been recourse to obligatory adjudication. Consideration of the Permanent Court of Arbitration from the perspective of obligatory arbitration leaves few lasting impressions. Of the 114 contentious cases considered by the Permanent Court of International Justice and the International Court of Justice, 26 were brought forward under the provisions of Article 36(1) relating to compromissory clauses. A further 25 cases were considered under the optional-clause system of Article 36(2). As Hersch Lauterpacht has pointed out, the legacy of the World Court is not without importance:

> The very existence of the Court, in particular when coupled with the substantial measure of obligatory jurisdiction already conferred upon it, must tend to be a factor of importance in maintaining the rule of law[98].

This importance, which Lauterpacht alluded to, may well be growing for, as the President of the International Court has noted towards the end of the twentieth Century, the docket has never been heavier[99]. Yet, despite this current upsurge, one must not lose sight of the fact that if the rule of law is to reign supreme on the international level, obligatory adjudication must be fully realized. Important as the current system may be, consent to be bound to the optional-clause system

[98] Hersch Lauterpacht, *The Development of International Law by International Courts*, 1958, p. 3.

[99] It should be noted that while the caseload of the Court's docket has increased, its budget has not kept pace. This was highlighted in President Schwebel's 1999 address to the United Nations General Assembly:

> While the caseload of the Court has significantly increased, it has not enjoyed a proportional growth in its resources. ... Today its total budget is of the order of $11,000,000 a year, a smaller percentage of the budget of the Organization than in 1946. This has resulted in an enlarging gap between the conclusion of the written, and the opening of the oral, phase of a case, a gap caused by the backlog in the work of the Court. It is trite but true to say that justice delayed may be justice denied. ... [I]f the Court is to fulfil its potential as the Organization's principal judicial organ, then it must be afforded the resources to work as intensively and expeditiously as burgeoning international recourse to the Court demands. Those resources will be effectively employed, in conformity with the principles of justice and international law, to promote the settlement of international disputes and thus further the first purpose of the United Nations."

United Nations, *Report of the International Court of Justice: 1 August 1998 – 31 July 1999*, 1999, U.N. Doc. A/54/4, para. 267.

of the International Court of Justice is far from universal. Despite the fact that, since the end of the Cold War, more than a dozen States have made declarations under Article 36(2) accepting the compulsory jurisdiction of the International Court of Justice, there remained more than two thirds of the members of the international community who have not done so. Furthermore, as opposed to the League of Nations era, where reservations to declarations accepting the Permanent Court's jurisdiction were quite banal, reservations to Article 36(2) had, during the latter part of the twentieth century, robbed the International Court of Justice of much of its jurisdiction.

States have always tended to obstruct the institutionalization of the rule of law by precluding the establishment of a universal system of obligatory adjudication. This rejection has manifested itself in the dichotomy that exists between what States assert as being a proclivity towards obligatory adjudication and their unwillingness to translate those assertions into action. While Lauterpacht may be right to the extent that the rule of law is strengthened by the 'Hague System', the rule of law demands more. That rule cannot be said to truly to exist on the international level when it is left to individual States to determine if and to what extent they will subscribe to obligatory adjudication. This structural flaw hampers the rule of law. Thus there must be a realization that the rule of law cannot effectively be implemented on the international plane without instituting obligatory recourse to third-party dispute settlement. The rule of law demands more.

Chapter 3
THE CENTRAL AMERICAN COURT OF JUSTICE

1. Introduction

The preceding examination of the 'Hague System' of international adjudication pertained to a fundamental limit to the rule of law. This limitation – the voluntary nature of the international system of dispute settlement –, while being the most far-reaching encumbrance on achieving full respect for the rule of law, is but one factor to have affected the progress of international adjudication. A further limit placed on the rule of law is the inability of a decentralized international system to ensure compliance with judgments of international courts[1] or even to have States appear before such adjudicative bodies[2], no matter what obligations they may have previously undertaken. By seeking to undermine the effectiveness of such organs, through non-cooperation, individual States place international adjudication at peril. This danger was made most evident during the tenure of the first permanent international court of law – the Central American Court of Justice. Established in 1908, that body was at the forefront of the movement which aimed at consolidating the rule of law on the international plane. Coming on the heels of the Hague Peace Conferences, the Court was a natural product of peace advocates and statesmen who sought to have international disputes settled by pacific means.

The legacy of the Court, however, reveals that the era, and more so the region, were not ripe for full acceptance of the rule of law. Instead, the Central American Court of Justice is a reminder that international law, beyond its voluntary nature, allows individual States "a very large degree of freedom of action whenever they

---

[1] In the following cases States did not abide by judgments rendered by the International Court of Justice: *Corfu Channel* case, *I.C.J. Reports*, 1949, p. 244; Albania settled in 1992 after a protracted period; *Icelandic Fisheries* case, *I.C.J. Reports*, 1974, p. 3; Iceland has not abided by this Judgement; *Iranian Hostages* case, I.*C.J. Reports*, 1980, p. 3; the Algiers Accord establishing the Iran-United States Claims Tribunal has by-passed this judgment; *Nicaragua* case, *I.C.J. Reports*, 1986, p. 3; a bilateral agreements settled this issue, by-passing the judgment.

[2] States did not participate fully in the following cases, having decided not to present oral pleadings in one or another of the phases of proceeding: Albania in the *Corfu Channel* case (United Kingdom and Northern Ireland. v. Albania), I.C.J. Reports, 1949, (Compensation); Iran in the *Anglo-Iranian Oil Company* case (United Kingdom v. Iran), I.C.J. Reports, 1952, (Interim Protection); Guatemala in the *Nottebohm* case (Liechtenstein v. Guatemala), I.C.J. Reports, 1953, (Preliminary Objections); Iceland in the *Fisheries Jurisdiction* case (United Kingdom v. Iceland), I.C.J. Reports, 1972 and 1974, (All phases); India in the *Trial of Pakistani Prisoners of War* case (Pakistan v. India), I.C.J. Reports 1973, (Interim Protection); France in the *Nuclear Tests* case (Australia v. France), I.C.J. Reports, 1974, (Interim Protection); Iran in the *U.S. Diplomatic and Consular Staff in Tehran* case (United States of America. v. Iran), I.C.J. Reports, 1980, (Merits); and the United States of America in the *Nicaragua* case (Nicaragua v. United States of America), I.C.J. Reports, 1986, (Merits).

are called upon to comply"[3] with their legal obligations. During the ten year existence of this regional Court, the notion that law should prevail found little fertile ground. In the end, the aspirations of those who advocated the primacy of law on the isthmus saw their dreams wither, as the Central American States were unable to make the transition from an international system based on complete political freedom of action to one limited by the rule of law and the pronouncements of a third-party dispute settlement mechanism.

The Central American region, since its independence from Spain on 15 September 1821, has been an area of political instability. Shortly after independence, the isthmus States formed a Central American Union shortly to be followed by dissolution, which in turn was followed by attempts to re-establish a political federation. The product of this political instability was a preoccupation with invasions and domestic turmoil. As a result of the discord reigning at the turn of the century, agreement was reached in September 1907 to hold a Central American Peace Conference between the Republics of Costa Rica, El Salvador, Guatemala, Honduras, and Nicaragua, in Washington, D.C. The United States of America and Mexico, "in order to devise the means of preserving the good relations among said Republics and bring about permanent peace in those Countries"[4], hosted the Conference. United States Secretary of State, Elihu Root, in his opening address to the Peace Conference, hinted at an American desire to see some form of international mechanism establishing itself in the region:

> It would ill become me to attempt to propose or suggest the steps you should take [however] you shall devise also some practical methods under which it will be possible to secure the performance of those agreements [...]. The declaration that a man is entitled to his liberty would be of little value with us in this country were it not for the writ of *habeas corpus* that makes it the duty of a specific judge, when applied to, to inquire into the cause of his detention and set him at liberty if he is unjustly detained[5].

James Brown Scott concluded that the Conference had been a success, not the least because of the influence exercised by the United States and Mexico over the Central American delegations. When evaluating the meeting, he wrote that the conventions concerning peace and amity, extradition, communication, future conferences, and the establishment of a pedagogical institute "would have been sufficient in themselves to justify the calling of an international conference to

[3] Hans J. Morgenthau, *Politics Among Nations: The Struggle for Power and Peace*, 1978, p. 329.

[4] Preamble, Protocol Providing for a General Conference Between the Republics of Costa Rica, Salvador, Guatemala, Honduras, and Nicaragua, *The American Journal of International Law*, Vol. 1 (Supplement), 1907, pp. 406-407.

[5] James Brown Scott, "The Central American Peace Conference of 1907", *The American Journal of International Law*, Vol. 2, 1908, p. 129.

deal with Central American affairs, but the crowning glory is the convention for the Central American court of justice"[6]. Scott was correct when, in his 1908 article, he attempted to explain why the peace negotiated at Washington was different from other Central American peace initiatives which, as Root claimed, "seemed to have been written on water"[7]:

> In the present case, the treaties and conventions would seem to be the crystallization of a public spirit and sentiment already existing, and *that the two great Republics lying to the north* have not only lent their friendly aid in the negotiation of the treaties and conventions, but *are prepared by peaceful and proper means to guarantee their execution*[8].

The willingness of the "two great Republics lying to the north" and, more specifically, the United States[9] to guarantee the execution of the decisions of the newly established Central American Court of Justice insured its early success and, as we shall see, its later demise.

2. The Central American Court of Justice

By virtue of the Article 27 of the Convention for the Establishment of a Central American Court of Justice, the Court came into existence when the last of the five States ratified the Convention, and it was to remain in existence for a period of ten years. The Central American Court of Justice was inaugurated on 25 May 1908 in Cartago, Costa Rica. A courthouse was erected thanks to a gift of $100,000 made by Andrew Carnegie[10]. Based on a Salvadorian proposal, the Statute of the Central American Court, although adopted in the months following

[6] *Ibid.*, p. 134.

[7] *Ibid.*, p. 129.

[8] *Ibid.*, p. 143. Emphasis added.

[9] Diana G. Munro, utilizing correspondence of the then US Secretary of State, Elihu Root, explains – in her book *Intervention and Dollar Diplomacy in the Caribbean 1900-1921,* 1964 – the United States' strategy in dealing with the isthmus. She notes that "[a]s usual, he [Root] sought to avoid the appearance of North American dictation by letting Mexico take the lead" (p. 147). Although the United States and Mexico are often mentioned in unison in their role with respect to the Central American Court of Justice, Mexico clearly played the role of proxy. Therefore, even though the writings related to the Court often speak of the United States and Mexico together, it should be understood, as will became evident as this chapter progresses, that the United States played *the* major and pivotal role in the establishment, rise, and subsequent fall of the Central American Court of Justice.

[10] The Central American Court of Justice, along with the Costa Rican capital, were later moved to present-day San José, 30 km northeast, which had proven geologically more stable. Andrew Carnegie, at the time of the Court's move, prompted by the decimation of Cartago by an earthquake, provided another $100,000 for the building of a new courthouse. That building, which still exists, is now utilized by Costa Rica's Foreign Ministry to receive dignitaries.

the 1907 Hague Peace Conference, was not influenced by the schemes presented there[11]. Instead of failing to come to an agreement as to the establishment of an arbitral tribunal – as had been the case on the "old continent" – the isthmus States created a court of law "for the purpose of efficaciously guaranteeing their rights and maintaining peace and harmony inalterably in their relations, without being obliged to resort in any case to the employment of force"[12].

2.1. The Jurisdiction of the Court

The jurisdiction of the Court was by any standard (be it today or at the time of its establishment) very broad. Pursuant to Article 1 of the Convention for the Establishment of a Central American Court of Justice, the latter's jurisdiction *ratione materiae* included "all controversies or questions which may arise among them, of whatsoever nature and no matter what their origin may be", the sole limitation being that the parties must attempt to settle their dispute beforehand by diplomatic means. Beyond the jurisdiction *ratione materiae* thus established, the Court could also be seized of international questions between Central American States and any other foreign States if they were submitted by common agreement. Furthermore, by means of an "annexed article", the Central American delegations to the Washington Peace Conference provided States with the option of allowing the Court to have jurisdiction over disputes involving the legislative, executive, and judicial branches of their respective municipal governments[13]. The final provision of the Convention for the Establishment of a Central American Court of Justice stated:

> *Provisionary Article*
> As a recommendation of the five Delegations an Article is annexed which contains amplification of the Central American Court of Justice, in order that the Legislatures

---

[11] Manley O. Hudson, *The Permanent Court of International Justice 1920-1942: A Treatise*, 1943, p. 44. James Brown Scott and subsequent authors, who base their analysis on his work, have noted that the establishment of the Court "was essentially an American project", *The American Journal of International Law*, Vol. 2, 1908, p. 26. Scott's opinion as to the United States' willingness to exercise leadership in the area of permanent international courts at the Hague Peace Conferences and in the creation of the Central American Court of Justice appears to be over-stated. For an examination of the two Hague Peace Conferences, see above Chapter 1; as to the influence of those Conferences on the creation of the Central American Court, Hudson writes that the "influence seems to have been confined to a stimulus to action", p. 44.

[12] Preamble, Convention for the establishment of a Central American Court of Justice, *Documentos relativos á la Conferencia de Paz Centroamericana: Tratodos y Convenciones*, 1907, p. 10. See Appendix 3 for the full text of the Convention.

[13] The Court was also given the power to determine its own competence in jurisdictional matters (*compétence de la compétence*). Article 22 of the Convention provided, in part, that the Court is empowered to "determine its jurisdiction, interpreting the treaties and conventions germane to the matter in dispute, and applying the principles of international law". Further, Articles 14 and 15 provided for challenges to the jurisdiction of the Court.

that may deem it proper may see fit to inc1ude it upon ratifying this Convention.

Annexed Article
The Central American Court of Justice shall also have jurisdiction over the conflicts which may arise between the Legislative, Executive and Judicial Powers, and when as a matter of fact the judicial decisions and congressional resolutions are not respected[14].

The jurisdiction *ratione personae* of the Central American Court of Justice was not limited to States; individuals were also allowed to bring claims forward against isthmus States of which they were not nationals if they had exhausted local remedies or could demonstrate a denial of justice[15]. By virtue of Article 3, individuals could also present claims against their own governments, but only by common accord[16]. While no cases were brought forward on the basis of such common accord, five cases instituted by individuals were placed on the docket during the Court's ten-year life-span. Of these five cases, four revolved around the issue of arbitrary imprisonment and expulsion.

The first three of these cases, *Fornos Diaz v. Guatemala*[17], *Cedra v. Costa Rica*[18], and *Molina Larios v. Honduras*[19], where found inadmissible by the Court, as the individuals concerned had failed to exhaust local remedies. A fourth case, *Bermúdez Nuñez v. Cost Rica*[20], saw Costa Rica waive the local remedies rule only to have the Court decide against the plaintiff on the basis that Mr. Bermúdez Nuñez had failed to demonstrate the restraint required of an alien. The plaintiff, it appears, had been expulsed from Nicaragua for his part in plotting to overthrow the Government of that State. The fifth case, the *Election of González*

[14] Hudson notes that it was unclear whether ratification of the Annexed Article was required to bring it into force. He goes on to note that Guatemala had expressly accepted the Article, while Costa Rica had expressly rejected it, which was to have an effect on *Election of González Flores* case. Hudson, *op. cit.* n. 11, p. 45, n. 31.

[15] Article 2, Convention for the Establishment of a Central American Court of Justice, pp. 10-11. Note that while the English version of the Convention reads: "provided that the remedies which the laws of the respective country provide against such violation shall have been exhausted *and* that a denial of justice shall be shown", this is clearly an error, as the Spanish text provides: "contra tal violación, *ó* se demonstrate denegación de justicia". Regardless, if both texts were authentic, the case-law, even at the turn of the century, indicates that exhaustion of local remedies and denial of justice are separate issues – they are not cumulative. For the authentication of treaties concluded in two or more languages, see Article 33, Vienna Convention on the Law of Treaties of 1969.

[16] Note that, because of an error in Article 3 of the Convention for the Establishment of a Central American Court of Justice, an Additional Protocol was signed which provides the authentic Article 3. See Additional Protocol to the Convention for the establishment of a Central American Court of Justice, *Documentos relativos á la Conferencia de Paz Centroamericana: Tratodos y Convenciones*, 1907, pp. 18-19.

[17] "*Fornos Diaz v. Guatemala* case", *The American Journal of International Law*, Vol. 3, 1909, pp. 737-747.

[18] Hudson, *op. cit.* n. 11, p. 55.

[19] *Ibid.*, p. 56.

[20] *Ibid.*, pp. 56-57.

Flores case, was brought by five individuals representing Central American States who challenged the election of a President of Costa Rica. The Court also found the case inadmissible, declaring that such an *actio popularis constitutionalis* was not within its jurisdiction, as Costa Rica was not a Party to the Annexed Article, which would have allowed the Court to consider conflicts between the municipal branches of a State[21].

The extent of the jurisdiction granted to the Central American of Justice was unheard of at the time and has not been heard of since. The following are examples of how far-reaching the jurisdiction was understood to be. The Minister of Foreign Relations of Colombia wrote with respect to the creation of the Court:

> The Central American Court of Justice, in the form established by the pacts we are studying, will give reality to an ideal that has not been reached by the three Pan American Conferences or even the Hague Conferences. To that tribunal are submitted, without restriction, all controversies or questions that may arise between the contracting parties, whatever their nature and whatever their origin. This is international arbitration in its amplest form [...] [22].

United States Ambassador Enrique Creel, writing to the President and the Minister of Foreign Relations of Mexico, congratulated them on the achievements of the Washington Conference, noting that the "Permanent Court of Justice will decide all international questions, *without exception,* and will be the first tribunal possessing the highest of jurisdictions to be organized on earth"[23]. Writing in the 1920s, historian Samuel Inman stated that:

> The Central American Court of Justice had the broadest jurisdiction ever instituted in a permanent system between nations. In some respects it was even boarder than any temporal international tribunal has ever had, and compares favorably with that of national courts. Therefore it marked an advance in a world where enlightened opinion was rapidly crystallizing around the idea that an international legal system, definite in character and operating with certainty, was absolutely necessary[24].

While some have argued that a main drawback of the Central American Court of Justice was that its jurisdiction was too large, this argument only seems to hold water in retrospect[25]. Because it was the first ever international and permanent court of law, it was breaking new ground in the field. Had the Central American Court survived beyond its original mandate and flourished, subsequent

---

[21] *Ibid.*, pp. 57-58.

[22] Manuel Echeverria, Secretary of the Central American Court of Justice, "Note addressed by the Central American Court of Justice to the Governments of Costa Rica, El Salvador, Honduras and Guatemala", *The American Journal of International Law*, Vol. 11 (Supplement), 1917, p. 6.

[23] *Ibid.*, p. 6. Emphasis in the original.

[24] Samual Guy Inman, *Problems in Pan-Americanism*, 1926, p. 302.

[25] Jean Eyma, *La Cour de justice centre américaine*, 1928, pp. 40-58.

international courts would have, in all likelihood, benefited from the vastness of its jurisdiction. Due to its failure, however, future attempts to establish international courts led to far more restricted areas of jurisdiction[26].

2.2. **The Rise of the Central American Court of Justice**

The earliest success of the Central American Court of Justice was its ability to end hostilities between three isthmus States involving an insurrection movement and a border dispute. However, this apex was illusory, as it was the influence of the United States which ensured that the decision, and, more specifically, the interlocutory orders handed down by the Court were respected. The rise of the Central American Court of Justice was illusionary in that the isthmus States were not prepared to abide by the orders pursuant to their own will. The acceptance of the rulings of the Court under pressure from the United States meant that the Central American countries might well disregard such rulings whenever the United States showed no inclination towards enforcement.

2.2.1. *Honduras v. El Salvador and Guatemala*

As noted in an editorial comment of the *American Journal of International Law*,

> [a]fter its inauguration, the Court was almost immediately called upon to hear and settle a dispute between Honduras [...], on one side, and El Salvador and Guatemala, on the other.

Thus, for the first time in world history, we see a permanent court of law sitting in judgment of nations, parties appearing before it. This was evidently a great step forward, in line with the hopes of those advocating obligatory adjudication, although it was a regional court; but it constituted a definite progress on the road to a court with universal jurisdiction. It was the first constituted judicial body of a permanent organization to sit in judgment of nations as municipal tribunals do of individuals[27].

The Court, taking seriously the mandate given it by the States at Washington, went beyond the jurisdiction to which it had been confined, setting out to solicit its first case. "The Court, before its jurisdiction was formally invoked by any of

---

[26] See Chapter 2, in particular the section dealing with the work of the Advisory Committee of Jurists in drafting the Statute of the Permanent Court of International Justice.

[27] Editorial Comment, "The First Case Before the Central American Court of Justice", *The American Journal of International Law*, Vol. 2, 1908, p. 836; see also M. Basdevant, "Premier litige porté devant la Cour de justice permanente centre-américaine", *Revue générale de droit international public*, vol. 16, 1909, pp. 99-106.

the Central American States, itself urged the contending nations to appear before it"[28]. The solicitation of the Court was by way of telegram and read, in part:

> This court can not, certainly, exercise in any case its attributes of arbiter unless at the solicitation of an interested party; but it considers itself bound by its high mission to exhaust the resources of its friendly and well-intentioned intervention for the maintenance of peace and harmony in the five brother States [...][29].

The Court noted that the case in point revolved around the claim that Guatemala and El Salvador were aiding the revolutionary movements within the Honduran border and that these events, having "unfortunately begun in Honduras, bring on complications of international importance, for which noble ends it suffices that recourse be had to this court"[30].

The Court, having received word shortly thereafter that the States were, in fact, prepared to utilize the Court as their dispute-settling mechanism, issued interlocutory orders. The Government of Honduras, having filed an action with the Court against Guatemala and El Salvador, sought to halt the hostilities. It asserted that the two States had "protected and fomented the revolutionary movement which [is] now astir against the constituted authorities of the nation"[31]. The Court ordered Guatemala and El Salvador to halt all military action and to make sure that those revolutionary forces, be they national or foreign, remain neutral. The effect of these orders, in retrospect, was no small achievement, as some authors at the turn of the century have asserted – the orders had the effect of saving the region from war[32]. As noted in the *American Journal of International Law*:

> Although there was no manifestation on the part of the Governments of Salvador and Guatemala to refuse to submit to these interlocutory decrees of the court, the President of El Salvador intimated that the order was, in reality, an unnecessary one. Whatever may have been the feeling with respect to these orders of the court, *the revolution in Honduras promptly subsided*[33].

Following these interlocutory orders, the Court rendered its decision in December of that year, finding that El Salvador and Guatemala were in fact not guilty of,

---

[28] *AJIL*, *ibid.*, p. 836; Basdevant, p. 100. Note that the Court solicited two further cases; this did not, however, contribute to bringing about a settlement. See *1910 Revolution in Nicaragua* case and *1912 Revolution in Nicaragua* case, Hudson, *op. cit.* n. 11, p. 54-56.

[29] Telegram dated 8 July 1908, *AJIL*, *ibid.*, p. 836.

[30] *Ibid.*, p. 837.

[31] *Ibid.*, p. 838.

[32] Primary among those contemporary scholars was James Brown Scott; others, however, give tacit support to his opinions on this matter, including Jean Eyma, *op. cit.* n. 25, and Hudson, "Central American Court of Justice", *The American Journal of International Law*, Vol. 26, 1932, pp. 759-786.

[33] *AJIL*, *op. cit.* n. 27, p. 841. Emphasis added.

among other items, "protecting or encouraging the [...] insurrection movement" by not "arresting and trying the Honduran emigrants who were threatening the peace of their country"[34]. This decision raised to a new level the notion of international adjudication. The Court, it was perceived, had taken an important step in consolidating the rule of law on the international level and in dealing with issues "of vital interest and national honor such as many powers had repeatedly asserted could not ever be settled [...]"[35]. As Jean Eyma has asserted, the Central American Court took a leading role in attempting to find a pacific settlement to the dispute, a situation never before seen internationally[36]. Professor Basdevant, writing in 1909, mentioned four reasons for which this case and the decision of the Court were of importance from a historical and legal perspective. Primary among these reasons was the fact that the case proceeded without the need for a *compromis*, the Court being endowed with obligatory jurisdiction. Second, the issue at hand was one which, up until this case, would have been excluded from adjudication, as it touched upon the "honour" of a State. Third, the interlocutory orders avoided war; and fourth and finally, it placed adjudication on the level of diplomacy as a means for settling a dispute at a time when adjudication was seen by the international community as a last-resort mechanism.[37]

To say that the decision in *Honduras v. El Salvador and Guatemala* case was a beacon of hope for the establishment of an international order based on the primacy of law would, however, be an overstatement. Instead, the decision of the Central American Court of Justice can be seen as an aberration, later to be corrected by bringing the Court back into the fold of a State-centric international system in which the Court would play a role subordinate to the United States' geopolitical and economic interests. The decision, the first ever rendered by a permanent international court of law, despite its apparent jurisprudential value, was tainted by politics. How might one explain the successful implementation of the first decision brought before the Central American Court of Justice? A simple answer could lie in the consent of the States Parties to the Court's jurisdiction given during the 1907 Central American Peace Conference. It will be recalled that each State had agreed to limit its sovereignty in exchange for corresponding limitations agreed to by the other concerned States. Yet this does not explain why the Court succeeded in its first case while subsequent decisions rendered by it went unenforced. A better answer would be one which takes account of the political aspect of what Hans Morgenthau has termed the "vague and ambiguous" nature of international law, which allows States "a very great degree of freedom of action" to "comply with a rule of international law"[38]. In *Honduras v. El Salva-*

---

[34] *Honduras v. Salvador and Guatemala*, 19 December 1909, *The American Journal of International Law*, Vol. 3, 1909, pp. 734-736.

[35] Helen May Cory, *Compulsory Arbitration of International Disputes*, 1932, p. 92.

[36] Eyma, *op. cit.* n. 25, p. 66.

[37] Basdevant, *op. cit.* n. 27, p. 66.

[38] Morgenthau, *op. cit.* n. 3, p. 329.

dor and Guatemala, consideration must be given to actions, subsequent to the issuing by the Central American Court of interlocutory orders, that prompted the hostilities in Honduras to subside.

Article 25 of the Convention establishing the Central American Court provides the following with regard to the implementation of its decisions:

> The judgments of the Court shall be communicated to the five Governments of the contracting Republics. The interested parties solemnly bind themselves to submit to said judgments, and all agree to lend all moral support that may be necessary in order that they may be properly fulfilled, thereby constituting a real and positive guarantee of respect for this Convention and for the Central American Court of Justice.

As a result, the only recourse the Court had, for calling upon States to comply with its decisions was to solicit the "moral support" of each State to respect the Convention. Can the fact that all the Parties to this dispute agreed to abide by the orders of the Court be attributed to the moral imperative to respect the Convention? To answer this question in the affirmative would, in hindsight, seem naive. What, then, were the factors ensuring compliance?

Beyond the invitation of the Court to make the parties appear before it, and beyond the moral imperative to respect the judgments of the Court, there are two factors which should be further expanded upon to explain the uniqueness of this case. The first is the relatively short time-period which had elapsed between the States' binding commitment to the Peace of Washington, thus ensuring a measure of goodwill between them. Yet this, in and of itself, is not enough to explain the compliance shown by the isthmus States. In reality, a second factor weighed much more heavily on the States' willingness to appear before the Central American Court and to comply with its orders and decisions. That second factor was the willingness of the United States of America and Mexico to act as coercive powers to insure that the judgments of the Court would be respected.

With less than a year having elapsed between the establishment of the Court and the claims being brought before it by Honduras, the Central American States had a positive, if somewhat cautious, view of the Court. The goodwill evidenced by those States was based, in part, on the fact that as signatories of the Peace of Washington, each felt compelled to attempt to make the new peace a workable one. Nor was the positive attitude of the Central American States towards the Court diminished by the uncertainty over the outcome of the Court's deliberation in this first case. Up until the commencement of the first session, the Court had been a theoretical entity, the first modern international court, with no historical precedent by which to gauge the outcome of its deliberations. Out of a sense of goodwill and curiosity about the role that the Court would play in Central America, States, then, were prepared to follow through with an untested way of proceeding. Goodwill and curiosity brought the parties to the Court. What made them stick around for long enough to comply with its interlocutory orders and decisions, and what caused them to respect their treaty obligations?

The parties to *Honduras v. El Salvador and Guatemala* chose to heed the orders that were issued by the Court because, in James Brown Scott's words, "the two great Republics lying to the north were prepared to guarantee their execution". Diana Munro described the events as follows:

> When the Court demanded that all of the governments withdraw their troops from the frontiers, the State Department and the Mexican Ambassador at Washington backed up its action by forceful representations to the Central American diplomatic representatives and discussed a proposal to send a strongly worded cable, signed by [United States President] Roosevelt and [Mexican President] Díaz, to demand respect for the Court's decisions[39].

What was witnessed in this first case before the Court was that the United States and Mexico were acting as coercive agents, not unlike municipal police forces, to insure compliance with a court order. By acting in such a manner, the North American States were challenging an essential element of international law – the sovereignty of the isthmus States. Munro notes that Root "was willing to pledge the influence of the United States and Mexico to the fullest extent and to say that a failure to obey the mandate of the Court would be a violation of most solemn obligations upon which the United States and Mexico were entitled to insist and did insist"[40]. The Central American countries got the message: "the telegram was never sent, because the governments withdrew their forces and the revolution in Honduras soon afterward collapsed"[41].

While it may be true that "the action of the court [in this case] is thus a confirmation of the partisans of arbitration, that an international tribunal can not only insure peace, but in appropriate cases prevent war"[42]. But at what cost? One must question the process which led to the prevention of war in this instance. If the primacy of international law was to prevail before this international court, the States concerned should have been prepared to comply with the Court's ruling of their own volition. Regardless of the outcome on the issuing of the interlocutory orders, the political interference which characterized this case must be seen as an obstacle to the advancement of international adjudication. This case can hardly be called, as it was in the *American Journal of International Law*, a step marking "great progress towards the judicial settlement of international disputes"[43]. In fact, it clearly demonstrates that behind the façade of international law lurked the political reality of a hegemonic State imposing its will on the weaker isthmus countries.

---

[39] Diana G. Munro, *Intervention and Dollar Diplomacy in the Caribbean 1900-1921*, 1964, p. 157.

[40] *Ibid.*, p. 157. Note here that it appears that US Secretary Root could speak for his State as well as for Mexico.

[41] *Ibid.*, p. 157.

[42] *AJIL*, *op. cit.* n. 27, p. 436.

[43] *Ibid.*, p. 436.

That the Central American Court of Justice did not survive past its original ten-year mandate is not surprising in view of the political foundation upon which its first case was built. With the role that the United States had played and was to play in Central America, it is clear that the Court, sooner of later, would run foul of the interests of the United States. When its own interests were at stake, it was not at all astonishing that the United States would chose not to utilize political pressure, as it had in *Honduras v. El Salvador and Guatemala*, to "demand respect for the Court's decision"[44].

2.3. **The Fall of the Central American Court of Justice**

The Central American Court of Justice lasted for a ten-year period; *Honduras v. El Salvador and Guatemala* was the highlight of the first five-year judicial term. The second five-year period, however, would be quite different, as it led to the Court's fall from grace. The decline of the Central American Court of Justice started on 18 February 1916. From this day on, the United States would no longer lend its weight to ensure compliance with the Court's decisions. With the United States turning its back on the Court, the Central American States – and more specifically the proxy of the United States – Nicaragua no longer felt compelled to accept the jurisdiction of the Court. On 18 February 1916, the United States Senate approved what is known as the Chamorro-Bryan Treaty. This convention, which quickly came to represent the imperialistic tendencies of the United States in Central America, was not greeted warmly on the isthmus. "In Central America, the establishment of the Chamorro-Bryan Treaty ignited protests and was, at its peak, the cause of demonstrations, public rallies, and speeches attacking United States imperialism"[45].

The Chamorro-Bryan Treaty reads, *inter alia*:

> The Government of the United States of America and the Government of Nicaragua being animated by the desire to strengthen their ancient and cordial friendship by the most sincere coöperation for all purposes of their mutual advantage and interest and to provide for the possible future construction of an interoceanic ship canal by way of the San Juan River and the great Lake of Nicaragua, or by any route over Nicaraguan territory, whenever the construction of such canal shall be deemed by the Government of the United States conducive to the interests of both countries[...]. [T]he two Governments have resolved to conclude a convention to these ends[...].

---

[44] See n. 39.

[45] Carlos Jose Gultierrez, *La Corte de Justicia Centroamericana*, 1978, p. 111. My translation. For more information regarding the Treaty, consider P. Walp, "The Central American Court of Justice", *Revue de droit international*, Vol. 1, 1927, pp. 89-108, at 102-107.

Article I
The Government of Nicaragua grants in perpetuity to the Government of the United States, forever free from all taxation or other public charge, the exclusive proprietary rights necessary and convenient for the construction, operation, and maintenance of an interoceanic canal by way of the San Juan River and the great Lake of Nicaragua, or by any route over Nicaraguan territory, the details of the terms upon which such canal shall be constructed, operated, and maintained to be agreed to by the two governments whenever the Government of the United States shall notify the Government of Nicaragua of its desire or intention to construct such an canal.

Article II
To enable the Government of the United States to protect the Panama Canal and the proprietary rights granted to the Government of the United States by the foregoing article, and also to enable the Government of the United States to take any measure necessary to ends contemplated herein, the Government of Nicaragua hereby leases for a term of 99 years to the Government of the United States, the islands in the Caribbean Sea known as Great Corn Island and Little Corn Island; and the Government of Nicaragua further grants to the Government of the United States for a like period of 99 years the right to establish, operate and maintain a naval base at such a place on the territory of Nicaragua bordering upon the Gulf of Fonseca as Government of the United States may select. The Government of the United States shall have the option of renewing for a further term of 99 years the above leases and grants upon the expiration of their respective terms, it being expressly agreed that the territory hereby aforesaid shall be subject exclusively to the laws and sovereign authority of the United States during the terms of such a lease and grant and of any renewal or renewals thereof.

Article III
[...] the Government of the United States shall, upon the date of the exchange of ratification of this convention, pay for the benefit of the Republic of Nicaragua the sum of $3,000,000 United States gold coin [...][46].

"The general objections" of Central Americans to the Chamorro-Bryan Treaty "were to the effect that the treaty would convert Nicaragua to all intents and purposes into a protectorate of the United States, and that such a relationship would make forever impossible the long-cherished union of the Central American Republics under one government"[47]. In reality, Nicaragua was already a protectorate of the United States, the Chamorro-Bryan Treaty only making it obvious to the outside world. As early as 1911, Nicaragua was little more than a

[46] Treaty concerning the Construction of an Interoceanic Canal through the Territory of the Republic of Nicaragua, 5 August 1914, G.-F. de Martens, *Nouveau Recueil Général de Traités*, Vol. 9, 1919, pp. 350-353.

[47] George A Finch, "The Treaty with Nicaragua Granting Canal and Other Rights to The United States", *American Journal of International Law*, Vol. 10, 1916, p. 345.

[48] John H. Latané and David W. Wainhouse, *A History of American Foreign Policy, 1776-1940*, 1941, p. 552.

lap dog of the United States, which occupied it for nearly 15 years. "From 1911 to 1925 a legation guard of one hundred marines was maintained at the capital of Nicaragua" wrote John Latané and David Wainhouse[48]. This helped, the historians stated, to maintain a government supported by few in Nicaragua but beneficial to United States' interests. The Secretary of State of the United States, Elihu Root, acknowledged as much, saying that "the present government with which we are making this treaty is really maintained in office by the presence of the United States marines in Nicaragua"[49]. As will become apparent from an examination of the following two cases, the interests of the United States weighed more heavily on the side of economics and geopolitics than on a willingness to respect the rule of law. As noted historian, Howard Zinn, has pointed out:

> Nicaragua was a vivid example of marine diplomacy at work. Her proximity to Panama, and the ever-present possibility of a trans-Nicaraguan canal, gave Nicaragua a special place in the plans of the State Department, while fruit and lumber investments gave American private business groups a sphere of interest there. Ever since 1909, when a United States-aided revolution had overthrown the Liberal Zelaya government, a pattern of Yankee intervention was established with bank credits and marines standing guard alternately over shaky conservative governments"[50].

2.3.1. *Costa Rica v. Nicaragua*

On 24 March 1916, the Government of Costa Rica commenced an action in the Central American Court of Justice against the Government of Nicaragua for the signing of the Chamorro-Byran Treaty and relating to the construction of the interoceanic canal. Costa Rica believed that the contents of the Treaty "were notoriously contradictory to the unquestionable rights of Costa Rica established in the Cañas-Jerez Treaty, the Cleveland Award, and the Central American Treaty of Washington"[51]. What was at the heart of Costa Rica's complaint before the Court was Article I of the Chamorro-Byran Treaty, which dealt with: "the construction, operation, and maintenance of an interoceanic canal by way of the San Juan River". The Government of Costa Rica argued before the Court that:

> in a word, Nicaragua has placed under the control of the United States, or sold to her,

[49] Council on Foreign Relations, *Survey on American Foreign Relations 1929*, p. 167, as quoted in: Howard Zinn, "LaGuardia and the Jazz Age", *The Zinn Reader*, p. 174.

[50] *Ibid.*, p. 174. John Latané states: "under the Knox regime [the United States State Department] exploited the situation in Central America for the benefit of American capitalists, and that the Wilson administration has for years maintained a minority party in power through the presence of a body of American Marines at the capital and a warship at Corinto". As quoted in P. Wasp, *op. cit.* n. 45, p. 103.

[51] "*Costa Rica v. Nicaragua* before the Central American Court of Justice", *American Journal of International Law*, Vol. 11, 1917, p. 191.

> the San Juan River, unreservedly, just as though the former were the absolute owner of that stream and of its banks, and Costa Rica, who possesses the unquestionable rights to navigate freely throughout the greater part of those waters, and who is the owner of the greater part of the southern banks of that river, has not been taken into account[52].

Costa Rica was totally taken aback by the signing of the Chamorro-Byran Treaty. An earlier attempt had been made, in 1913, at ratifying an analogous instrument, the Weitzel-Chamorro Treaty, about which Costa Rica made vigorous representations to "different [U.S.] Senators to the end that when the treaty should be debated in the Senate and the treaty ratified, the rights of [Costa Rica] in relation to the construction of any interoceanic canal should not only not be lost sight of but should be respected and guaranteed"[53]. As Costa Rica noted in its arguments before the Court, "the Government of Costa Rica was assured that the treaty for the canal across Nicaragua had been in fact tacitly withdrawn from consideration by the Senate of the United States"[54]. Yet Costa Rica went on to state that:

> while [its] mind was at rest on the subject the [Washington] *Evening Star* [...] announced that the Committee on Foreign Relations of the North American Senate had recommended to that body the ratification of the treaty that had been concluded more than a year before by the Government of the United States with the Government of Nicaragua, among other objects, for the construction of an interoceanic canal through Nicaraguan territory[55].

The Government of Costa Rica argued that the Treaty should be voided on the grounds that the actions of Nicaragua infringed, in part, upon three separate international agreements. The first, the Cañas-Jenez Treaty of 15 April 1858, stipulated:

> *Article 6*
> The Republic of Nicaragua shall have exclusive dominion and the highest sovereignty over the waters of the San Juan River for their issue out of the lake to their discharge into the Atlantic; but the Republic of Costa Rica shall have in those waters perpetual rights of free navigation from the said mouth of the river up to a point three English miles [inland] [...] for the purpose of commerce.
> [...]
>
> *Article 8*
> If the contracts of canalization or transit entered into before the Nicaraguan Government had knowledge of this convention should for any cause cease to be in force, Nicaragua agrees not to conclude any other relating to the objects above stated

---

52 *Ibid.*, p. 195.
53 *Ibid.*, p. 188.
54 *Ibid.*
55 *Ibid.*, p. 189.

> without first hearing the opinion of the Costa Rican Government respecting the disadvantages that may result to the two countries, [...] and in the event that the enterprise should cause no injury to the natural rights of Costa Rica, that opinion shall be advisory.

Second, an award, clarifying a subsequent treaty between Nicaragua and Costa Rica, made by the then United States President Cleveland, on 22 March 1888, stated:

> *Second*
> The Republic of Costa Rica under said [Esquivel-Román Convention] has not the right of navigation of the River San Juan with vessels of war; but she may navigate said river with such vessels of the revenue service as may be related to...the "purpose of commerce".
>
> *Third*
> With respect to the point of doubtful interpretation communicated as aforesaid by the Republic of Nicaragua, I decide as follow:
> [...]
>
> *Tenth*
> The Republic of Nicaragua remains bound not to make any grants for canal purposes across her territory without first asking the opinion of the Republic of Costa Rica [...].
>
> *Eleventh*
> The Treaty [...] does not give the Republic of Costa Rica the right to be party to grants which Nicaragua may make for interoceanic canals; though in cases where the construction of the canal will involve an injury to the natural rights of Costa Rica, her opinion or advice, [...] should be more than "advisory" or "consultative". It would seem in such cases that her consent is necessary, and that she may thereupon demand compensation for the concession she is asked to make [...].

The third major international agreement which was utilized, in part, to buttress the arguments of Costa Rica was a convention which was signed at the same time as the text bringing the Court into existence: the General Treaty of Peace and Amity concluded at the 1907 Central American Peace Conference. A provision within this Treaty dealing with navigation was meant to ensure that no State, Central American or other, would be discriminated when navigating in Central America. The Court wrote: "it is evident, said the complainant, that in matters relating to navigation, any [...] convention [...] which neglects to reserve to merchant vessels of Costa Rica, El Salvador, Guatemala, and Honduras, plying her waters, privileges and advantages identical with those enjoyed by her, openly violates [...] the Treaty"[56].

[56] *Ibid.*, p. 196.

Beyond these three international agreements, the Costa Rican Government added "that the treaty and conventions of Washington of 1907 having furthermore been conceived, debated and concluded through the friendly intervention of the Government of the United States of America, those pacts carry with them the moral guaranty of that Great Republic"[57]. That the United States was involved as a host to the Peace Conference of Washington of 1907 is an important point which, Salvador Rodríguez argued, forced the United States to ensure compliance with the Treaty.

> it is impossible not to admit the legal rôle of mediators which the Governments of the United States and Mexico actually and effectively assumed in the conference.
>
> Now then, the first duty of a mediator is to see to it that the undertakings in which he intervened are fulfilled, and, therefore, to oppose any acts which might tend to destroy the results of his mediation. From this primary duty is derived another which is no less positive, imperative as necessary, namely, that of refraining from annulling or destroying, by his own acts, the undertakings in which he intervened as mediator[58].

The decision of the Court rendered in the *Costa Rica v. Nicaragua* case "completely sustained the main contentions of Costa Rica"[59]. "It is declared that the Government of Nicaragua has violated, to the injury of Costa Rica, the rights granted to the latter by the Cañas-Jerez Treaty [...], by the Cleveland Award [...], and by the Central American Treaty of Peace and Amity"[60]. However, the Court found that it was not in its power to annul the Chamorro-Bryan Treaty, as was requested by the Costa Rica, for one of the Contracting Parties – the United States – did not come under the jurisdiction of the Court. The political outcome of this case, in which Nicaragua chose not to appear before the Court, nor to recognize its binding decision, shall be examined shortly. First, the salient facts of a second case dealing with the Chamorro-Bryan Treaty, will be considered.

2.3.2. *El Salvador v. Nicaragua*

The utilization of the Court by Costa Rica and later by El Salvador had the effect of isolating Nicaragua. On the Atlantic side, Costa Rica argued successfully that it had an advisory right over the main entrance route contemplated in the

---

[57] *Ibid.* This may well have been a reference to U.S. Ambassador Creel's statement at the inauguration of the new Court, when he pledged the United States' moral support. See Warren, *infra.*, n. 85.

[58] Salvador Rodríguez González, "The Neutrality of Honduras and the Question of the Gulf of Fonseca". *American Journal of International Law*, Vol. 10, 1916, p. 534.

[59] *AJIL*, *op. cit.* n. 51, p. 156.

[60] *Costa Rica v. Nicaragua*, 30 September 1916, *Papers relating to the Foreign Relations of the United States 1916*, 1925, pp. 862-886, at p. 886.

Chamorro-Bryan Treaty. For its part, El Salvador seized the Court contending that the Treaty provisions dealing with the Pacific Ocean section of any proposed canal were injurious to its interests. On 28 August 1916, the Government of El Salvador commenced an action before the Central American Court of Justice against Nicaragua asserting that some of "the stipulations of [the Chamorro-Bryan Treaty] are held by El Salvador to be highly prejudicial to its supreme interests, in that they endanger her security and preservation, violate her right to co-ownership of the Gulf of Fonseca and strike at her legitimate hopes for the future as a Central American nation"[61]. The stipulations of the Chamorro-Byran Treaty, which El Salvador said were violated by Nicaragua, were the following:

> the Government of Nicaragua further grants to the Government of the United States for a like period of 99 years the right to establish, operate and maintain a naval base at such a place on the territory of Nicaragua bordering upon the Gulf of Fonseca as the Government of the United States may select.

El Salvador filed a formal notice with the United States Government establishing that "it does not recognize the validity of the Nicaraguan treaty, which establishes a naval base in the Gulf of Fonseca, and that consequently the Government of El Salvador will always work against the said treaty, with all the means and lawful procedures which existing conventions, international law and justice grant it, in order to invalidate [...] its effects"[62]. El Salvador maintained that Nicaragua did not "confine itself to its own exclusive territorial jurisdiction by negotiating for a naval base to be built in the Gulf of Fonseca"[63]. Allowing the United States to establish a naval base upon which it would be a "sovereign authority" would be contrary, El Salvador argued, to the fact that the Gulf was not owned by Nicaragua but was shared by the States of Honduras, Nicaragua and El Salvador. Finally, El Salvador contended that by ceding the right to establish a naval base in the Gulf of Fonseca, Nicaragua was endangering the national security of El Salvador while violating its contractual obligations under the Treaty of Amity and Peace signed at the 1907 Washington Conference.

The Central American Court of Justice, in a decision dated 29 March 1917, found, in favour of El Salvador (with the Nicaraguan judge dissenting), that the Gulf of Fonseca belonged to the special category of historical bays and "is the exclusive property of the three countries surrounding it"[64]. Further it held that the establishment of a naval base inside the Gulf did, in fact, cause a menace to El Salvador's security. Finally, the Court found that the conclusion of the

---

[61] "The Republic of El Salvador v. The Republic of Nicaragua", *American Journal of International Law*, Vol. 11, 1917, p. 675.

[62] Finch, *op. cit.* n. 47, pp. 350-351.

[63] *AJIL*, *op. cit.* n. 61, p. 676.

[64] *El Salvador v. Nicaragua*, 9 March 1917, *Papers relating to the Foreign Relations of the United States (1917)*, 1926, pp. 1100-1104 at p. 1102.

Chamorro-Bryan Treaty violated specific articles of the Treaty of Amity and Peace. The Court, in this instance, as it had in the Costa Rican case, decided in favour of the plaintiff, against Nicaragua, yet was unwilling to annul the Chamorro-Byran Treaty, as the United States was not a Party to the dispute before the Court.

2.3.3. *Nicaragua Challenges the Jurisdiction of the Court*

Having described the facts of *Costa Rica v. Nicaragua* and *El Salvador v. Nicaragua*, it is now time to consider once again the jurisdiction of the Court, which came under attack as the Government of Nicaragua sought to consolidate its gains made under the Chamorro-Byran Treaty while distancing itself from the Court and the rule of law. It should be remembered that these gains, which the Court ruled were contrary to international law, were obtained at the expense of Nicaragua's Central American neighbors and were fully endorsed by the United States of America[65]. Although, in both instances, the Court decided that it had jurisdiction[66], Nicaragua challenged this, arguing that the Court could not interfere as it was infringing upon Nicaragua's sovereign right to enter into a treaty. Donning the mantle of State sovereignty, it hastened to declare that Nicaragua not only:

> has always been, and will always be, possessed of full legal capacity to enter into and fulfill conventions of this character, but holds as offensive to her dignity as a free and independent nation any discussion of acts pertaining to her sovereignty – acts which in no case could become the subject of arbitrament[67].

The Nicaraguan Government later reaffirmed its intention not to accept to the results of the case brought forward by Costa Rica:

> [The Government of Nicaragua] does not, and cannot, admit the unrestricted power that the Court arrogates to itself to take cognizance of all the differences that may arise between the Central American States, because nothing that affects the sovereignty and

[65] See Christian Tomuschat, "International Courts and Tribunals with Regionally Restricted and/or Specialized Jurisdiction", in: H. Mosler, and R. Bernhardt (eds.), *Judicial Settlement of International Disputes*, 1974, p. 321, where he states that: as "Nicaragua could rely on American assistance it was able to give absolute priority to national interests without making any sacrifices and without regard for its neighbours".

[66] In its decision in *Costa Rica v. Nicaragua*, the Court wrote: "this Court is competent to decide the complaint brought by the Government of Costa Rica", p. 229. In *El Salvador v. Nicaragua*, the Court stated that it was "competent to take cognizance of, and decide the present action brought by the Government of The Republic of El Salvador ", *American Journal of International Law*, Vol. 11, p. 730.

[67] *Ibid.*, p. 184.

> integrity of the five republics is involved in the treaty stipulations; because no nation on earth would submit to the arbitrament of strangers, its security and preservation[68].

The confrontation between the Court and the Government of Nicaragua in this case was conducted in a less than diplomatic manner. The Court, having called upon the Government of Nicaragua to answer the complaints against it, as prescribed by Article 14 of the Court's Statute, received in reply an official *communiqué* from the Nicaraguan Ministry of Foreign Relations. The Court noted, in part, that the *communiqué* read:

> [the Minster] is constrained also to express the surprise of his government in noting that the Central American Court of Justice should have admitted the complaint, the incompetency of the Court being so manifest, as he then undertakes to show: The convention that created the Court, he said, is a fundamental code. It cannot be ignored, and the Court must subject itself to the provisions of that convention or its proceedings will be null and void[69].

Further, the Court relates that Nicaragua asserted that:

> the Central America Court of Justice could not, and cannot, legally prescribed from that legal requirement without overstepping its powers [...]without bringing about the absolute nullity of all its acts; and that everything it shall decide, if it should reach the stage of decision, will be absolutely null and void for want of jurisdiction.

[…]

> And finally, that [...] Nicaragua has proceeded within her rights, that the Central American Court is without jurisdiction, and, in the event of a decision adverse to her, Nicaragua declares that she will be unable to abide by it[70].

At this point, the Court, too dignified to respond to the harsh wording of the *communiqué* in its judgment, instructed its Secretary, Manuel Echeverria:

> to present for the consideration of Your Excellency's illustrious Government a brief analysis of the arguments whereby the decision is impugned, which arguments in fact constitute grave charges against the Court, imputing, as they do, violations of its organic law, breaches of international law, contradictions in its decisions and even inferred affronts to the Republic of Nicaragua[71].

---

[68] Echeverria, *op. cit.* n. 22, p. 5.
[69] *AJIL*, *op. cit.* n. 51, p. 204.
[70] *Ibid.*, pp. 205, 207.
[71] Echeverria, *op. cit.* n. 22, p. 4.

The Secretary, in an attempt to have the four other Central American States lend their moral support to this judgment in accordance with Article 25, went on to provide a scathing critique, citing the fact that, although Nicaragua claimed that the Court did not have jurisdiction over the affairs pertaining to *Costa Rica v. Nicaragua*, its own delegation at the 1907 Conference in Washington had noted that: "Article I fixes the permanent character of the Court of Justice and the principal object of its jurisdiction, which is to take cognizance of all questions that arise between the Central Government, *without a single exception*"[72]. The Secretary further noted:

> that no one has been of the opinion that customary limitations in the conclusion of international arbitral conventions were retained in negotiating these memorable conventions – pacts that consecrated obligatory judicial arbitration in form more ample and unrestricted that may heretofore be adopted in the history of the world.
>
> Now, therefore, can the Government of Nicaragua demand the exclusion from the cognizance of the Court of questions that affect sovereignty [...]. The Treaties of Washington are not impressed with those limitations, either expressly or tacitly; and hence contrary to the clear, precise, and conclusive texts of those pacts[73].

As opposed to its conduct in *Costa Rica v. Nicaragua*, the Government of Nicaragua did appear before the Court in the *El Salvador v. Nicaragua* case. However, it did so only in a limited manner. As the Court noted in its documentation of the proceedings:

> That counsel for the high party defendant, before analyzing the arguments on which the Government of El Salvador relied in support of its complaint, protested that it was not his intention to answer the said complaint in its entirety, nor to acknowledge in any manner that the Central American Court of Justice had acquired jurisdiction to decide the case [...][74].

The Court further noted that Nicaragua "through its counsel, makes the following exceptions:
[...]

> Second. – That the Court is incompetent, for lack of jurisdiction, to take cognizance of, and decide, the complaint and the additions thereto presented by the Government of El Salvador[75].

In March of 1917, the Government of Nicaragua filed documents with the Court to the effect that it considered the decision null and void and would not respect it.

---

72 *Ibid.*, p. 6. Emphasis in the original.

73 *Ibid.*, p. 7.

74 *AJIL*, *op. cit.* n. 61, p. 686.

2.4. **The Closing of the Central American Court of Justice**

Article 27 of the Convention for the Establishment of a Central American Court of Justice reads in part: "The High Contracting Parties solemnly declare that on no ground nor in any case will they consider the present Convention as void; and that, therefore, they will consider it as being always in force during the term of ten years counted from the last ratification". Yet, as a result of the bad blood created by the litigants over the Chamorro-Bryan Treaty, on

> March 17, 1918, it was announced in the press that the judges of the Central American Court of Justice paid their respects to the President of Costa Rica and took leave of the court, which had ceased to exist because of the failure of a contracting Power [Nicaragua] to renew the convention creating the court when the term of ten years for which it was concluded had elapsed[76].

The closing of the Central American Court of Justice took place despite attempts by the judges to save it by proposing to "clarify" its Statute. The Court took it upon itself to suggest limits to its own jurisdiction. Beyond purely administrative proposals, it sought to "clarify" Article 1 so as to ensure that States had exhausted all "efforts at diplomatic settlement"[77] before having recourse to the Court. Coupled with this concession, there was a proposal "to forbid any state to enter into treaties affecting other states without previous consent"[78]. The lack of any true concessions to States' interests and a proposal to ensure that the cases surrounding the Chamorro-Bryan Treaty would not be adjudicated again, however, were apparently not enough to ensure the survival of the Court.

The legacy of the Court has been characterized in two ways. Some authors have pointed to the success of the Court in preserving the peace in *Honduras v. El Salvador and Guatemala.* James Brown Scott notes that it is "proper to express regret that the court should close its doors, inasmuch as it was avowedly the first international court of justice which had been created, and as its successful operation was constantly pointed to as a demonstration of the possibility of judicial settlement of disputes between nations"[79]. Likewise, Helen Cory wrote that "the Court had justified its existence by the equitable decision of three important cases of international character"[80], while Nicolas Politis believed that the Court's decisions were "just, strongly reasoned, and perfectly correct"[81]. Other authors,

---

[75] *Ibid.*, p. 691.

[76] James Brown Scott, "The Closing of the Central American Court of Justice", *American Journal of International Law*, Vol. 12, 1918, p. 380.

[77] Hudson, *op. cit.* n. 32, p. 782.

[78] *Ibid.*, p. 782.

[79] Scott, *op. cit.* n. 76, p. 381.

[80] Cory, *op. cit.* n. 35, p. 97.

[81] Nicolas Politis, *La justice internationale*, 1924, p. 152. My translation.

notably Manley Hudson and Jean Eyma, commented less favorably on the achievements of the Court. They argued that the Court was doomed from the start because the Convention which established it was flawed. These authors asserted in particular that the Court was not sufficiently independent and pointed to its jurisdiction as being too broad[82].

Although it would be simple to say that the true legacy of the Court lies somewhere in between these two poles; a further point of view could consist of examining the larger picture. Consideration of the motives and the interplay of the States involved and their engagement with the Court would appear to lead to a better understanding of the historical significance of the Central American Court. The analysis of the Court has been left in large part to scholars who have sought to highlight the United States' role in the establishment of the Court and to downplay that country's leading role in its demise. These scholars have tended to evaluate the Court solely on its own merits and to omit externalities. Yet this analysis does not do full justice to it and is akin to having dealt with the symptoms of the disease rather than its cause. The fact that the Court has played a minor role on the international level was not due to defects in the Convention which established it. A more balanced appraisal must include an examination of the role played by the United States of America, which left a permanent imprint on the Court's legacy.

2.4.1. *The Role of the United States of America*

A disproportionate amount of blame for rendering the Court ineffective must be placed on the United States of America. This is because the "United States refused to back the very agency for settling disputes to whose establishment it had given such hearty encouragement", writes Graham Stuart, a specialist in U.S.-Latin American relations, "simply because the decision interfered with her own selfish interests"[83]. The United States encouraged the establishment of the Central American Court of Justice, not in the interest of truly attempting to maintain the peace on the isthmus but, instead, as a diplomatic demonstration that it had emerged, at the start of the 20th century, from under the shadow of dominance of the European powers. The United States, through its sponsorship of the Court, was attempting to establish itself, at the expense of Central America, as a power which could set a course clearly different from that proposed by the European States. In establishing the Court on the isthmus, United States diplomats, it would seem, did not have their thoughts centered on the Western hemisphere; instead they "wanted to show Europe that the concepts

---

[82] Hudson, *op. cit.* n. 32, "Appreciation of the Court", pp. 785-786, and Eyma, *op. cit.* n. 25, "Conclusion", pp. 171-176.

[83] Graham Stuart, *Latin America and the United States*, 1922, p. 276.

which it [the United States] had defended [in 1899 and 1907] and which were not well received were perfectly realizable on the other side of the Atlantic"[84].

Having lent much of its weight to the establishment of the Central American Court, the United States sought to ensure its success during the early part of its mandate. However, when overriding economic and geopolitical interests came into conflict with the Court's rulings, the United States no longer felt obligated to ensure their respect, despite assurances, made when the Central American Court was first established, that the United States had "accepted a serious moral responsibility in this international undertaking"[85]. The observations of Jean Eyma on this point seem perceptive:

> It really served no purpose for the United States to wish to be progressive in establishing "ideal" international adjudication as an example for the people of Europe. The United States, in fact, but a few years later, helped insure the failure of this very institution which was to show that the American spirit for establishing an "ideal" international adjudication had matured more than Europe's[86].

The fact that the United States, while having been a force for establishing the Court, later played a critical role in its demise did not escape scrutiny. As Samual Inman noted, in his 1926 evaluation of the failure of the Court, that "this most remarkable experiment in international good will ever known to history was terminated ten years later largely because the United States, the sponsor of the whole idea, refused to abide by one of its decisions, thus robbing it of its prestige, is one of the strangest tricks of fate"[87]. In retrospect, the cases brought by Costa Rica and El Salvador clearly demonstrate a shift in United States policy. As Eduardo Crawley noted in *Nicaragua in Perspective*: "times had obviously changed [...] the criteria of international law came a poor second to the dictates of United States national interest"[88]. The Chamorro-Bryan Treaty and its importance to the United States economic and geopolitical interests would relegate international adjudication and the rule of law, as manifested in the work of the Central American Court, to a subservient role.

It is at this point that the analysis of the Court's legacy faces a dilemma. The Central American Court of Justice as the first attempt at overall international adjudication leaves one with a choice between two equally unsatisfactory alternatives. When the United States was not willing to enforce its decisions, the Court was ineffective in that Nicaragua did not feel compelled to abide by its judgments. Yet even when it was effective, as in *Honduras v. El Salvador* and *Guate-*

---

[84] Scott, *op. cit.* n. 11, pp. 53-54.

[85] Tully Evans Warren, *The Projected Inter-American Court of Justice as a Part of the Inter-American Peace Machinery,* 1950, p. 44.

[86] Eyma, *op. cit.* n. 25, p. 176. My translation.

[87] Inman, *op. cit.* n. 24, p. 302.

[88] Eduardo Crawley, *Nicaragua in Perspective*, 1984, p. 45.

mala, that effectiveness was due, in large part, to the threat of enforcement provided by the United States and Mexico. What of this dilemma? John Stoessinger argues that the "establishment of the rule of law can help knit the bonds of social and political order [and] can weave the fabric of community"[89]. The Central American States, as well as the United States, demonstrated through their actions that they were not prepared to establish community ties based on the rule of law. Instead, political accommodation dictated the inter-relationship existing between the States concerned during the era of the Central American Court of Justice. Fundamentally, then, the rule of law did not prevail during the mandate of the Court, as its judgements remained subordinated to political accommodation.

It may be argued that, had the Court been able to function without interference from the United States, it could have been successful. Jean Eyma alluded to this when he wrote: "if the wish to arbitrate disputes was in the thought of nations which had between them no real affinity [European States], it is then natural that there exists a more acute wish in peoples who are united through common origins, race, and demure"[90]. Further, the discrepancy in power which divided the Central American Republics was negligible, no State being able to dominate another. It would seem that the region was ripe for the introduction of a successful international court.

However, the manner in which the Court was established, with United States and Mexican involvement, did not endear it to the isthmus States. Instead, as became clear with *Honduras v. El Salvador and Guatemala*, the enforcement of judgments would not be ensured by the simple respect of treaty obligations, but would be achieved with the assistance of "the two great Republics lying to the north". That assistance would, in turn, be based, not on the primacy of law, as shown by *Costa Rica v. Nicaragua* and *El Salvador v. Nicaragua*, but on a great power's willingness to support or not to support the Court. As Hans Morgenthau has rightly noted, whether "such assistance will be forthcoming is not a matter of international law but of national interest as conceived by individual nations"[91]. An examination of the state of international adjudication during the tenure of the Central American Court of Justice demonstrates that, although the Court was meant to have jurisdiction over all international legal issues on the isthmus, what became apparent as its mandate drew to a close was that the Court was at the mercy of States and their willingness to comply with its judgments.

---

[89] John G. Stoessinger, *The Might of Nations*, 1967, p. 234.
[90] Eyma, *op. cit.* n. 25, p. 7. My translation.
[91] Morgenthau, *op. cit.* n. 3, p. 312.

3. Conclusion

The limits of the rule of law which have been considered in this evaluation of the Central American Court of Justice are to some extent a relics of a by-gone era, at least as regards the overt behaviour of the United States of America during the life-span of this first international judicial organ[92]. Yet the unwillingness of States to accept, in certain situations, decisions or orders, or even to accept the jurisdiction of adjudicative organs persists to this day. Beyond the voluntary nature of international adjudication, a secondary encumbrance to the full respect for the rule of law are the actions of States attempting to manipulate the use of law for their own gain. If law is to be paramount on the international level, States must respect international obligations in the domain of adjudication by their own will. Yet the demise of the Central American Court of Justice has not resulted, unfortunately, in the end of non-compliance with judgments or of non-appearance before international adjudicative organs[93].

That the role of ensuring compliance with the decisions of international courts of law has been taken out of the hands of individual States and placed in those of international organs means that enforcement is now to be undertaken in concert[94]. However today, as during the era of the Central American Court of Justice, those factors which influence the effectiveness of the international rule of law – a State's willingness to appear before a court and its willingness to recognize a decision – remain overtly political elements which should have no place in an international system governed by the rule of law.

[92] Note, however, the lack of respect for the International Court of Justice by the United States in the *Case concerning Military and Paramilitary Activities in and against Nicaragua*, and the *Breard* and *LaGrand* cases.

[93] See notes 1 and 2.

[94] For the International Court of Justice, enforcement is left to the UN Security Council (Article 94, Charter of the United Nations); for the Court of Justice of the European Communities, enforcement is entrusted to the European Commission (Article 228, *Treaty on European Union "Maastricht Treaty");* regarding the European Court of Human Rights, enforcement is ensured by the Committee of Ministers of the Council of Europe (Article 46(2), European Convention for the Protection of Human Rights and Fundamental Freedoms); and in the case of the Inter-American Court of Human Rights, enforcement is an attribution of the General Assembly of the Organization of American States (Article 30, Statute of the Inter-American Court of Human Rights).

Chapter 4
THE EUROPEAN COURT OF HUMAN RIGHTS AND THE INTER-AMERICAN COURT OF HUMAN RIGHTS

1. Introduction

Previously, consideration has been given to two issues that limit full respect for the rule of law. The voluntary nature of international adjudication allowing States to auto-determine whether they subscribe to any court's jurisdiction is the most fundamental limit to the rule of law. Beyond this encumbrance, the legacy of the Central American Court of Justice demonstrates how non-cooperation with international courts places in peril, not only institutions, but also the very essence of international adjudication. These limitations directly challenge the system of international adjudication. By seeking to remain outside that system, States devalue the legitimacy of international courts and the rule of law. States, however, have also sought to limit the effectiveness of the rule of law while being subject to the jurisdiction of a court, appearing before it, and respecting and implementing its judgments. The best example of this may be found in a comparison of regional human rights courts, where the constitutive instruments were essentially analogous, yet their ability to ensure the respect of the rule of law varied.

To establish the differences in the ability for the European Court of Human Rights and the Inter-American Court of Human Rights to function effectively may well be the best case-study available for students of international adjudication who seek to understand how legal instruments, similar in nature, can vary in implementation. These two Courts, along with the nascent African Court of Human and Peoples' Rights, also provide an instructive continuum illustrating the evolution of human rights courts. While the European system dismantled the European Commission of Human Rights in 1998, thus allowing individuals increased access to the European Court, African countries decided in the late 1990s, to establish a court – having relied exclusively on its Commission to garner respect for human rights. Between these two poles lies the Inter-American system where – this will be emphasized in this study – both an Inter-American Commission and Court are mandated to ensure compliance with human rights norms in the Americas.

2. The Human Rights Systems[1]

The establishment of regional human rights courts is a result of the events in Europe in the late 1930s and early 1940s, and of the subsequent failure of the international community, as a whole, to provide for a universal human rights court within the framework of the newly created United Nations Organization. The atrocities of the National Socialist Government in Germany against its own people were perpetrated:

> with complete legality under [its] legislation: the domestic laws authorized, and paralleled, the pernicious injustices of the acts. Moreover, those laws had been enacted by a legislature lawfully installed under the constitution of a sovereign State. According to the strict doctrine of national sovereignty, any foreign criticism of those laws was therefore formally illegitimate[2].

Out of the ravages of the Second World War came a movement "to introduce into international law new concepts designed to outlaw such events for the future, in order to make their recurrence at least less probable"[3]. Beyond the *ad hoc* international war crimes tribunals performing at Nuremberg and Tokyo, and the establishment of a new legal order with the United Nations Organization; the real novelty in international law, which would have an impact on international adjudication at the regional level, was the emergence of the notion of "human rights". The fact that the Charter of the United Nations mentions the promotion and encouragement of respect for human rights as one of its main purposes, yet failed to establish, within the Charter, a mechanism to ensure its "faith in fundamental human rights"; together with the 1948 Universal Declaration of Human Rights, which was not a legally binding document, meant that those who advocated the international "judicialization" of the respect for human rights would have to look elsewhere for their implementation.

---

[1] See generally Héctor Gros Espiell, "La Convention américaine et la Convention européenne des droits de l'homme", *Collected Courses of The Hague Academy of International Law*, Vol. 89, 1989, pp. 175-410, and "La Cour interaméricaine et la Cour européenne des droits de l'homme", *Liber Amicorum Marc-André Eissen*, 1995, pp. 233-246; Jochen A. Frowein, "The European and the American Conventions on Human Rights – A Comparison", *Human Rights Law Journal*, Vol. 1, 1980, pp. 44-65; A. Glenn Mower, *Regional Human Rights: A Comparative Study of the West European and Inter-American Systems*, 1991; and Burns Weston, Robin Lukes, and Kelly Hnatt, "Regional Human Rights Regimes: A Comparison and Appraisal", *Vanderbilt Journal of Transnational Law*, Vol. 20, 1987, pp. 585-638.

[2] Paul Sieghart, *International Law of Human Rights*, 1983, p. 14.

[3] *Ibid.*, p. 14.

2.1. Evolution of Human Rights Courts

At the end of the Second World War, it was left to the Council of Europe to establish a human rights regime at the regional level, as Europe had witnessed first-hand the violations that States could perpetrate against their own people. Thus, the European Convention for Protection of Human Rights and Fundamental Freedoms entered into force in 1953 to "take the first steps for the collective enforcement of certain of the rights stated in the Universal Declaration"[4]. European States agreed, at that time, that a European Commission of Human Rights and a European Court of Human Rights would be created to "ensure the observance of the engagements undertaken"[5].

The Inter-American community, for its part, adopted the American Declaration on the Rights and Duties of Man some seven months before the 1948 Universal Declaration of Human Rights[6], but would have to wait until 1959 for the creation of the Inter-American Commission on Human Rights and until 1980 for the establishment of the Inter-American Court of Human Rights. Still slower to develop was the African regime that saw the African Charter on Human and Peoples Rights enter into force in 1986, creating an African Commission on Human and Peoples Rights[7], and the agreement to establish the African Court on Human and Peoples Rights having come as late as 1996[8]. Thus, the notion of human rights would evolve during the second half of the twentieth century in an uneven manner, both in time and in effectiveness. Despite this uneven evolution, the notion of "human rights" maintains a unique position within the realm of international law. A regional regime has developed, with the consent of States, to respect and protect the rights of individuals within the territories of those States. Also by consent, States have provided international organs with the responsibility to ensure – albeit with varying degrees of success – the respect of their conventional undertakings. It may be said that in the area of international human rights law,

> the strict doctrine [of State sovereignty was] cut down in two crucial respects. First, how a State treats its own subjects is now the legitimate concern of international law.

[4] Preamble, Convention for Protection of Human Rights and Fundamental Freedoms, 4 November 1950, ETS n. 5. The text of the Convention was completed by Protocol No. 2 (ETS n. 44), 6 May 1963, and amended by Protocol No. 3 (ETS n. 45), 6 May 1963, Protocol No. 5 (ETS n. 55), 20 January 1966, Protocol No. 8 (ETS n. 118) of 19 March 1985, and Protocol no. 11 (ETS n. 155), 1 November 1998. See Appendix 4.

[5] *Ibid.*, Article 19.

[6] Weston *et al.* (eds.), *op. cit.* n. 1, p. 593.

[7] Article 30, African Charter on Human and Peoples Rights, P. R. Ghandhi (ed.), *Blackstone's International Human Rights Documents*, 1995, pp. 175- 185.

[8] See Resolution on the African Commission on Human and Peoples' Rights, 64th Session of the Council of Ministers of the Organization of African Unity, 1-5 July 1996, Yaoundé, Cameroon. Note that the Court had yet to be established by 31 December 1999.

Secondly, there is now a superior international standard, established by common consent, which may be used for judging the domestic laws and the actual conduct of sovereign States within their own territories and in the exercise of their internal jurisdictions[9].

2.1.1. *The European Convention for the Protection of Human Rights and Fundamental Freedoms*

In May 1948, a "Congress of Europe" was held in The Hague that proposed the creation of a European charter of rights and a European court of human rights. The outcome of this Congress was the establishment of the Council of Europe, "a sort of social and ideological counterpart"[10] to NATO and the body that would prepare the European Convention to be signed at Rome in 1950 and brought into force three years later[11]. Since that time, the European system for the protection of human rights has been continuously reinventing itself. Not satisfied with either the substantive rights guaranteed or with the monitoring mechanisms established, the European States have added eleven protocols to the 1950 Convention either amending it or adding to its scope[12].

Protocol 1 guarantees individual property and provides that the right to education shall be part of the Convention; and it calls on States Parties to "undertake to hold free elections"[13]. Protocol 4 adds further substantive rights, which for the Parties having accepted it are to "regard as additional article to the Convention"[14]. Those rights revolve around the concept of nationality and include the right to liberty of movement and the prohibition of collective expulsion of aliens. Protocol 6 seeks to abolish the death penalty[15], while Protocol 7 deals with a variety of matters, including the refining of the rights respecting aliens, the acceptance of the right to appeal in criminal matters, and the equality of spouses[16]. Beyond these additions to the substantive rights

---

[9] Sieghart, *op. cit.* n. 2, p. 15.

[10] Ian Brownlie, *Basic Documents on Human Rights*, 1992, p. 325.

[11] Gros Espiell, *op. cit.* n. 1, pp. 216-217.

[12] For Protocols 1 through 10, see Ian Brownlie, *Basic Documents on Human Rights*, 1992, pp. 341-363; for the European Convention as amended by Protocols n. 3, 5, 8 and 11, see Ghandhi, *op. cit.* n. 7, pp. 125-134.

[13] Protocol to the Convention for Protection of Human Rights and Fundamental Freedoms: Enforcement of Certain Rights and Freedoms Not Included in Section I of the Convention, 20 March 1952, ETS n. 9.

[14] Article 6(1), Protocol 4 to the Convention for Protection of Human Rights and Fundamental Freedoms: Securing Certain Rights and Freedoms Other than Those Included in the Convention and in Protocol 1, 16 November 1963, ETS n. 46.

[15] Article 1, Protocol 6 to the Convention for Protection of Human Rights and Fundamental Freedoms: Concerning the Abolition of the Death Penalty, 28 April 1983, ETS n. 114.

[16] Articles 1, 2 and 5, Protocol 7 to the Convention for Protection of Human Rights and Fundamental Freedoms: Concerning Various Matters, 22 November 1984, ETS n. 117.

enshrined in the European Convention, Protocols 2, 3, 5, and 8-10 provide refinements to the system and its organs. Protocol 2 grants the Court the competence to deliver advisory opinions[17], while Protocol 9 gives individuals direct access to the Court[18]. Protocols 3, 5 and 8 seek, *inter alia*, to develop and clarify the mandate of the European Commission on Human Rights[19]. Finally, Protocol 11, which came into force on 1 November 1998, dismantled the Commission in favour of a revamped European Court of Human Rights and incorporated various Protocols into the Convention[20].

2.1.2. *The American Convention on Human Rights*

The Inter-American human rights system originated in the 1948 Bogotá Conference, which saw the setting up of the Organization of American States (OAS). The creation of the OAS was a further evolution in the regional organization of the Americas; the "present Organization of American States has its origins in a resolution of the First International Conference of American States convened in Washington by the United States in 1899"[21]. Out of this Conference emerged the Commercial Bureau of the American Republics which, in 1910, became the Pan American Union and which would later evolve into the Secretariat of the Organization of American States[22]. It has been pointed out that "the Inter-American System would have probably continued its gradual evolutionary growth"[23], had it not been for the move towards establishing the United Nations Organization. Fearful that the Inter-American system would be absorbed by the United Nations, American States reorganized and strengthened their regional structure.

Margaret Ball, one of the few English-language writers to have dealt with the OAS in depth, wrote that at the 1948 Bogotá Conference three fundamental issues were being raised concerning the incorporation of human rights into the new Charter of the Organization of American States:

---

[17] Protocol 2 to the Convention for Protection of Human Rights and Fundamental Freedoms: Conferring upon the European Court of Human Rights Competence to Give Advisory Opinions, 6 May 1963, ETS n. 44.

[18] Protocol 9 to the Convention for Protection of Human Rights and Fundamental Freedoms: Concerning Access to the Court by Individuals, 6 September 1990, ETS n. 140.

[19] See Articles 1 and 2, Protocol 3 to the Convention for Protection of Human Rights and Fundamental Freedoms: Amending Articles 29, 30 and 94 of the Convention, 6 May 1963, ETS n. 45; Articles 1 and 2, Protocol 5, Amending Articles 22 and 40 of the Convention, 20 January 1966, ETS n. 55; and Articles 1 to 8, Protocol 8 to the Convention for Protection of Human Rights and Fundamental Freedoms: Concerning Various Matters, 19 March 1985, ETS n. 118.

[20] Protocol No. 11 to the Convention for Protection of Human Rights and Fundamental Freedoms: Restructuring the Control Machinery Established thereby, 1 November 1998, ETS n. 155.

[21] M. Margaret Ball, *The OAS in Transition*, 1969, p. 10.

[22] O. Carlos Stoetzer, *The Organization of American States: An Introduction*, 1966, p. 6.

[23] Ann Van Wynen Thomas and A.J. Thomas, Jr., *The Organization of American States*, 1963, p. 36.

1) whether any statement of human rights should be included in the Charter;
2) if handled outside the Charter, whether the statement should take the form of a declaration or a convention; and,
3) whether the rights should be simply "recognized" internationally, or whether some effort should be made to protect them through the efforts of some sort of international tribunal"[24].

Thomas Buergenthal, former President of the Inter-American Court, answers these questions in part in noting that "the 1948 OAS Charter contained very few provisions relating to human rights, and all of them were phrased in very general terms"[25]. Rather than being included in the Charter, a statement on human rights – The American Declaration of Rights and Duties of Man – "was proclaimed at the same Bogotá Conference that produced the 1948 Charter, but the Declaration was adopted in the form of a simple conference resolution; [hence it] did not form part of the Charter itself"[26]. As to the third of Ball's issues, a request was made to the Inter-American Juridical Committee to "prepare a draft statute providing for the creation and functioning of an Inter-American Court to guarantee the rights of man to be submitted first to the governments then to the Tenth Conference"[27]. It was considered at that Conference that in the "absence of a convention on the subject [i.e. human rights] creating positive substantive law, the time had not arrived for the drafting of a statute of the court"[28].

Instead, the members of the OAS agreed, in 1959, to establish a human rights commission as an "interim measure", until a human rights court could be created[29]. The Inter-American Commission on Human Rights was to be an "autonomous entity" within the Inter-American system, and later in 1970, it became an organ of the Organization of American States by virtue of the Protocol of Buenos Aires amending the Charter of the OAS[30]. The Commission was directed by the main organ of the OAS, the General Assembly, to prepare a draft which would later become the American Convention on Human Rights, adopted in 1969, which entered into force in 1978[31]. Buergenthal notes that the "American Convention is patterned on the European Convention of Human

[24] Ball, *op. cit.* n. 21, p. 503.

[25] Thomas Buergenthal, "The Inter-American System for the Protection of Human Rights", in Buergenthal *et al.* (eds.), *Protecting Human Rights in the Americas: Select Problems*, 1990, p. 4.

[26] *Ibid.*, p. 4.

[27] *Ibid.*, pp. 503-504.

[28] C. G. Fenwick, "The Tenth Inter-American Conference at Caracas", *The American Journal of International Law*, Vol. 48, 1954, p. 139.

[29] Christina M. Cerna, "The Inter-American Commission of Human Rights", *Connecticut Journal of International Law*,Vol. 2, 1987, p. 312.

[30] Charter of the Organization of American States, 1948, amended by the Protocol of Buenos Aires, 1967, and by the Protocol of Cartagena de Indias, 1985, OAS Doc. OEA Ser. A/E/2 Rev.

[31] American Convention on Human Rights, signed November 22, 1969, entered into force 18 July 1978, O.A.S. no. 36, OAS Doc. OEA Ser. L./V/II. 23 Rev. 2. See Appendix 5 for full text.

Rights. This is true in particular of its institutional framework which is quite similar to its European counterpart"[32]. The American Convention on Human Rights gave the Inter-American Commission a different role, however, and made way for the creation of the Inter-American Court of Human Rights[33]. The Statute of the Inter-American Court, drafted by the newly elected judges, was approved by the OAS General Assembly in October 1979, while the original Rules of the Court were adopted in August 1980[34].

2.1.3. *African Charter on Human and Peoples' Rights*

The pressure to establish a regional human rights regime in Africa came in the wake of the dismantling of the colonial system. Having removed the yoke of colonialism, African States established the Organization of African Unity (OAU) to "promote solidarity in Africa; to cooperate in an attempt to better the lives of Africans; to defend State sovereignty and territorial integrity; to eliminate all forms of colonialism from Africa; and to promote international cooperation with regard to the UN and the Universal Declaration of Human Rights"[35]. The OAU emphasized, however, the preoccupation of its members to ensure political stability and territorial integrity, often at the expense of violations of human rights:

> Notwithstanding the genuine concern of African Leaders to maintain their national sovereignty and territorial integrity, the African public, NGOs and the international community were justifiably outraged by the OAU's inaction if not indifference to massive human rights violations in Africa.[36]

As a result of this type of criticism, the OAU Secretary-General requested the drafting of an African human rights treaty. The African Charter of Human and Peoples' Rights was thus produced in 1981 and entered into force on 21 October 1986[37]. This instrument differs in two significant respects from its counterparts in Europe and the Americas. Beyond first-generation (political and civil) and second-generation (economic, social and cultural) rights that are found in all three instruments, the African Charter ensures third-generation (solidarity or "peoples") rights, which include the right of peoples to self-determination, the free disposition of wealth and natural resources, and the right to international

---

[32] Buergenthal, *op. cit.* n. 25, pp. 8-9.

[33] See Chapters 6, 7, and 8 of the American Convention on Human Rights, *ibid.*

[34] The Rule of the Court may be found at Inter-American Court of Human Rights: Rule of the Court, adopted July 30 to 9 August 1980, OAS Doc. OEA Ser. L./V/III. 3.

[35] Article 2, Charter of the Organization of African Unity, 23 May 1963, *International Legal Materials*, Vol. 2, 1963, p. 776.

[36] Evelyn Ankumah, *The African Commission on Human and Peoples' Rights*, 1996, p. 5.

[37] The African Charter of Human and Peoples' Rights, *op. cit.* n. 7.

peace and security[38]. A further distinction is to be found in the enforcement mechanisms provided for under the African Charter. As opposed to the European and Inter-American Conventions, the African Charter has provided for only an African Commission on Human and Peoples' Rights. The African Court of Human and Peoples' Rights, which was agreed upon in 1996, was given formal consent by the African States through the signing of the Protocol to the African Charter on Human and Peoples' Rights on the Establishment of an African Court of Human and Peoples' Rights during the 34th Ordinary Session of the Assembly of Heads of States and Governments of the OAU in June 1998[39], had not seen the light of day by the end of 1999.

3. Comparing the European and Inter-American Courts, 1980–1998

While the African Court of Human and Peoples' Rights had not yet been established by the latter part of the twentieth century, the courts within the European and American systems have been functioning for some time. Until November 1998, the European and Inter-American human rights systems had analogous constitutive instruments[40]. The active presence of nearly identical human rights courts in the Americas and in Europe during an eighteen-year period from 1980 to 1998 allows for comparisons which shed light on why the Inter-American Court, while appearing to be similar to its European counterpart, in reality evolved in a fundamentally different manner. The first difference, which relates to the inability of contentious cases to reach the Inter-American Court is, of course, the voluntary nature of international adjudication. Article 62(1) of the American Convention allows State Parties to recognize as binding the jurisdiction of the Court. Further, Article 63(3) reads:

> The jurisdiction of the Court shall comprise all cases concerning the interpretation and application of the provisions of the Convention that are submitted to it, provided that the State Parties to the case recognize or have recognized such declaration pursuant to the preceding paragraphs, or by a special agreement.

While the European system remained voluntary (until November 1998), thirty-nine States subscribed to the Court's contentious jurisdiction under Article 46. By contrast, by that same date only sixteen American States had recognized the

[38] Articles 19, 21, and 23, *ibid.*

[39] By the end of 1999, 35 States had signed the Protocol and 3 States had ratified it: Burkina Faso, Gambia, and Senegal. Information received from Ben Kioko, Legal Counsel, the Organization of African Unity.

[40] See Protocols n. 9 and n. 11 to the Convention for Protection of Human Rights and Fundamental Freedoms.

jurisdiction of the Inter-American Court[41]. Thomas Buergenthal, as President of the Inter-American Court of Human Rights, noted in a 1986 address before the OAS Permanent Council that there are "many hurdles"[42] surrounding the Court's contentious jurisdiction. At the time, he stated that the biggest obstacle to having more cases heard before the Court was the lack of Parties which had accepted the Court's contentious jurisdiction. However, in the years following his address, the number of States accepting the jurisdiction of the Court doubled from eight to sixteen and therefore, by the end of the century, included almost half of the thirty-five OAS member States.

Having consented to the jurisdiction of the Court, American and European States, during the period 1980-1998, saw their obligations under the applicable human rights conventions enforced by way of proceedings initiated by the Commissions. As Héctor Fix-Zamundio, a judge of the Inter-American Court, stated, the latter does "not have a direct jurisdictional function; there is no direct access to the Court. Access is through the Commission, and we have jurisdiction only when the Commission send us cases"[43]. Before a case could reach either of the Courts, it must first have been dealt with by the Commission which, like a gatekeeper, would make the determination of allowing a case to proceed to the Court. Although "any person or group of persons, or any non-governmental entity"[44] may come forward complaining that their Convention rights have been violated, they cannot bring such complaints directly before the Court[45]. Thus, in the period under review, a case started its road towards either the European or Inter-American Court as a petition before the relevant Commission.

Before either the European or the Inter-American Commission could consider a petition, the petitioner would have to ensure that all domestic remedies available had been exhausted in accordance with the rules of international law and that the petition had been lodged within a six-month period from the time of

---

[41] The sixteen countries which had accepted the jurisdiction of the Court are: Argentina, Bolivia, Chile, Colombia, Costa Rica, Ecuador, Guatemala, Honduras, Nicaragua, Panama, Paraguay, Peru, Surinam, Trinidad and Tobago, Uruguay, and Venezuela. See "State of Ratification of Major Human Rights Conventions", *Netherlands Quarterly of Human Rights*, Vol. 14, 1996, pp. 360-373.

[42] Thomas Buergenthal, "The Inter-American Court, Human Rights and the OAS", *Human Rights Law Journal*, Vol. 7, 1986, p. 158.

[43] Lynda E. Frost, "The Evolution of the Inter-American Court of Human Rights: Reflections of Present and Former Judges", *Human Rights Quarterly*, Vol. 14, 1992, p. 178.

[44] Article 44, American Convention on Human Rights; Article 25, Convention for Protection of Human Rights and Fundamental Freedoms.

[45] In the first contentious case to be brought before the Inter-American Court, Costa Rica – in a case against itself – asked the Court to deliberate, without having gone through the Commission's procedures, on the death of one of its nationals, Viviana Gallardo, killed while in detention by National Guardsmen. By submitting this case directly to the Court and bypassing the Commission, Costa Rica rendered the case inadmissible. The Court decided that the Commission "is the channel through which" cases must proceed if they are to reach the Court. *In the Matter of Viviana Gallardo*, I/A Court H.R., 13 November 1981, p. 85.

the exhaustion of those local remedies[46]. Having thus gone through a domestic judicial system, the case would then become something of a political issue before the Commissions, thereby losing its judicial nature, until it would again appear before a human rights court. If the Commissions considered a petition admissible, it would inform the State accused and ask it to provide information. Regardless of whether the Commissions received information back from the State, after a set period of time, they could decide whether grounds existed to proceed with the petition. The Commissions could at this time end the procedure if they considered the petition totally unfounded[47].

Further in the petition process, the Commissions were called upon to undertake fact-finding missions and to seek friendly settlement[48]. To this point in the process, by which a petition could be heard before either the Inter-American or European Courts, the systems were analogous. If a friendly settlement could not be reached, within the Inter-American system then the Commission was to draw up a confidential report outlining facts and drawing conclusions, which was to be made available to the parties[49]. Under certain conditions, including a waiting period, the Commission could then publish the report making recommendations where appropriate and establishing a period in which a State was to remedy the situation. Within the former European system, reports were forwarded not only to the parties but also to the Committee of Ministers for consideration and possible action[50]. Finally, it was at this point, when no settlement was possible, that a petition could, upon the decision of either of the Commissions, proceed to a Court.

3.1. **The New European Human Rights System**

One of the main reasons the Inter-American Court of Human Rights had not functioned to its potential has been the lack of coordination with the Inter-American Commission; both mechanisms of European system, by contrast, worked in a complementary manner. In fact, the European system functioned to such a degree that it became overburdened and major reforms became necessary,

---

[46] Article 46(1)(a) and (b), American Convention on Human Rights; Article 26, Convention for Protection of Human Rights and Fundamental Freedoms.

[47] Article 48(1)(b), American Convention on Human Rights. Article 27, Convention for Protection of Human Rights and Fundamental Freedoms.

[48] Article 48, American Convention on Human Rights; Article 28, Convention for Protection of Human Rights and Fundamental Freedoms.

[49] Article 50, American Convention on Human Rights; Article 31, Convention for Protection of Human Rights and Fundamental Freedoms.

[50] Articles 31 and 32(3) and (4), Convention for Protection of Human Rights and Fundamental Freedoms.

> so as not to collapse under its own weight, be this as a result of the enormous increase in individual applications now coupled with a 48 per cent increase of State Parties [to the Convention] since 1989 or the interrelated problem of the clogging–up with unacceptable delays in the processing of applications in Strasbourg[51].

A major determination in the reforming of the European human rights system was that the Commission was expendable. This is in direct contrast to the Inter-American mechanism, where Inter-American Judge Gros Espiell has noted that:

> In America, we do not foresee the modification of the bi-organizational system (the Commission and the Court). It is true that there has been some thought as to the improving and to better coordination between the two organs. But there are no attempts to assimilate the two organs or to eliminate the Commission[52].

In contrast to this stance, the phasing-out of the European Commission commenced in 1990 with the signing of Protocol No. 9 to the European Human Rights Convention. For those States which became Parties to that Protocol, the Convention allowed "the person, non-governmental organization or group of individuals having lodged the complaint with the Commission" to refer a case directly to the Court[53]. In such cases, the judges formed a panel effectively to carry out the duties that had been attributed to the Commission; they considered whether the cases raised "serious questions affecting the interpretation or application of the Convention" and thus became the "gatekeepers", determining the admissibility of the case before going to the full Court[54].

By 1993, the members of the Council of Europe had decided that further reforms were necessary "to enhance the efficiency of the means of protection, to shorten procedures and to maintain the present high quality of human rights protection"[55]. Protocol No. 11 was signed at the meeting of Heads of State and Governments of the Council of Europe on 11 May 1994. The Protocol, which came into force on 1 November 1998, one year after the last of the State Parties to the Convention had consented to be bound by it, dismantled both the European Commission and the part-time Court. In their stead, a new full-time European Court of Human Rights was created which receives applications directly from

---

[51] Andrew Drzemczewski, "The Major Overhaul of the European Human Rights Convention Control Mechanism: Protocol No. 11", *Collected Courses of the Academy of European Law*, Vol. 6, 1995, pp. 121-245, p. 127.

[52] Gros Espiell, *op. cit.* n. 1, p. 236.

[53] Article 5(1), Protocol 9 to the Convention for Protection of Human Rights and Fundamental Freedoms. Concerning Access to the Court by Individuals, 6 September 1990, ETS n. 140. Protocol 9 came into force on 1 October 1994 and, before it was repealed by Article 2(8) of Protocol 11, had been ratified by 23 States.

[54] Article 5(2), Protocol 9 to the Convention for Protection of Human Rights and Fundamental Freedoms.

[55] Vienna Declaration, 9 October 1993, as cited in Drzemczewski, *op. cit.* n. 51, p. 203.

"persons, non-governmental organizations or group of individuals claiming to be victim of a violation by one of the High Contracting Parties of the rights set forth in the Convention or protocols thereto"[56]. This new body was meant to streamline and render more efficient a system which was burdened with over 5000 cases in 1996[57].

While the European system was on the verge of collapse due to its success, the Inter-American system, though the means of bringing a case before its Court were similar, seemed to have been still-born. It appears that whereas the European Commission evolved in parallel to the European Court, in developing an effective coordinated system for the protection of human rights, the mechanisms in the Americas took a distinctly opposite course. The difference in the evolution of the Inter-American system led to a curbing of the effectiveness of the rule of law in the Western Hemisphere. With final judgment being given in only sixteen cases over an eighteen-year period, it appears that factors other than the constitutive documents of the Inter-American system influence respect for the rule of law. These other factors, the development of the Inter-American Commission and the financing of the Inter-American Court, demonstrate that while international adjudication may appear strong on paper, it can be very ineffective in practice.

4. The Inter-American Court of Human Rights

The previous section demonstrated that between 1980 and November 1998 the European Court of Human Rights and its Inter-American counterpart functioned with an analogous procedural regime under which cases started as petitions to the Commission before the could be considered by a judicial organ. Despite the similarities in the constitutive instruments of these judicial bodies, the Inter-American Court has only been able to render final judgment on the merits in seventeen cases in an eighteen-year period while the European Court dealt with 737 cases during the same period[58]. What will now be considered are the impediments which have been faced by the Inter-American Court of Human Rights and which are responsible for the fact that during its existence of nearly twenty years, it came nowhere close to matching the effectiveness of the European Court of Human Rights. To contrast the two Courts is to find that while

[56] Article 1, Protocol No. 11 to the Convention for Protection of Human Rights and Fundamental Freedoms: Restructuring the Control Machinery established thereby, 1 November 1998, ETS n.155. New Article 34 (Individual applications) of the Convention for Protection of Human Rights and Fundamental Freedoms.

[57] Drzemczewski, *op. cit.* n. 51, pp. 134-135.

[58] See the Judgments and Decision section of the European Court of Human Rights website at: http:// www.dhcour.coe.fr.

they were similar on paper, the amount of decisions delivered demonstrates a wide disparity in practice. The lack of effective judicial remedies before the Inter-American Court of Human Rights was best summarized by a Judge of that Court, who wrote:

> I have come to the conclusion that unfortunately the system of the Convention appears to make [human rights protection] impossible because the American States in drafting it did not wish to accept the establishment of a swift and effective jurisdictional system but rather they hobbled it by interposing the impediment of the Commission, by establishing a veritable obstacle course that is almost insurmountable, on the long and arduous road that the basic rights of the individual are forced to travel[59].

The obstacle course to which Judge Piza alludes includes the procedural regime discussed, which attributes a key role to the Inter-American Commission. Further, the Organization of American States (OAS) must be criticized for having established the Inter-American Court of Human Rights without funding it in a manner which would allow it to function effectively. Despite the fact that non-governmental human rights organizations, such as Amnesty International and Human Rights Watch, have drawn attention to, and documented, systematic State-sponsored abuses during the 1980s and 1990s, which have lead to literally millions of human rights violations in Latin America while the Inter-American Court was forced to live in near-splendid isolation, giving judgment in less than two dozen contentious cases[60].

The limitations on the rule of law imposed by States becomes evident when examining the establishment and functioning of the Inter-American Court. Beyond the procedural road a case must travel before reaching the Court, the administrative and political impediments meeting cases upon their arrival explains why the Inter-American Court – as opposed to its European counterpart – has had little tangible impact as a judicial organ meant to uphold the rule of law. How is it that in an area of the world fraught with human rights violations only a handful of contentious cases had been decided? To answer the question, different factors should be highlighted. First, the evolution of the Court as related to its gatekeeper – the Commission – inhibited a number of cases from being forwarded to the Court. Second, the OAS member States had further reduced the ability of the Court to deal with adjudicative matters by administrative limitations. Through these impediments, the American States sought to ensure that major obstacles would have to be overcome before a case could reach the Inter-American Court of Human Rights.

---

[59] Concurring Opinion, Judge Rodolfo Piza Escalante, *In the Matter of Viviana Gallardo*, 13 November 1981, I/A Court H.R., p. 99.

[60] See for instance Amnesty International, *Crime without Punishment: Impunity in Latin America*, AMR 01/08/96, 1996; Latin American country reports in Human Rights Watch, *World Report 1999*, 1999, and, more specifically, the situation reports from Human Rights Watch/Americas.

4.1. **Organizational Impediments**

The evolution of both the European Court and the Inter-American Court were conditioned by the relationships with their respective Commissions. While both the European and the Inter-American Commission appeared *prima facie* to have the same responsibilities, the evolution of their mandates demonstrated that they were fundamentally different. The fact that the European Commission has been recently dismantled does not affect the following evaluation, which seeks to identify the factors which have caused the Inter-American Court to take a fundamental different course from that of its European counterpart.

The European Commission of Human Rights, during the 45 years of existence, consisted of the same number of commissioners as there were Parties to the European Convention. Originally composed of eleven members, the Commission would grow to have thirty-nine by the end of its mandate[61]. By way of contrast, Articles 34 to 36 of the American Convention provide for a set number of members – seven – who are to act as Human Rights Commissioners in their personal capacity but, at the same time, as representatives of all the member States of the OAS, regardless of whether a State has ratified the American Convention. Both bodies were empowered to receive petitions from any person, group of persons, or non-governmental organizations claiming to be victim of violations of the Conventions[62]. Having received a petition, the Commissions were to determine the admissibility of the claim; if the latter was judged admissible, the Commissions were to ascertain the facts and to seek a friendly settlement[63]. If such friendly settlement was not forthcoming, they were empowered either to bring the petition to their Courts as contentious cases or to submit a report to their respective executive organs for action[64].

Despite these similarities, the fundamental difference in the establishment and evolution of the European and Inter-American Commissions meant that these institutions, which acted as "filters", would play significant roles in any success which a Court might have in fulfilling its mandate. While the European Com-

---

[61] Chart of Signatures and Ratifications, Convention for the Protection of Human Rights and Fundamental Freedoms, http://www.dhcour.coe.fr.

[62] Article 25, European Convention; Article 44, American Convention.

[63] For admissibility, see Articles 26-28 of the European Convention and Articles 46 and 47 of the American Convention; for friendly settlement, Article 30 of the European Convention and Article 49 of the American Convention.

[64] Provisions for friendly settlement are found at Article 30 of the European Convention and Article 48 of the American Convention; the provision related to the referral to the European Courts or the filing of a Report with the Committee of Ministers (Article 32 of the European Convention), while Article 51 of the American Convention allows the Commission to refer a petition to the Inter-American Court as a case or, by virtue of Articles 49-51, to make a report and forward it to the State accused of violations of the Convention and to the Secretary-General of the OAS, and to make it public if, after a set period of time, no action has been taken.

mission of Human Rights was a creation of the European Convention, as was the European Court, the Inter-American Commission was established twenty years earlier than the Inter-American Court. This resulted in a situation where the European mechanisms matured as complementary organs, while the Inter-American system evolved in a less than harmonious manner. Despite its having been established in 1959, the Inter-American Commission always functioned in the shadow of an Inter-American Court. This is due, in large part, to the fact that originally the American States wished to create a human rights court but settled for a commission instead.

4.1.1. *The Evolution of the Inter-American Commission on Human Rights*

Although attempts were made at the Tenth Inter-American Conference held at Caracas, Venezuela, in 1954, "to have the question of an Inter-American Court to Protect the Rights of Man included on the agenda", these came to naught[65]. This was, in large part, a result of a meeting of the Inter-American Council of Jurists in the previous year, where it was decided that without a human rights convention it made no sense to establish a judicial mechanism[66]. Anna Schreiber notes that:

> The fate of the proposal to prepare a draft statute for an inter-American court to protect human rights indicates that in 1953 most governments were still unwilling to move rapidly to establish international guarantees for human rights. Although the proposal came within one vote of being placed on the agenda of the Tenth Inter-American Conference, the mood of the majority was mirrored in the title of the human rights item which was placed on that agenda: "Human Rights – Measures Tending to Promote Human Rights Without Detriment to National Sovereignty and the Principle of Non-Intervention". Few States were willing to modify their traditional adherence to the doctrine of non-intervention by approving measures that would give international bodies the power to pass judgment on their domestic activities[67].

Schreiber points out that during the next five years, up until 1959, "no major steps towards the construction of an inter-American system for the protection of human rights were taken"[68]. At the Fifth Meeting of Consultation of the Ministers of Foreign Affairs held at Santiago, Chile, in 1959, the delegates called on the Inter-American Council of Jurists to forge a link between a court and a convention by drafting first a "convention on human rights and another convention for the establishment of an Inter-American Court for the Protection of

[65] Fenwick, *op. cit.* n. 28, p. 139.
[66] See n. 28.
[67] Anna P. Schreiber, *The Inter-American Commission of Human Right*, 1970, p. 24.
[68] *Ibid.*, p. 26.

Human Rights and of any other organs suitable for that same task"[69]. The second paragraph of the draft resolution provided for the creation of:

> an Inter-American Commission on Human Rights, composed of seven members elected as individuals by the Council of the Organization of American States from panels of three names presented by the governments. The Commission, which shall be organized by the Council of the Organization and have the specific functions that the Council assigns it, shall be charged with furthering respect for such rights"[70].

The draft resolution calling for the establishment of the Inter-American Commission on Human Rights appears to have been a setback to the movement towards creating a human rights court. Although the founding of the Commission was secondary to the task of developing a convention on human rights and the establishment of a court, the Commission would come to play a prominent role in the protection of human rights in the Americas. However, the creation of the Inter-American Commission on Human Rights would also become an obstacle in the path of creating a properly functioning human rights court. The Commission would, with its solid work in promoting human rights, sidetrack the wishes of proponents of international adjudication for a twenty-year period; it would become the gatekeeper which would determine which cases could reach the Court; and it would become the *locus* of a labyrinth of procedures both slowing down and limiting the number of cases reaching the Inter-American Court. Finally, the Commission, feeling threatened by the establishment of the Inter-American Court of Human Rights, would involve itself in a "turf war" with the Court. This struggle affected both the amount of international adjudication taking place in the Americas and the impact which the Court would have on human rights in the Western Hemisphere.

"The Inter-American Commission on Human Rights was born almost by accident and without special design. There was no definite plan for its creation, no prior studies"[71]. The happenstance manner in which the Commission originated and would later evolve belies the fact that it did so as a response to a functional and pragmatic approach taken by the States of the Western Hemisphere. A staff attorney for the Commission noted in a 1987 article that, at the 1959 Santiago Meeting of Consultation, "the drafters considered a court the primary instrument for the promotion and protection of human rights in the

[69] *Ibid.*

[70] Cecilia Medina, *The Battle of Human Rights: Gross, Systematic Violations and the Inter-American System*, 1988, p. 67.

[71] César Sepúlveda, "The Inter-American Commission on Human Rights (1969-1981)", *Israel Yearbook on Human Rights*, Vol. 12, 1982, p. 47. Note that M. Margaret Ball wrote, however, that the establishment of the Commission was not without precedent, a like plan having been put forward by the Uruguayan delegation at the Tenth International Conference of American States at Caracas in 1954. *Op. cit.* n. 21, p. 373.

Americas, while the Commission was considered only an interim measure until the creation of such a court"[72]. With such an auspicious beginning, it is interesting to note the critique leveled by the delegate from Uruguay, at the 1959 Santiago Meeting of Consultation of the Ministers of Foreign Affairs, to the paragraph of the draft resolution, noted above, creating the Commission. The Uruguayan delegate took up the argument mentioned earlier by the Inter-American Council of Jurists[73], stating that "to create an organ to promote the rights before respect of the rights become a precise and clear legal obligation [i.e. a convention on human rights] would be illogical"[74]. Yet, the argument, which had been strong enough to derail the movement toward an Inter-American Court, was not sufficient to stop the creation of the Inter-American Commission on Human Rights.

The battle for legitimacy that the Commission waged after the Council of the OAS approved its Statute in 1960 is important to an understanding of the response which the Commission would later have towards the establishment of the Inter-American Court. The Commission, through an arduous process, moved from being a temporary entity, "which, sooner or later, would disappear at the expense of a system which would establish a convention on human rights"[75], to becoming an OAS Charter organ[76]. How did the Commission leave such unstable ground to become a foundation for the promotion of human rights within the Inter-American system?

Karel Vasak argues that the Commission's "actions, prudent and daring at times, had the effect of proving, if not the compatibility, at least the possibility of conciliation, between the principles of non-intervention and the international protection of human rights in the Western Hemisphere"[77]. It was within this atmosphere of finding a balance between human rights and State sovereignty that the Commission would come to prosper within the Inter-American system. As José Cabranes notes, the establishment of the Commission

> gave little hint of the role which the new body would fashion for itself within the inter-American system, and indicates that some of the Members of the O.A.S. may have supposed that in voting to create the Commission they had merely voted for the establishment of one more "study group":
>
> > In carrying out its assignment of promoting respect for human rights, the Commission shall have the following functions and powers:

[72] Cerna, *op. cit.* n. 29, p. 312.

[73] See *supra*, n. 26.

[74] Medina, *op. cit.* n. 70, p. 67.

[75] Karel Vasak, *La Commission interaméricanne des droits de l'homme*, 1968, p. 175. My translation.

[76] Articles 52 and 111, Charter of the Organization of American States.

[77] Vasak, *op. cit.* n. 75, p. 87. My translation.

a. To develop an awareness of human rights among the peoples of America;

b. To make recommendations to the Governments of the members states in general, if it considers such action advisable, for the adoption of progressive measures in favor of human rights within the framework of their domestic legislation and in accordance with their constitutional precepts, appropriate measures to further the faithful observance of those rights;

c. To prepare such studies or reports as it considers advisable in the performance of its duties;

d. To urge the Governments of the member states to supply it with information on the measures adopted by them in matters of human rights;

e. To serve the Organization of American States as an advisory body in respect of human rights.

By its own interpretation and application of its Statute, however, the Commission has received and reviews communications from individuals and groups within member States, studied conditions and held sessions and public hearings in particular states, and made findings and recommendations thereon to the State or States involved. This interpretation of its own Statute, as one of the Commission's members noted, "laid a foundation for visitations, examinations, and recommendations with respect to conditions involving flagrant and persistent violations of human rights in individual countries"[78].

The evolution of the Commission from its early form of an "entity" to become an important part of the Inter-American system clearly demonstrates the mistrust which American States fostered towards the notion of international adjudication. The Commission would come to play a significant role within the OAS as a quasi-political go-between, linking States and the Inter-American Court. The establishment and evolution of the Inter-American Commission was a pragmatic means used by American States for dealing with human rights without having to submit to the jurisdiction of a court. Yet the growth in stature of the Commission would become a double-edged sword.

During its early years, American States saw the Commission's actions as being "political" in nature. This eased the pressure which had been building in favour of setting up a tribunal by dealing with human rights within the political realm. However, by the late 1960s, the Commission was, "if not in the process of solidifying, at least acquiring, the powers of a juridical organ"[79]. In so doing, the Commission forced the American States to follow through on the establishment of the Inter-American Court or face the consequences of placing formal judicial powers in the hands of a very powerful organ of the OAS. The final thrust toward

---

[78] José A. Cabranes, "The Protection of Human Rights by the Organization of American States", *The American Journal of International Law*, Vol. 62, 1982, pp. 894-895.

[79] Vasak, *op. cit.* n. 75, p. 140. My translation.

creating the Inter-American Court of Human Rights was, therefore, not born out of any affinity for a judicial mechanism to protect human rights. Instead, a proper evaluation would lead to the conclusion that the States of the Americas sought to curb the judicial powers that the Commission was acquiring and, in so doing, developed an awkward system for the protection of human rights which further shielded States from having to defend themselves in front of an international court.

The hasty creation of the Inter-American Commission can be attributed to the fall of the Batista dictatorial regime in Cuba on 1 January 1959. The theme of the Meeting of Consultations of the American Ministers of Foreign Affairs, which took place that year, was "the rupture of democracy in various parts of the Hemisphere, and the delegates, or at least the majority, were convinced that if human rights were reinforced, the democratic system would function better"[80]. The Commission rode this wave of anti-communism and Cold War rhetoric, enabling it to secure strong institutional foundation:

> The development during [the first sessions of the Commission, 1961-65] show that the Commission had assumed several powers which were not explicit in its Statutes, but which it felt were implied powers needed for the better fulfillment of its functions. The OAS political organs, by not questioning these powers, had tacitly agreed on their validity. A powerful reason for this attitude was the fact that most cases handled by the Commission at that time concerned [Fidel Castro's] Cuba, and there the issue was [...] fighting communism. [...] For the cause of human rights it was fortunate that Cuba's cases were the first to be examined by the Commission; the activities undertaken in this respect formed a precedent that was very difficult to challenge when the Commission started handling other cases in the same fashion[81].

By 1965, the actions that the Commission had taken were incorporated into its Statute. A Guatemalan representative, when asking for a discussion of the Commission's status to be placed on the agenda of an upcoming conference, explained that: "the Commission was in no position to give efficient protection to human rights due to its lack of powers [and] that this body could only be considered a temporary Commission"[82]. At the Second Special Inter-American Conference held at Rio de Janeiro in 1965, the Statute of the Commission was amended to legitimize the expanded role it had already assumed. The increased mandate included: ensuring the observance of specific rights as set out in the American Declaration of Rights and Duties of Man; examining communications which were sent to it; seeking information from governments; making recommendations for bringing about a more effective observance of human rights;

---

[80] Sepúlveda, *op. cit.* n. 71, p. 47. Note that dictatorial regimes in a state of imminent collapse in the late 1950s, included, besides Cuba, the Dominican Republic and Haiti.

[81] Medina, *op. cit.* n. 70, pp. 74-75.

[82] *Ibid.*, p. 77.

submitting an annual report noting any progress or setbacks with respect to States' obligations under the American Declaration; and making "explicit decisions about the merits of a complaint"[83].

American States justified this increased mandate by pointing out that the ratification of a convention on human rights was still many years away and that there had been "agreement among American governments about the positive role that the Commission had already played in the [human rights] field"[84]. Karel Vasak argued that "due to the authorization – resembling a blank check – which it received at Rio de Janeiro"[85], the Commission was quickly moving from a quasi-political entity to a quasi-judicial one. Vasak notes that "[i]f some doubt still remains, it is that the jurisprudence – not the actions of the Commission – had not, as of yet, confirmed the evolution which would allow for a comparison between the writings which have emanated from the Inter-American Commission with those of the European Commission"[86].

Cecilia Medina, in her work *The Battle Of Human Rights: Gross, Systematic Violations and the Inter-American System*, notes that the Commission had acquired quasi-judicial functions and points out that:

> [It] had special competence to examine individual communications concerning the violations of human rights. [...] This competence comprised more elements of a judicial nature. On the one hand, there were preliminary legal requirements. [...] On the other hand, its purposes were to lead to an opinion as to whether a violation [...] had been committed. Finally the competence had another judicial element; as a sanction against a government failing to carry out the recommendations, the Commission was empowered to publish a report on the violation.[87]

Vasak likewise shared the opinion of Medina with respect to the evolution towards a judicial mandate which the Commission was undergoing. He notes that the latter already had at its disposal all the elements of a judicial procedure:

> a written phase in the form of an exchange of "information" which is supplied to the Commission by each of the antagonists; an oral phase in the form of an audience accorded often by the Commission to individual petitioners [as] well as the on-site investigation. [...] Even the presumption of truth which, according to Article 51 of the Regulations of the Commission, is attached to the facts not in dispute by the State accused[88].

---

[83] Schreiber, *op. cit.* n. 67, pp. 54-55.
[84] Medina, *op. cit.* n. 70, p. 77.
[85] Vasak, *op. cit.* n. 75, p. 140. My translation.
[86] *Ibid.*, p. 140.
[87] Medina, *op. cit.* n. 70, at p. 84.
[88] Vasak, *op. cit.* n. 75, at p. 147. My translation.

Further, he points out that "violations which were not addressed voluntarily by the specific States, [were to be published in the] yearly report, a "judicial document" which, as is, constitutes a decision"[89].

Vasak argues that the Commission had not, as of yet, taken an overtly judicial character because, although judicial elements existed in its mandate, they were of "variable judicial worth" and were "quite dispersed"[90]: some were to be found in the Commission's Statute, others in its Regulations, and still others were customary in nature, having emerged through the Commission's practice. Vasak contends that the Commission was evolving into a strong entity within the Inter-American system and was solidifying its judicial base. "Already the 1967 revisions of its Regulations, compared to the previous year, traces a clear division between the Commission's function of investigation and its function of protection [...] of human rights"[91]. Vasak ventures the observation that the Commission's status would have to be reformed eventually, lest the Commission attempt to "judicialize its actions"[92]. Thus, in June 1968, the main political body of the OAS, the Council, "approved a resolution by which the Commission was requested to prepare a draft convention on human rights that was to serve as a working document for the Inter-American Specialized Conference on Human Rights"[93].

4.1.2. *The Conflict between the Commission and the Court*

Through its achievements in the protection and promotion of human rights, the Commission not only had gained legitimacy as an OAS Organ, but had been directed to prepare the draft of a human rights convention; thus assuring its own survival. On 22 November 1969, at the Inter-American Specialized Conference on Human Rights in San José, Costa Rica, twelve OAS members signed the "American Convention on Human Rights" based on a draft convention prepared by the Inter-American Commission. It is worth recalling, at this point, that the American Convention closely resembles the European Convention of Human Rights. As Héctor Gros Espiell points out, there "is no doubt that all of Chapter VIII of the American Convention, which deals with the Inter-American Court (Arts. 52-69), is inspired by the European model, which had already been adopted and running, when the Pact of San José was opened for signatures in 1969"[94].

---

[89] *Ibid.*, p. 150.
[90] *Ibid.*, p. 148.
[91] *Ibid.*
[92] *Ibid.*
[93] Medina, *op. cit.* n. 70, p. 96.
[94] Gros Espiell, *op. cit.* n. 1, p. 235.

With the coming into existence of the Inter-American Court of Human Rights in 1980, the means by which human rights abuses were to be dealt within the Inter-American system fundamentally changed. The Inter-American Commission, which had been vested solely with the responsibility of insuring the promotion, and later the protection, of human rights since 1959, was forced to cede to the Court what had been its growing judicial character. Since the establishment of the Court, the Commission witnessed its actions becoming less and less "judicalized", to the point where it questioned the force of its own recommendations.

The Commission's recommendations, adopted pursuant to in Article 51(2) of the Convention, are to be incorporated in a report which is to be issued confidentially to the parties towards the end of the petition procedure. By the late 1960s, this had taken on the flavour of what Cecilia Medina termed "a sanction" and what Vasak called "a "judicial document" that is, a decision"[95]. Yet, by 1994, the Commission had become unsure of the status of such Reports[96]. The movement towards the judicialization of the Commission, which Vasak foresaw in his 1968 text, did not materialize, as the Court stepped in to create a clear distinction between the judicial and political roles which the Convention organs were to fulfill.

Cecilia Medina points out that, from the earliest period of the Court's existence, tension had existed between it and the Commission. That tension reduced the likelihood of a case being heard before the Inter-American Court. In its first contentious case before the Court, *In the Matter of Viviana Gallardo,* the Commission, having had its jurisdiction upheld by the Court and hence established itself as the channel by which cases were to proceed to the Court, decided after a two-year deliberation that the *Gallardo* petition was inadmissible. Medina notes that the "Commission's decision could be perceived as aimed at preventing the Court from exercising its powers"[97]. This hypothesis would seem to be confirmed by the fact that the Commission – the main channel through which contentious cases are to proceed to the Court – did not refer a contentious case to the Court until 1986, six years after it had been constituted. Although the Commission did submit, for its consideration, a number of advisory questions, the Court was obviously being under-utilized at the time. As Scott Davidson noted in 1992, it "is perhaps an abuse of speech to refer to the 'lack of the use' of

---

[95] Medina, *op. cit.* n. 70 and Vasak, *op. cit.* n. 75.

[96] See *El Amparo* case, I/A Court H.R., 18 January 1995. The *El Amparo* case, submitted by the Commission to the Court on 15 January 1994, dealt with the attack and subsequent attempted cover up, in 1988, of a Venezuelan commando unit on fishermen of their own country whom they mistook for Colombia drug-runners.

[97] Cecilia Medina, "The Inter-American Commission on Human Rights and the Inter-American Court on Human Rights: Reflections on a Joint Venture", *Human Rights Quarterly*, Vol. 12, 1990, p. 450.

the Court's contentious jurisdiction. It is possibly more accurate to describe the prevailing situation as one of 'non use'"[98].

The Court, in its advisory opinion on *Compulsory Membership in an Association Prescribed by Law for the Practice of Journalism*, criticized the Commission for not taking advantage of its ability to refer cases to the Court:

> Although the Convention does not specify under what circumstances a case should be referred to the Court by the Commission, it is implicit in the functions that the Convention assigns to the Commission and the Court that certain cases should be referred by the former to the Court[99].

In a separate opinion, Judge Máximo Cisneros went further, stating that he was disappointed, having sat on the Court for six years and now retiring: "I feel [a sense of frustration] in leaving the Court before it has had the opportunity to hear a single case of a violation of human rights, in spite of the sad realities of our America in this field"[100]. He then concurred with the Court's judgment by restating that "the Commission has a special duty to consider the advisability of coming to the Court"[101].

4.1.3. *The Commission accepts the Court*

Since the early 1990s, the political impediments to adjudication, which the Court suffered during its early years, have been slowly disappearing, allowing it to become more active in attempting to protect human rights. If this trend is to continue, the Court will face a situation where there are no longer any overt political impediments preventing cases from reaching it. This, however, appears to be a blessing in disguise, as the Court will be called upon to perform more and more work while remaining within the limited budget provided by the Organizations of American States. As shall be seen in the next section on "administrative impediments", while the Inter-American Commission was willing, in the 1990s, to recognize the contentious jurisdiction of the Court, the OAS was slow to supply the Court with the resources required for fulfilling its task of dealing with a burgeoning caseload.

In a 1990 article, entitled "The Inter-American Commission on Human Rights and the Inter-American Court on Human Rights: Reflections on a Joint Venture", Cecilia Medina wrote that 1986 was the year when "the Commission seized the Court"[102]. However, in hindsight, the disappearance of friction between the

[98] Scott Davidson, *The Inter-American Court of Human Rights*, 1992, p. 195.
[99] I/A Court H.R., 1 November 1985, p. 96.
[100] *Ibid.*, p. 145.
[101] *Ibid.*, p. 145.
[102] Medina, *op. cit.* n. 97, p. 453.

Commission and the Court did not become tangible until the 1990s. Medina's only basis for stating that the Court had been "seized" by the Commission was that it had, for the first time, presented to the Court a series of contentious cases related to the same incident[103]. However, after having submitted these cases, it would take the Commission another four years to forward another.

In 1990, the "turf war" between the Commission and the Court appeared to have ceased for all intents and purposes. Since that time, the Inter-American Commission has been active before the Court as it had never been during the 1980s. The increased activities of the Court can be attributed to its acceptance, by the Inter-American Commission, as a vital tool in the protection of human rights. After an extended period of hesitation, the Commission recognized, in a series of cases dealing with "disappearances" in Honduras, the important role that the Court could play in the Americas. Medina confirms this when she states:

> the Court is a welcome and necessary addition. The importance of legally binding decisions against states needs not be emphasized. Not only do binding decisions provide authoritative interpretations of the rights in the Convention, but the Court's decisions may have an enormous political importance as well, making it more difficult for governments to persistently disregard human rights. The *Velásquez* case shows how important it is for the system to receive and rule on individual cases[104].

The Commission, during the 1990s, consistently utilized the Court's contentious jurisdiction and called on the Court to adopt provisional measures in urgent matters to prevent harm to individuals. During in the 1990s, it has forwarded to the Court twenty-two contentious cases in which various American States were accused of having violated the American Convention on Human Rights[105]. In addition to submitting such cases, the Commission requested the Court to use its powers of issuing provisional measures. Article 63 (2) of the American Convention reads:

---

[103] The cases submitted dealt with the issue of 'disappearances' in Honduras. *Velasquez Rodriguez Case*, I/A Court H.R., 17 August 1990; *Cadinez Cruz Case*, I/A Court H.R., 17 August, 1990; and *Fairan Garbi and Solis Corrales Case*, I/A Court H.R., 21 July 1989.

[104] Medina, *op. cit.* n. 97, p. 461.

[105] The following are the thirteen contentious cases for which the Court has rendered judgment on the merits in the 1990s: *Gangaram Panday* case, I/A Court H.R., 4 December 1991; *Aloeboetoe et al.* case, I/A Court H.R., 10 September 1993; *Cayara* case, I/A Court H.R., 3 February 1993; *El Amparo* case, I/A Court H.R., 18 January 1995; *Neira Alegría et al.* case, I/A Court H.R., 19 January 1995; *Caballero Delgado and Santana* case, I/A Court H.R., 8 December 1995; and *Garrido and Baigorria* case, I/A Court H.R., 2 February 1996; *Genie Lacayo* case, I/A Court H.R., 29 January 1997; *Loayza Tamayo* case, I/A Court H.R., 17 September 1997; *Castillo Paez* case, I/A Court H.R., 3 November 1997; *Suárez Rosero* case, I/A Court H.R., 12 November 1997; *Blake* case, I/A Court H.R., 24 January 1998; *Paniagua Morales y Otros* case, I/A Court H.R., 8 March 1998, *Castillo Petruzzi et al.* Case, I/A Court H.R., 30 May 1999. For information regarding the Inter-American Court of Human Rights consider its website at: http://corteidh-oea.nu.or.cr/ci/HOME_ING.HTM .

> In cases of extreme gravity and urgency, and when necessary to avoid irreparable damages to persons, the Court shall adopt such provisional measures as it deems pertinent in matters it has under consideration. With respect to a case not yet submitted to the Court, it may act at the request of the Commission[106].

Since the Inter-American Commission first used the provision in Article 63(2) in 1991, it had, by 1999, asked the Court to take such measures on more than two dozen occasions[107]. This willingness, since the early 1990s, to request the Court to adopt provisional measures, coupled with the use by the Inter-American Commission of the Court's contentious jurisdiction, demonstrates that the organizational impediments which hampered its ability to adjudicate internationally in the Americas during the 1980s had vanished.

4.2. **Administrative Impediments**

In the wake of the dissipation of the organizational impediments, administrative hurdles had emerged that restrict access to the Court. Thus as the Court, by the late end of the 1990s, was functioning at or near capacity, that capacity was set at a very low threshold. The Court's part-time basis and the lack of budgetary support required to fulfill its mandate places more strain on the Court as its caseload increases. The removal of political impediments, far from aiding the Court, simply reveals fundamental flaws regarding the manner in which the OAS sought to establish and maintain the Inter-American Court of Human Rights. The then Vice-President of the Inter-American Court, Judge Sonia Picado Sotela, alluded to these fundamental problems during a 1991 interview:

> [t]he budget situation of the Court is very bad [...]. The Court will keep getting more cases, but they come in and it is not until one year later that there is an audience on those cases. That is very frustrating [...] the staff of the Court is very small; there is a secretary and an undersecretary and three or four other persons. It really makes it very inefficient[108].

Beyond the political impediments associated with the Inter-American Commission, which have prevented the Court from attempting to fulfill its mandate, the manner in which it is constituted is another hazard on the road to proper respect for the rule of law in the Inter-American system. Despite the numerous violations of human rights, the Court did not sit full-time, although it does have a permanent seat and secretariat. In presenting its draft statute to the OAS General

---

[106] Article 63(2), American Convention on Human Rights.

[107] For an early study of provisional measures, see Jo. M. Pasqualucci, "Provisional Measures in the Inter-American Human Rights System: An Innovative Development in International Law", *Vanderbilt Journal of Transnational Law*, Vol. 26, 1993, pp. 846-874.

[108] Frost, *op. cit.* n. 43, p. 189.

Assembly, the Court attempted to obtain full-time status; however, the General Assembly found this proposal unacceptable, "ostensibly on the grounds that a full-time court would be too expensive and was unjustified until the Court had a substantial caseload"[109]. The Court had sought full-time status in an attempt to exude "prestige and legitimacy"[110], yet "since its inception [it] has functioned on a part-time basis, holding two, and sometimes three regular two-week sessions per year"[111].

Beyond establishing the Court as a part-time tribunal, the OAS member States, through their lack of budgetary support, had erected other administrative impediments to full respect of the rule of law. For the Inter-American Court to function properly as the Convention organ mandated with delivering authoritative judgments on human rights cases in the Americas, it must first and foremost have a budget allowing it to carry out that mandate. By the end of the century, the OAS had not provided the Court with the amount of money essential to its functioning. Thus, the Inter-American Court was forced to seek other budgetary sources to ensure the fulfillment of its function and, in so doing, placed itself in a position whereby its status as an independent court could be brought into question.

4.2.1. *The Organization of American States*

Article 72 of the American Convention on Human Rights reads in part: "the Court shall draw up its own budget and submit it for approval to the General Assembly through the General Secretariat. The latter may not introduce any changes in it"[112]. Throughout the period under review, the Court was the recipient of an erratically fluctuating budget provided from the Organization of American States. During the first five years of the Court's existence, stretching from 1983 to 1987, the Court's OAS budget allocations were reduced by 4.4%. During a ten-year period, from 1983 to 1993, the budget provided by the OAS to the Inter-American Court increased on average 3% annually, but this does not take into account the inflation rate which, if taken into account, demonstrates a clear decline in the funding of the Court over that period. While it was not uncommon for public institutions to have their budgets cut during the 1980s, the Inter-American Court was hit particularly hard as it already functioned on very limited funds.

In 1993, the budget provided by the OAS to the Inter-American Court was US$ 429,000. More than half of this – US$ 235,000 – was earmarked for the

[109] Buergenthal, *op. cit.* n. 25, p. 18.
[110] *Ibid.*, p. 18.
[111] Pasqualucci, *op. cit.* n. 107, p. 860.
[112] Article 72, American Convention on Human Rights.

payment of salaries[113]. Consequently, the Organization of American States, which established the Court as an "autonomous judicial institution"[114], has determined that, apart from the judges, the Court is to function with only four employees[115]. The employment positions which the OAS has established at the Court are: Secretary of the Inter-American Court, its Deputy-Secretary, a Principal Secretary (administrative officer) and a Secretary (support) to the Secretary of the Court. Accordingly, the OAS has not seen fit to provide funds for clerks to assist the judges, for librarians, or for any other support staff. The frustration caused by the lack of OAS funding is apparent when one considers what the members of the Court have had to say on this matter.

Judges have often found themselves lobbying for sufficient funds to allow the Court to fulfill its mandate. In 1981, the budget of US$ 356,700 proposed by the Court was reduced by the OAS Advisory Commission on Administration and Budgetary Matters to US$ 290,500, then further lowered by the OAS Commission on Program-Budget to US$ 284,100. Only through representations made before the latter Commission by the President of the Court, Judge Thomas Buergenthal, was the budget for 1982 increased, albeit marginally, to US$ 300,000[116]. Five years later, Judge Buergenthal, as President of the Court, was still fighting the good fight. This time, in his 1986 address before the OAS Permanent Council, Buergenthal pointed out that:

> the Court currently confronts a very serious crisis. I realize, of course, that the Organization as a whole faces serious financial problems, but the 20% across-the-board budget cuts mandated by the OAS (10% this year and 10% next year) hit the Court particularity hard. This is due to the fact that the Court's 1980-81 start-up budget and those that followed were very small, and rightly so, because the Court did not have much work. Now that our work load has significantly increased, our already small budget is being automatically reduced to a level that has a paralyzing effect on the Court and its ability to properly discharge its obligations[117].

The frustration, felt by the judges over the years is reflected in the reality of the budgetary means supplied to the Inter-American Court of Human Rights by the

---

[113] See the section on the Inter-American Court of Human Rights in Secretaria General de los Organizacion de los Estados Americanos, *Programa-Presupuest de la Organizacion, 1992-93*, 1992, p. 64. An explanations of the methodology used on p. 64 is explained in General Secretariat Organization of American States, *Proposed Program-Budget of the Organization, 1980-81*, 1981, OAS/D.Ser./II.1-1980-81, p. 17.

[114] Article 1, American Convention on Human Rights.

[115] Secretary-General of the Organization of American States, "Approved Posts – Regular Fund by Area and Object (1997)" *Annual Report 1996-1997*, p. 224.

[116] Organization of American States, *Annual Report of the Inter-American Court of Human Rights 1981*, OAS Doc. OEA/Ser.L/III.5 doc 13, pp. 6-7.

[117] Thomas Buergenthal, "The Inter-American Court, Human Rights and the OAS", *Human Rights Law Journal*, Vol. 7, 1986, p. 163.

OAS. The Organization has never provided the Court with the required funds or personnel, despite the overwhelming number of violations of the American Convention. Since its inception, the Court has been unable to function with its limited administrative staff. Consequently, it has been forced to rely on other sources of income, including grants from its host State, Costa Rica.

4.2.2. *The Republic of Costa Rica*

The fact that Costa Rica – which to date is the only State to have both brought a contentious case before the Court and to have utilized its advisory jurisdiction[118] – provides an essential source of income to the Court must be examined in the light of the Court's independence. Through its lack of funding, the OAS has placed the Court in a situation whereby it must rely on money provided to it by Costa Rica to ensure that it can function on a daily basis. In so doing, the Court has been forced to accept, annually, an average of 20% of its budget from a State Party to the American Convention on Human Rights, which is also one of the sixteen States which had accepted the contentious jurisdiction of the Court. In reality, the Inter-American Court has never been able to function with an administrative staff of only four OAS employees. To carry out its mandate, it has had to utilize other sources of income and personnel which, although intended for non-essential matters, have become vital in ensuring that the Court fulfill its most basic function: garnering respect for the American Convention. Following the coming into force of the American Convention, the Government of Costa Rica entered into a headquarters agreement with the Inter-American Court. Article 28 of that Agreement reads:

> As a contribution of the host country to the functioning of the Court, the Government of the Republic of Costa Rica shall:
>
> a) Continue to make an annual grant of an amount not less than that allotted to the Court during its first year in operation, and which was included in Law of the General Budget of the Republic of Costa Rica for the year 1980.
>
> b) Make available to the Court an appropriate locale for its operation[119].

The Headquarters Agreement demonstrates to what extent Costa Rica was willing to back the establishment of the Inter-American Court of Human Rights. The Republic of Costa Rica has, on occasion, given more in grant money to the Inter-

---

[118] *Proposed Amendments to the Naturalization Provisions of the Political Constitution of Costa Rica*, I/A Court H.R., 19 January 1984 and *Compulsory Membership in an Association Prescribed by Law for the Practice of Journalism,* I/A Court H.R., 1 November 1985.

[119] Agreement Between the Government of the Republic of Costa Rica and the Inter-American Court of Human Rights, Organization of American States, *Annual Report of the Inter-American Court of Human Rights*, 1981, OAS Doc. OEA/Ser.L/III.5 doc 13, p. 16.

American Court than it has paid to maintain its membership within the Organization of American States. For example, during the year 1992, Costa Rica paid US$ 81 200 in regular funds to the OAS while donating US$ 94 753 to the Court. However, the Court's host country has been hard pressed by economic problems to transfer its support for international adjudication into real money terms. Costa Rica has been generous, arguably beyond its means. In 1980, during the Court's first year of operation, it pledged the amount of US$ 100,000. Yet Costa Rica had only been able to meet its treaty obligation to provide an annual amount of no less than US$ 100,000 three times and did not do so at all during the 1980s. Far from being critical of Costa Rica, the fact that this State had found it hard to provide the promised funding to the Court demonstrates that the latter should not have to use any given State as a source of vital income. That the Court must rely on a specific State to increase its OAS budget allotment to a tolerable level effectively jeopardizes the Court's independence.

Costa Rica has emerged, not only as an important source of income for the Court, but beyond a doubt as a vital one. Since 1982, Costa Rica has provided the Court with an average of 20% of its yearly budget. Without this yearly contribution/donation, the Court could not carry out its mandate. Thanks to these annual grants, the Court had been able to complete its staff, more than doubling it. It hired, albeit on a contractual basis, a librarian, a civil law lawyer, an additional secretary, along with the Court's receptionist and driver. Through these yearly supplements, the Court shored up the lack of personnel required to fulfill its mandate. The fact that Costa Rica – which, during the period under review, had been the most active State before the Court – provided an essential source of income must be examined in the light of the Court's independence. Through lack of funding, the OAS has placed the Court in a situation whereby it must rely on money provided to it by its best client.

According to the legal adage, "justice must not only be done, but must also be seen to be done"[120]. To function effectively the Inter-American Court must not only act independently but also dissociate itself from situations that might make it appear dependent. It must ensure that it garners the respect of American States so that they will abide by its judgments. Although there is no indication that the Court's independence had been affected by the money supplied by Costa Rica, this is not the issue. The issue is the appearance of a lack of independence with respect to the Inter-American Court of Human Rights when one of the sixteen countries having accepted the Court's contentious jurisdiction provided a vital part of its budget.

[120] For an outline of the norms governing judicial independence consider Jean Allain, "Judicial Independence in Practice: The Case of Judge Odio Benito, Vice-President of Costa Rica", *Revue de droit international de science diplomatiques et politiques*, Vol. 77, 1999, pp. 1-22.

4.2.3. *The European Union*

From 1994 onwards, the European Union financed a project known as "Support the Inter-American Court of Human Rights" which, in 1997, entered its third and final phase. The project had "as its fundamental purpose the development of activities which would strengthen and modernize the Inter-American System for the Protection of Human Rights through supporting the work of the Inter-American Court"[121]. During the earlier stages, the European Union financed the publication of the basic documents and case-law of the Court, and further assisted in updating and expanding the library. The purpose of the third stage of the project was "to consolidate the system of circulation of the publications of the Court and to develop and consolidate new resources and sources of information" at the Court[122]. Without the assistance of the European Union, which amounts to 630 000 ECUs[123], the Court would have had no means of disseminating its work and making itself known to the citizens of the Americas.

4.2.4. *The Inter-American Institute of Human Rights*

A further budgetary source, albeit an indirect one, was the Inter-American Institute of Human Rights (IIDH). On 17 November 1980, the Inter-American Institute was established through an agreement between Costa Rica and the Inter-American Court. "The Institute is an autonomous international academic institution with a global, multidisciplinary approach to the teaching, research and promotion of human rights"[124]. The Institute maintains a close relationship with the Court, as one of the judges acts as the Institute's Executive Director; and, until 1991, individuals who were elected judges to the Court became *ex officio* members of the Institute's Board of Directors[125]. The Institute utilizes the premises of the Court to store its documentation centre while using the Court's library as its resource center. In this manner the library, on the site of the Court, has an additional two employees, an assistant librarian and a staff librarian, to ensure its effective functioning. There is no denying that the Court and its librarian (paid for through the yearly Costa Rican grants) have greatly benefited from the IIDH employees. Although the IIDH does not contribute directly to the

[121] Inter-American Court of Human Rights, *Press Release: Activities of the Inter-American Court of Human Rights*, June 1997, CDH-CP5/97 English.

[122] *Ibid.*

[123] Manuel Ventura-Robles, "Evolución Institucional de la Corte Interamerican de Derechos Humanos durante los Anõs 1987-1997", *Contribución del Juez Héctor Fix-Zamudio a la Evolución Institucional de la Corte Interamericana de Derechos Humanos*, 1998, p. 30.

[124] Organization of American States, *Annual Report of the Inter-American Court of Human Rights* 1991, OAS Doc. OEA/Ser.L/V/III.25 doc 7, 1991, p. 8.

[125] See Douglass W. Cassel, Jr., "Somoza's Revenge: A New Judge for the Inter-American Court of Human Rights", *Human Rights Law Journal*, Vol. 13, 1992, p. 139.

financing of the Inter-American Court, it provides, through this joint venture, personnel who, together with the employees provided by the Costa Rican grants, ensure that the Court can function on a daily basis.

Although the Inter-American Court was envisioned in its Statute as an autonomous judicial institution, an examination of its budgeting sources leads to another conclusion. While the Organization of American States provides the Court with its primary budget, the amount provided has never allowed it to meet all its obligations under the American Convention on Human Rights. The Court has had to rely on Costa Rica as a secondary budget source, thus raising the issue of its independence. Beyond these primary and secondary sources, the Court has received indirect budgetary support through the initiative of the European Union and the staffing of its library by the Inter-American Institute of Human Rights. Without these further sources of income the Court would be expected to function with the resources provided solely by the OAS: an unrealistic proposition.

The staffing and budgetary limits faced by the Inter-American Court has been accentuated in the last decade of the century by the increased amount of cases on the docket. The Court had evolved to the point where it stretched the resources provided to it from various sources. The Secretary of the Court, Manuel Ventura-Robles, noted, in a letter to the President of the Commission on Administration and Budgetary Matters of the OAS, that "it is very hard to believe that the Court continues to provide quality professional work, today internationally recognized, with the human resources that the Court has at its disposal"[126]. Further, the then President of the Court, Rafael Nieto Navia, acknowledged the lack of resources, for which the OAS was responsible, and that this lack of funding might affect the Court's ability to adjudicate properly. In correspondence with the Secretary-General of the OAS, João Clemente Baena Soares, the President pointed out:

> The reality is that the personnel of the Court regularly work 10 hour days which is increased to 14 to 16 hours including Saturdays and Sundays while the Court is in session. This situation can not be allowed to continue much longer without affecting the level of the judgments and consequently the prestige of the Court[127].

Despite the added contributions of Costa Rica, the overall budget was not sufficient to ensure that the Court perform in the manner which is expected of an international tribunal. The moneys first budgeted by the OAS were meant for a Court without cases. In the 18 years that passed, however, the docket increased to a point where it was necessary for the OAS to step in and provide more funds. To

---

126 Correspondence between the Secretary of the Inter-American Court of Human Rights, Manuel Ventura-Robles, and the President of the Commission on Administration and Budgetary Matters, Ambassador Ricardo Toledo, 27 April 1993, CDH-S/352.

127 Correspondence between the President of the Inter-American Court of Human Rights, Rafeal Nieto Navia, and the Secretary-General of the OAS, João Clemente Baena Soares, 6 November 1993, CDH-S/401.

that end, in a meeting on 4 December 1996 the Secretary-General of the OAS agreed with a delegation of judges from the Inter-American Court that the latter "be given complete administrative independence and budgetary autonomy"[128]. As a result, the Court submitted a larger budget meant to cover "the basics it must have to accomplish its lofty purposes"[129]. In the OAS General Assembly Resolution approving the Court's Annual Report for 1996, the Organization decided to "support appropriate financing to the Inter-American Court of Human Rights within the available resources of the Organization, so it can continue to fulfill the high functions entrusted to it by the American Convention on Human Rights"[130]. Despite this rhetoric, and despite its receiving more funding from the OAS since 1995, the Court still functioned by the end of the decade with only four persons paid by the OAS and receives a large portion of its total budget from other sources[131]. The OAS did not see fit to fund the Court to a proper level and thus continued to place administrative impediments in the way of full respect for the rule of law and of human rights in Western Hemisphere.

5. Conclusion

The preceding study has considered the evolution of the Inter-American Court of Human Rights and sought to identify the factors which have inhibited its ability, within the domain of human rights, to ensure even limited respect for the rule of law in the Americas. A comparison between the Inter-American and the European human rights systems, during the 1980-1998 period, shows that international courts, despite their similar constitutive instruments, can vary much in their effectiveness. Thus, when attempting to understand the limitations to full respect for the rule of law on the international level one must go beyond the legal texts and consider how obligations are implemented. The functioning of the Inter-American Court demonstrates that States can establish adjudicative organs yet hobble them by the introduction of various impediments.

The Inter-American Commission on Human Rights, its establishment and evolution have limited the number of cases that reached the Court. Through this "organizational" obstacle, the Court remained under-employed for more than a decade. When the obstacle was finally removed, in the early 1990s, other impediments emerged in the form of a lack of staffing and budgetary support from the Organization of American States. The consequence of these "admin-

---

[128] Secretary General of the Organization of American States, *Annual Report 1996-1997*, p. 36.

[129] *Ibid.*, p. 36.

[130] Inter-American Court of Human Rights, *Press Release: Activities of the Inter-American Court of Human Rights*, June 1997, CDH-CP5/97 English.

[131] Between 1995 and 1997 the Courts overall budget has increased from US$ 585.700 to US$1.120.000. I/A Press Release, *op. cit.* n. 120, pp. 19-32.

istrative" obstructions is that, as the docket increases its case-load, the Court may not be able to handle the cases in a manner that does not affect the "level of the judgments" or its "prestige"[132]. Such impediments and the manner in which they have affected the evolution of the Inter-American Court demonstrate that the effectiveness of the rule of law can be limited even when States do agree to international adjudication. The comparison of the evolution of the Inter-American Court during the period 1980-1998 with that of the European Court shows that factors other than the voluntary nature of the international adjudication, or non-cooperation with such organs, can prevent full respect for the rule of law.

[132] *Op. cit.*, n. 125.

Chapter 5
THE INTERNATIONAL CRIMINAL TRIBUNAL FOR THE FORMER YUGOSLAVIA

1. Introduction

The previous chapters have sought to demonstrate how the basic structure of the international system, premised on voluntary adjudication, along with political manoeuvres, can limit the effectiveness of adjudication and, by extension, the rule of law on the international level. It is now time to consider situations where the effectiveness of international adjudication has been hampered, not by States but by the guardians of international law. The following chapter considers the role of the judge, the judicial decision-making process, and the way in which these elements can affect the rule of law on the international level.

Consideration is given in this chapter to the rights of the accused indicted by the International Criminal Tribunal for the former Yugoslavia. It will be shown that there exists, at the heart of burgeoning international criminal law, a structural paradox whereby the right to a fair trial has been supplanted by the "higher calling" of ensuring the establishment of a *prima facie* "effective" international criminal law system aimed at placing individuals behind bars. The fact that this paradox existed at Nuremberg and at Tokyo demonstrates that if judges do not respect the rule of law, proceedings will be nothing more than show trials. The various examples presented of the failings of the Yugoslav Tribunal to ensure full respect for the rule of law seem to indicate that this Tribunal is heading down the same path. Individuals mistakenly detained for months, kidnapped, or wrongly accused, appear to give credence to the view that the Tribunal has sought to prosecute individuals at the expense of their rights. The chapter that follows makes it clear that as guardians of an international rule of law, judges have a responsibility not to limit its effectiveness.

2. Evolution of International Criminal Law

Over the last century, there has been growing momentum towards States granting international personality to individuals. One fundamental tenet in the implementation of this has been – beyond the evolution of human rights – the notion that individuals can be held internationally responsible for committing certain crimes. As was noted at the Nuremberg Tribunal:

> Crimes against international law are committed by men, not by abstract entities, and only by punishing individuals who commit such crimes can the provisions of international law be enforced[1].

If courts are to try individuals at the international level, it is axiomatic that they should ensure that the proceedings are conducted so that the rule of law is respected in its integrity. Yet there exists, at the heart of the burgeoning international criminal law, a structural paradox which pits the wishes of the international judge to establish an effective criminal law system against the rights of those who find themselves in the dock, accused of international crimes.

This structural paradox manifests itself in the fact that international criminal law is, for all intents and purposes, a new field. While there have been, for at least half a century, various offenses which constitute the essence of international criminal law, those offenses have not been – at least until recently – tried internationally. Thus, while international criminal law is relatively clear on what constitutes an international crime for which an individual may be held responsible, the actual limits of those provisions and the means and modalities for finding a person guilty of such crimes have, for a long time, been the basis of little more than academic conjecture.

It is at the level of implementation – the right to a fair trial – that international criminal law is most vulnerable. This is so because of the lack of precedent from which international judges can base their decisions. With this lack of case-law comes a greater reliance on international judges to determine the parameters of the law to be applied. Further, the case-law developed by these judges will, in turn, become the basis of future precedent. The daily blank slate which is offered to the international judges requires that the right to a fair trial be protected *de rigore juris*.

The following section will consider the evolution of international criminal law and demonstrate to what extent the right to a fair trial has been supplanted. Tracing the development of international criminal law through the 20th century, it will become evident that expediency in establishing a criminal law system has, time and again, take precedent over the right to a fair trial. Few would argue with the assessment of B.V.A. Röling, who sat in judgment during the Tokyo Trials, to the effect that those proceedings, along with the Nuremberg Trials, "had sinister origins; they were misused for political purposes; and [...] they were somewhat unfair"[2]. Röling sought to justify the flaws of these military trials as establishing

[1] The Trial of Major War Criminals: Proceedings of the International Military Tribunal Sitting at Nuremberg Germany, Part 22, 1950, p. 447, referred to in the *Decision on Defence Motion for Interlocutory Appeal on Jurisdiction*, IT-94-1-T (*Tadic* case), 2 October 1995, para. 128.

[2] B.V.A. Röling and Antonio Cassese, *The Tokyo Trial and Beyond: Reflections of a Peacemonger*, 1993, p. 89.

a precedent upon which the international community could travel in attempting to establish an international system based on the rule of law. Yet, by the time the International Criminal Tribunal for the former Yugoslavia (ICTY) was established, such a rationale, it will be argued, could no longer be upheld.

By the 1990s, the general principles of law governing individuals accused of international crimes were well defined, as were the various international treaty rules. The ability to ride roughshod over the right to a fair trial at Nuremberg and Tokyo was, in large part, due to an international community that had not, as yet, agreed upon international standards. Between the period at which these trials came to an end and the time which, in 1993, the ICTY was established, various international instruments had been forged which formulated specific rights granted to an accused in criminal proceedings. Taking as a basis the 1948 Universal Declaration of Human Rights[3], the rules governing the right of the accused have been incorporated into various international instruments, including the 1949 Geneva Conventions (and Additional Protocols of 1977), the 1967 International Covenant on Civil and Political Rights, the 1984 Convention against Torture and Other Cruel, Inhuman and Degrading Treatment or Punishment, as well as regional arrangements such as the 1950 European Convention for the Protection of Human Rights and Fundamental Freedoms, the 1969 American Convention on Human Rights, and the 1981 African Charter on Human and Peoples' Rights.

As will become apparent from the various cases that will be considered shortly, the Yugoslav Tribunal has, on occasion, given less weight to these international rules related to the right to a fair trial, giving priority instead to fulfilling its mandate of "prosecution of persons responsible for serious violations of inter-

[3] Regarding the customary nature of the Universal Declaration, see the conclusion drawn by Hurst Hannum, Report of the International Law Association's Committee on the Enforcement of Human Rights Law (Final Report on the Status of the Universal Declaration of Human Rights in National and International Law), International Law Association Report of the Sixty-Sixth Conference, 1994, pp. 22-23.

The provisions related to the rights of the accused incorporated in the Universal Declaration are the following:

Article 9
No one shall be subjected to arbitrary arrest, detention or exile.

Article 10
Everyone is entitled in full equality to a fair and public hearing by an independent and impartial tribunal, in the determination of his rights and obligations and of any criminal charge against him.

Article 11
1. Everyone charged with a penal offence has the right to be presumed innocent until proved guilty according to law in a public trial at which he has had all the guarantees necessary for his defence.
2. No one shall be held guilty of any penal offence on account of any act or omission which did not constitute a penal offence, under national or international law, at the time when it was committed. Nor shall a heavier penalty be imposed than the one that was applicable at the time the penal offence was committed.

national humanitarian law committed in the territory of the former Yugoslavia"[4]. While the judges of the ICTY have always maintained their allegiance to the notion of the right to a fair trial and have, in general, sought the respect of that right, the rule of law demands more. It demands that respect for the right to a fair trial, especially in what the noted legal philosopher Ronald Dworkin has called the "hard cases", be absolute[5]. That policy considerations have been at the forefront of the chambers of the ICTY has meant that, in certain situations, the rights of the accused have been disregarded so as to ensure an "effective" criminal justice system in the sense of a mechanism aimed at finding persons guilty of international crimes.

2.1. **International Military Tribunals**

While the Nuremberg and Tokyo Trials are at the forefront of our collective memories when considering the earliest manifestations of international criminal courts, the idea of resorting to such adjudicative organs precedes those proceedings by nearly fifty years. "As early as the Hague Peace Conference of 1899 the concept of the establishment of a criminal court and its place in the international legal order were discussed"[6]. While these discussions did not bear fruit, as no follow-up debate took place at the 1907 Hague Peace Conference, the idea did re-surface at the end of the World War I. The first inclusion, in an international instrument, of provisions relating to the establishment of an international court with criminal jurisdiction over individuals is found in Article 227 of the Treaty of Versailles, whereby:

> The Allied and Associate Powers publicly arraigned Kaiser Wilheim II of Hohenzollern, formerly German Emperor, of a supreme offence against international morality and sanctity of treaties.
>
> A special tribunal will be constituted to try the accused, thereby assuring him the guarantees essential to the right of defence. It will be composed of five judges, one appointed by each of the following Powers: namely, the United States of America, Great Britain, France, Italy, and Japan.
>
> In its decisions the tribunal will be guided by the highest motives of international policy, with a view to indicating the solemn obligations of international undertakings and the validity of international morality. It will be its duty to fix the punishment which it considers should be imposed.

[4] The quotation comes from the full length title of the Yugoslav Tribunal: "International Tribunal for the Prosecution of Persons Responsible for Serious Violations of International Humanitarian Law Committed in the Territory of the Former Yugoslavia". U.N. Doc. S/RES/808, 22 February 1993.

[5] See, generally, Ronald Dworkin, *Taking Rights Seriously*, 1978.

[6] T.L.H. McCormack and G.J. Simpson, "A New International Criminal Regime?", *Netherlands International Law Review*, Vol. 42, 1995, p. 181.

> The Allied and Associated Powers will address a request to the Government of the Netherlands for the surrender to them the ex-Emperor in order that he may be put on trial[7].

Further, under Articles 228 and 229, the Allied and Associate Powers reserved the right to try individuals before military tribunals for violations of the laws and customs of war. As a result of these provisions, a mere twelve individuals were brought before a court after the World War I. The former German Emperor found refuge with the Government of the Netherlands, which considered the charge to be in the nature of a "political offence" and was unwilling to surrender him to the victorious powers[8]. Of the twelve members of the *Bundeswehr* who stood accused of war crimes, in what has since come to be known as the "Leipzig Trials", six were convicted, but only token sentences were meted out[9]. While these proceedings made a mockery of the notion of justice, the Treaty of Lausanne signed between the Allied and Associated Powers and Turkey on 24 July 1923 did not even contain provisions for the trial of the individuals responsible for the 1915 genocide of the Armenians[10]. This amnesty of Turkish military and political leaders was granted in 1923, despite Articles 226-230 of the Treaty of Sèvres (signed in 1920, but never ratified) which had called on the Turks to surrender the accused for war crimes proceedings as part of the treaty attempting to impose settlement of World War I by the Allied powers on Turkey[11].

With the establishment of the League of Nations, in the wake of the First World War, came the creation of the Permanent Court of International Justice as

[7] Article 227, Peace Treaty signed at Versailles on 28 June 1919. See Draft Code of Offences against the Peace and Security Of Mankind: Compendium of Relevant International Instruments, U.N. Doc. A/CN.4/368, 13 April 1983, p. 11.

[8] Quincy Wright, "The Legality of the Kaiser", *American Political Sience Review*, Vol. 8, 1919, p. 121.

[9] For the definitive study of the Leipzig Trials, see Claude Mullins, *The Leipzig Trials: An Account of the War Criminals Trials and a Study of German Mentality*, 1921. Note also Cherif Bassiouni's statement that the "maximum sentence imposed was three years, erasing any hope that this formal exercise could serve as a future deterrent to others". Cherif Bassiouni, "Former Yugoslavia: Investigating Violations of International Humanitarian Law and Establishing an International Criminal Tribunal", *Security Dialogue*, Vol. 25, 1994, p. 419, n. 11.

[10] Treaty of Peace between the Allied Powers and Turkey, 24 July 1923, League of Nations Treaty, Series, Vol. 28, p.11, reprinted in *American Journal of International Law* (Supplement), Vol.18, 1924, pp.1-26. This ghost would later come to haunt European Powers as Adolf Hitler, less than 20 years hence, remarked when calling for the extermination of the Polish-speaking race: "After all," he stated "who remembers today the extermination of the Armenians?". Mercedeh Momeni, "Balancing the Procedural Rights of the Accused Against a Mandate to Protect Victims and Witnesses: An Examination of the Anonymity Rules of the International Criminal Tribunal for the former Yugoslavia", *Howard Law Journal*, Vol. 41, 1997, p. 155, n. 1.

[11] Treaty of Peace between the Allied Powers and Turkey of 10 August 1920, *American Journal of International Law* (Supplement), Vol. 15, 1921, pp. 179-196.

well as a movement considering the establishment of an international criminal court under the banner of the League. To that end, the Advisory Committee of Jurists appointed to prepare the Statute of the Permanent Court of International Justice adopted a resolution calling on the League's Council and Assembly to create a "High Court of International Justice [...] competent to try crimes constituting a breach of international public order or against the universal law of nations"[12]. However, this Resolution was rejected by the League bodies, which considered that such proceedings should be left to municipal law and that it was "premature" as "there is not yet any international penal law recognized by all nations"[13].

As the movement towards an international criminal tribunal stalled within the League of Nations, another organization, the Inter-Parliamentary Union, in cooperation with the International Association of Penal Law and the International Law Association, delivered the first draft statute for an international criminal court to the 1926 Conference of the International Law Association[14]. As these organizations had no intergovernmental status, the draft statute was an academic exercise rather than a concrete move to establish an international criminal court. Yet such moves prompted the League of Nations to retake the lead by adopting the Convention for the Creation of an International Criminal Court at the International Conference on the Repression of Terrorism in 1937. However, as this treaty-based court was established in the midst of a terrorist scare which had seen the King of Yugoslavia and the French Foreign Minister assassinated, when these acts subsided, so to did interest in such a court[15]. As this International Criminal Court was to be "seized as soon as a High Contracting Party has committed an accused person to it for trial"[16], and the treaty saw only one ratification[17], the Convention and its companion, the Convention for the Prevention and Punishment of Terrorism were shelved.

It was not until 1942, with the occupation of much of Europe by the Axis powers, that the Allied Governments, by the so-called London Declaration, made

---

[12] See "Proces-verbaux of the Proceedings of the Advisory Committee of Jurists", 1920, as found in Historical Survey of the Question of International Criminal Jurisdiction, U.N. Doc. A/CN.4/7/Rev. 1, pp. 49-50.

[13] Herman von Hebel, "An International Tribunal for the Former Yugoslavia; An Act of Powerlessness or a New Challenge for the International Community?", *Netherlands Quarterly of Human Rights*, Vol. 11, 1993, p. 439.

[14] International Law Association, "Proposal for an International Criminal Court, Report of the Thirty-Fourth Conference of the International Law Association, Vienna, 11 August 1926", as reprinted in Benjamin Ferencz, "The Draft Code of Offences Against the Peace and Security of Mankind", *American Journal of International Law*, Vol. 75, 1981, pp. 674-682.

[15] See von Hebel, *op. cit.* n. 13, p. 439.

[16] See Article 25(1) of the Convention for the Creation of an International Criminal Court, Geneva, 16 November 1937, see Compendium, *op. cit.* n. 7, p. 24.

[17] Bassiouni, *op. cit.* n. 9, p. 410. The lone State to ratify the Convention for the Creation of an International Criminal Court was India.

it known that "among their principal war aims [was] the punishment, through the channel of organized justice, of those guilty of or responsible for these crimes [undertaken in the occupied countries], whether they have ordered them, perpetrated them or participated in them"[18]. At the end of World War II in Europe, the four major victorious powers signed the London Agreement calling for the "prosecution and punishment of the major war criminals of the European Axis"[19]. Annexed to this Agreement was a statute of a tribunal entitled the Charter of the International Military Tribunal (IMT). That Charter established an *ad hoc* tribunal which has come to be known as the Nuremberg Tribunal. This Tribunal conducted the trials of twenty-two high-ranking political and military officials, mostly members of the National Socialist Party, finding nineteen guilty and sentencing twelve to death by hanging[20]. Further, over a thousand lesser accused war criminals were tried "in one of the countries in which they had committed war crimes or in Germany by one of the four Occupying Powers [...] based on the so called "Law No. 10" decrees, issued by the Allied Control Council, which was largely based on the Charter of the London Agreement"[21].

In the other major theatre of war, as a result of the capitulation of Japan ending World War II in Asia, United States General Douglas MacArthur, acting as Supreme Allied Commander, established, in 1946, the *ad hoc* International Military Tribunal for the Far East "in order to implement the Terms of Surrender which requires the meting out of stern justice to war criminals"[22]. As a result of the proceedings of the Tokyo Tribunal, which found twenty-eight high-ranking officials in the dock, all were found guilty and seven were hanged[23]. While much criticism has been directed at the proceedings at Nuremberg, more was heard of the Tokyo Tribunal, which was established by a unilateral act of United States

---

[18] See para. 3 of the Resolution by Allied Governments Condemning German Terror and Demanding Retribution, London, 13 January 1942, see Compendium, *op. cit.* n. 7, p. 28.

[19] Agreement by the Government of the United Kingdom of Great Britain and Northern Ireland, the Government of the United States of American, the Provisional Government of the French Republic and the Government of the Union of Soviet Socialist Republics for the Prosecution and Punishment of the Major War Criminals of the European Axis, see Compendium, *op. cit.* n. 7, pp. 30-31. See also Moscow Declaration on German Atrocities, 30 October 1943, *ibid.*, p. 29.

[20] Virginia Morris and Michael Scharf, *An Insider's Guide to The International Criminal Tribunal for the former Yugoslavia*, Vol.1, 1994, pp. 3 (n. 13) and 8.

[21] See Von Hebel, *op. cit.* n. 13, p. 440.

[22] See General Order No. 1, General Headquarters, Supreme Commander for the Allied Powers at Tokyo, 19 January 1946, amended 26 April 1946, Compendium, *op. cit.* n. 7, p. 41.

On the Tokyo Tribunal, see generally: Andrew Brackman, *The Other Nuremberg: The Untold Story of the Tokyo War Crimes Trials*, 1987; C. Hoyosa *et al.* (eds.), *The Tokyo War Crimes Trial: An International Symposium*, 1986; Richard Minear, *Victor's Justice: The Tokyo War Crimes Trials*, 1971; Röling and Rüter (eds.), *The International Military Tribunal for the Far East*, 1997; and Röling and Cassese, *op. cit.* n. 2.

[23] Leslie Mansfield, "Crimes against Humanity: Reflections on the Fiftieth Anniversary of Nuremberg and a Forgotten Legacy", *Nordic Journal of International Law*, Vol. 64, 1995, p. 313.

General MacArthur "without prior approval of the other allied nations"[24]. The criticism leveled at both IMTs stems from the fact that they failed, in large part, to pay heed to the rule of law. The two prevalent items which academics have taken issue with were the composition of the Tribunals and their jurisdiction *ratione materiae,* which were considered as violating the rule of *nullum crimen sine lege*. For example, both IMTs were composed of a representative of each of the four victorious powers, which brought into question the independence and impartiality of those judges who were called upon to apply laws established by the very same victorious powers.

Yet the persistent and most vocal opposition to the legality of these proceedings were those based on the subject-matter jurisdiction of the Tribunal, which was defined as follows:

> *Crimes against the peace:* namely, planning preparation, initiation or waging of a war of aggression, *or* a war in violation *of international* treaties, agreements *or* assurances, or participation in a common plan or conspiracy for accomplishment of any of the foregoing;
>
> *War crimes:* namely, violations of the laws and customs of war. Such violations shall include, but not be limited to murder, ill treatment or deportation of slave labour or for any other purpose of civilian population of or in occupied territory, murder or ill-treatment of prisoners of war or persons on the seas, killing of hostages, plunder of public or private property, wanton destruction of cities, towns or villages, or devastation not justified by military necessity;
>
> *Crimes against humanity:* namely, murder, extermination, enslavement, deportation, and other inhumane acts committed against any civilian population, before or during the war, or persecutions on political, racial or religious grounds in execution of or in connection with any crime within the jurisdiction of the Tribunal, whether or not in violation of domestic law of the country where perpetrated[25].

Most observers have contended that while the provisions regarding war crimes partly reflected existing conventional and customary rules, those on crimes against the peace and against humanity were laws *ex post facto*[26]. The shadow

---

[24] See von Hebel, *op. cit.* n. 13, p. 440. Note however, that the Allies had decided at the Potsdam Conference, during July and August 1945, to utilize the Nuremberg precedent with respect to any agreement of surrender which would be imposed upon Japan. Further, Morris and Scharf note that the judgment rendered at Tokyo was considered by the French Judge, in his dissenting opinion, as violating "so many principles of justice [...] that the Court's judgment certainly would be nullified on legal grounds in most civilized countries". *Op. cit.* n. 20, p. 9 n. 42.

[25] Article 6, Charter of the International Military Tribunal, see Compendium, *op. cit.* n. 7, p. 33. Note that while the subject-matter of the jurisdiction remained the same at Tokyo, the content of these provisions was different. See Article 5, the Charter of the International Military Tribunal for the Far East, see Compendium, *op. cit.* n. 7, p. 47.

[26] For discussion regarding the legal validity of the Nuremberg and Tokyo Trials, see generally: Richard Conot, *Justice at Nuremberg*, 1983; Robert K. Woetzel, *The Nuremberg Trials in International Law*, 1962; Minear, *op. cit.* n. 22; and Röling and Cassese, *op. cit.* n. 2.

which was cast over Nuremberg and Tokyo is a long one and persists to this day[27]; yet, until the early 1990s, these were the only criminal trials to have been given effect on the international plane.

2.2. United Nations Era

When the proceedings at Nuremberg ended, the newly established United Nations Organization sought to codify as international law the provision founding the jurisdiction *ratione materiae* of this IMT. The General Assembly, in its Resolution 95(1), affirmed "the principles of international law recognized by the Charter of the Nuremberg Tribunal and the judgment of the Tribunal"[28]. In the same Resolution, the General Assembly instructed the Committee on the Progressive Development of International Law and its Codification, which it had created the same day, to formulate "in the context of a general codification of offences against the peace and security of mankind, or of an International Criminal Code, the principles recognized in the Charter of the Nuremberg Tribunal and the judgement of the Tribunal"[29]. By 1947, with the Committee unable to agree on substantive issues[30], the General Assembly resolved to have the Committee's heir – the International Law Commission (ILC) – formulate those Nuremberg principles and prepare a draft code of offences against the peace and security of mankind.

Moving ever forward, in 1948, the General Assembly adopted the Convention on the Prevention and Punishment of the Crime of Genocide, which included a provision calling for the jurisdiction over persons charged with genocide to be vested, not only for a municipal court, but also for "such international penal tribunal as may have jurisdiction"[31]. In effect, what this Convention did, as did subsequent treaties[32], was to bank on the establishment of an international criminal tribunal which might someday assert its competence over the subject-matter of the Convention. However, the latter did not seek to establish within its framework an international criminal court with limited jurisdiction, because there

---

[27] Consider, for instance, the preoccupation of the UN Secretary-General over the issue of *nullum crimen sine lege*. Report of the Secretary-General Pursuant to Paragraph 2 of Security Council Resolution 808 (1993), U.N. Doc. 5/25704, para. 34, International Criminal Tribunal for the former Yugoslavia, *Basic Documents: 1995*, p. 175. For the full text of the ICTY Statute, see Appendix 6.

[28] Affirmation of the Principles of International Law recognized by the Charter of the Nuremberg Tribunal, 11 December 1946, U.N. Doc. A/1195, see Compendium, *op. cit.* n. 7, p. 71.

[29] *Ibid.*

[30] See von Hebel, *op. cit.* n. 13, p. 441.

[31] Article 6, The Convention on the Pevention and Punishment of the Crime of Genocide, and Text of 9 December 1948.

[32] See, for example, the Geneva Conventions of 12 August 1949, with respect to its grave breaches provisions, or Article 5 of the 1972 Convention on the Suppression and Punishment of the Crime of Apartheid, 9 December 1948.

seemed to be a movement toward establishing a general international criminal court. This was made abundantly clear to those who adopted the Genocide Convention, as on the same day, the General Assembly requested the International Law Commission to undertake a "study of the desirability and the feasibility of establishing an international criminal court"[33].

In 1950, by Resolution 489, the General Assembly created a special committee composed of the representatives of 17 States to study and prepare a draft statute for an international criminal court[34]. This Special Committee on International Criminal Jurisdiction submitted its first Draft Statute to the UN General Assembly in 1951[35]. However, the General Assembly, considering that text to be "insufficient", created a second special committee, which presented an amended version of the 1951 draft two years later[36]. The 1953 Draft Statute provided for jurisdiction *ratione personae*, as called for the contemplated Code of Offences against the Peace and Security of Mankind[37]. Jurisdiction over an individual was to be established by treaty or by unilateral declarations of States[38]. The Court was to have five judges who would confirm the indictment prepared by a prosecuting attorney from the State against which the transgression took place, with no appeals being envisioned. Despite progress, the first Statute for an international criminal court drafted within the United Nations system raised problems over what exactly would be the jurisdiction *ratione personae* of such an international criminal court.

As Morris and Scharf write, "the 1953 Draft Statute was shelved due to the absence of an internationally accepted definition of the crime of aggression [...]"[39]. The definition of aggression was also at the heart of the delay which stalled the Draft Code of Offences against the Peace and Security of Mankind[40]. The drafting of such a code had been entrusted to the International Law Commission by General Assembly Resolution 177 which, as will be recalled, also requested the elaboration of the Nuremberg Principles[41]. While the ILC was relatively quick to

---

33 U.N. Doc. A/III/260B, 9 December 1948.

34 See U.N. Doc. A/V/489, 12 December 1950.

35 Draft Statute for an International Criminal Court, U.N. Doc. A/AC.48/4, Annex 1, 7 December 1951.

36 Brigitte Stern, "La Cour criminelle internationale dans le projet de la Commission du droit international", N. Al-Nauimi and R. Meese (eds.), *International Legal Issues Arising under the United Nations Decade of International Law*, 1995, p. 744. For the establishment of the second Special Committee on International Criminal Jurisdiction, see U.N. Doc. A/VII/678, 5 December 1952.

37 Morris and Scharf, *op. cit.* n. 20, p. 12.

38 Article 27, Revised Draft Statute for an International Criminal Court (annexed to the Report of the Committee of International Criminal Jurisdiction), U.N. Doc. A/IX/2645, 10 December 1953.

39 Morris and Scharf, *op. cit.* n. 20, p. 13.

40 See Cherif Bassiouni, *Commentaries on the International Law Commission's 1991 Draft Code of Crimes Against the Peace and Security of Mankind*, 1993, p. 12.

41 U.N. Doc. A/II/177, 21 November 1947. The Nuremberg Principles retain *verbatim* the jurisdiction *ratione materiae* of the Nuremberg Tribunal, *i.e.*: crimes against the peace, against humanity,

present the Nuremberg Principles to the General Assembly, it was not until 1954, that the Assembly, conscious of the problems which the Commissions experienced over the drafting of the Code, established a Special Committee to prepare a draft definition of aggression[42]. However, the Special Committee's preparation of this definition, which resulted in the adoption by consensus of a resolution by the General Assembly, was twenty years in the making[43]. While the International Law Commission, at the request of the UN General Assembly, once again took up its study of the Draft Code of Offences against the Peace and Security of Mankind in 1981, no progress was made while the Cold War lasted[44].

2.2.1. *Post-Cold War Era and the March to Rome*

The momentum, which ultimately culminated in the signing of the Rome Statute of the International Court[45] on 17 July 1998, followed two trajectories[46]. Free from the obfuscation of Russia and the United States and their client States, which defined the Cold War era, concrete steps were taken towards establishing an international criminal court. The UN Security Council constituted two *ad hoc* tribunals related to violations of humanitarian law, in 1993 in the former Yugoslavia and a year later in Rwanda[47]. This, in turn, gave renewed impetus to the ILC to work toward drafting a statute for an international criminal court.

---

and war crimes. See Principles of International Law Recognized in the Charter of the Nuremberg Tribunal and in the Judgement of the Tribunal, see Compendium, *op. cit.* n. 7, pp. 74-75.

[42] See von Hebel, *op. cit.* n. 13, p. 441.

[43] U.N. Doc. A/29/3314, 21 November 1974.

[44] U.N. Doc. A/36/106, 10 December 1981. The ILC presented the General Assembly with a Draft Code of Crimes Against the Peace and Security of Mankind in 1991. This Code was forwarded to UN member States for comment. Based on these comments, a revised 1996 Draft Code of Crimes Against the Peace and Security of Mankind was formulated, but this text received the death knell with the signing of the Rome Statute of the International Criminal Court, U.N. Doc. A/Conf.183/9, 17 July 1998.

[45] U.N. Doc. A/Conf.183/9, 17 July 1998.

[46] David Krieger, "A Permanent International Criminal Court and the United Nations System", N. AI-Nauimi and R. Meese (eds.), *International Legal Issues Arising under the United Nations Decade of International Law*, 1995, p. 761.

[47] The International Criminal Tribunal for Rwanda (ICTR) was established on 8 November 1994 by the UN Security Council (U.N. Doc. S/RES/995). The ICTR will not be considered in this work, as information pertaining to its activities within the domain of the rights of the accused is scant to non-existent. However, as both the ICTR Statute and Rules are based on the Statute of ICTY, and the ICTR has demonstrated its willingness to examine and utilize the Decisions of the ICTY as precedents, it would appear that any insights drawn from this study might well be analogous to the situation of individuals accused before the Arusha Tribunal. See Decision on the Preliminary Motion submitted by the Prosecutor on Protective Measures for Witnesses, where the ICTR Trial Chamber (Judges Aspergen, Ostrovsky (presiding) and Pillary), in the *Rutaganda* case, noted in its preamble: "TAKING INTO CONSIDERATION the jurisprudence of the International Criminal Tribunal for the former Yugoslavia, notably its decisions of 10 August 1995 and 14 November 1995", ICTR-96-3-T, 26 September 1996, p. 2.

With the end of the Cold War, the United Nations placed the work of the ILC on two tracks, one concerned with the Draft Code, the other urging the ILC "to address the question of establishing an international criminal court"[48]. With respect to the first, the Commission, for the first time since 1954, presented the General Assembly with a Draft Code of Crimes Against the Peace and Security of Mankind in 1991. Based on comments made by UN member States, a revised 1996 Draft Code of Crimes against the Peace and Security of Mankind was formulated. When it became apparent that momentum was building towards the creation of an international criminal court, the Draft Code became moot as it was evident that the subject-matter jurisdiction of an international criminal court would ultimately be determined by States at a plenipotentiary meeting meant to bring such a court into being[49].

With the mandate to address the issue of establishing an international criminal court, the ILC established a Working Group with the aim of drafting a statute for such a court. The General Assembly subsequently requested the Commission to start drafting a statute based on the Working Group's recommendations[50]. The ILC completed the Draft Statute in 1994 and submitted it to the General Assembly with the recommendation that an international conference be convened, at which time the Statute could be included in a universal treaty[51]. To that end, the General Assembly, basing itself on the further recommendation of a 1995 *ad hoc* Committee, created the Preparatory Committee on the Establishment of an International Criminal Court, entrusted with "preparing a widely acceptable consolidated text of a convention for an international criminal court as a next step towards consideration by a conference of plenipotentiaries"[52]. This Committee, which held six sessions from between 1996 to 1998, drafted the working document used at the Rome Conference held between 15 June to 17 July 1998[53].

2.2.2. *Establishment of the International Criminal Tribunal for the Former Yugoslavia*

Parallel to the discussions regarding the drafting of a statute for a permanent international criminal court, many deliberations took place in the wake of the Cold War regarding the establishment of *ad hoc* international criminal tribunals.

---

[48] U.N. Doc. A/44/39, 4 December 1989.

[49] For the predicted demise of the Draft Code, see Jean Allain and John R.W.D. Jones, "A Patchwork of Norms: A Commentary on the 1996 Draft Code of Crimes against the Peace and Security of Mankind", *European Journal of International Law*, Vol. 8, 1997, pp. 100-117.

[50] See U.N. Doc. A/47/33, 25 November 1992.

[51] U.N. Doc. A/49/10, 4 December 1994.

[52] U.N. Doc. A/50/46, 11 December 1995.

[53] For information regarding the International Criminal Court, see the official United Nations website at: *www.un.org/law/icc/*; for further information, consider the website of the non-governmental Coalition for an International Criminal Court at: *www.igc.org/icc/*.

The cooperation within the international community, as reflected in the UN Security Council's response to the Iraqi invasion of Kuwait, allowed leaders to express themselves openly about the rekindling of the Nuremberg precedent. In the late summer of 1990, both British Prime Minister Margaret Thatcher and United States President George Bush expressed such views[54]. The Council of Ministers of the European Community asked UN Secretary-General Perez de Cuellar to "examine the question of the personal responsibility of the Iraqi leaders in the tragedy that is unfolding [i.e.: the use of chemical weapons against Iraqi Kurds] in particular on the basis of the Genocide Convention"[55]. However, this attempt proved a false start as no further action was taken by the United Nations. The issue was however revived after Croatia and Slovenia had declared their independence from the Socialist Federal Republic of Yugoslavia on 25 June 1991.

As the war in the former Yugoslavia moved from Slovenia and Croatia to focus around a newly independent Bosnia-Herzegovia in the summer of 1992, the UN Security Council, amidst persistent evidence of atrocities, made clear to the parties, through its Resolution 764, that those violating international humanitarian law would be held individually responsible[56]. This was followed, in August 1992, by Resolution 771 whereby "the Council strongly condemned violations of international humanitarian law"[57] and used, for the first time with respect to this conflict, its powers under Chapter VII of the Charter, calling on the parties to comply or face the possibility of the "Council taking further measures"[58]. With the utter disregard for the rules of international humanitarian law shown by the parties, the Security Council undertook to prescribe such further measures.

By Resolution 780, the Security Council called for the establishment of what has come to be known as the Kalshoven Commission. This impartial Commission of experts[59] was established to gather information related to violations of international humanitarian law generally and, more specifically, violations of the grave breaches provisions of the 1949 Geneva Conventions. In its first Interim Report to the Security Council, in early 1993, the Commission, beyond concluding that mass violations of humanitarian law were occurring in the former Yugo-

[54] International Criminal Tribunal for the former Yugoslavia, *The Path to the Hague: Selected Documents on the Origins of the ICTY*, 1996, p. 9.

[55] See Letter from Mr. Poos, President-in-Office of the Council of Ministers of the European Communities, to the Secretary-General of the United Nations, *ibid.*, p. 15.

[56] U.N. Doc. 5/47/764, 13 July 1992.

[57] Christopher Greenwood, "The International Tribunal for former Yugoslavia", *International Affairs*, Vol. 69, 1993, p. 642.

[58] Juan José Quintana, "Les violations du droit international humanitaire et leur répression: Le Tribunal pénal international pour l'ex-Yougoslavie", *Revue internationale de la Croix-Rouge* No. 807, 1994, p. 249.

[59] See Alain Pellet, "Le Tribunal criminel international pour l'ex-Yougoslavie: Poudre aux yeux ou avencée décisive?", *Revue générale de droit international public*, Vol. 98, 1994, p.16.

slavia, proposed the establishment of an *ad hoc* international tribunal that it said would be "consistent with the direction of its work"[60]. This endorsement of the creation of an *ad hoc* international criminal tribunal made formally to the Security Council added "further weight to similar recommendations" proffered by individuals with official ties to the Balkan conflict[61].

Despite these recommendations, it was not until 16 December 1992, with the public pronouncement by the then United States Secretary of State, Lawrence Eagleburger, calling for the establishment of Nuremberg-type tribunal, that true diplomatic activity commenced towards the drafting of a statute for an *ad hoc* tribunal having jurisdiction over acts taking place in the former Yugoslavia[62]. France, whose Foreign Minister had called for the creation of an international criminal tribunal on the occasion of the adoption of Security Council Resolution 780, was first off the mark in presenting a draft statute to the Secretary-General on 10 February 1993. This draft was followed over the following days by proposals from Italy and Sweden[63].

As a consequence of the momentum which was building, the Security Council, in its Resolution 808 of 22 February 1993, decided to establish an *ad hoc* tribunal, and to that end requested:

> [...] the Secretary-General to submit for consideration by the Council at the earliest possible date, and if possible no later than 60 days after the adoption of the present resolution, a report on all aspects of this matter, including specific proposals and where appropriate options for the effective and expeditious implementation of the decisions to establishing a tribunal, taking into account suggestions put forward in this regard by Member States.

Nine States put forward their views on the content of the future statute for a Yugoslavia tribunal. These views and suggestions from "intergovernmental, non-governmental organizations and individuals" were synthesized by the Secretary-General into a report which he presented to the Security Council on 25 May 1993[64]. Annexed to the Report of the Secretary-General, pursuant to paragraph 2

---

[60] Paragraph 74, Letter dated 9 February, 1993 from the Secretary-General Addressed to the President of the Security Council, U.N. Doc. S/25274.

[61] Morris and Scharf, *op. cit.* n. 20, p. 29. These two authors cite the following recommendations: from the CSCE Rapporteurs in October 1992; the Special Rapporteurs appointed by the United Nations Human Rights Commission to investigate the human rights situation in former Yugoslavia, Mr. Tadeuz Mazowiecki, in November 1992; and the Co-Chairmen of the International Conference on the former Yugoslavia, Mr. Cyrus Vance and Sir David Owen.

[62] See ICTY, *op. cit.* n. 55, p. 11.

[63] See Morris and Scharf, *op. cit.* n. 20, pp. 477-478.

[64] Daphna Shraga and Ralph Zacklin, "The International Criminal Tribunal for the former Yugoslavia", *European Journal of International Law*, Vol. 5, 1994, p 362. The States making proposals and suggestions were: Brazil, Canada, Egypt, Mexico, Netherlands, Russia, Slovenia, Switzerland, United States of America, and Yugoslavia, *op. cit.* n. 20, pp. 477-478.

of Security Council Resolution 808 (1993), was the Secretary-General's proposal of a statute for the International Criminal Tribunal for former Yugoslavia[65]. The Report, with the annexed Statute, was approved without modification by the Security Council in Resolution 827 which established the Tribunal on the basis of chapter VII of the UN Charter[66].

The paths taken by the international community, manifest in the establishment of *ad hoc* Tribunals by the UN Security Council and the work of the UN General Assembly and the ILC, met in Rome in the summer of 1998 where the proposed Statute of an International Criminal Court was adopted by some 120 States[67].

3. The Right to a Fair Trail

The provisions regarding the right to a fair trial found within the Rome Statute will now be examined in greater detail, so as to give an indication of the *opinio juris* which exists within this domain. By highlighting these new standards, it will become apparent to what extent the provisions of the ICTY are skeletal. By comparing the standards that States believe are the minimum guarantees provided to an accused to ensure a fair trial in the Rome Statute, it becomes evident that much leeway is given to the judges of the ICTY by its Statute when setting the parameters of what are understood to be limits to the right to a fair trial. The provisions of the Rome Statute related to the rights of the accused are as follows:

> *Article 67 – Rights of the accused*
> 1. In the determination of any charge, the accused shall be entitled to a public hearing, having regard to the provisions of this Statute, to a fair hearing conducted impartially, and to the following minimum guarantees, in full equality:
>
> (a) To be informed promptly and in detail of the nature, cause and content of the charge, in a language which the accused fully understands and speaks;
> (b) To have adequate time and facilities for the preparation of the defence and to communicate freely with counsel of the accused's choosing in confidence;
> (c) To be tried without undue delay;
> (d) Subject to article 63, paragraph 2, to be present at the trial, to conduct the defence in person or through legal assistance of the accused's choosing, to be informed, if the accused does not have legal assistance, of this right and to have legal assis-

---

[65] Statute of the International Criminal Tribunal for the Former Yugoslavia, Annex to the Report of the Secretary-General Pursuant to Paragraph 2 of Security Council Resolution 808 (1993), U.N. Doc. S/48/25704.

[66] U.N. Doc. S/RES/827, 25 May 1993.

[67] "The Statute was adopted by non-recorded vote of 120 in favour, 7 against, 21 abstentions". See Rome Conference Press Release, U.N. Doc. L/2889, 20 July 1998. By the end of 1999, 91 States had signed and 5 had ratified the Rome Statute (Fiji, Italy, San Marino, Senegal, and Trinidad and Tobago).

tance assigned by the Court in any case where the interests of justice so require, and without payment if the accused lacks sufficient means to pay for it;

(e) To examine, or have examined, the witnesses against him or her and to obtain the attendance and examination of witnesses on his or her behalf under the same conditions as witnesses against him or her. The accused shall also be entitled to raise defences and to present other evidence admissible under this Statute;

(f) To have, free of any cost, the assistance of a competent interpreter and such translations as are necessary to meet the requirements of fairness, if any of the proceedings of or documents presented to the Court are not in a language which the accused fully understands and speaks;

(g) Not to be compelled to testify or to confess guilt and to remain silent, without such silence being a consideration in the determination of guilt or innocence;

(h) To make an unsworn oral or written statement in his or her defence; and

(i) Not to have imposed on him or her any reversal of the burden of proof or any onus of rebuttal.

2. In addition to any other disclosure provided for in this Statute, the Prosecutor shall, as soon as practicable, disclose to the defence evidence in the Prosecutor's possession or control which he or she believes shows or tends to show the innocence of the accused, or to mitigate the guilt of the accused, or which may affect the credibility of prosecution evidence. In case of doubt as to the application of this paragraph, the Court shall decide[68].

Beyond these specific rights subsumed under the title "Rights of the Accused", the International Criminal Court (ICC) provides for various other rights insuring a fair trial, including provisions related to the concepts of *nullum crimen, nulla poena sine lege*, and the non-retroactivity of the jurisdiction of the Court *ratione personae*[69]. Further, the international community gathered in the Italian capital saw fit to adopt various provisions to safeguard the rights of individuals in the pre-arrest to pre-indictment stages[70].

The rights as provided for in the Rome Statute have a long history. That a person accused of a criminal offence should be given specific guarantees against those who seek to prosecute that person has been a basis of every municipal criminal system which respects the rule of law. This concept goes back in the English speaking world to 1215, with the provisions of the *Magna Carta*, in which the King agreed that:

no free man shall be taken or imprisoned or deprived of his freehold or his liberties or free customs or outlawed or exiled or in any manner destroyed, nor shall we come

[68] U.N. Doc. A/Conf.183/9, 17 July 1998. The provision of Article 67(1)(d) which notes that the accused it to be present at trial "Subject to article 63, paragraph 2" refers to situations where the accused is deemed to be continuing to "disrupt the trial".

[69] Articles 22, 23, and 24 respectively.

[70] See Articles 59, 60, and 61.

> upon him or send against him, except by legal judgment of his peers and by the law of the land[71].

Since the end of World War II, there has been a cross pollinization in the evolution of the rules on the right to a fair trial between municipal jurisdictions and the international system. While general principles of municipal law have been amalgamated into various provisions of international instruments; the likes of the Universal Declaration and the International Covenant on Civil and Political Rights have prompted further elaboration of what rights an accused is due municipally. It was only in 1993, with the creation of the Yugoslavia Tribunal, that the right to a fair trial, as defined in international instruments, was given application on the international plane.

The link between international rules of fair trial and the ICTY is manifest in an observation of the latter's Appeal Chamber which noted that the "fair trial guarantees in Article 14 of the International Covenant on Civil and Political Rights have been adopted almost *verbatim* in Article 21 of the Statute"[72]. Thus, the minimum guarantees provided to individuals indicted by the ICTY are standards that had been agreed upon by the UN General Assembly in 1966. It is, therefore, left to the judges of the ICTY to fill the 30-years gap in the evolution of the law of fair trial by fleshing out to the provisions of Article 21 of its Statute.

The Statute of the ICTY does not go beyond the rights of the accused to ensure that individuals receive a fair trial[73]. The Statute of the Yugoslavia Tribunal attributes rights to individuals only after indictment. There are no statutory provisions related to the pre-indictment stage when – as will be demonstrated – the rights of individuals suspected of atrocities (but of course remaining innocent until proven guilty) are most likely to be violated. The fair trial rules for individuals who appear before the ICTY are limited to the following Article 21 provisions:

> *Right of the Accused*
>
> 1. All persons shall be equal before the International Tribunal.
>
> 2. In the determination of charges against him, the accused shall be entitled to a fair and public hearing, subject to article 22 of the Statute.
>
> 3. The accused shall be presumed innocent until proved guilty according to the provisions of the present Statute.
>
> 4. In the determination of any charge against the accused pursuant to the present Statute, the accused shall be entitled to the following minimum guarantees, in full equality:

---

[71] Pieter van Dijk, *The Right of the Accused to a Fair Trial under International Law*, 1983, p. 1.

[72] *Defence Motion for Interlocutory Appeal on Jurisdiction,* IT-94-1-T (*Tadic* case), 2 October 1995, para. 46.

[73] This despite a Trial Chambers mandate to "ensure that a trial is fair and expeditious". See Article 20(1) of the Statute of the ICTY.

(a) to be informed promptly and in detail in a language which he understands of the nature and cause of the charge against him;
(b) to have adequate time and facilities for the preparation of his defence and to communicate with counsel of his own choosing;
(c) to be tried without undue delay;
(d) to be tried in his presence, and to defend himself in person or through legal assistance of his own choosing; to be informed, if he does not have legal assistance, of this right; and to have legal assistance assigned to him, in any case where the interests of justice so require, and without payment by him in any such case if he does not have sufficient means to pay for it;
(e) to examine, or have examined, the witnesses against him and to obtain the attendance and examination of witnesses on his behalf under the same conditions as witnesses against him;
(f) to have the free assistance of an interpreter if he cannot understand or speak the language used in the International Tribunal;
(g) not to be compelled to testify against himself or to confess guilt.

The application by the ICTY of the above provisions has been, on notable occasions, accomplished in a manner which reflects more the policy needs of the Tribunal than the *rights* of the accused. The following examination of a number of sub-sections of Article 21 of the ICTY Statute will show to what extent the Tribunal, both in Chambers and in the Office of the Prosecutor, has applied such provisions in its own interest and, as a result, has violated fundamental tenets of the very law it is mandated to uphold.

3.1. Article 21(1): All Persons Shall Be Equal before the Tribunal

Where the ICTY falls short of providing ultimate respect for the rule of law is in areas where the UN Security Council failed to adopted fair trial standards beyond those specific to the accused. Ultimately, the fact that it may be uncertain whether an individual receives a fair trial before the ICTY is due to the fact that the Statute of this *ad hoc* tribunal was drafted over a 60-day period[74]. The lack of a well defined Statute means that it is left to the judges themselves, through rules of procedure and evidence, to determine to what extent an individual accused of grave violations of humanitarian law is afforded a fair trial. That the Tribunal has had to amend its Rules of Procedure and Evidence more than a dozen times since they were first adopted in 1994 means that the goal posts have been shifting constantly for those individuals who have had the misfortune of finding

[74] Ralph Zacklin, "Trials and Tribulations: Some Legal and Constitutional Problems in the Making of an International War Crimes Tribunal", N. Al-Nauimi and R. Meese (eds.), *International Legal Issues Arising under the United Nations Decade of International Law*, 1995, p. 722.

themselves in the dock early in the mandate of the ICTY[75]. While each individual is to receive equal treatment before the ICTY, it is clear that this has not been the case, as the Rules have been modified time and again, ensuring an expeditious system of justice often at the expense of the right to a fair trial.

As a result of the duration of the *Celebici* case and the lessons learnt during the proceedings, the judges decided to amend the Rules of Procedure and Evidence in a number of ways. Defense teams, having been allowed to prepare their response to the Prosecutor's case in an unfettered manner, are now finding their defense conducted under judicial supervision. The Tribunal has sought to streamline defense counsel actions through Rule 73 *ter*, which introduces the concept of a "Pre-Defence Conference" where the Trial Chamber may order the defense, *inter alia*, to prepare a statement of the contested matters of fact and law and a list of its witnesses. Based on this Conference, the Trial Chamber can require the defence to limit the number of witnesses and shorten the estimated length of its examination-in-chief[76]. The outcome of this new legislation is that, despite the fact the Tribunal "adopted a largely adversarial approach in its procedure"[77], the new Rules introduce a civil law concept of judicial management notwithstanding the maintenance of the Office of the Prosecutor which acts as an antagonist to the defence.

3.2. Article 21(2): In the determination of charges against him, the accused shall be entitled to a fair and public hearing, subject to article 22 of the Statute

Although Article 14(3) the ICCPR, Article 6(3) of the European Convention for the Protection of Human Rights and Fundamental Freedoms, and Article 67(1) of the Rome Statute determine that the rights of the accused enumerated are to be considered "minimum guarantees" afforded to the accused, the Yugoslav Tribunal has seen fit to legislate that the provisions of its Statute related to the rights of the accused are not "minimum guarantees". Despite objections from the defence in the *Tadic* case, the Trial Chamber decided that it will interpret its Statute and Rules "within [their] own context"[78], discarding the rules elaborated in various international instruments regarding these minimum guarantees. The

[75] By the end of 1999, the Rules of Procedure and Evidence had been amended 17 times. See Rules of Procedure and Evidence IT/32/REV.17, 7 December 1999. See the ICTY website under the heading Basic Legal Documents at: http://www.un.org/icty/.

[76] The Rules of Procedure and Evidence, IT/32/REV.13, 9 and 10 July 1998. International Criminal Tribunal for the former Yugoslavia, *Basic Documents 1998*, 1998, pp. 106-108. Subsequently amended on 7 December 1999.

[77] See the Tribunal's First Annual Report, 29 August 1994, (A/49/342), para. 71, *Yearbook 1994*, p 99.

[78] *Decision on the Prosecutor's Motion Requesting Protective Measures for Victims and Witnesses*, IT-95-1-T (*Tadic* case), 10 August 1995, para. 30.

Chamber justified this, using as a basis the rules of treaty interpretation as found in the Vienna Convention on the Law of Treaties while acknowledging that this can only take place by analogy as the Tribunal's governing documents are "*sui generis* legal instrument[s]"[79]. As a result, the ICTY is prepared to forgo the minimum guarantees of an accused in a balancing act with the rights of victims and witnesses.

The majority of the Trial Chamber was heavily criticized by writers for its willingness to characterize the accused's right to a "fair" trial as being subject to Article 22 of the Statute: the protection of victims and witnesses[80]. The majority, Judges McDonald and Vohrah stated that:

> the Trial Chamber agrees with the Prosecutor that the International Tribunal must interpret its provisions within its own context and determine where the balance lies between the accused's right to a fair and public trial and the protection of victims and witnesses within its unique legal framework. While the jurisprudence of other international judicial bodies is relevant when examining the meaning of concepts such as "fair trial", whether or not the proper balance is met depends on the context of the legal system in which the concepts are being applied[81].

The extent to which the ICTY was prepared to abrogate international norms of what constitutes a fair trial will be considered in due time[82]; for the moment it is worth considering the statement made by Paul Hoffman, the Chairman of the Board of Directors (USA), Amnesty International:

> Essentially, the majority of the tribunal declared that international human rights standards do not apply. The body of standards created in treaties, such as the ICCPR, stands in opposition to the tribunal's interpretation. This is a serious consequence to the past fifty years work in international human rights law. It is futile to create international human rights standards if international courts or tribunals do not implement their provisions[83].

---

[79] *Ibid.*, para. 18.

[80] Natasha Affolder, "*Tadic*, The Anonymous Witness and the Source of International Procedural Law", *Michigan Journal of International Law*, Vol. 19, 1998, pp. 445-495; Monroe Leigh, "Witness Anonymity Is Inconsistent with Due Process", *The American Journal of International Law*, Vol. 91, 1997, pp. 80-83; and Mark S. Zaid, "Trial of the Century? Assessing the Case of Dusko Tadic before the International Criminal Tribunal for the Former Yugoslavia", *ILSA Journal of International & Comparative Law*, Vol. 3, 1997, p. 619. The provisions of Article 22 – Protection of victims and witnesses – reads:

> The International Tribunal shall provide in its rules of procedure and evidence for the protection of victims and witnesses. Such protection measures shall include, but shall not be limited to, the conduct of in camera proceedings and the protection of the victim's identity.

[81] See the *Tadic* case, *op. cit.* n. 78, para. 30.

[82] *Infra.*, Section 3.6, dealing with Article 21(4)(e).

[83] Paul Hoffman, "The Dusko Tadic Trial and Due Process Issues", *Whittier Law Review*, Vol. 19, 1997, p. 316.

The willingness to disregard the work of the United Nations in the area of human rights seems curious as the ICTY itself has noted in its first Annual Report that:

> The United Nations, which over the years has accumulated an impressive corpus of international standards enjoining States and individuals to conduct themselves humanely, has now set up an institution to put those standards to the test, to transform them into living reality. A whole body of lofty, if remote, United Nations ideals will be brought to bear upon human beings [...]. Through the Tribunal, those imperatives will be turned from abstract tenets into inescapable commands[84].

In a separate opinion, Judge Sir Ninian Stephen, however, was not prepared to consider a "teleological"[85] approach which would dilute the international standards already established to guarantee a right to a fair trial at the expense of seeking to fulfill the mandate of the ICTY, which is to "prosecute" those responsible for international humanitarian law violations in the former Yugoslavia:

> That phrase "subject to Article 22" itself repays analysis. What it is in Article 21(2) that is to be subject to Article 22 can scarcely be the combined concept which precedes that phrase, the concept of "a fair and public hearing". It must rather be only one component of that concept, the public quality of the hearing and not its fairness, that is made subject to Article 22, and this for two reasons: first, because, while Article 22 specifically contemplates non-public hearings, it certainly does not contemplate unfair hearings; secondly, because Article 20(1) itself, unqualifedly and quite separately from Article 21 requires a Trial Chamber to ensure that a trial is "fair". If this understanding of the phrase "subject to Article 22" be correct and it is primarily the public quality, not the fairness, of a hearing that may have to give way to the need to protect victims and witnesses, that in turn suggests that the kind of protection being thought of in Article 22 is essentially those measures that will affect the public nature of the trial, rather than its fairness[86].

3.3. Article 21(3): The accused shall be presumed innocent until proved guilty according to the provisions of the present Statute

If the pursuit of individuals accused of violations of international humanitarian law degenerates into little more than a witch-hunt, clearly the aims of the inter-

---

[84] First Annual Report of the International Criminal Tribunal for the former Yugoslavia, 29 August 1994, U.N. Doc. A/49/342, p. 49 as cited in Michael Scharf, "*The Prosecutor v. Dusko Tadic*: An Appraisal of the First International War Crimes Trial Since Nuremberg" *Albany Law Review*, Vol. 60, 1997, p. 864.

[85] The teleological approach to judicial decision-making is meant to emphasize the sociological perspective: The object and goal of the international actor is to be emphasized over the content of conventional undertakings. See Judge Tanaka dissenting opinion in the *North Sea Continental Shelf* cases, *ICJ Reports* 1969, p. 230.

[86] Separate Opinion, Judge Sir Ninian Stephen, IT-95-1-T, 10 August 1995, p. 5027.

national community to have an international system premised on the rule of law will not be served. Yet the Office of the Prosecutor, along with those assisting in apprehending the persons wanted by the Tribunal, have acted more like sheriffs and posses than law enforcement officials acting under international rules of policing[87]. Throughout the process, from the point at which an individual is prosecuted to that of judgment before the ICTY, clear examples have emerged of an Office of the Prosecutor which is acting in an over-zealous manner.

The case of Goran Lajic is illustrative. When brought before the ICTY in June 1996, Mr. Lajic pleaded not guilty at his initial appearance before a Trial Chamber, stating that an error had been committed over his identity. Yet as late as 17 May 1996, the Prosecutor was sure "that the accused was the person mentioned in the indictment"[88]. It was only after three months in detention that Mr. Lajic's claims were recognized: He was, in fact, *not* the "Goran Lajic" wanted by the Tribunal. Mr. Lajic, having spent from 18 March till 17 June 1996 in pre-trial detention, was freed by the Tribunal; the Prosecution having admitted a case of mistaken identity.

Since this incident, it appears that the Prosecutor has streamlined the process relating to individuals mistakenly identified as accused persons wanted by the Tribunal. In July of 1998, the Office of the Prosecutor took only 24 hours to realize they were detaining innocent persons. On 22 July, identical twins were served with warrants of arrest by British special forces and brought from Prijedor, Bosnia-Herzegovina to the Netherlands. *The Sunday Times* reported that one of the persons arrested, Milan Vucicevic, when pleading his innocence, was manhandled: "When I said I'm not that man, one of the British took my hair and hit my head on the ground"[89]. London's *Evening Standard* wrote: "They were the Serb war criminals no one could miss"; and yet as an official from the ICTY announced: "These two persons [Milan and Miroslav Vucicevic] are not the Banovic brothers" accused of war crimes against prisoners of war"[90]. *The Times* went on to state that after "a round trip to The Hague, the Vucicevics ended up back in Prijedor, hospitalized"[91]. By comparison, the Vucicevic twins and Mr. Lajic have been lucky. Two other suspects, Dragan Gagovic and Simo Drljaca, have been killed by NATO troops enforcing the Dayton Accord. Both men, sus-

---

[87] For international rules of policing, see Cees de Rover, *To Serve and Protect: Human Rights and Humanitarian Law for Police and Security Forces*, 1998.

[88] *Order for the Withdrawal of the Charges Against the Person Named Goran Lajic and for his Release*, IT-95-8-T (*Lajic* case), 17 June 1996, p. 2.

[89] Marie Colvin, "The Hague Court Hit by Blunders", *The Sunday Times*, 16 August 1998, p. 13.

[90] Charles Reiss, "War Crimes Troops Round Up Wrong Serb Twins", *The Evening Standard*, 23 July 1998, p. 2.

[91] See Colvin, *op. cit.* n. 89, p. 13.

pected of violations of humanitarian law and wanted by the Tribunal, were killed during attempts at arrest[92].

The fervour of the Office of the Prosecutor has also been manifest when luring Mr. Slavko Dokmanovic from his native Serbia to Croatia. The "methods employed" by the Prosecutor, notes Leslie Green, a humanitarian law expert, "have little in common with what is generally regarded as due process in the most general meaning of that term"[93]. Michael Scharf sets the scene:

> [...] in June 1997, Kevin Curtis, an OTP [ICTY's Office of the Prosecutor] investigator, met with Dokmanovic at his home in the FRY [Federal Republic of Yugoslavia] in an effort to lure Dokmanovic into Eastern Slavonia for arrest by UNTAES [United Nations Transitional Administration for Eastern Slavonia]. Curtis purported to set up a meeting between Dokmanovic and General Jacques Klein, the Transitional Administrator of Eastern Slavonia, for the stated purpose of arranging for possible compensation for Dokmanovic's property in Eastern Slavonia, which he had been forced to abandon. In accordance with this arrangement, on the afternoon of 27 June 1997, Dokmanovic crossed the border into Eastern Slavonia under what he believed was a promise of safe conduct, and voluntarily entered an UNTAES vehicle which was to take him to meet General Klein at the UNTAES base in the town of Erdut. Upon arriving at Erdut, UNTAES soldiers removed Dokmanovic from the vehicle at gunpoint and handcuffed him, while a member of the OTP advised him of his rights and the charges against him. Dokmanovic was then flown on board an UNTAES airplane to The Hague and handed over to the ICTY for trial[94].

In such a case, Scharf, co-author of the *Inside Guide to the International Criminal Tribunal for the former Yugoslavia*, has noted that the Trial Chamber decision to maintain the detention of Mr. Dokmanovic "rests on an artificial distinction between luring and abductions" which is against "the internationally recognized human rights of the accused"[95]. Despite a general principle of law existing regarding the concept of *male captus, bene judicatus*, the trial of Mr. Dokmanovic was allowed to proceed[96].

---

[92] For Dragan Gagovic, see Charles Trueheart, "A Serb War-Crimes Suspect Is Killed" *The International Herald Tribune*, 11 January 1999, p.1; and Associated Press, "French NATO Troops Kill Bosnia War-Crime Suspect", *The Boston Globe*, 10 January 1999, p. 3. For Simo Drljaca, see Philip Smucker, "Alleged War Criminal's Death Creates a Backlash in Bosnia", *The Houston Chronicle*, 13 July 1997, p. 27; and Karen Coleman, "Thousands Mourn Bosnian Serb 'Hero' of Genocide", *The Guardian* (London), 14 July 1997, p. 10.

[93] Leslie Green, "Erdemovic – Tadic – Dokmanovic: Jurisdiction and Early Practice of the Yugoslav War Crimes Tribunal", *Israel Yearbook of Human Rights*, Vol. 27, p. 364.

[94] Michael Scharf, "*The Prosecutor v. Slavko Dokmanovic*: Irregular Rendition and the ICTY", *Leiden Journal of International Law*, Vol. 11, 1998, p. 370.

[95] *Ibid.*, pp. 382 and 380. *Decision on the Motion for Release*, IT-95-13a-PT (*Dokmanovic* case), 22 October 1997.

[96] Mr. Dokmanovic may well have been making a statement regarding the ICTY's version of justice when he committed suicide on the night of 28 –29 June 1998, "three days after the completion of his trial". See "Dokmanovic Case Terminated", *ICTY Bulletin*, Vol. 21, 27 July 1998.

Once detained by the ICTY and brought to trial, the zeal of the Office of the Prosecutor has been made evident by the judgments of the Trial Chambers. In the *Tadic* case, the Prosecutor appealed the Trial Chamber's verdict, as Mr. Tadic was found guilty of only 11 out of an original 34 counts[97]. Despite having been sentenced to 20 years for having been found guilty of "persecution" and beatings, which constituted crimes against humanity and violations of the laws and customs of war, Mr. Tadic was acquitted on all charges of murder[98]. Having been persistently referred to as a "small fry"[99] before the judgment, it would appear that, in the light of having been convicted on less than one third of the counts, the Prosecutor may well have gone overboard in even having brought Mr. Tadic to trial before the ICTY. Despite a mandate to prosecute only "serious" violations of humanitarian law, the Tribunal went forward in a case that would have been better heard by a municipal court in the former Yugoslavia.

In the second case that has been tried fully before the ICTY, the Tribunal found two Bosnian Muslims and one Croat guilty of grave breaches of the 1949 Geneva Conventions and violations of the laws of war for their participation in acts committed in the Celebici detention camp (Konijc, Bosnia-Herzegovina). However, the *Celebici* case also found a fourth defendant in the dock. Mr. Zejnil Delalic was acquitted on all 12 counts after having spent nearly three years in detention[100]. He walked away from the ICTY after having spent 980 days in jail for crimes he had not committed[101]. The prosecution, not willing to let sleeping dogs lie, has appealed. The case of Mr. Delalic may well be the clearest example of a Prosecutor rushing to indict while giving little thought to the presumption of innocence.

---

[97] Jose E. Alvarez, "Rush to Closure: Lessons of the Tadic Judgment" *Michigan Law Review*, Vol. 96, 1998, p. 2042.

[98] *Opinion and Judgment*, IT-94-1-T(*Tadic* case,), 7 May 1997; and Sentencing Judgment, IT-94-1-T, 14 July 1997. Note that nine counts for which the Trial Chamber found Mr. Tadic innocent were reversed by the Appeals Chamber. See *Judgment* of the Appeals Chamber, IT-94-1-A, *Tadic* case, 15 July 1999.

[99] The use of the term small fry to describe Tadic was first used by the President of the ICTY, Antonio Cassese, when he stated: "[if] the major powers of the world are not consistent and don't make arrests in the next ten months, we are prepared to pack up and go home. We think our job is to try leaders, not small fry." Raymond Brown, "*A fronte praecipitium a tergo tulpi*: Towards an Assessment of the Trial of Dusko Tadic before the ICTY", *ILSA Journal of International & Comparative Law*, Vol. 2, p. 599.

[100] *Judgment*, IT-96-21-T(*Celebici* case), 16 November 1998.

[101] Statement by counsel of Mr. Delalic, Edina Residovic, after her client's acquittal and an attempt by the Prosecutor to have Mr. Delalic detained pending appeal. Transcripts, IT-96-21-T (*Celebici* case), 16 November 1998, p. 16409, lines 14-15.

3.4. Article 21(4)(a): to be informed promptly and in detail in a language which he understands of the nature and cause of the charge against him

To be informed promptly of the charges against an accused is a right which is considered to have an international character. Provisions related to the giving of "notice" include Article 9(2) of the ICCPR[102] which provides that anyone "who is arrested shall be informed, at the time of arrest, of the reasons for his arrest and shall be promptly informed of any charges against him", and, Article 14(3) which sets out the minimum guarantee that an individual being charged shall "be informed promptly and in detail in a language which he understands of the nature and cause of the charge against him". The ICTY reproduces Article 14(3) as Article 21(4)(a); however, there is no provision that parallels Article 9(2) of the International Covenant on Civil and Political Rights.

As the Yugoslav Tribunal is of an international character, there is a question of geography and coordination which places practical obstacles in the way of the right to be informed promptly of the charges. When one considers that the Office of the Prosecutor is located at The Hague, while those suspected of serious violations of international humanitarian law may have scattered to the four corners of the planet; it may be too much to expect that every port-of-call or border control has the names of indictees wanted on an international arrest warrant and will also have a copy of the indictments which has been issued by the ICTY. As such, individuals who are detained under the jurisdiction of the Tribunal by municipal or international police forces may have to wait for some time before receiving proper notice. The UN Human Rights Committee has noted that a detention without notification for 50 hours is in violation of Article 9(2) of the ICCPR. It remains to be seen whether the Prosecutor will be able to met this criterion, let alone inform an individual promptly of the charges laid against him[103].

What may be problematic for the *ad hoc* Tribunals and for a future international criminal court may be the delegation of the arrest to third parties who may well violate an individual's right to being promptly informed of criminal charges against him. Consider for instance, the Memorandum of Understanding between the International Criminal Tribunal for the Former Yugoslavia and the Supreme Headquarters Allied Powers Europe (re: NATO) which provides initial and secondary cautions to be read "as soon as is practicable after detention" and "as soon as is practicable after the initial detention [after having been moved to a secure

---

[102] Article 9(2) of the ICCPR reads: "Anyone who is arrested shall be informed, at the time of arrest, of the reasons for his arrest and shall be promptly informed of any charges against him".

[103] With respect to the 50-hour criterion, see *Portorreal v. Dominican Republic*, Report of the Human Rights Committee, Official Record of the General Assembly, Forty-third Session, Supplement No. 40, (A/43/40), Annex VII.D.

location]"[104]. This secondary caution, which is the more substantive of the two, states: "you are detained as a person believed to be indicted for war crimes by the International Criminal Tribunal for the former Yugoslavia", thus meeting the first obligation under Article 9(2) of the ICCPR, that of being "informed, at the time of arrest, of the reasons for [the] arrest". However, the second obligation to be "promptly informed of any charges" may be violated as the caution goes on to say that "[t]he Tribunal has been informed of your detention, and members of the Prosecutor's Office will meet you as soon as possible. They will give you full details of the charges against you when they arrive"[105].

This situation in which a policing force informs a detainee of the reason of the arrest while a member of the Office of the Prosecutor is required to provide information on the charges which are being laid seems to be a cause for time-lags and hence for violations of the accused's right to be promptly informed of charges against him. The fact that a representative of the Office of the Prosecutor will be found at the side of an accused simply to read the charges before that detainee has had time to consult with a lawyer may lead to abuses of the accused's rights. Recalling that the function of notice is to allow an individual to secure release if the charges against him are invalid, one may ask whether steps should be taken to ensure that any notice includes details of the charges beyond simply stating that an arrest is being made for "serious violations of humanitarian law". As the eyes of the international community are focused on the actions of the Office of the Prosecutor, the use of facsimile machines and telephone communication should render respect for the rights of the accused's a manageable process. Furthermore, the Office of the Prosecutor should be removed completely from the process of notice, leaving this task to the Tribunal's "neutral" Registry.

3.5. Article 21(4)(d): to be tried in his presence, and to defend himself in person or through legal assistance of his own choosing; to be informed, if he does not have legal assistance, of this right; and to have legal assistance assigned to him, in any case where the interests of justice so require, and without payment by him in any such case if he does not have sufficient means to pay for it

The Tribunals, lacking the equivalent of a municipal "legal-aid" programme to ensure that indictees who cannot afford their own lawyers are provided one, established a regime for assigning counsel to indigent persons. This programme is initiated through Rule 45 (Assignment of Counsel) and, in the case of the

---

[104] Articles 2.3 and 2.7, Memorandum of Understanding between the International Criminal Tribunal for the Former Yugoslavia and the Supreme Headquarters Allied Powers Europe Concerning Practical Arrangements for the Detention and Transfer to the Tribunal of Persons Indicted for War Crimes by the Tribunal, dated 9 May 1996.

[105] *Ibid.*, Annex B

ICTY, are detailed in the Registrar's *Directive on the Assignment of Defence Counsel*.[106] This Directive establishes the criteria for determining the indigency of the accused, remuneration of counsel assigned, and prerequisites for assigned counsel. One issue of concern respecting the right to effective representation was the movement within the ICTY Registry to have assigned counsel sign-on to a code of ethics controlling their behaviour. While this, in and of itself, may not be reprehensible, the fact that only those counsel assigned by the Registrar, and not counsel from the Office of the Prosecutor nor counsel remunerated by the accused, would be bound by this code does not agree with the concept of equality of arms and could adversely affect the rights of accused persons who are indigent.

To continue with the theme of effective legal representation, while Rule 44 ensures that qualified counsel represent the accused, a fundamental question must be raised as to the accused having a lawyer present from the earliest possible moment of the Prosecutor's investigation. Rule 63 (Questioning the Accused) states that:

> Questioning by the Prosecutor of an accused, including after the initial appearance, shall not proceed without the presence of counsel unless the accused has voluntarily and expressly agreed to proceed without counsel present [...].

and Rule 42(B), concerning the rights of suspects during investigation, makes it clear that

> Questioning of a suspect shall not proceed without the presence of counsel unless the suspect has voluntarily waived his right to counsel.

Here is a case in point where the international community, having the means, should also have the fortitude to make a right non-derogable, i.e. to consider any statements made to the Office of the Prosecutor or to any national authority without the presence of counsel considered as inadmissible. Why? Because any international criminal system established will have elements which do not correspond to a domestic legal system. This being so, the accused will have very little concept of what rights are available within this international jurisdiction. This is true for suspects and accused from the former Yugoslavia who live under a civil law – inquisitorial system – in which the *juge d'instruction* is seen as an ally. The suspect or the accused may well be willing to co-operate with the Prosecutor on the assumption that the latter is there to help him. This assumption may be inferred by an accused, as it is a member of the Office of the Prosecutor who, it will be recalled, is called upon to provide details of the charges against the individual. This situation arises before the individual is transported to The

[106] T1/94, adopted 11 February 1994 and amended various times.

Hague to make arrangements to provide him with counsel. During this time period of uncertainty for the accused, the representative for the Office of the Prosecutor may very well be perceived by the accused as being there to aid him and thus lead to a violation of the right to have effective legal representation.

Under an international mandate, there should be no room for prosecutorial games which lead, as has been the case for most of the accused in the *Celebici* case, to give statements to the Office of the Prosecutor without counsel being present. The fact that these men were indigent and arrested away from The Hague, where the Registrar could not provide them with assigned counsel, does not contribute to an appearance that justice is being served. Further, by not ensuring that suspects and accused are accompanied by their lawyers when giving any statement which could be admissible in court, the international community may be denying fundamental rights. Individuals arrested could be detained and questioned by national authorities acting as proxies for the Office of the Prosecutor and would therefore find themselves between jurisdictions, and not in a position to draw benefit from ICTY Rules 42(B).

3.6. Article 21(4)(e): to examine, or have examined, the witnesses against him and to obtain the attendance and examination of witnesses on his behalf under the same conditions as witnesses against him

As noted earlier[107], the ICTY has, on occasion, been prepared to abrogate the international rules governing the right to a fair trial to the detriment of the accused. This was made most evident in the *Tadic* case where, as Michael Scharf noted, "at times, the Tribunal tread dangerously close to denying Tadic a fair trial, most conspicuously by its decision to allow certain prosecution witnesses to testify anonymously"[108]. In its *Decision on the Prosecutor's Motion Requesting Protective Measures for Victims and Witnesses*, the ICTY Trial Chamber found, by a majority vote of two to one that witnesses could testify, as Paul Hoffman noted, "without public or media present and their identities would never by disclosed to the defense"[109].

Monroe Leigh, in an editorial of the American Journal of International Law, makes a persuasive argument that "neither the text of the Statute of the Yugoslav Tribunal nor its published rules authorize the use of witnesses whose names are withheld from the accused"[110]. Leigh notes elsewhere that such witness anonymity is incompatible with constructing a proper defense:

---

[107] *Supra*, Section 3.2.
[108] See Scharf, *op. cit.* n. 84, p. 871.
[109] Hoffman, *op. cit.* n. 83, p. 315.
[110] See Leigh, *op. cit.* n. 80, p. 80.

> It is an almost impossible task to cross-examine an adverse witness effectively without knowing that witness' name, background, habitual residence, or whereabouts at the time of the events to which he testifies[111].

The dangers of having witnesses testify anonymously, and the repercussions this could have on a defense were never more in evidence than on the day which Tadic took the stand in his own defense.

During the Prosecution case, "Witness L", Dragan Opacic, had been granted partial anonymity to testify. His testimony "contained shocking eyewitness descriptions of Tadic's personal participation in murders, beatings, and rapes"[112]. Yet the defense, having been given the details of the witness' identity only thirty days before the trial commenced[113], was able to establish, in the interim period, that the witness had lied under oath[114]. As Paul Hoffman correctly points out: "If [Opacic] had [had] complete anonymity, his testimony would have stood and Tadic would have been convicted of crimes based on a false testimony"[115]. In a most spectacular morning session of 25 October 1996, minutes before Tadic was to take the stand in a surprise move by the defense, the prosecution moved to have the Chamber disregard the testimony of "Witness L" as having been false.

The granting of anonymity as an expression of the ICTY's willingness to balance the rights of the accused with those of victims and witnesses has been heavily criticized. Monroe Leigh posits that not only is the validity of the *Tadic* judgment in question but that of the legitimacy of the Tribunal is at stake:

> [...] at this time it is of overriding importance that the first international criminal tribunal established since Nuremberg should exercise its jurisdiction in such a way as to establish the credibility of international criminal tribunals on a basis that cannot be criticized from a due process point of view. This is important not only from the assurance of justice to the accused, but also from the reputation of this Tribunal, and for the effect the record of this Tribunal will have on public acceptance of a permanent international criminal court[116].

---

[111] Monroe Leigh, "The Yugoslav Tribunal: Use of Unnamed Witnesses Against Accused", *American Journal of International Law*, Vol. 90, 1996, p. 236.

[112] See Brown, *op. cit.* n. 99, p. 610.

[113] *Decision on the Prosecutor's Motion Requesting Protective Measures for Witness L*, IT-96-21-T, 14 November 1995.

[114] As an outcome of this revelation, all protective measures were withdrawn and Dragan Opacic was placed in detention awaiting perjury charges. See *Decision on the Prosecutor's Motion to Withdraw Protective Measures for Witness "L"*, IT-96-21-T, 5 December 1996; and *Trial Chamber II: Order for the Prosecution to Investigate False Testimony of Dragan Opacic (Witness "L")*, IT-96-21-T, 10 December 1996.

[115] See Hoffman, *op. cit.* n. 83, p. 315.

[116] Leigh, *op. cit.* n. 111, p. 236.

4. Conclusion

If courts are to try individuals at the international level, it is axiomatic that they must ensure that the proceedings are conducted so that the rule of law is respected in its integrity. Yet the consolidation of the rule of law, within the domain of international criminal law, has been hampered by a structural paradox: international judges at times attempt to establish an effective criminal law system at the expense of the right of those accused of international crimes. Both the Chief Prosecutor at Nuremberg, Justice Robert H. Jackson, and B.V.A. Röling, the Dutch Judge in the Tokyo Trials, used the maxim "The power of the precedent is the power of the beaten path"[117] as a justification for playing fast and loose with the rights of the accused during the IMT trials after the Second World War. Yet the danger of not fully respecting the rule of law was pointed out in elegant terms by Robert H. Jackson himself in his opening statement at Nuremberg:

> We must never forget that the record on which we judge these defendants is the record on which history will judge us tomorrow. To pass these defendants a poisoned chalice is to put it to our lips as well[118].

The legacy of the Nuremberg and Tokyo Trials is that the term "justice" was modified by "victor's", as a recognition by scholars that the IMT trials lacked full respect for the primacy of law. The International Criminal Tribunal for the former Yugoslavia has also sought to establish "victim's justice"[119] instead of simply "justice". This chapter has considered the functioning of the ICTY and demonstrated to what extent the right to a fair trial has been supplanted by the "higher calling" of ensuring the establishment of a *prima facie* "effective" international criminal law system. The legacy of the development of international criminal law throughout the 20th century has demonstrated that the establishment of a criminal law system has always taken precedence over the right to a fair trial. Through the collaboration in the book *The Tokyo Trials and Beyond: Reflections of a Peacemonger*, it appears that the poisoned chalice has been handed down from B.V.A. Röling to the first President of the ICTY, Antonio Cassese. The examples that have been presented of the failings of the Yugoslavia Tribunal to ensure full respect for the rule of law show that individuals have been subjected to hardships in the name of international justice. In this respect, the last word will be given to Michail Wladimiroff, the highly respected Dutch criminal attorney who acted on Dusko Tadic's behalf:

---

[117] See Röling and Cassese, *op. cit.* n. 2, p. 90, and Zaid, *op. cit.* n. 80, p. 591.

[118] Telford Taylor, *The Anatomy of the Nurember Trials*, 1992, p. 168.

[119] Address of Antonio Cassese, President of International Criminal Tribunal for the former Yugoslavia, to the General Assembly of the United Nations, 19 November 1996, p. 3.

> For those who would respond to criticisms of the Tribunal by saying you have to start somewhere [...] I say that's no good enough when you're dealing with a person whose life and liberty are at stake"[120].

Having thus considered the role of international judges, and demonstrated how their actions can impede the rule of law at the international level, it is now time to examine an international court which has avoided many of the pitfalls that have hobbled other judicial organs. The final substantive chapter of this study will consider the evolution of the European Court of Justice and demonstrate how the willingness of European States to ensure the success of European integration has resulted in the creation of a court which – at least in the domain of economic integration – has demonstrated its ability to govern a society based on the rule of law. As such, the European Court of Justice may be seen as a beacon for those who advocate the consolidation of the rule of law on the international plane.

---

[120] See Scharf, *op. cit.* n. 84, p. 871.

Chapter 6
THE EUROPEAN COURT OF JUSTICE*

1. Introduction

Thus far, this study has been witness to the various means by which the rule of law can be and is limited on the international plane. The apparent lack of effectiveness of international adjudication is, for the most part, not inherent: it is a manifestation of a State-centric system. Ultimately, if States wish an international court to function effectively, to ensure respect for the rule of law, it will happen. Such is the case for the Court of Justice of the European Communities. So effective was this Court, during its first four decades, that the Communities were seen as being a phenomenon apart from traditional international law: as being *sui generis*. In fact, until the Maastricht Treaty of 1992, academics, following the pronouncements of the Court, sought to classify it as being the constitutional court of a new "supranational" order which had slipped from the ultimate control of States.

With the conclusion of the Maastricht Treaty and again with the Amsterdam Treaty, it has become evident that the creation of what is today termed the "European Union" is governed by international law and that, ultimately, it is the States and not the European institutions – foremost among them the Court of Justice – which are the "*Herren der Verträge*". For nearly forty years, European institutions, led in large part by the pronouncements of the Court, found themselves sovereign in the area of economic integration. The Court was heard to say that the EEC [European Economic Community] Treaty, "albeit concluded in the form of an international agreement, nonetheless constitutes the constitutional charter of a Community based on the rule of law"[1]. It thus came as a shock to those advocating a distinct European legal order when, with the Maastricht and Amsterdam Treaties, States created the European Union while limiting the jurisdiction of the Court in various areas and excluding it outright from others. It thus became evident that the Court of Justice, for all its inroads, is no different from other courts existing within a State-centric international order.

Yet in the domain of economic integration, the European Court has acted in a truly revolutionary manner for an international court. Examining the achieve-

* This Chapter, in substance, was first published as "The European Court of Justice is an International Court" in *Nordic Journal of International Law*, Vol. 68, 1999, pp. 249-274. ©2000, Kluwer Law International.

[1] *Re the Draft Treaty on a European Economic Area*, Opinion 1/91, 1991, *Reports of the Cases before the Court*, p. I-6084.

ments of the Luxembourg Court in this field makes it possible to realize to what extent international law can be dynamic. The lesson to be learnt from the function of the European Court within the field of economic integration is that if there is consensus within States to achieve a result, an international court can promote and ensure the rule of law. The other side of the coin is that international courts can only be as effective in upholding the rule of law as States are willing to allow them. The Court of Justice of the European Communities is no exception, as the member States of the European Union have decided that its jurisdiction should be excluded in major areas, and thus established that it remains, above all else, an international court.

2. The European Framework

The genesis of the system of European integration, which today manifests itself in the European Union,[2] can be seen as dating from 9 May 1950. On that day, the French Foreign Minister, Robert Schuman, proposed the pooling of Franco-German coal and steel resources under the supervision of a treaty based on "higher authority". Thus France attempted to neutralize the strategic and historical importance of the coal-producing regions of the Ruhr and Saar while, at the same time, ensuring that the raw materials of the German armaments industry would be placed in joint control[3]. In essence, the Schuman Plan, the brainchild of Jean Monnet, was meant to have Europe turn its back on the notion of nationalism, blamed, as it was, for leading the continent down the path to a major war, not once but twice, during the first half of the twentieth century. The signing of the European Coal and Steel Community Treaty (ECSC) in 1951 was to be the first significant step toward European integration whereby a "supranational" authority – independent from the parties and holding the power to make binding decisions – would replace parochial nationalism[4]. In other words, this was "the establishment, in limited fields, of elements of common government"[5].

The European Coal and Steel Community was followed in 1957 by the Treaty Establishing a European Atomic Energy Community (Euratom) and the Treaty Establishing a European Economic Community (EEC). While these new treaty regimes shared the Parliamentary Assembly and the Court of Justice with the ECSC – which had establishmed them – each maintained separate executive insti-

---

[2] See the Treaty of Amsterdam amending the Treaty on European Union, the Treaties establishing the European Communities and Certain Related Acts, 10 November 1997.

[3] Paul Craig and Cráinne de Búrca, *EU Law: Texts, Cases, and Materials* (2nd ed.), 1998, p. 9.

[4] The original six States of the ECSC were: Belgium, France, German, Italy, Luxembourg, and Netherlands.

[5] Andrew Duff, *Reforming the European Union*, 1997, p. 1.

tutions[6]. It was not until 1965 that the European institutions would merge so as to function within the three European Communities[7]. The subsequent twenty years would see few reforms to the legal framework of the European movement. While the depth of the process of European integration was stalled, the breadth of the union expanded as Denmark, Greece, Ireland, Portugal, Spain and the United Kingdom would join the European Communities before the coming into force of the Single European Act in 1986. This Act, "the most important revision of the Treaties since they were first adopted [...], heralded the revival of the Community momentum towards integration which continued apace thereafter"[8]. That momentum would widen the breadth of the Community, carrying in its wake the accessions of Austria, Finland, and Sweden by the early 1990s.

The pace of economic integration initiated in the Single European Act was pursued with vigour with a proposal being put forward by Jacques Delors in 1989 for a three-stage plan to reach economic and monetary union. It was decided that an inter-governmental conference would be held to consider this plan as well as the furthering of political integration. On the basis of those negotiations, the Treaty on European Union (TEU) was signed at Maastricht in 1992:

> Apart from the detailed commitment to full economic and monetary union, the most obvious features of the TEU was the institutional change it brought about, establishing a "three-pillar" structure for what was henceforth to be called the European Union, with the Communities as the first of these pillars[9].

Thus, the achievements of European integration have now been consolidated into the first pillar of the Union, the only change of note being the rebaptizing of the European Economic Community as "European Community" (EC). The second and third pillars established at Maastricht are, by comparison, inter-governmental in nature. They are outside the supranational (institutional and legal) framework of European integration as it had evolved before Maastricht. The second pillar, Common Foreign and Security Policy and the third pillar, Justice and Home Affairs are meant to allow for cooperation between States without compulsion. That is, both pillars allow for joint action to be taken without these fields coming under the scrutiny of the European institutions.

Built into the TEU was a provision to review, in 1996, the progress of Maastricht at an inter-governmental conference[10]. The outcome of this confer-

---

[6] See Convention on certain Institutions common to the European Communities, 25 March 1957.

[7] P.J.G. Kapteyn and P. VerLoren van Themaat, *Introduction to the Law of the European Communities* (3rd ed.), 1998, p. 74.

[8] Craig and de Búrca, *op. cit.* n. 3, p. 20. The Single European Act created the Court of First Instance to the Court of Justice.

[9] *Ibid.*, pp. 24-25.

[10] Article N(2), Treaty of European Union, 1 November 1993.

ence was the Treaty of Amsterdam[11] which moves certain elements relating to "common visa, immigration and asylum policy from the intergovernmental third pillar of Maastricht to the first pillar of the European Community"[12]; while renaming the third pillar: Police and Judicial Cooperation in Criminal Matters. The other significance of Amsterdam is that the Schengen Agreement – allowing for the free movement of people within the Union, previous placed outside the framework of the European Communities, has been brought into the fold. As such, the Treaty of Amsterdam constitutes the most recent addition to the *acquis communautaire*[13]: the *corpus juris europaeum*[14].

3. The Court of Justice of the European Communities

The Court of Justice of the European Communities, otherwise known as the European Court of Justice (ECJ), is comprised of 16 judges, one selected by each of the 15 member States plus one chosen by the five largest States of the Union[15]. In situations where the Court comprises an even number of judges, as was the case at the end of 1999, the judge selected in concert becomes an Advocate-General. The role of the Advocate-General[16] is to act "with complete impartiality and independence, to make, in open court, reasoned submissions [both oral and written] on cases brought before the Court of Justice, in order to assist the Court

---

[11] Treaty of Amsterdam amending the Treaty on European Union, The Treaties establishing the European Communities and Certain related Acts, 1 May 1999. Provisions which fall under the Amsterdam Treaty will be cited as EU law; provisions falling under the new European Community they will called EC law.

[12] Andrew Duff, *The Treaty of Amsterdam: Text and Commentary*, 1997, p. xxxiii.

[13] *Aquis communautaire* is the patrimony of the Union: "the whole body of rules, principles, agreements, declarations, resolutions, positions, opinions, objectives, and principles" related to the European Union. The most important part the *aquis* plays in the Union is in times of enlargement, when States acceding to the Union must accept it without reservation. For the complete definition of aquis communautaire, see A.G. Toth, *The Oxford Encyclopaedia of European Community Law*, Vol. 1, 1990, p. 9.

[14] Consider the following explanation of the evolution of EU law: "The process of treaty building in the European Union has been simply to pile one treaty on top of another without care for consolidation. After the Treaty of Paris in 1951 there have been five major new Treaties (EEC, Euratom, Single Act, Maastricht and Amsterdam) as well as five revisions of major consequence [...] plus four sets of complex accession treaties. Numerous protocols and declarations have been added on: at Amsterdam alone there were thirteen of the former and fifty-seven of the latter. The corpus of treaty provisions now runs to three 'pillars', scores of parts, sections, titles and chapters, thousands of juxtaposed articles and tens of thousands of pages. Accessible the Treaties are not". Duff, *op. cit.* n. 12, p. 200.

[15] Craig and de Búrca, *op. cit.* n. 3, p. 80. The five States are: France, Germany, Italy, Spain and the United Kingdom.

[16] The existence of positions of Advocates-General within the ECJ belies the assertion that the structure of the Court of Justice is modelled on the continental system of civil law and more precisely on that of French law.

in the performance of the task assigned to it"[17]. Thus, beyond the submissions by the applicant and the respondent, the Advocates-General also forward their views to the Court. Excluding the possible additional Advocate-General, the Court has eight Advocates-General, five appointed by the large States and three chosen in rotation by the other States. The status of the Advocates-General as full fledged member of the Court is illustrated by the fact that their appointment, and the "terms and conditions of [their] office, including dismissal, are governed by the same provisions as those of the judges"[18].

The members of the Court are selected by the States for a six-year renewable term. While this period may seem to be too short to guarantee judicial independence, the fact that the Court renders its decisions by consensus – allowing for no dissenting or concurring opinions – means that judges remain insulated by their anonymity[19]. While the Court often sits in Chambers, no allowance is made to ensure that a judge, national of a party to the dispute, sits in the case. As a result, the notion of an *ad hoc* judge is foreign to this Court. The latter not only has jurisdiction to interpret and apply the instruments constituting the *corpus* of European Law; it also has the power under the EC to "impose a lump sum or penalty payment" on States which fail to comply with its judgements[20]. The jurisdiction of the Court, and the manner in which it has interpreted its mandate, has meant that the Court has been at the forefront of a movement to establish a *sui generis* legal system.

4. The Community Court as a Constitutional Court

> Tucked away in the fairyland Duchy of Luxembourg and blessed, until recently, with benign neglect by the powers that be and the mass media, the Court of Justice of the European Communities has fashioned a constitutional framework for a federal-type structure of Europe[21].

---

[17] Article 222 EC.

[18] L. Neville Brown and Tom Kennedy, *The Court of Justice of the European Communities* (4th ed.), 1994, p. 62.

[19] Takis Tridimas writes that there "are three reasons which explain the collegiality of the judgment. The Court is modelled on the judicial system of the continental Member States, in particular the *Conseil d'Etat*, where collegiate judgments are the rule. The multilingual character of Community law makes it practically very difficult to introduce a system of individual judgments. Finally, collegiality is seen as a guarantee of impartiality and of ensuring that the judges remain free from political pressure from their Member States". Takis Tridimas, "The Court of Justice and Judicial Activism", *European Law Review*, Vol. 21, 1996, p. 210.

[20] Article 228 EC.

[21] Eric Stein, "Lawyers, Judges, and the Making of a Transnational Constitution", *American Journal of International Law*, Vol. 75, 1981, p. 1.

This splendid isolation afforded to the European Court of Justice during its formative years allowed it to develop case-law specific to the European Economic Community (EEC); which it professed was neither international law nor municipal law. As Paul Craig and Cráinne de Búrca have noted in their leading volume, *EU Law: Texts, Cases, and Materials*, much of "the development of the Community's legal system has been brought about not by the express agreement of the States which founded the Community nor by means of a detailed plan for an integrated legal system, but through the interpretative practice and influence of the European Court of Justice"[22]. Thus the Court noted in *van Gend and Loos* that the:

> objective of the EEC Treaty, which is to establish a Common Market, the functioning of which is of direct concern to interested parties in the Community, implies that this Treaty is more than an agreement which merely creates mutual obligations between the contracting parties.
> [...]
> The conclusion to be drawn from this is that *the Community constitutes a new legal order of international law* for the benefit of which the States have limited their sovereign rights, albeit within limited fields, and the subjects of which comprise not only Member States but also their nationals[23].

Later, the Court would drop the qualifier "international law" and would move towards recognizing the Treaty Establishing the European Economic Community as amounting to a constitution:

> The European Economic Community is a Community based on the rule of law, inasmuch as neither its Member States nor its institutions can avoid a review of the question whether the measures adopted by them are in conformity with the *basic constitutional charter*, the Treaty[24].

This great leap forward was confirmed in 1991, when the Court stated that "the ECC Treaty, albeit concluded in the form of an international agreement, nonetheless constitutes the *constitutional charter of a Community* based on the rule of law"[25].

The metamorphosis toward constitutionalization of the Treaty governing the ECC occurred as the Court took a leading role in moving the integration of European economic life forward. The result has been an ECC which today has "devel-

---

[22] Craig and de Búrca, *op. cit.* n. 3, p. 163.

[23] *Van Gend en Loos v. Nederlandse Administratie der Belastingen*, *Reports of the Cases before the Court* 1963, p. 12. Emphasis added.

[24] *Parti écologiste 'Les Verts' v. The European Parliament*, *Reports of the Cases before the Court* 1986, p. 1365. Emphasis added.

[25] *Re the Draft on a European Economic Area*, Opinon 1/91, *Reports of the Cases before the Court* 1991, p. I-6084. Emphasis added.

oped into an organization of States with a relatively autonomous legal system, a system of norms which bind each of the States"[26]. How did the Court effect this transition to a constitutional court from one which, at the onset, appeared to be little more than a court of "limited international jurisdiction"[27], cut from much the same cloth as the International Court of Justice, to acting as a constitutional court?

> It is the ECJ itself that is popularly credited with the transformation of the Treaty of Rome from an international agreement into the constitution of the European Union, by convincing national courts to apply European Union law directly and supremely to national law. The ECJ benefited greatly from the structural relations with national courts that Article 177 created, providing a ready-made entrée into national legal systems[28].

4.1. **The Doctrine of Direct Effect**

The Court of Justice, lacking a mandate to hear appeals from national jurisdictions, sought to coax municipal judges into accepting what was, at the time an obscure provision of the EEC: Article 177[29]. Article 177 (now Article 234 EC) reads:

> The Court of Justice shall have jurisdiction to give preliminary rulings concerning:
>
> a. the interpretation of this Treaty;
> b. the validity and interpretation of acts of the institutions of the Community and of the ECB;
> c. the interpretation of the statutes of bodies established by an act of the Council, where those statutes so provide.
>
> Where such a question is raised before any court or tribunal of a member State, that court or tribunal may, if it considers that a decision on the question is necessary to enable it to give judgment, request the Court of Justice to give a ruling thereon.
>
> Where any such question is raised in a case pending before a court or tribunal of a member State against whose decisions there is no judicial remedy under national law, that court or tribunal shall bring the matter before the Court of Justice.

In the words of Judge Mancini, the "Court's first preoccupation"[30] was to win over national judges in an effort to have them make referrals to the Court of

[26] Craig and de Búrca, *op. cit.* n. 3, p. 163.

[27] Laurence R. Helfer and Anne-Marie Slaughter, "Towards a Theory of Effective Supranational Adjudication", *Yale Law Journal*, vol. 107, 1997, pp. 290-291.

[28] *Ibid.*, pp. 308-309.

[29] See Thomas de la Mare, "Article 177 in Social and Political Context", in Paul Craig and Cráinne de Búrca (eds.), *The Evolution of EU Law*, 1999, pp. 215-261.

[30] G. Federico Mancini, "The Making of A Constitution for Europe", *Common Market Law Review*, Vol. 26, 1989, p. 605.

Justice following the dictates of Article 177. The ability of the Court to render preliminary rulings was achieved through what has been euphemistically called a "generous information campaign"[31] or an "extensive education campaign"[32], which included "seminars, dinners, regular invitations to Luxembourg, and visits around the Community"[33]. As a result of this judicial lobbying, municipal courts started to send preliminary references to the Luxembourg; the rulings emanating from those referrals were then accepted by those courts as the law of the land and implemented through the municipal systems.

Via the *van Gend and Loos* case, the Court determined that individuals could apply directly – as opposed to the filter of the State and the regime of *exequatur* – to municipal courts to have EEC law enforced[34]. Thus, the Court not only concluded that individuals, like the State Parties, had rights, but also granted them the means of giving those rights direct effect at the municipal level. From this ground-breaking judgment in 1963, the Court has gone on to expand and broaden the concept of direct effect to include much of what is today referred to as European Community law[35]. It is from the vantage point of this penetration of EC law into municipal systems that the Court, as well as those studying European integration, are willing to consider the system as having a constitutional basis[36]. Yet the integration of European Community law among the States Parties to that Treaty could only take place if it was applied uniformly among the Parties. This need for uniformity, although hinted at in *van Gend and Loos*, was made plain one year later in *Costa* v. *ENEL*.

4.2. **The Doctrine of Supremacy**

In its 1964 decision in the *Costa* v. *ENEL* case, the European Court of Justice articulated one of the fundamental principles of Community Law: the supremacy of that law over municipal law. It determined that EC Law would not only prevail

[31] Hjalte Rasmussen, *On Law and Policy in the European Court of Justice*, 1986, p. 247.

[32] Helfer and Slaughter, *op. cit.* n. 27, p. 302.

[33] *Ibid.*

[34] Or, as the Oxford Encyclopaedia of European Community Law indicates: "The question of whether certain provisions of the EEC Treaty, an international agreement concluded between sovereign States, is capable of producing enforceable rights in favour of individuals was first raised in Case 26/62 *Van Gend en Loos* [1963] ECR 1". *Supra*, n. 23, p. 166.

[35] Bruno de Witte, "Direct Effect, Supremacy, and the Nature of the Legal Order", in Craig and de Búrca , *op. cit.* n. 29, pp. 177-213.

[36] Weiler argues that Community law should be considered as a 'new legal order' because the quantitative change within the system is "of such a magnitude that it is quantitative in nature". But making the leap to constitutionalization of the European Community requires more: "the system of judicial remedies and enforcement. It is this system, as interpreted and opertionalized by the European judicial branch, that truly differentiates the Community legal order from [...] classical public international law": Joseph Weiler, "The Transformation of Europe", *Yale Law Journal*, Vol. 100, 1991, p. 2418.

over municipal law in the litigating State, but would be applicable in all other Community member States as part of a superior legal order:

> By contrast with ordinary international treaties, the EEC Treaty has created it own legal system which, on the entry into force of the Treaty, became an integral part of the legal system of the member States and which their courts are bound to apply.
>
> By creating a Community of unlimited duration, having it own institutions, its own personality, its own legal capacity and capacity of representation on the international plane and, more particularly, real powers stemming from a limitation of sovereignty or a transfer of powers from the States to the Community, the member States have limited their sovereign rights, albeit within limited fields, and have thus created a body of law which binds both their nationals and themselves.
>
> The integration into the laws of each member State of provisions which derive from the Community, and more generally the terms and the spirit of the Treaty, make it impossible for the States, as a corollary, to accord precedence to an unilateral and subsequent measure over a legal system accepted by them on the basis of reciprocity. [...] The executive force of Community law cannot vary from one State to another in deference to subsequent domestic law, without jeopardising the attainment of the objectives of the Treaty [...].
>
> It follows from all these observations that the law stemming from the Treaty, an independent source of law, could not, because of its special and original nature, be overridden by domestic legal provisions, however framed, without being deprived of its character as Community law and without the legal basis of the Community itself being called into question. [37]

By using such forceful language, the Court established a doctrine which allowed this "new legal order" to prevail over, not only municipal legislation, but also over a State's constitution if an element of that *Grundnorm* violated Community law. The Court did not make its findings of supremacy, as the above excerpt indicates, based on a claim that the Treaty was an international instrument and, as such, trumped municipal law. Instead it held that supremacy was based on the fact that a "new legal system" had been created with "real power" based on the consent of States to "limit their sovereignty" in the area of economic integration. As a result, the Court asserted itself as being the final arbiter of a system beyond the reach of municipal law, a European constitutional court within the Community framework.

Yet the simple pronouncement of the doctrine of supremacy was not enough to solidify the "constitutional" nature of the European system. Municipal courts were required to accept it. As Joseph Weiler has noted, this acceptance "amounts in effect to a quiet revolution in the legal orders of the member States"[38]. Within

---

[37] *Flaminio Costa v. ENEL*, *Reports of the Cases before the Court*, 1964, p. 585.

[38] Joseph Weiler, "The Community System: the Dual Character of Supernationalism", *Yearbook of European Law*, Vol. 1, 1981, p. 275.

the European Community, a symbiotic relationship has thus been created whereby municipal courts are willing to make references to the European Court and to accept its pronouncements as having a binding effect upon them[39]. This new order, accessible to both States and individuals[40], and given direct effect municipally, constitutes, in the discourse of the European Court and European scholars, the essence of a system that escapes its founding instruments: a legal system *sui generis*.

4.3. **The Need for Such a Constitutional Order**

As will be shown shortly, the notion of "direct effect" and "supremacy" are not unknown to public international law. Yet, the European Court of Justice utilized them as a foundation for the establishment of a new constitutional order. The construction of this legal fiction was necessary because of the nature of the European States, whose systems were not uniform when it came to integrating international law into their municipal orders. The monist/dualist dichotomy existing amongst various European constitutional orders would have meant a piecemeal application of European integration: some States would have accepted the Community treaties as automatically binding while others would have required specific domestic legislation to give it effect. The Court, going beyond the prescriptions of the Treaty and emphasizing the teleological interpretation of its provisions, squared that circle by declaring that the system was beyond reach of the traditional understanding of the integration of international instruments into municipal systems. Craig and de Búrca write:

> The ECJ however avoided the problem of member States' differing constitutional approaches to international treaties by describing the legal order created by them under the Treaty as an entirely new system which was different in nature from international law. Disregarding the specific constitutional perspectives of the individual member States, the Court instead spoke broadly of a constitutional transfer of power from the member States. The novel nature of the Treaty and of the legal order it had created derived, on the Court's analysis, from a voluntary limitation of their sovereign right by the member States, which had chosen to create and endow new political institutions with such sovereign rights[41].

---

[39] Eric Stein notes that the "European judicial process, characterized by a symbiotic relationship between national courts and the Court of Justice, is a complex dialectic process". Stein, *op. cit.* n. 21, p. 1.

[40] Consider de Witte's assessment of the role of the individual within the European Community: "in contrast with other regimes of international co-operation, where individuals are mainly looking from the sidelines at the action taken on their behalf by governments and international institutions, the individual has been made a direct participant in the European integration process thanks, in large part, to the principles of supremacy and direct effect". De Witte, *op. cit.* n. 35, p. 205.

[41] Craig and de Búrca, *op. cit.* n. 3, p. 257.

While some States, notably those of the Benelux, considered a ratified international treaty as being part and parcel of their municipal law, others, most notably Italy and Germany, were of a dualist tradition. Within the dualist system, a clear break exists between international law and municipal law, and domestic courts may only apply domestic legislation[42]. The European Court, by creating a "mid-level" law, allowed dualist States to integrate European law while still maintaining their fundamental constitutional framework prohibiting the direct application of international law[43]. As Bruno de Witte points out: "The message in *Costa* [v. *ENEL*], was primarily addressed to the Italian Constitutional Court. This court has gradually come to recognize the supremacy of Community law over national legislation, on the basis of its special nature which distinguishes it from other international treaties"[44].

Through the development of the doctrines of direct effect and supremacy the Court of Justice was able, through its case-law which emphasized States' need to implement the spirit of the Community treaties, to establish a "new legal order". Yet, as has been noted, this new order was based on a legal fiction which allowed for economic integration among all Community members. The removal of this legal fiction reveals that the underlying basis of this "new" Community legal order is none other than public international law. What sets apart the "new legal order" from public international law, generally speaking, is not the law itself but the way in which it is being applied. Essentially, European Community law is public international law applied in a quantitatively different manner. But this fact in no way alters the international legal nature of the system. Confirmation of this is found in the existence, within the realm of public international law, of both the principles of direct "self-executing" effect and supremacy.

[42] The dualist system is explained in *Oppenheim's* in the following terms: "international law and internal law of States are totally separate legal systems. Being separate systems international law would not *as such* from part of the internal law of the State: to the extent that in particular instances rule of international law may apply within a State they do so by virtue of their adoption by the internal law of the States, and apply as part of that internal law and not as international law. Such a view avoids any question of the supremacy of the one system of law over the other since they share no common field of application: each is supreme in its own sphere". Robert Jennings and Arthur Watts (eds.), *Oppenheim's International Law*, Vol. 1, 1996, p. 53. Emphasis in the original.

[43] Bruno de Witte explains that the States with a dualist tradition do not accept the supremacy of the treaties as emanating from the international plain: "Thus we find an enlargement of the *scope* of the principle of supremacy: to the simple notion of *international supremacy*, *Costa* adds what we might term the supremacy in the internal application or *internal supremacy*. See "Retour à «Costa»: La primauté du droit communautaire à la lumière du droit international", *Revue trimestrielle de droit européen*, Vol. 20, 184, p. 427.

[44] De Witte, *op. cit.* n. 35, p. 197. De Witte goes on to say that a "similar evolution took place in Germany". *Ibid.*

5. The European Court of Justice as an International Court

At the most fundamental level, the European Community law is public international law, the European Court an international court. As the European Communities were established by treaties, consolidated into the first pillar of the European Union by another treaty, it is plain that the European Community, like the Union itself, is governed by treaty law as found in the Vienna Convention on the Law of Treaties, itself a fundamental instrument of public international law[45]. The device of dropping the qualifier after *van Gend and Loos*, to the effect that the Community constitutes a new legal order "of international law", was in stark contrast to one of the most fundamental tenets of public international law as expressed by the Permanent Court of International Justice in the *Wimbledon* case:

> The Court declines to see, in the conclusion of any treaty by which a State undertakes to perform or refrain from performing a particular act, an abandonment of its sovereignty [...]. The right of entering into international engagements is an attribute of state sovereignty.[46]

By removing this phrase, the Court was created a *prima facie* "new legal order" but not a new order "of international law". Yet member States had not, in fact, abandoned their sovereignty to this new legal order; instead they demonstrated their sovereignty by establishing the European Community. Regardless of what the European Court of Justice wishes to term[47] the regime over which it maintains jurisdiction – a new legal order or a constitutional charter – the European Community remains, as it always has, a treaty-based regime governed by public international law.

5.1. Examination of the Doctrines

That Community law is fundamentally public international law is made evident when consideration is given to the doctrines upon which the Court attempts to justify the uniqueness of the law. The doctrine of direct effect has existed for some time in public international law under the rubric of "self-executing"

---

[45] Vienna Convention on the Law of Treaties, 23 May 1969; Eric Suy, *Corpus iuris gentium*, 1996, pp. 99-120.

[46] *Wimbledon* case, *PCIJ Reports*, 1923, Series A, No. 1, p. 25.

[47] Consider the following quotation: "The notion of the 'new legal order' owes less to an objective assessment of the legal characteristics of the Community law than to the descriptive language used by the European Court, and an understandable concern lest the familiar design of the Treaty be misunderstood by national tribunals more familiar with international instruments of more limited and specialised ambit". Derek Wyatt, "New Legal Order or Old", *European Law Review*, Vol. 7, 1982, p. 147.

treaties[48]. Some treaties – or provisions therein – are meant to have immediate effect at the municipal level once they have been ratified[49]. The Permanent Court of International Justice, in its 1928 opinion on *Jursidiction of the Courts of Danzig*, considered whether an international agreement creates rights or obligations only for the parties or could create rights or obligations be created for individuals and directly applicable in municipal courts. The Court stated that treaties do not, simply by their nature, provide for direct effect. They are not self-executing:

> It may be readily admitted that, according to well established principles of international law, [the agreement], being an international agreement, cannot, as such, create direct rights and obligations on private individuals[50].

However, the Court noted that in the case at hand, it appeared that the Parties had wished it to be so, and thus the sovereign right of States to undertake international agreements allowed for such direct effect:

> But it cannot be disputed that the very object of an international agreement, according to the intention of the contracting Parties, may be the adoption by the Parties of some definite rules creating individual rights and obligations and enforceable by the national courts. That there is such an intention in the present case can be established by reference to the terms of [the agreement][51].

In the same manner that the notion of "direct effect" is not unique to the European Community law, the notion of "supremacy" has had a long history and remains one of the bulwarks for determining jurisdiction of international courts. The International Court of Justice has noted that:

> It would be sufficient to recall the fundamental principle of international law that international law prevails over *domestic law*. This principle was endorsed by judicial deci-

[48] The notion of self-executing treaties is not foreign to the law of nations, however, as Pierre Pescatore rightly points out "the concept is nevertheless exceptional as far as international law is concerned". This affirms the proposition that the Community law is not qualitatively different, but given application in a quantitatively different manner. Pierre Pescatore, "International Law and Community Law – A Comparative Analysis", *Common Market Law Review*, Vol. 7, 1970, p. 174.

[49] Consider the following understanding of self-executing treaties that Carlos Vazquez puts forward as having evolved from United States' case-law: "At a general level, a self-executing treaty may be defined as a treaty that may be enforced in the courts without prior legislation by Congress [...]". Carlos Manuel Vazquez, "The Four Doctrines of Self-Executing Treaties", *The American Journal International Law*, Vol. 89, 1995, p. 695; see also Thomas Buergenthal, "Self-Executing and Non-Self-Executing Treaties in National and International Law", *Collected Courses of The Hague Academy of International Law*, Vol. 235, 1992, pp. 315-316.

[50] *Jursidiction of the Courts of Danzig*, *PCIJ Reports*, 1928, Series B, No. 15, p. 17.

[51] *Ibid.* Note that "[the agreement]" was a *Beamtenabkommen*: an agreement relating to officials as between the international city of Danzig and Poland.

> sion as long ago as the arbitral award of 14 September 1872 in the *Alabama* case between Great Britain and the United States, and has frequently been recalled since, for example in the case concerning the *Greco-Bulgarian "Communities"* in which the Permanent Court of International Justice laid it down that "it is a generally accepted principle of international law that in the relations between Powers who are contracting Parties to a treaty, the provisions of municipal law cannot prevail over those of the treaty"[52].

Community law, therefore, does not prevail over domestic law because it is a new legal order over and beyond that of the municipal systems of Community Members. It has supremacy because it is grounded in international treaties which, by their very nature, are to prevail over domestic law.

5.2. **The Aftermath of Maastricht**

If the Court maintained a fairyland existence during is early years, allowing it to build a near self-encapsulated system of law which it considered to be based on a constitutional charter, the international character of European law was driven home with the conclusion of the Maastricht Treaty. Later confirmed at Amsterdam, European integration in the post-Maastricht era has taken on a decidedly public international law bent. The fact that the European Court of Justice has been excluded completely from the second pillar and provided with limited jurisdiction over matters in the third pillar confirms its status as an international court. Beyond this, post-Maastricht sees a European Union which is no longer moving in concert towards European integration. The European Union is very much a reflection of a decentralized international system, whereby States are allowed to determine the obligations which they will subscribe to and the means by which they will assume them.

5.2.1. *Limited Jurisdiction*

While the Court of Justice maintained its jurisdiction over Community law (EC Law), it was in the newly created domain of European Law (EU Law) that confirmation emerged that that Court was functioning within the realm of public international law. It was not the jurisdiction that the Court of Justice was granted under Maastricht and Amsterdam which confirmed that it was acting as an international court; it was the jurisdiction that it was denied[53]. As Weiler and Trachtman point out:

---

[52] *Applicability of the Obligation to Arbitrate under Section 21 of the United Nations Headquarters Agreement of 26 June 1947, I.C.J. Reports*, 1988, p. 12.

[53] For the changes in the Court's jurisdiction after Amsterdam, consider: Ole Due, "The Impact

> Maastricht does represent a "rebellion" against that image of constitutionalism. It is clear that the principal raison d'être of the pillar structure, with the meticulous and explicit attempt to exclude the Court, was the wish of member States to operate outside the European constitutional structure[54].

The realization that member States could transform the fundamental character of European law called for a re-evaluation of the constitutional nature of the system. Those who advocated a "supranational" understanding of Communities based on a constitutional precept had to make way, under the three-pillar system, for the "intergovernmental" elements of the European Union. As Francis Synder notes in his general course at the European Academy of Law:

> [...] the debate still flickers with regard to the novelty of EC law as compared to international and national law. More importantly for the present purposes, it can in fact be suggested that the Maastricht Treaty on European Union (TEU) has altered significantly the terms of this debate. In particular, it expanded the intergovernmental – and hence public international law – features of the system, giving it much greater weight than ever before in relations to supranationalism and Community law[55].

Regarding pillars two and three, the States demonstrated that they, and not the Community institutions, maintained ultimate and sovereign control over the European Union. With respect to the second pillar (Title V) – Common Foreign and Security Policy (CFSP) – the Court has been denied any jurisdiction. The Court itself argued against this "artificial compartmentalization entailed by the system of three pillars"[56], but to no avail. As Anthony Arnull notes when considering the Report presented by the Court and leading up to the 1996 Conference which resulted in the Maastricht Treaty: "One is left in little doubt that the Court would prefer the pillar structure of the Union to be abandoned and its own jurisdiction to be extended to every aspect of the Union's activities"[57]. Yet the preference of the member States prevailed, and, as a result, their actions

of the Amsterdam Treaty upon the Court of Justice", *Fordham International Law Journal*, Vol. 22, 1999, pp. S48-S71; and Melchior Wathelet, "La Cour de justice: Acteur et objet des réformes du Traité d'Amsterdam", Yves Lejeune (ed.), *Le Traité d'Amsterdam*, 1999, pp. 127-144.

[54] Joseph Weiler with Joel P. Trachtman, "Symposium – Institutions for International Economic Integration: European Constitutionalism and its Discontents", *Journal of International Law & Business*, Vol. 17, 1996-1997, p. 371.

[55] Francis Snyder, "General Course on Constitutional Law of the European Union", *Collected Courses of the Academy of European Law*, Vol. 6, 1995, p. 51.

[56] As noted in Anthony Arnull, "The Community Judicature and the 1996 IGC", *European Law Review*, Vol. 20, 1995, p. 600.

[57] *Ibid.*

in foreign and security matters do not find their way into the provision establishing the jurisdiction of the European Court of Justice[58].

With the transfer of provisions related to visas, asylum and immigration policies from the third to the first pillar under the Amsterdam Treaty, the Court of Justice gained jurisdiction over these items[59]. What was left of the third pillar (Title VI) – Police and Judicial Cooperation in Criminal Matters – gave the Court variable amounts of limited jurisdiction[60]. The Court is excluded specifically from considering "the validity or proportionality" of measures taken by security forces "with regard to the maintenance of law and order and the safeguarding of internal security"[61]. On the other hand, the Court was given jurisdiction to provide preliminary rulings (as under Article 177) "on the validity and interpretation" of the other actions taken under the third pillar. The rub is, however, that this jurisdiction – unlike Community law – is not compulsory. Article 35(2) establishes a veritable "optional-clause" system whereby each State may "accept the jurisdiction of the Court to give preliminary rulings" regarding those actions. Having accepted the Court's jurisdiction to give preliminary rulings, States may allow any court to make referrals or may limit such requests to courts of last instance.

The "optional-clause" system as established by the third pillar of the EU Treaty is very much a concept derived from public international law. The International Court of Justice (ICJ) does not benefit, as the European Court of Justice, does from compulsory jurisdiction. Apart from gaining jurisdiction through the agreement of the parties or by way of compromissory clauses, the International Court of Justice may establish jurisdiction by reference to Article 36(2) of its Statute, i.e. the optional clause. The optional-clause system under the Statute of the ICJ is, by comparison to that of Article 35(2) EU, much more limiting. Under

[58] The Court's jurisdiction as is established by Article 46 EU:

The provisions of the Treaty establishing the European Community, the Treaty establishing the European Coal and Steel Community and the Treaty establishing the European Atomic Energy Community concerning the powers of the Court of Justice of the European Communities and the exercise of those powers shall apply only to the following provisions of this Treaty:

(a) provisions amending the Treaty establishing the European Economic Community with a view to establishing the European Community, the Treaty establishing the European Coal and Steel Community and the Treaty establishing the European Atomic Energy Community;
(b) provisions of Title VI, under the conditions provided for by Article 35;
(c) provisions of Title VII, under the conditions provided for by Article 11 of the Treaty establishing the European Community and Article 40 of this Treaty;
(d) Article 6(2) with regard to action of the institutions, insofar as the Court has jurisdiction under the Treaties establishing the European Communities and under this Treaty;
(e) Articles 46 to 53.

[59] At Maastricht, the third pillar had been headed: 'Justice and Home Affairs'.

[60] As noted in Article 46(b) EU, the Court's jurisdiction within the Provisions of Police and Judicial Cooperation in Criminal Matters is limited by provision of Article 35. See Appendix 6 for those provisions.

[61] Article 35(5) EU.

the system of the ICJ, States go beyond a simple unilateral declaration as to whether or not they will accept the jurisdiction of the Court; through reservations to their declarations, they also determine (and very often substantially limit) the parameters of that undertaking[62].

The States Parties' ability to penetrate even the constitutional order of EC law was made evident by Protocols to the Maastricht and Amsterdam treaties which aimed at "clos[ing] the door that seemed to have been left ajar"[63] by the Court. By the so-called "Barber" Protocol, States Parties amended the EC Treaty in such a manner as to reinterpret the European Court's judgment in the *Barber* case[64]. Such amendments, the prerogative of the Community members, has been seen as a "*hijacking of the acquis communautaire*", as it goes against the established case-law of the European Court and thus violates the "constitutional order" that exists[65]. Through such treaty amendments[66], it was demonstrated that even the self-encapsulated "constitutional" system of European Community Law was not impregnable to changes proposed by the State Parties[67]. The fact that even EC law is not impervious to the dictates of public international law owing to the ability of States to amend the "constitutional" order confirms its nature as deriving from the law of nations.

5.2.2. *Decentralization of the Union*

Despite its name, the European Union is decentralized by comparison with the European Community. The buzzwords "flexibility" and "variable geometry" have altered the fundamental precepts of European integration, allowing States to proceed at various speeds and on various levels. The disintegration of the ideal of one Europe is best demonstrated by the provisions of Title VII, regarding "Closer Cooperation", which provides, under the rubrics of "flexibility", that "some member States should be able, if they so wish, to integrate more closely than the

---

[62] See generally: Renata Szafarz, *The Compulsory Jurisdiction of the International Court of Justice*, 1993.

[63] Deirdre Curtin, "The Constitutional Structure of the Union: A Europe of Bits and Pieces", *Common Market Law Review*, Vol. 30, 1993, p. 49.

[64] *Barber v. Guardian Royal Exchange, Reports of the Cases before the Court*, 1990, p. 1889.

[65] Curtin, *op. cit.* n. 63, p. 46.

[66] Consider also the "Irish Abortion" Protocol as well as addition provisions which affect the jurisdiction of the Court within EC Law as noted in J. Weiler and Ulrich R. Haltern, "Constitutional or International? The Foundations of the Community Legal Order and the Question of Judicial *Kompetenz-Kompetenz*", in Anne-Marie Slaughter, A.S. Sweet, and J. Weiler (eds.), *The European Courts and National Courts*, 1998, pp. 335-336, n. 23.

[67] For a view from the European law perspective, see Tamara K Hervey, "Legal Issues concerning the *Barber* Protocol", David O'Keeffe and P.M. Twomey (eds.), *Legal Issues of the Maastricht Treaty*, 1994, pp. 329-337.

rest in some fields by means of an enhanced cooperation between them"[68]. By allowing States to proceed at various speeds the European Union is becoming decentralized, reflecting the nature of international relations rather than a movement toward a European federation.

The relationships established between member States which undermine communal integration in the post-Maastricht era has been termed "variable geometry". This notion has been defined as:

> attempts by member States to escape [the intensification of certain fundamentals of the EC legal order] through non-EC forms of cooperation in the framework of the European Union, the development of the idea that not all the rules of the EC Treaty apply to all the member States, and the entry by the majority of the member States into a separate Treaty, the Schengen Agreement, dealing with matters which might be thought to fall under the EC Treaty [...] all of which might generically be referred to as variable geometry[69].

While the Schengen Agreement has now been made part of EC Law by the Treaty of Amsterdam; the notion that European integration does not have to include all States is confirmed rather than rescinded by that Treaty. A case in point is this Agreement, as Schengen does not bind Ireland nor the United Kingdom, although it is now EC law[70]. The third phase of the Economic and Monetary Union (EMU) is a further example of "*Europe à la carte*" in that the United Kingdom decided to remain outside the movement toward full monetary integration with an option to opt into the "Euro" at some future time. The flip side of that coin is the stance of Denmark, which opted-out of the third phase of the EMU[71].

European integration has been significantly affected by the "intergovernmental" nature of the European Union. Yet, the European Union has focused the fact that it is grounded in international agreements, grounded in public international law. While it is regrettable that the

> result of the Maastricht summit is an umbrella Union threatening to lead to constitutional chaos; the potential victims are the cohesiveness and the unity and the concomitant power of a legal system painstakingly constructed over the course of some 30 odd years[72].

---

[68] Albertina Albors-Llorens, "Changes in the Jurisdiction of the European Court of Justice under the Treaty of Amsterdam", *Common Market Law Review*, Vol. 35, 1998, p. 1283.

[69] J.A. Usher, "Variable Geometry or Concentric Circles: Patterns for the European Union", *International and Comparative Law Quarterly*, Vol. 46, 1997, p. 243.

[70] Article 4, Protocol Integrating the Schengen *Acquis* into the Framework of the European Union (part of Protocol B.), Treaty of Amsterdam.

[71] Deirdre Curtin and Ronald van Ooik, "Denmark and the Edinburgh Summit: Maastricht without tears: A Legal Analysis", O'Keeffe and Twomey, *op. cit.* n. 67, pp. 361-362.

[72] Curtin, *op. cit.* n. 63, p. 67.

Yet this should not come as a surprise. The exclusion of the jurisdiction of the Court from the second pillar and the introduction of the optional-clause system for the third lays to waste the myth of the "constitutional charter of a Community". Andrew Duff writes that giving member States the possibility, under the third pillar, to "volunteer whether to agree or not to references by national courts to the Court of Justice [...] is an unprecedented provision, and may force the Court into delivering variable jurisprudence within the Union – with obvious attendant dangers for the integrity of the corpus of European Community law"[73].

The decentralization of the Union, allowing States to opt-in and opt-out of various provisions, is yet another reminder – if one were needed – that European law is international law[74]. Deirdre Curtin best summarizes the rude awakening, which has befallen those advocating the constitutional framework of European Law, when she writes:

> It must be said, at the heart of all this chaos and fragmentation [brought on by the Maastricht Treaty], the unique *sui generis* nature of the European Community, its true world historical significance, is being destroyed. The whole future and credibility of the Communities as a cohesive legal unit which confers rights on *individuals* and which enters into their national legal systems as an integral part of those systems, is at stake[75].

5.3. *"Herren der Verträge"*

As has been mentioned earlier, at its most fundamental level, the European Community law, and much more obviously European Union law, is public international law; thus confirming that the European Court is an international one. That is not to say that the European Court of Justice has not built for itself a sphere of competence over which it maintains exclusive jurisdiction. At the most fundamental level, however, it is the States, having created the treaty regime of the European Union, which maintain ultimate control over that Union. It is at the level of what H.L.A. Hart called the secondary rules – rules of change – that EU law is governed by international law. While EU and EC law may be termed the "primary rules" which set the activities that can or cannot be undertaken within

[73] Andrew Duff, *op. cit.* n. 12, p. 162.

[74] Paul Demaret writes: "Member States have in several instances been allowed to proceed at different speeds on the road towards greater integration on account of their varying degree of social and economic development. [...] Variable geometry or "l'Europe à la carte" means something else, in that the member States are not required to move towards the same objective. The Treaty of Maastricht offers concrete examples of both the variable speed and variable geometry concepts. The spread of the latter has some troublesome implications for the future of the Community as a coherent entity". Paul Demaret, "The Treaty Framework", O'Keeffe and Twomey, *op. cit.* n. 6, p. 8.

[75] Curtin, *op. cit.* n. 63, p. 67. Emphasis in the original.

the Union, it falls to public international law, as the rules of change, to "introduce new rules of the primary type, extinguish or modify old ones, or in various ways determine their incidence or control their operations"[76].

The ability for member States ultimately to "extinguish" the Union, the Community or the European Court itself if they see fit was noted during the ratification process of the Maastricht Treaty, when German nationals brought a case before their Constitutional Court, asking whether that Treaty conflicted with Germany's Basic Law. The Karlsruhe Court stated:

> The Federal Republic of Germany, therefore, even, after the Union Treaty comes into force, will remain a member of a federation of States, the common authority of which is derived from the States and can have binding effects within the German sovereign sphere by virtue of the German instruction that its law be applied. Germany is one of the "Masters of the Treaties" [Herren der Verträge], which have established their adherence to the Union Treaty concluded "for an unlimited period" with the intention of long-term membership, *but could also ultimately revoke that adherence by a contrary act.* [...] Germany thus preservers the quality of a sovereign State in its own right and the status of sovereign equality with other States within the meaning of Article 2(1) of the United Nations Charter of 26 June 1945[77].

Thus, as "*Herren der Verträge*", States Parties have the power to dissolve the system for the integration of Europe. Ultimately it is the dictates of States within the framework of public international law and not those emanating from the Court of Justice which carry the day[78]. To make this point plain, consider the unlikely scenario whereby the European Court would seek to maintain its status *sui generis* over the objections of the member States: would it not simply be a matter of the States turning off the financial tap to Luxembourg to witness the withering of the Court; leading eventually to its demise?

The ability to "modify" the Union has been discussed in great detail when considering the limitations on the jurisdiction of the European Court in the post-Maastricht era. It has been demonstrated that the States Parties have, for all in-

---

[76] Hart continues: "Rules of the first type impose duties; rules of the second type confer powers, public or private. Rules of the first type concern actions involving physical movement or changes; rules of the second type provide for operations which lead not merely to physical movement or change, but to the creation or variation of duties or obligations". H.L.A. Hart, *The Concept of Law*, 1961, p. 79.

[77] *Brunner et al. v. The European Union Treaty*, 12 October 1993, as in translation in *Common Market Law Review*, Vol. 31, 1994, pp.258-259. Emphasis added.

[78] Mattli and Slaugther point out the significance of the *Bundesverfassungsgericht* decision: "Many analysts of EU law are likely to reengage the debate concerning the relationship of EU law to international law more generally. The revisiting of these issues will be fueld by the German Constitutional Court's rejection of the landmark depiction by the ECJ of the EU legal order of *sui generis* in *Van Gend en Loos*, reemphasizing the status of the Treaty of Rome as a treaty and the role of the member states as the 'masters of the treaty' ". Walter Mattli and Anne-Marie Slaughter, "Revisiting the European Court of Justice", *International Organizations*, vol. 52, 1998, p. 206.

tents and purposes, "de-constitutionalized" European integration through amendments inserted in the Maastricht and Amsterdam Treaties. Bruno de Witte adds credence to this proposition when he writes that the Maastricht Treaty "confirmed the States' nearly unlimited control over the amendment procedure"[79]. De Witte goes on to conclude that the amending process is governed by international law:

> It is hard to deny that European Community law is a *very special* branch of international law. Yet, this Article is more concerned with the slightly different question of whether Community law *is* still a branch of international law. Many authors, particularly among the specialists of Community law, tend to deny this by pointing to the gradual constitutionalization of the Community system. But one crucial element of the Community legal order is still dominated by the spirit of international law, namely the procedure for its amendment[80].

One may ask, however, what is to be gained by demonstrating that the European Union, the European Community and the European Court of Justice are ultimately governed by public international law. The deconstruction of the edifice of European Law to demonstrate its public international law character may scandalize European lawyers, but it demonstrates to what extent international law can be metamorphosed. The European experience and the role that the European Court of Justice has played in promoting the rule of law within Europe can serve as a beacon for those who advocate the progressive development of the rule of law in other spheres of international relations.

6. The European Court of Justice and the Rule of Law

The success of the European Court of Justice as a supranational adjudicative organ cannot be denied. Within the sphere of European economic integration, it may well be said that the rule of law reigns. Why has the European Court been successful where the other courts and tribunals in this study have not? The answer lies in the willingness of States to allow it to be successful. The elements which typically limit the rule of law on the international level, be they *structural* in the form of voluntary adjudication or be they *political* in the various forms of non-cooperation by States; have all been absent from the evolution of the European Court. Thus, while the member States could have limited the mandate or effectiveness of the European Court at any time, they chose not to because it benefited their interest: the economic integration of Europe. Geoffrey Garrett points this out when he writes, "member governments could, if they so chose,

---

[79] Bruno De Witte, "Rules of Change in International Law: How Special is the European Community?", *Netherlands Yearbook of International Law*, Vol. 25, 1994, p. 320.

[80] *Ibid.*, p. 331. Emphasis in the original.

either ignore ECJ decisions or amend the legal order through multilateral action. The fact that governments have done neither to any important degree thus implies that the extant order serves their interests"[81].

Using the "executive-political branch of the Community [the Commission] as a political bellwether"[82], the Court pushed for economic integration where States themselves could not. Going beyond what had traditionally been considered the limits of international adjudication, by having municipal courts act as their proxies in giving direct effect to Community law, was tolerated because it was the outcome that States wished to achieve[83]. Hjalte Rasmussen writes, in his groundbreaking *On the Law and Policy in the European Court of Justice,* that:

> It is crucially important to note the indisputable successes which the Court has scored in converting the States to its own integrationist legal positions. Viewing how easily the States as a rule might be converted, *the Court's individual Members might legitimately have come to the conclusion that the States tacitly welcome integration by judicial fiat.*[84]

Had economic integration not been what the Member States wanted to achieve, they could have limited the Court by any one of the means which have been highlighted in this study. In fact, the post-Maastricht era demonstrates that where economic integration is concerned, the rule of law should persist, but where the issue is political integration in the form of a common internal and external policies, the States have balked. Excluding the second and third pillars from the obligatory jurisdiction of the European Court, simply reinforces willingness to allow the rule of law to reign where it benefits the political and economic elite: European economic integration.

7. Conclusion

The achievements of the European Court of Justice in upholding the rule of law in the domain of economic integration bear witness to the extent to which public international law can be dynamic. As Weiler and Trachtman put it, while

---

[81] Geoffrey Garrett, "The Politics of Legal Integration in the European Union", *International Organizations*, Vol. 49, 1995, p. 172.

[82] Helfer and Slaughter, *op. cit.* n. 27, p. 315. The notion of the Commission acting as a political bellwether is also mentioned in Garrett, *ibid.*, p. 178 and n. 17.

[83] Shapiro writes: "But the strong suspicion also arises that to some degree the member States knew what was happening and deliberately fostered a pro-integrationist judicial review as one element in the melange of pro- and anti-integrationist constitutional elements they were assembling in the Treaties". Martin Shapiro, "The European Court of Justice", in Craig and de Búrca, *op. cit.* n. 29, p. 333.

[84] Rasmussen, *op. cit.* n. 31, p. 291. Emphasis in the original.

"European Community law is no nirvana, it has contributed to our world-view both as a substantive demonstration of one development path and as the instrument of reformation of our perceptions of international law. It is time to recognize that European Community law is not a different species of law, but is a mutation of the same species"[85]. There is no reason to believe that the deviation from the course of the application of public international law, which has occurred in EC law, could not be reproduced elsewhere. The supranational character of European law, which allows for the European Court of Justice to put the municipal legal systems of States at the service of economic integration, could be used in most any sphere of public international law.

How could this be achieved? Helfer and Slaughter may provide some insights, as they have put forward a theoretical basis for achieving effective supranational adjudication in which they propose a checklist of items which can assist or impair attempts to bring the European experience to bear internationally[86]. The transfer of the experience of the European Court to public international law "may still seem a pipe dream to many, part of a utopian vision of global governance"[87]. Nevertheless Helfer and Slaughter argue that what is required is to shift the debate "away from the familiar tropes of realism versus idealism and towards the pragmatics of building regional and, perhaps, ultimately global communities of law"[88].

While the uniqueness of the European experience and that of the European Court of Justice may not be transplanted – as is – to the international level or even to other regions of the world, what the evolution of the European Court does provide is a new way of *thinking* about international law. The supranational elements, those "constitutional" areas of European law, demonstrate to what extent public international law can be dynamic. The challenge is not simply to try to lift the European experience to the international level. The challenge is to rethink the fundamental precepts of what international law is: and what it can achieve. The experience of the European Court of Justice shows us but one way out of this mental straitjacket.

---

[85] Weiler and Trachtman, *op. cit.* n. 54, p. 354.

[86] Laurence R. Helfer and Anne-Marie Slaughter, "Towards a Theory of Effective Supranational Adjudication", *Yale Law Journal*, vol. 107, 1997, pp. 276-391.

[87] *Ibid.*, p. 391.

[88] *Ibid.*

CONCLUSIONS

This examination of international adjudication has sought to highlight a number of international courts which were established during the twentieth century and to demonstrate the limits to their effectiveness. Despite the growth in the number of international courts which were established during the period under review, little progress was achieved in moving States towards accepting the principle that the rule of law should govern international relations. In fact, the powers which States have bestowed upon international adjudicative organs best reflect their reluctance towards being bound by the rule of law. The numerous impediments which have been highlighted throughout this study demonstrate the extent to which States, in a most fundamental manner, reject the dictates of fully integrating the rule of law on the international plane. Even in situations where adjudication has been consented to by States, various factors have limited its effectiveness and thus nullified full respect for the rule of law.

The sad reality of the deconstruction of the rule of law which resulted from the first five chapters of this study is that it is solely the intransigence of States which limits international adjudication and, by extension, the rule of law. The mental straitjacket in which international law currently finds itself in, is based on the way in which the notion of sovereignty is understood and applied. The existence of the European Court of Justice, however, demonstrates that sovereignty need not be an obstacle to promoting and implementing the rule of law. As a result, no plausible reason emerges that would preclude a move by international jurists to calling upon States to respect the rule of law in its integrity. It is simply a matter of unbridling international law so that it may serve the purposes of an international society based not on whims of power politics but on the agreed dictates of the rule of law.

The themes, which recur throughout this study, relate to the notion of sovereignty as a means of avoiding unwanted advances related to strengthening the rule of law through adjudication. While the case-study approach of examining various international courts has allowed this monograph to highlight the historical evolution of adjudication over the past one hundred years, this study's underlying motivation was to show the various limitations hampering the implementation of the rule of law.

Throughout most of the 1800s, the concept of sovereignty held a tight grip on international affairs. Despite efforts by various peace movements and other non-governmental groups, calls for obligatory arbitration could be rebuffed as the States' unfettered right to undertake war was unchallengable. This was so because the aim of introducing the notion of obligatory arbitration was not so much related to seeking an international community based on the rule of law, as it was providing an alternative to war as a means of settling disputes. The earliest attempts at limiting the edifice of State sovereignty to allow for adjudication as an alternative to war were achieved not by non-governmental actors, but by parliamentarians. The latter, having taken up the cause of various European and United States national arbitration leagues, sought and achieved the inclusion of compromissory clauses in a significant number of international treaties. While in Latin America, States flirted with the idea of general obligatory arbitration treaties, these agreements amounted to little more than paper tigers, as the States of Central and South America increasingly inserted into these treaties clauses which limited access to the process of arbitration. These limitations to allowing arbitration to go forward were, not surprisingly, couched in terms of 'sovereignty' or 'independence'.

The turning point for international arbitration – if not obligatory arbitration – can be dated from the late nineteenth century when, during its last three decades, a number of events allowed for a consolidation of voluntary arbitration within bounds acceptable to States. It was not until the 1872 *Alabama* arbitration that States came to realise that arbitration could be utilised fully as an instrument of international relations. This, coupled with the work of the Institute of International Law and the Inter-Parliamentary Union –, which was taking the notion of obligatory arbitration out of the hands of "Jews, Socialists, and hysterical women"[1] and making it more palatable to States by ridding it of most of its 'obligatory' nature.

The newly found taste for arbitration manifested itself during the Hague Peace Conferences of 1899 and 1907 where voluntary arbitration was made a talking point. Despite the fact that obligatory arbitration was discussed, States, however, proved unwilling to allow for obligatory arbitration in any circumstance. States were simply not going to allow the rule of law, that is, the application of law by third parties, to override their sovereign right to achieve their aims by the methods of their choice. As the German Kaiser put it, referring to the lead role of the Czar Nicholas II in the establishment of the Permanent Court of Arbitration: "to prevent the disgrace of the Tsar in the face of Europe I vote for this nonsense. But in my actions, now and hereafter, I shall trust and invoke only God and my sharp sword"[2]. Despite the pressure applied by the peace movements, the States had the game well in hand; not willing to sacrifice their unfettered (i.e.: sovereign) right to act internationally, they established the Permanent Court of Arbitration with its lack of permanence and its completely voluntary nature. The establishment and subsequent record of the Permanent Court of Arbitration over the last one hundred years speaks volumes as a testimony to the mentality of States

[1] Russian Foreign Minister Isvolski's private correspondence regarding the Second Hague Peace Conference. See Chapter 1, n. 84.

[2] See Chapter 1, n. 66.

and statesmen of the nineteenth century who started to pay lip service to the notion of the rule of law, but were, in all reality, not willing to give an inch towards its realisation.

Having consolidated the concept of arbitration *qua* adjudication as a tool of international relations, European States, having lived through the horrors of World War I, sought to solidify the peaceful settlement of disputes. Yet the Covenant of the League of Nations emphasised the notion that State sovereignty would override the obligation to respect the rule of law in its integrity by allowing the establishment of an international court which would only "be competent to hear and determine any dispute of an international character which the parties thereto submit to it"[3]. Despite attempts while drafting the Statute of the Permanent Court of Justice, by the Advisory Committee of Jurists in 1920, to orient the momentum established during the preceding fifty years towards obligatory adjudication, this was not to be. While the President of the Advisory Committee considered the time ripe for the conferring of obligatory jurisdiction to an international court, he based his assertion on the rhetoric used by States, in part, during the Hague Peace Conferences. As has been noted, the political organs of the League would have none of it.

As a result of negotiations mainly within the League Assembly, a compromise was reached which is very much in line with the decentralised nature of international relations: the 'optional-clause' system[4]. This compromise, which allows States to opt for obligatory adjudication, corresponds to the prerogatives inherent in the notion of State sovereignty. As Nicolas Politis noted in 1924, regarding the optional-clauses system, "if the League of Nations did not bless obligatory [adjudication], it did make place for the idea of an obligation within its judicial organization"[5]. Yet the idea has had limited effect on the international plane. This is especially true for the United Nations era, where but a limited number of newly independent States have made declarations under the optional-clause system, thus limiting the obligatory jurisdiction internationally. Further limits to the scope of obligatory jurisdiction result from the "multiplication of reservations [to declarations accepting the provision of Article 36(2)], and their willingness to give them the most extensive formulation possible"[6].

The examination of what has been termed the 'Hague System' of adjudication comprising the Permanent Court of Arbitration and the World Court, has shown that States have been unwilling to turn their rhetoric into reality. Given the opportunity to do so in 1899, 1907, 1920, and again in 1945, to establish an interna-

[3] Article 14 of the Covenant of the League of Nations, see Chapter 2, n. 2.

[4] The optional-clause system is found in Articles 36(2) of the Statute of the Permanent Court and, later, of the International Court of Justice.

[5] See Chapter 2, n. 4.

[6] Dailler, Patrick and Alain Pellet (eds.), *Nguen Quoc Dinh: Droit International Public*, 1994, p. 848. My translation.

tional system based on obligatory adjudication, they balked. Unwilling to give up the sovereign prerogative to deal with disputes as they saw fit, States drew what they saw as the indispensable limits to the expansion of a universal application of the rule of law. That the rule of law plays a lowly second to the concept of State sovereignty in international relations today, however, is not only evident from the limitations flowing from the voluntary nature of international adjudication. Even where States have established international courts and agreed to appear before them, the invocation of State sovereignty has allowed them, in certain situations, to further limit their effectiveness.

Mention has been made of the decentralised nature of international relations which not only enables States to limit their obligations *vis-à-vis* international courts, but also allows them, through the invocation of their sovereignty, not to appear before a court or not to comply with that court's orders or judgements. As an international adjudicative organ has limited power in the post-adjudicative phase, it is often up to the States themselves to determine whether they will respect the dictates of a court[7]. The legacy of the Central American Court of Justice is the most pertinent example of what can happen when a State, though having accepted the jurisdiction of an international court, no longer respects its rulings.

With the tacit support of the United States of America, Nicaragua, having accepted the jurisdiction of the Central American Court of Justice in 1908, sought to challenge that Court's competence to render judgements in cases involving Costa Rica and El Salvador regarding the Chamorro-Bryan Treaty. As has been noted, Nicaragua challenged the Court's competence as "infringing upon Nicaragua's sovereign right to enter into a treaty"[8]. By donning the mantle of State sovereignty, Nicaragua defied the Court, leaving this first-ever permanent international court with compulsory jurisdiction to its fate – it folded when its ten-year mandate was not renewed. Under the pretence that it "holds as offensive to her dignity as a free and independent nation any discussion of acts pertaining to her sovereignty"[9], Nicaragua flaunted the authority of this international body. Yet, as the Court's Registrar rightly noted that despite Nicaragua's demand for "the exclusion from the cognizance of the Court of questions that affect sovereignty", the Statute of the Court is "not impressed with those limitations, either expressly or tacitly"[10]. No matter, as shown by the legacy of the Central American Court of Justice, the extent to which sovereignty allows a State to determine itself whether it will or – as the case at hand poignantly attests – will not respect the rule of law, knows no bounds.

---

[7] With, of course, the proviso, noted at Chapter 3, n. 94, regarding the political organs of international organisations which have been given the responsible for ensuring compliance of decisions of international courts.

[8] See Chapter 3, n. 73.

[9] See Chapter 3, n. 67.

[10] See Chapter 3, n. 73.

The sovereign right to enter into a treaty, which Nicaragua attempted to use as a justification for its unwillingness to follow the Court's dictates, has been used in a more general manner by States to limit access to international adjudication. This is made plain in the evaluation of the Inter-American system for the protection of human right where, as opposed to the European system which both shared a Commission and Court from 1980-1998, the Inter-American mechanisms appear to have been designed to limit the effective redress of human rights violations. Confirmation of this assertion may be found in the concurring opinion of Judge Rodolfo Piza Escalante, accompanying the Judgement in the first contentious case dealt with by the Court:

> I have come to the conclusion that unfortunately the system of the Convention appears to make [human rights protection] impossible because the American States in drafting it did not wish to accept the establishment of a swift and effective jurisdictional system but rather they hobbled it by interposing the impediment of the Commission, by establishing a veritable obstacle course that is almost insurmountable, on the long and arduous road that the basic rights of the individual are forced to travel[11].

Likewise, the inability of the Inter-American Court even to hear a case during its early life was also considered worthy of comment by a member of the Court. Judge Máximo Cisneros, having sat on the Court for six years noted:

> I feel [a sense of frustration] in leaving the Court before it has had the opportunity to hear a single case of a violation of human rights, in spite of the sad realities of our America in this field[12].

One must note at this point the words of Daniel Bardonnet who states that it is "appropriate to remember the common-sense reality that international disputes are not settled by magic formulas or by the proliferation of institutions. Bodies of this type have only such powers as are bestowed upon them by States"[13]. Thus we have witnessed the limiting of the effectiveness of international adjudicative organs by States through the establishment of constitutive documents which, for instance, have endowed judicial organs with voluntary jurisdiction, or instituted an optional-clause system, or laid down labyrinthine procedures. Further, States have sought to limit the output of adjudicative organs by way of insufficient financing. The study on the Inter-American Court of Human Rights clearly indicates that that Court's ability to function and its very independence remains at the mercy of funding provided by the community of American States, as represented

---

[11] See Chapter 4, n. 59.

[12] See Chapter 4, n. 100.

[13] Daniel Bardonnet, "Introduction of the Subject", Daniel Bardonnet (ed.), *The Peaceful Settlement of International Disputes in Europe: Future Prospects*, Workshop at the Hague Academy of International Law, 6-8 September 1990, 1991, p. 19.

by the OAS General Assembly, or by its host State, Costa Rica. The conclusions to be drawn from the comparison between the American and European systems during the 1980-1998 period is that, despite similar constitutive instruments, their effectiveness greatly varied. Thus, even when States have accepted the principle of international adjudication and subscribed to its precepts, one must go beyond the texts to gauge the true extent of respect for the rule of law.

Beyond the limitations which are imposed by States on a full realization of the rule of law within the international system, this study has considered the role of the judge as guardians of, not only international law, but international justice. An examination of the case-law of the International Criminal Tribunal for the former Yugoslavia has shown that State sovereignty was not the only factor limiting full respect for the rule of law on the international level. Various examples brought forward seem to show that individuals were mistakenly detained, kidnapped, or wrongly accused. This appears to demonstrate a pattern whereby the accused's right to a fair trial has been supplanted by the aim of seeking to establish a visibly effective international criminal law system, the main goal of which is placing individuals behind bars. By moving to establish "victim's justice"[14] instead of simply "justice", the members of the Tribunal find themselves on the same slippery path which was followed at Nuremberg and Tokyo. The rule of law, then, as has been made evident in Chapter 5, is ultimately in the hands of international judges; it is for them to guard it, insulated as it may be by the dictates of State sovereignty, and to apply it to its fullest extent, lest they themselves be judged too harshly by posterity.

In many respects the examination devoted to the functioning of the European Court of Justice is an implicit conclusion to this study. The supranational jurisdiction bestowed by European States makes the European Court the true guardian of the rule of law where the European Community is concerned[15]. Yet, for the Court to be able to consolidate its position as the guardian of the European system, it had to create a legal fiction, seeking as it did to slip from its public international law origins to that of a "new legal order"[16]. This new order was one "based on the rule of law, inasmuch as neither its Member States nor its institutions can avoid a review of the question whether the measures adopted by them are in conformity with the basic constitutional charter, the Treaty [Establishing the European Economic Community (1957)]"[17]. Yet the pronouncement by the German Constitutional Court in the *Brunner et al.* case, coupled with the changes to the European order brought by the Maastricht and Amsterdam Treaties, clearly reflect that the Court has not escaped its international law origins.

The reason for emphasising the public international law nature of the European Union is to demonstrate to what extent international law can be dynamic.

---

[14] See Chapter 5, n. 119.

[16] See the excerpt of the *Van Gend en Loos* case as cited at n. 23, Chapter 6.

[17] See the excerpt of the *Les Verts* case as cited at n. 24, Chapter 6.

The role of the European Court shows the extent to which international adjudication can further the rule of law if States lift the veil of sovereignty. In reality, very little prevents States from respecting the rule of international law and the European Court of Justice presents us with one way out of this mental straitjacket. The one-hundredth anniversary of the establishment of the first international adjudicative organ, the Permanent Court of Arbitration, should be a time to reflect on the evolution of international adjudication which has taken place over the past century. Having studied international adjudication from the perspective of the attainment of full respect for the rule of law, no plausible reason emerges which would preclude striving for that goal. The experience of the European Court of Justice confirms this assertion.

States, it would seem, are limited only by their own intransigence to be bound by the rules of international law, using 'sovereignty' as their excuse. While the conclusion of international legal instruments will, in all probability, not only continue but accelerate in the future, can this be said to be true progress? No evolution in the nature of international law will occur by increasing the quantity of measures; it is their quality of application that matters. Any progress of international law passes through progress in international adjudication. This study has highlighted the limitation to the rule of law; but it has also made clear, through the examination of the European Court of Justice, that such limits can be overcome. It is up to those who would advocate the rule of law on the international level to make this plain to States, to learn from the mistakes of the early peace movements, and to be insistent that the rule of law be respected in its integality despite assertions that sovereignty must triumph.

APPENDICES

APPENDIX 1

Part IV. (International Arbitration) of the 1907 Convention for the Pacific Settlement of International Disputes[1]

Chapter I. The System of Arbitration

Article 37

International arbitration has for its object the settlement of disputes between States by Judges of their own choice and on the basis of respect for law. Recourse to arbitration implies an engagement to submit in good faith to the Award.

Article 38

In questions of a legal nature, and especially in the interpretation or application of International Conventions, arbitration is recognized by the Contracting Powers as the most effective, and, at the same time, the most equitable means of settling disputes which diplomacy has failed to settle.

Consequently, it would be desirable that, in disputes about the above-mentioned questions, the Contracting Powers should, if the case arose, have recourse to arbitration, in so far as circumstances permit.

Article 39

The Arbitration Convention is concluded for questions already existing or for questions which may arise eventually.

It may embrace any dispute or only disputes of a certain category.

Article 40

Independently of general or private Treaties expressly stipulating recourse to arbitration as obligatory on the Contracting Powers, the said Powers reserve to themselves the right of concluding new Agreements, general or particular, with a view to extending compulsory arbitration to all cases which they may consider it possible to submit to it.

Chapter II. The Permanent Court of Arbitration

Article 41

With the object of facilitating an immediate recourse to arbitration for international differences, which it has not been possible to settle by diplomacy, the Contracting Powers undertake to maintain the Permanent Court of Arbitration, as established by the First

[1] Permanent Court of Arbitration, *Basic Documents: Conventions, Rules, Model Clauses and Guidelines*, 1998.

Peace Conference, accessible at all times, and operating, unless otherwise stipulated by the parties, in accordance with the rules of procedure inserted in the present Convention.

Article 42

The Permanent Court is competent for all arbitration cases, unless the parties agree to institute a special Tribunal.

Article 43

The Permanent Court sits at The Hague.

An International Bureau serves as registry for the Court. It is the channel for communications relative to the meetings of the Court; it has charge of the archives and conducts all the administrative business.

The Contracting Powers undertake to communicate to the Bureau, as soon as possible, a certified copy of any conditions of arbitration arrived at between them and of any Award concerning them delivered by a special Tribunal.

They likewise undertake to communicate to the Bureau the laws, regulations, and documents eventually showing the execution of the Awards given by the Court.

Article 44

Each Contracting Power selects four persons at the most, of known competency in questions of international law, of the highest moral reputation, and disposed to accept the duties of Arbitrator.

The persons thus elected are inscribed, as Members of the Court, in a list which shall be notified to all the Contracting Powers by the Bureau.

Any alteration in the list of Arbitrators is brought by the Bureau to the knowledge of the Contracting Powers.

Two or more Powers may agree on the selection in common of one or more Members.

The same person can be selected by different Powers. The Members of the Court are appointed for a term of six years. These appointments are renewable.

Should a Member of the Court die or resign, the same procedure is followed for filling the vacancy as was followed for appointing him. In this case the appointment is made for a fresh period of six years.

Article 45

When the Contracting Powers wish to have recourse to the Permanent Court for the settlement of a difference which has arisen between them, the Arbitrators called upon to form the Tribunal with jurisdiction to decide this difference must be chosen from the general list of Members of the Court.

Failing the direct agreement of the parties on the composition of the Arbitration Tribunal, the following course shall be pursued:

> Each party appoints two Arbitrators, of whom one only can be its national or chosen from among the persons selected by it as Members of the Permanent Court. These Arbitrators together choose an Umpire.
>
> If the votes are equally divided, the choice of the Umpire is intrusted to a third Power, selected by the parties by common accord.
>
> If an agreement is not arrived at on this subject each party selects a different Power, and the choice of the Umpire is made in concert by the Powers thus selected.

If, within two months' time, these two Powers cannot come to an agreement, each of them presents two candidates taken from the list of Members of the Permanent Court, exclusive of the members selected by the parties and not being nationals of either of them. Drawing lots determines which of the candidates thus presented shall be Umpire.

Article 46

The Tribunal being thus composed, the parties notify to the Bureau their determination to have recourse to the Court, the text of their 'Compromis', and the names of the Arbitrators.

The Bureau communicates without delay to each Arbitrator the 'Compromis', and the names of the other members of the Tribunal.

The Tribunal assembles at the date fixed by the parties. The Bureau makes the necessary arrangements for the meeting.

The members of the Tribunal, in the exercise of their duties and out of their own country, enjoy diplomatic privileges and immunities.

Article 47

The Bureau is authorized to place its offices and staff at the disposal of the Contracting Powers for the use of any special Board of Arbitration.

The jurisdiction of the Permanent Court may, within the conditions laid down in the regulations, be extended to disputes between non-Contracting Powers or between Contracting Powers and non-Contracting Powers, if the parties are agreed on recourse to this Tribunal.

Article 48

The Contracting Powers consider it their duty, if a serious dispute threatens to break out between two or more of them, to remind these latter that the Permanent Court is open to them.

Consequently, they declare that the fact of reminding the parties at variance of the provisions of the present Convention, and the advice given to them, in the highest interests of peace, to have recourse to the Permanent Court, can only be regarded as friendly actions.

In case of dispute between two Powers, one of them can always address to the International Bureau a note containing a declaration that it would be ready to submit the dispute to arbitration.

The Bureau must at once inform the other Power of the declaration.

Article 49

The Permanent Administrative Council, composed of the Diplomatic Representatives of the Contracting Powers accredited to The Hague and of the Netherland Minister for Foreign Affairs, who will act as President, is charged with the direction and control of the International Bureau.

The Council settles its rules of procedure and all other necessary regulations.

It decides all questions of administration which may arise with regard to the operations of the Court.

It has entire control over the appointment, suspension, or dismissal of the officials and employees of the Bureau.

It fixes the payments and salaries, and controls the general expenditure.

At meetings duly summoned the presence of nine members is sufficient to render valid the discussions of the Council. The decisions are taken by a majority of votes.

The Council communicates to the Contracting Powers without delay the regulations adopted by it. It furnishes them with an annual Report on the labours of the Court, the working of the administration, and the expenditure. The Report likewise contains a résumé of what is important in the documents communicated to the Bureau by the Powers in virtue of Article 43, paragraphs 3 and 4.

Article 50

The expenses of the Bureau shall be borne by the Contracting Powers in the proportion fixed for the International Bureau of the Universal Postal Union.

The expenses to be charged to the adhering Powers shall be reckoned from the date on which their adhesion comes into force.

Chapter III. Arbitration Procedure

Article 51

With a view to encouraging the development of arbitration, the Contracting Powers have agreed on the following rules, which are applicable to arbitration procedure, unless other rules have been agreed on by the parties.

Article 52

The Powers which have recourse to arbitration sign a 'Compromis', in which the subject of the dispute is clearly defined, the time allowed for appointing Arbitrators, the form, order, and time in which the communication referred to in Article 63 must be made, and the amount of the sum which each party must deposit in advance to defray the expenses.

The 'Compromis' likewise defines, if there is occasion, the manner of appointing Arbitrators, any special powers which may eventually belong to the Tribunal, where it shall meet, the language it shall use, and the languages the employment of which shall be authorized before it, and, generally speaking, all the conditions on which the parties are agreed.

Article 53

The Permanent Court is competent to settle the 'Compromis', if the parties are agreed to have recourse to it for the purpose.

It is similarly competent, even if the request is only made by one of the parties, when all attempts to reach an understanding through the diplomatic channel have failed, in the case of:

1. A dispute covered by a general Treaty of Arbitration concluded or renewed after the present Convention has come into force, and providing for a 'Compromis' in all disputes and not either explicitly or implicitly excluding the settlement of the 'Compromis' from the competence of the Court. Recourse cannot, however, be had to the Court if the other party declares that in its opinion the dispute does not belong to the category of disputes which can be submitted to compulsory arbitration, unless the Treaty of Arbitration confers upon the Arbitration Tribunal the power of deciding this preliminary question.
2. A dispute arising from contract debts claimed from one Power by another Power as

due to its nationals, and for the settlement of which the offer of arbitration has been accepted. This arrangement is not applicable if acceptance is subject to the condition that the 'Compromis' should be settled in some other way.

Article 54

In the cases contemplated in the preceding Article, the 'Compromis' shall be settled by a Commission consisting of five members selected in the manner arranged for in Article 45, paragraphs 3 to 6.

The fifth member is President of the Commission ex officio.

Article 55

The duties of Arbitrator may be conferred on one Arbitrator alone or on several Arbitrators selected by the parties as they please, or chosen by them from the Members of the Permanent Court of Arbitration established by the present Convention.

Failing the constitution of the Tribunal by direct agreement between the parties, the course referred to in Article 45, paragraphs 3 to 6, is followed.

Article 56

When a Sovereign or the Chief of a State is chosen as Arbitrator, the arbitration procedure is settled by him.

Article 57

The Umpire is President of the Tribunal ex officio.

When the Tribunal does not include an Umpire, it appoints its own President.

Article 58

When the 'Compromis' is settled by a Commission, as contemplated in Article 54, and in the absence of an agreement to the contrary, the Commission itself shall form the Arbitration Tribunal.

Article 59

Should one of the Arbitrators either die, retire, or be unable for any reason whatever to discharge his functions, the same procedure is followed for filling the vacancy as was followed for appointing him.

Article 60

The Tribunal sits at The Hague, unless some other place is selected by the parties.

The Tribunal can only sit in the territory of a third Power with the latter's consent.

The place of meeting once fixed cannot be altered by the Tribunal, except with the consent of the parties.

Article 61

If the question as to what languages are to be used has not been settled by the 'Compromis', it shall be decided by the Tribunal.

Article 62

The parties are entitled to appoint special agents to attend the Tribunal to act as intermediaries between themselves and the Tribunal.

They are further authorized to retain for the defence of their rights and interests before the Tribunal counsel or advocates appointed by themselves for this purpose.

The Members of the permanent Court may not act as agents, counsel, or advocates except on behalf of the Power which appointed them Members of the Court.

Article 63

As a general rule, arbitration procedure comprises two distinct phases: pleadings and oral discussions.

The pleadings consist in the communication by the respective agents to the members of the Tribunal and the opposite party of cases, counter-cases, and, if necessary, of replies; the parties annex thereto all papers and documents called for in the case. This communication shall be made either directly or through the intermediary of the International Bureau, in the order and within the time fixed by the 'Compromis'.

The time fixed by the 'Compromis' may be extended by mutual agreement by the parties, or by the Tribunal when the latter considers it necessary for the purpose of reaching a just decision.

The discussions consists in the oral development before the Tribunal of the arguments of the parties.

Article 64

A certified copy of every document produced by one party must be communicated to the other party.

Article 65

Unless special circumstances arise, the Tribunal does not meet until the pleadings are closed.

Article 66

The discussions are under the control of the President. They are only public if it be so decided by the Tribunal, with the assent of the parties.

They are recorded in minutes drawn up by the Secretaries appointed by the President. These minutes are signed by the President and by one of the Secretaries and alone have an authentic character.

Article 67

After the close of the pleadings, the Tribunal is entitled to refuse discussion of all new papers or documents which one of the parties may wish to submit to it without the consent of the other party.

Article 68

The Tribunal is free to take into consideration new papers of documents to which its attention may be drawn by the agents or counsel of the parties.

In this case, the Tribunal has the right to require the production of these papers or documents, but is obliged to make them known to the opposite party.

Article 69

The Tribunal can, besides, require from the agents of the parties the production of all papers, and can demand all necessary explanations. In case of refusal the Tribunal takes note of it.

Article 70

The agents and the counsel of the parties are authorized to present orally to the Tribunal all the arguments they may consider expedient in defence of their case.

Article 71

They are entitled to raise objections and points. The decisions of the Tribunal on these points are final and cannot form the subject of any subsequent discussion.

Article 72

The members of the Tribunal are entitled to put questions to the agents and counsel of the parties, and to ask them for explanations on doubtful points.

Neither the questions put, nor the remarks made by members of the Tribunal in the course of the discussions, can be regarded as an expression of opinion by the Tribunal in general or by its members in particular.

Article 73

The Tribunal is authorized to declare its competence in interpreting the 'Compromis', as well as the other Treaties which may be invoked, and in applying the principles of law.

Article 74

The Tribunal is entitled to issue rules of procedure for the conduct of the case, to decide the forms, order, and time in which each party must conclude its arguments, and to arrange all the formalities required for dealing with the evidence.

Article 75

The parties undertake to supply the Tribunal, as fully as they consider possible, with all the information required for deciding the case.

Article 76

For all notices which the Tribunal has to serve in the territory of a third Contracting Power, the Tribunal shall apply direct to the Government of that Power. The same rule applies in the case of steps being taken to procure evidence on the spot.

The requests for this purpose are to be executed as far as the means at the disposal of the Power applied to under its municipal law allow. They cannot be rejected unless the Power in question considers them calculated to impair its own sovereign rights or its safety.

The Court will equally be always entitled to act through the Power on whose territory it sits.

Article 77

When the agents and counsel of the parties have submitted all the explanations and evidence in support of their case the President shall declare the discussion closed.

Article 78

The Tribunal considers its decisions in private and the proceedings remain secret.

All questions are decided by a majority of the members of the Tribunal.

Article 79

The Award must give the reasons on which it is based. It contains the names of the Arbitrators; it is signed by the President and Registrar or by the Secretary acting as Registrar.

Article 80

The Award is read out in public sitting, the agents and counsel of the parties being present or duly summoned to attend.

Article 81

The Award, duly pronounced and notified to the agents of the parties, settles the dispute definitively and without appeal.

Article 82

Any dispute arising between the parties as to the interpretation and execution of the Award shall, in the absence of an Agreement to the contrary, be submitted to the Tribunal which pronounced it.

Article 83

The parties can reserve in the 'Compromis' the right to demand the revision of the Award.

In this case and unless there be an Agreement to the contrary, the demand must be addressed to the Tribunal which pronounced the Award. It can only be made on the ground of the discovery of some new fact calculated to exercise a decisive influence upon the Award and which was unknown to the Tribunal and to the party which demanded the revision at the time the discussion was closed.

Proceedings for revision can only be instituted by a decision of the Tribunal expressly recording the existence of the new fact, recognizing in it the character described in the preceding paragraph, and declaring the demand admissible on this ground.

The 'Compromis' fixes the period within which the demand for revision must be made.

Article 84

The Award is not binding except on the parties in dispute.

When it concerns the interpretation of a Convention to which Powers other than those in dispute are parties, they shall inform all the Signatory Powers in good time. Each of these Powers is entitled to intervene in the case. If one or more avail themselves of this right, the interpretation contained in the Award is equally binding on them.

Article 85

Each party pays its own expenses and an equal share of the expenses of the Tribunal.

Chapter IV. Arbitration by Summary Procedure

Article 86

With a view to facilitating the working of the system of arbitration in disputes admitting of a summary procedure, the Contracting Powers adopt the following rules, which shall be observed in the absence of other arrangements and subject to the reservation that the provisions of Chapter III apply so far as may be.

Article 87

Each of the parties in dispute appoints an Arbitrator. The two Arbitrators thus selected choose an Umpire. If they do not agree on this point, each of them proposes two candidates taken from the general list of the Members of the Permanent Court exclusive of the members appointed by either of the parties and not being nationals of either of them; which of the candidates thus proposed shall be the Umpire is determined by lot.

The Umpire presides over the Tribunal, which gives its decisions by a majority of votes.

Article 88

In the absence of any previous agreement the Tribunal, as soon as it is formed, settles the time within which the two parties must submit their respective cases to it.

Article 89

Each party is represented before the Tribunal by an agent, who serves as intermediary between the Tribunal and the Government who appointed him.

Article 90

The proceedings are conducted exclusively in writing. Each party, however, is entitled to ask that witnesses and experts should be called. The Tribunal has, for its part, the right to demand oral explanations from the agents of the two parties, as well as from the experts and witnesses whose appearance in Court it may consider useful.

APPENDIX 2

Statute of the International Court of Justice

Article 1

The International Court of Justice established by the Charter of the United Nations as the principal judicial organ of the United Nations shall be constituted and shall function in accordance with the provisions of the present Statute.

Chapter I: Organization of the Court

Article 2

The Court shall be composed of a body of independent judges, elected regardless of their nationality from among persons of high moral character, who possess the qualifications required in their respective countries for appointment to the highest judicial offices, or are jurisconsults of recognized competence in international law.

Article 3

1. The Court shall consist of fifteen members, no two of whom may be nationals of the same state.
2. A person who for the purposes of membership in the Court could be regarded as a national of more than one state shall be deemed to be a national of the one in which he ordinarily exercises civil and political rights.

Article 4

1. The members of the Court shall be elected by the General Assembly and by the Security Council from a list of persons nominated by the national groups in the Permanent Court of Arbitration, in accordance with the following provisions.
2. In the case of Members of the United Nations not represented in the Permanent Court of Arbitration, candidates shall be nominated by national groups appointed for this purpose by their governments under the same conditions as those prescribed for members of the Permanent Court of Arbitration by Article 44 of the Convention of The Hague of 1907 for the pacific settlement of international disputes.
3. The conditions under which a state which is a party to the present Statute but is not a Member of the United Nations may participate in electing the members of the Court shall, in the absence of a special agreement, be laid down by the General Assembly upon recommendation of the Security Council.

Article 5

1. At least three months before the date of the election, the Secretary-General of the United Nations shall address a written request to the members of the Permanent Court of Arbitration belonging to the states which are parties to the present Statute, and to the members of the national groups appointed under Article 4, paragraph 2, inviting them to

undertake, within a given time, by national groups, the nomination of persons in a position to accept the duties of a member of the Court.
2. No group may nominate more than four persons, not more than two of whom shall be of their own nationality. In no case may the number of candidates nominated by a group be more than double the number of seats to be filled.

Article 6

Before making these nominations, each national group is recommended to consult its highest court of justice, its legal faculties and schools of law, and its national academies and national sections of international academies devoted to the study of law.

Article 7

1. The Secretary-General shall prepare a list in alphabetical order of all the persons thus nominated. Save as provided in Article 12, paragraph 2, these shall be the only persons eligible.
2. The Secretary-General shall submit this list to the General Assembly and to the Security Council.

Article 8

The General Assembly and the Security Council shall proceed independently of one another to elect the members of the Court.

Article 9

At every election, the electors shall bear in mind not only that the persons to be elected should individually possess the qualifications required, but also that in the body as a whole the representation of the main forms of civilization and of the principal legal systems of the world should be assured.

Article 10

1. Those candidates who obtain an absolute majority of votes in the General Assembly and in the Security Council shall be considered as elected.
2. Any vote of the Security Council, whether for the election of judges or for the appointment of members of the conference envisaged in Article 12, shall be taken without any distinction between permanent and non-permanent members of the Security Council.
3. In the event of more than one national of the same state obtaining an absolute majority of the votes both of the General Assembly and of the Security Council, the eldest of these only shall be considered as elected.

Article 11

If, after the first meeting held for the purpose of the election, one or more seats remain to be filled, a second and, if necessary, a third meeting shall take place.

Article 12

1. If, after the third meeting, one or more seats still remain unfilled, a joint conference consisting of six members, three appointed by the General Assembly and three by the Security Council, may be formed at any time at the request of either the General Assembly or the Security Council, for the purpose of choosing by the vote of an absolute majority

one name for each seat still vacant, to submit to the General Assembly and the Security Council for their respective acceptance.
2. If the joint conference is unanimously agreed upon any person who fulfills the required conditions, he may be included in its list, even though he was not included in the list of nominations referred to in Article 7.
3. If the joint conference is satisfied that it will not be successful in procuring an election, those members of the Court who have already been elected shall, within a period to be fixed by the Security Council, proceed to fill the vacant seats by selection from among those candidates who have obtained votes either in the General Assembly or in the Security Council.
4. In the event of an equality of votes among the judges, the eldest judge shall have a casting vote.

Article 13

1. The members of the Court shall be elected for nine years and may be re-elected; provided, however, that of the judges elected at the first election, the terms of five judges shall expire at the end of three years and the terms of five more judges shall expire at the end of six years.
2. The judges whose terms are to expire at the end of the above-mentioned initial periods of three and six years shall be chosen by lot to be drawn by the Secretary-General immediately after the first election has been completed.
3. The members of the Court shall continue to discharge their duties until their places have been filled. Though replaced, they shall finish any cases which they may have begun.
4. In the case of the resignation of a member of the Court, the resignation shall be addressed to the President of the Court for transmission to the Secretary-General. This last notification makes the place vacant.

Article 14

Vacancies shall be filled by the same method as that laid down for the first election subject to the following provision: the Secretary-General shall, within one month of the occurrence of the vacancy, proceed to issue the invitations provided for in Article 5, and the date of the election shall be fixed by the Security Council.

Article 15

A member of the Court elected to replace a member whose term of office has not expired shall hold office for the remainder of his predecessor's term.

Article 16

1. No member of the Court may exercise any political or administrative function, or engage in any other occupation of a professional nature.
2. Any doubt on this point shall be settled by the decision of the Court.

Article 17

1. No member of the Court may act as agent, counsel, or advocate in any case.
2. No member may participate in the decision of any case in which he has previously taken part as agent, counsel, or advocate for one of the parties, or as a member of a na-

tional or international court, or of a commission of enquiry, or in any other capacity.
3. Any doubt on this point shall be settled by the decision of the Court.

Article 18

1. No member of the Court can be dismissed unless, in the unanimous opinion of the other members, he has ceased to fulfill the required conditions.
2. Formal notification thereof shall be made to the Secretary-General by the Registrar.
3. This notification makes the place vacant.

Article 19

The members of the Court, when engaged on the business of the Court, shall enjoy diplomatic privileges and immunities.

Article 20

Every member of the Court shall, before taking up his duties, make a solemn declaration in open court that he will exercise his powers impartially and conscientiously.

Article 21

1. The Court shall elect its President and Vice-President for three years; they may be re-elected.
2. The Court shall appoint its Registrar and may provide for the appointment of such other officers as may be necessary.

Article 22

1. The seat of the Court shall be established at The Hague. This, however, shall not prevent the Court from sitting and exercising its functions elsewhere whenever the Court considers it desirable.
2. The President and the Registrar shall reside at the seat of the Court.

Article 23

1. The Court shall remain permanently in session, except during the judicial vacations, the dates and duration of which shall be fixed by the Court.
2. Members of the Court are entitled to periodic leave, the dates and duration of which shall be fixed by the Court, having in mind the distance between The Hague and the home of each judge.
3. Members of the Court shall be bound, unless they are on leave or prevented from attending by illness or other serious reasons duly explained to the President, to hold themselves permanently at the disposal of the Court.

Article 24

1. If, for some special reason, a member of the Court considers that he should not take part in the decision of a particular case, he shall so inform the President.
2. If the President considers that for some special reason one of the members of the Court should not sit in a particular case, he shall give him notice accordingly.
3. If in any such case the member Court and the President disagree, the matter shall be settled by the decision of the Court.

Article 25

1. The full Court shall sit except when it is expressly provided otherwise in the present Statute.
2. Subject to the condition that the number of judges available to constitute the Court is not thereby reduced below eleven, the Rules of the Court may provide for allowing one or more judges, according to circumstances and in rotation, to be dispensed from sitting.
3. A quorum of nine judges shall suffice to constitute the Court.

Article 26

1. The Court may from time to time form one or more chambers, composed of three or more judges as the Court may determine, for dealing with particular categories of cases; for example, labour cases and cases relating to transit and communications.
2. The Court may at any time form a chamber for dealing with a particular case. The number of judges to constitute such a chamber shall be determined by the Court with the approval of the parties.
3. Cases shall be heard and determined by the chambers provided for in this article if the parties so request.

Article 27

A judgment given by any of the chambers provided for in Articles 26 and 29 shall be considered as rendered by the Court.

Article 28

The chambers provided for in Articles 26 and 29 may, with the consent of the parties, sit and exercise their functions elsewhere than at The Hague.

Article 29

With a view to the speedy dispatch of business, the Court shall form annually a chamber composed of five judges which, at the request of the parties, may hear and determine cases by summary procedure. In addition, two judges shall be selected for the purpose of replacing judges who find it impossible to sit.

Article 30

1. The Court shall frame rules for carrying out its functions. In particular, it shall lay down rules of procedure.
2. The Rules of the Court may provide for assessors to sit with the Court or with any of its chambers, without the right to vote.

Article 31

1. Judges of the nationality of each of the parties shall retain their right to sit in the case before the Court.
2. If the Court includes upon the Bench a judge of the nationality of one of the parties, any other party may choose a person to sit as judge. Such person shall be chosen preferably from among those persons who have been nominated as candidates as provided in Articles 4 and 5.
3. If the Court includes upon the Bench no judge of the nationality of the parties, each of these parties may proceed to choose a judge as provided in paragraph 2 of this Article.

4. The provisions of this Article shall apply to the case of Articles 26 and 29. In such cases, the President shall request one or, if necessary, two of the members of the Court forming the chamber to give place to the members of the Court of the nationality of the parties concerned, and, failing such, or if they are unable to be present, to the judges specially chosen by the parties.
5. Should there be several parties in the same interest, they shall, for the purpose of the preceding provisions, be reckoned as one party only. Any doubt upon this point shall be settled by the decision of the Court.
6. Judges chosen as laid down in paragraphs 2, 3, and 4 of this Article shall fulfil the conditions required by Articles 2, 17 (paragraph 2), 20, and 24 of the present Statute. They shall take part in the decision on terms of complete equality with their colleagues.

Article 32

1. Each member of the Court shall receive an annual salary.
2. The President shall receive a special annual allowance.
3. The Vice-President shall receive a special allowance for every day on which he acts as President.
4. The judges chosen under Article 31, other than members of the Court, shall receive compensation for each day on which they exercise their functions.
5. These salaries, allowances, and compensation shall be fixed by the General Assembly. They may not be decreased during the term of office.
6. The salary of the Registrar shall be fixed by the General Assembly on the proposal of the Court.
7. Regulations made by the General Assembly shall fix the conditions under which retirement pensions may be given to members of the Court and to the Registrar, and the conditions under which members of the Court and the Registrar shall have their travelling expenses refunded.
8. The above salaries, allowances, and compensation shall be free of all taxation.

Article 33

The expenses of the Court shall be borne by the United Nations in such a manner as shall be decided by the General Assembly.

Chapter II: Competence of the Court

Article 34

1. Only states may be parties in cases before the Court.
2. The Court, subject to and in conformity with its Rules, may request of public international organizations information relevant to cases before it, and shall receive such information presented by such organizations on their own initiative.
3. Whenever the construction of the constituent instrument of a public international organization or of an international convention adopted thereunder is in question in a case before the Court, the Registrar shall so notify the public international organization concerned and shall communicate to it copies of all the written proceedings.

Article 35

1. The Court shall be open to the states parties to the present Statute.
2. The conditions under which the Court shall be open to other states shall, subject to the special provisions contained in treaties in force, be laid down by the Security Council, but in no case shall such conditions place the parties in a position of inequality before the Court.
3. When a state which is not a Member of the United Nations is a party to a case, the Court shall fix the amount which that party is to contribute towards the expenses of the Court. This provision shall not apply if such state is bearing a share of the expenses of the Court.

Article 36

1. The jurisdiction of the Court comprises all cases which the parties refer to it and all matters specially provided for in the Charter of the United Nations or in treaties and conventions in force.
2. he states parties to the present Statute may at any time declare that they recognize as compulsory *ipso facto* and without special agreement, in relation to any other state accepting the same obligation, the jurisdiction of the Court in all legal disputes concerning:
   a. the interpretation of a treaty;
   b. any question of international law;
   c. the existence of any fact which, if established, would constitute a breach of an international obligation;
   d. the nature or extent of the reparation to be made for the breach of an international obligation.
3. The declarations referred to above may be made unconditionally or on condition of reciprocity on the part of several orcertain states, or for a certain time.
4. Such declarations shall be deposited with the Secretary-General of the United Nations, who shall transmit copies thereof to the parties to the Statute and to the Registrar of the Court.
5. Declarations made under Article 36 of the Statute of the Permanent Court of International Justice and which are still in force shall be deemed, as between the parties to the present Statute, to be acceptances of the compulsory jurisdiction of the International Court of Justice for the period which they still have to run and in accordance with their terms.
6. In the event of a dispute as to whether the Court has jurisdiction, the matter shall be settled by the decision of the Court.

Article 37

Whenever a treaty or convention in force provides for reference of a matter to a tribunal to have been instituted by the League of Nations, or to the Permanent Court of International Justice, the matter shall, as between the parties to the present Statute, be referred to the International Court of Justice.

Article 38

1. The Court, whose function is to decide in accordance with international law such disputes as are submitted to it, shall apply:
   a. international conventions, whether general or particular, establishing rules expressly recognized by the contesting states;

b. International custom, as evidence of a general practice accepted as law;
c. the general principles of law recognized by civilized nations;
d. subject to the provisions of Article 59, judicial decisions and the teachings of the most highly qualified publicists of the various nations, as subsidiary means for the determination of rules of law.

2. This provision shall not prejudice the power of the Court to decide a case ex aequo et bono, if the parties agree thereto.

Chapter III: Procedure

Article 39

1. The official languages of the Court shall be French and English. If the parties agree that the case shall be conducted in French, the judgment shall be delivered in French. If the parties agree that the case shall be conducted in English, the judgment shall be delivered in English.
2. In the absence of an agreement as to which language shall be employed, each party may, in the pleadings, use the language which it prefers; the decision of the Court shall be given in French and English. In this case the Court shall at the same time determine which of the two texts shall be considered as authoritative.
3. The Court shall, at the request of any party, authorize a language other than French or English to be used by that party.

Article 40

1. Cases are brought before the Court, as the case may be, either by the notification of the special agreement or by a written application addressed to the Registrar. In either case the subject of the dispute and the parties shall be indicated.
2. The Registrar shall forthwith communicate the application to all concerned.
3. He shall also notify the Members of the United Nations through the Secretary-General, and also any other states entitled to appear before the Court.

Article 41

1. The Court shall have the power to indicate, if it considers that circumstances so require, any provisional measures which ought to be taken to preserve the respective rights of either party.
2. Pending the final decision, notice of the measures suggested shall forthwith be given to the parties and to the Security Council.

Article 42

1. The parties shall be represented by agents.
2. They may have the assistance of counsel or advocates before the Court.
3. The agents, counsel, and advocates of parties before the Court shall enjoy the privileges and immunities necessary to the independent exercise of their duties.

Article 43

1. The procedure shall consist of two parts: written and oral.
2. The written proceedings shall consist of the communication to the Court and to the

parties of memorials, counter-memorials and, if necessary, replies; also all papers and documents in support.

3. These communications shall be made through the Registrar, in the order and within the time fixed by the Court.

4. A certified copy of every document produced by one party shall be communicated to the other party.

5. The oral proceedings shall consist of the hearing by the Court of witnesses, experts, agents, counsel, and advocates.

Article 44

1. For the service of all notices upon persons other than the agents, counsel, and advocates, the Court shall apply direct to the government of the state upon whose territory the notice has to be served.

2. The same provision shall apply whenever steps are to be taken to procure evidence on the spot.

Article 45

The hearing shall be under the control of the President or, if he is unable to preside, of the Vice-President; if neither is able to preside, the senior judge present shall preside.

Article 46

The hearing in Court shall be public, unless the Court shall decide otherwise, or unless the parties demand that the public be not admitted.

Article 47

1. Minutes shall be made at each hearing and signed by the Registrar and the President.
2. These minutes alone shall be authentic.

Article 48

The Court shall make orders for the conduct of the case, shall decide the form and time in which each party must conclude its arguments, and make all arrangements connected with the taking of evidence.

Article 49

The Court may, even before the hearing begins, call upon the agents to produce any document or to supply any explanations. Formal note shall be taken of any refusal.

Article 50

The Court may, at any time, entrust any individual, body, bureau, commission, or other organization that it may select, with the task of carrying out an enquiry or giving an expert opinion.

Article 51

During the hearing any relevant questions are to be put to the witnesses and experts under the conditions laid down by the Court in the rules of procedure referred to in Article 30.

Article 52

After the Court has received the proofs and evidence within the time specified for the purpose, it may refuse to accept any further oral or written evidence that one party may desire to present unless the other side consents.

Article 53

1. Whenever one of the parties does not appear before the Court, or fails to defend its case, the other party may call upon the Court to decide in favour of its claim.
2. The Court must, before doing so, satisfy itself, not only that it has jurisdiction in accordance with Articles 36 and 37, but also that the claim is well founded in fact and law.

Article 54

1. When, subject to the control of the Court, the agents, counsel, and advocates have completed their presentation of the case, the President shall declare the hearing closed.
2. The Court shall withdraw to consider the judgment.
3. The deliberations of the Court shall take place in private and remain secret.

Article 55

1. All questions shall be decided by a majority of the judges present.
2. In the event of an equality of votes, the President or the judge who acts in his place shall have a casting vote.

Article 56

1. The judgment shall state the reasons on which it is based.
2. It shall contain the names of the judges who have taken part in the decision.

Article 57

If the judgment does not represent in whole or in part the unanimous opinion of the judges, any judge shall be entitled to deliver a separate opinion.

Article 58

The judgment shall be signed by the President and by the Registrar. It shall be read in open court, due notice having been given to the agents.

Article 59

The decision of the Court has no binding force except between the parties and in respect of that particular case.

Article 60

The judgment is final and without appeal. In the event of dispute as to the meaning or scope of the judgment, the Court shall construe it upon the request of any party.

Article 61

1. An application for revision of a judgment may be made only when it is based upon the discovery of some fact of such a nature as to be a decisive factor, which fact was, when the judgment was given, unknown to the Court and also to the party claiming revision, always provided that such ignorance was not due to negligence.

2. The proceedings for revision shall be opened by a judgment of the Court expressly recording the existence of the new fact, recognizing that it has such a character as to lay the case open to revision, and declaring the application admissible on this ground.
3. The Court may require previous compliance with the terms of the judgment before it admits proceedings in revision.
4. The application for revision must be made at latest within six months of the discovery of the new fact.
5. No application for revision may be made after the lapse of ten years from the date of the judgment.

Article 62

1. Should a state consider that it has an interest of a legal nature which may be affected by the decision in the case, it may submit a request to the Court to be permitted to intervene.
2. It shall be for the Court to decide upon this request.

Article 63

1. Whenever the construction of a convention to which states other than those concerned in the case are parties is in question, the Registrar shall notify all such states forthwith.
2. Every state so notified has the right to intervene in the proceedings; but if it uses this right, the construction given by the judgment will be equally binding upon it.

Article 64

Unless otherwise decided by the Court, each party shall bear its own costs.

Chapter IV: Advisory Opinions

Article 65

1. The Court may give an advisory opinion on any legal question at the request of whatever body may be authorized by or in accordance with the Charter of the United Nations to make such a request.
2. Questions upon which the advisory opinion of the Court is asked shall be laid before the Court by means of a written request containing an exact statement of the question upon which an opinion is required, and accompanied by all documents likely to throw light upon the question.

Article 66

1. The Registrar shall forthwith give notice of the request for an advisory opinion to all states entitled to appear before the Court.
2. The Registrar shall also, by means of a special and direct communication, notify any state entitled to appear before the Court or international organization considered by the Court, or, should it not be sitting, by the President, as likely to be able to furnish information on the question, that the Court will be prepared to receive, within a time limit to be fixed by the President, written statements, or to hear, at a public sitting to be held for the purpose, oral statements relating to the question.

3. Should any such state entitled to appear before the Court have failed to receive the special communication referred to in paragraph 2 of this Article, such state may express a desire to submit a written statement or to be heard; and the Court will decide.
4. States and organizations having presented written or oral statements or both shall be permitted to comment on the statements made by other states or organizations in the form, to the extent, and within the time limits which the Court, or, should it not be sitting, the President, shall decide in each particular case. Accordingly, the Registrar shall in due time communicate any such written statements to states and organizations having submitted similar statements.

Article 67

The Court shall deliver its advisory opinions in open court, notice having been given to the Secretary-General and to the representatives of Members of the United Nations, of other states and of international organizations immediately concerned.

Article 68

In the exercise of its advisory functions the Court shall further be guided by the provisions of the present Statute which apply in contentious cases to the extent to which it recognizes them to be applicable.

Chapter V: Amendment

Article 69

Amendments to the present Statute shall be effected by the same procedure as is provided by the Charter of the United Nations for amendments to that Charter, subject however to any provisions which the General Assembly upon recommendation of the Security Council may adopt concerning the participation of states which are parties to the present Statute but are not Members of the United Nations.

Article 70

The Court shall have power to propose such amendments to the present Statute as it may deem necessary, through written communications to the Secretary-General, for consideration in conformity with the provisions of Article 69.

APPENDIX 3

Convention for the establishment of a Central American Court of Justice[2]

The Governments of the Republics of El Salvador, Costa Rica, Guatemala, Honduras and Nicaragua, for the purpose of efficaciously guaranteeing their rights and maintaining peace and harmony inalterably in their relations, without being obliged to resort in any case to the employment of force, have agreed to celebrate a Convention for the constitution of a Court of Justice charged with attaining such high aims, and, to that end, have named as Delegates;

SALVADOR. — Their Excellencies Doctor Don Salvador Gallegos, Doctor Don Salvador Rodríguez González, and Don Federico Mejía;
COSTA RICA. — Their Excellencies Doctor Don Luis Anderson and Don Joaquín B. Calvo;
GUATEMALA. — Their Excellencies Doctor Don Antonio Batres Jáuregui, Doctor Don Luis Toledo Herrarte, and Don Victor Sánchez Ocaña;
HONDURAS. — Their Excellencies Doctor Don Policarpo Bonilla, Doctor Don Angel Ugarte, and Don E. Constantino Fiallos; and
NICARAGUA. — Their Excellencies Doctors Don José Madrix and Don Luis F. Corea.

By virtue of the invitation sent in accordance with Article II of the Protocol signed at Washington on September 17, 1907, by the Plenipotentiary Representatives of the five Central American Republics, their Excellencies, the Representative of the Government of the United Mexican States, Ambassador Don Enrique C. Creel, and the Representative of the Government of the United States of America, Mr. William I. Buchanan, were present at all the deliberations.

The Delegates, assembled in the Central American Peace Conference at Washington, after having communicated to each other their respective full powers, which they found to be in due form, have agreed to carry out said purpose in the following manner:

Article 1

The High Contracting Parties agree by the present Convention to constitute and maintain a permanent tribunal which shall be called the "Central American Court of Justice", to which they bind themselves to submit all controversies or questions which may arise among them, of whatsoever nature and no matter what their origin may be, in case the respective Departments of Foreign Affairs should not have been able to reach an understanding.

---

[2] Convention for the establishment of a Central American Court of Justice, *Documentos relativos á la Conferencia de Paz Centroamericana: Tratodos y Convenciones*, (including Additional Protocol), 1907, pp. 10-19.

Article 2

This Court shall also take cognizance of the questions which individuals of one Central American country may raise against any of the other Contracting Governments, because of the violation of Treaties or Conventions, and other cases of an international character; no matter whether his own Government supports said claim or not; and provided that the remedies which the laws of the respective country provide against such violation shall have been exhausted or that a denial of justice shall be shown[3].

Article 3

It shall also take cognizance of the cases which by common accord contracting Governments may submit to it, no matter whether they arise between two or more of them or between one of said Governments and individuals.

Article 4

The Court can likewise take cognizance of the international questions which by special agreement any one of the Central American Governments and a foreign Government may have determined to submit to it.

Article 5

The Central American Court of Justice shall sit at the City of Cartago in the Republic of Costa Rica, but it shall be authorized to transfer its residence to another point in Central America when it may deem it proper to do so for reasons of health, of guaranteeing the exercise of its functions, or of the personal security of its members.

Article 6

The Central American Court of Justice shall consist of five justices named, one from each Republic and selected from among the jurists who possess the qualifications which the laws of each country may exact for the exercise of high judicial functions, and enjoy the highest consideration, not only because of their moral character but also on account of their professional ability.

The vacancies shall be filled by substitute Justices named at the same time and in the same manner as the regular ones and who shall unite the same qualifications as the former.

The attendance of the five justices who constitute the Tribunal is indispensable in order to have a legal quorum in the judgments of the Court.

Article 7

The legislative power of each one of the five contracting Republics shall name one regular and two substitutes as their respective justices. The salary of each justice shall be eight thousand dollars, gold, per annum, which shall be paid them by the Treasury of the Court. The salary of the justice of the place where the Court resides shall be designated by the respective Government. Besides, each State shall contribute two thousand dollars, gold, annually for the ordinary and extraordinary expenses of the Tribunal. The Governments of the contracting Republics bind themselves to include their respective contribu-

---

[3] Note that the English text should read "exhausted or that a denial of justice shall be shown". The Spanish text reads: "contra tal violación, ó se demonstrate denegación de justicia".

tions in their budgets of expenses and to remit quarterly in advance to the Treasury of the Court the proportion which corresponds to them on account of such expenditures.

Article 8

The regular and substitute Justices shall be appointed for a term of five years. which shall be counted from the day on which they assume the discharge of their duties, and they may be reappointed.

In case of death, resignation or permanent incapacity of any one of them, steps shall be taken to fill the vacancy by the respective Legislature, and the Justice chosen shall complete the term of his predecessor.

Article 9

The regular and substitute Justices shall take oath or make a legal declaration before the authority that may have appointed them, and from that moment they shall enjoy the immunities and prerogatives which the present Convention confers upon them. The substitutes shall enjoy from then on the salary designated in Article VII.

Article 10

Whilst they remain in the country of their appointment the regular and substitute Justices shall enjoy the personal immunity which the respective laws grant to the magistrates of the Supreme Court of Justice, and in the other Contracting Republics they shall have the privileges and immunities of Diplomatic Agents.

Article 11

The office of Judge whilst acting is incompatible with the exercise of his profession and the discharge of public offices and employments. The same incompatibility is established for the substitute Justices during the time when they may actually perform their duties.

Article 12

At its first annual session the Court shall elect from amongst the Justices forming its body a President and Vice-President; and shall organize the personnel, including the designation of Secretary and Treasurer, and the other subordinate employees that it may deem necessary, and shall prepare the budget of expenses.

Article 13

The Central American Court of Justice represents the national conscience of Central America, wherefore the Justices who compose the Tribunal shall not consider themselves prohibited from the exercise of their functions because of the interest which the Republics, whence they derive their appointment, may have in any case or question. With regard to implications and challenges, the rules of procedure which the Court may fix shall make proper provision.

Article 14

When conditions or questions subject to the jurisdiction of the Tribunal arise, the interested party shall present a complaint which will contain all the points of fact and law relative to the matter, and present all pertinent evidence. The Tribunal shall communicate without loss of time a copy of the complaint to the Governments or individuals interested, and shall invite them to furnish their allegations and evidence within the term that it may indicate to them, which, in no case, shall exceed sixty days counted from the date of notice of the complaint.

Article 15

If the term designated shall have expired without answer having been made to the complaint, the Court shall require the complainant or complainants to do so within a further term which can not exceed twenty days more, after the expiration of which and in view of the evidence presented and of such evidence as it may officially have seen fit to obtain, the Tribunal shall pronounce the pro-per judgment, which shall be final.

Article 16

If the Government, Governments, or individuals sued shall have appeared in time before the Court, presenting their allegation and evidence, the Court shall decide the matter within thirty days following, without further process or procedure; but if a new term for the presentation of evidence is solicited, the Court shall decide if it is proper or not to grant it; and in case it decides affirmatively it shall designate therefor a proper time. The latter term having expired, the Court shall pronounce its final judgment within thirty days.

Article 17

Each one of the Governments or individual whom the questions which are about to be discussed in the Court directly concern the right to be represented before it by the person or persons of their confidence, who shall present evidence, formulate arguments, and shall do within the terms fixed by the Convention and by the rules of the Court of Justice everything that in their judgment shall be beneficial to the defense of the rights they represent.

Article 18

From the moment any suit may be instituted against one or more Governments, until it has been decided finally, the Court may fix the place wherein the contending parties shall abide, at the solicitation of any of them, to the end of not aggravating the difficulty, and with the object that things shall be preserved in status quo until the final judgment is pronounced.

Article 19

For all the purposes of this Convention, the Central American Court of Justice may address itself to the Governments or Tribunal of justice of the contracting States, through the medium of the Ministry of Foreign Relations or the office of the Clerk of the Supreme Court of Justice of the respective country, in accordance with the nature of the proceeding necessary to be had for the purpose of carrying out the measures that it may dictate within the scope of its jurisdiction.

Article 20

It may also name special commissioners to carry out the formalities above referred to, when it may decide that it is best for their proper fulfillment. In such case, it shall ask of the Government where the proceeding is to be had, its cooperation and assistance, in order that the Commissioner may fulfill his mission. The contracting Governments formally bind themselves to obey and to compel to be obeyed the orders of the Court, furnishing all the assistance that may be necessary for their best and most expeditious fulfillment.

Article 21

The Central American Court of Justice hall decide concerning questions of fact which may be discussed in accordance with it own judgment; and with respect to questions of law in accordance with the principles of international law. The official judgment cover each one of the points involved in the litigation.

Article 22

The Court is authorized to determine its jurisdiction, interpreting the Treaties and Conventions germane to the matter in dispute, applying the principles of international law.

Article 23

Every final or interlocutory decision shall be rendered in accordance with the agreement of at least three of the Justices of the Court. In case of disagreement, one of the substitute Justices shall be chosen by lot, and if still a majority of three be not obtained other Justices shall continue to be chosen by lot until three votes in the same sense shall have been obtained.

Article 24

The decision must be in writing and shall contain a statement of the reasons upon which they are based. They must be signed by all the Justices of the Court and countersigned by the Secretary. Once they have been published they can not be altered on any account; but, at the request of any of the parties the tribunal may decide the interpretation which must be given to its judgment.

Article 25

The judgments of the Court shall be communicated to the five Governments of the Contracting Republics. The interested parties solemnly bind themselves to submit to said judgment; and they all agree to lend every moral support that may be necessary in order that they may be properly fulfilled, in the manner constituting a real and positive guarantee of respect for this Convention and for the Central American Court of Justice.

Article 26

The Court is empowered to make its rules, to designate the order of procedure which may be necessary, and determine the forms and terms not prescribed in the present Convention All the decisions which may be rendered in this respect shall be communicated immediately to the High Contracting Parties.

Article 27

The High Contracting Parties solemnly declare that for no motive nor in any case will they consider the present Convention as lapsed; and that, therefore, they will consider it as being always in force during the term of ten years counted from the last ratification. In the event that the political entity of one or more of the Contracting Republics changed or altered, the attributes of the Central American Court of Justice created by this Convention shall be suspended *ipso facto*; and a conference to adjust the constitution of said Court to the new order of things shall be forthwith convoked by the respective Governments; in case they do not unanimously agree the present Convention shall be considered as rescinded.

Article 28

The exchange of ratification of the present Convention shall be made in accordance with Article XXI of the General Treaty of Peace and Amity concluded on this date.

Provisionary Article

As a recommendation of the five Delegations an Article is annexed which contains amplification of the Central American Court of Justice, in order that the Legislatures that may deem it proper may see fit to inc1ude it upon ratifying this Convention.

Annexed Article

The Central American Court of Justice shall also have jurisdiction over the conflicts which may arise between the Legislative, Executive and Judicial Powers, and when as a matter of fact the judicial decisions and congressional resolutions are not respected.

Signed at the city of Washington on the twentieth day of December, one thousand - nine hundred and seven.

Additional Protocol to the Convention for the establishment of a Central American Court of Justice.

At the city of Washington, at one o'clock in the afternoon of the twentieth day of December, one thousand nine hundred and seven. The undersigned Delegates to the Central American Peace Conference:

[Same delegates as noted at p. 210]

Noting that an error has been committed in copying the text of Article III of the Convention for the establishment of a Central American Court of Justice, concluded on this date, make it known that the authentic text of said Article III is as follows:

"It shall also have jurisdiction over cases arising between any of the contracting Governments and individuals, when by common accord they may have been submitted to it."

In testimony whereof they sign the present Protocol, which shall be considered as an integral part of the Convention.

APPENDIX 4

Convention for Protection of Human Rights and Fundamental Freedoms[4]

The governments signatory hereto, being members of the Council of Europe,

Considering the Universal Declaration of Human Rights proclaimed by the General Assembly of the United Nations on 10th December 1948;

Considering that this Declaration aims at securing the universal and effective recognition and observance of the Rights therein declared;

Considering that the aim of the Council of Europe is the achievement of greater unity between its members and that one of the methods by which that aim is to be pursued is the maintenance and further realisation of human rights and fundamental freedoms;

Reaffirming their profound belief in those fundamental freedoms which are the foundation of justice and peace in the world and are best maintained on the one hand by an effective political democracy and on the other by a common understanding and observance of the human rights upon which they depend;

Being resolved, as the governments of European countries which are like-minded and have a common heritage of political traditions, ideals, freedom and the rule of law, to take the first steps for the collective enforcement of certain of the rights stated in the Universal Declaration,

Have agreed as follows:

Article 1. Obligation to respect human rights

The High Contracting Parties shall secure to everyone within their jurisdiction the rights and freedoms defined in Section I of this Convention.

---

[4] Convention for Protection of Human Rights and Fundamental Freedoms, 4 November 1950, ETS n. 5. The text of the Conventions was completed by Protocol No. 2 (ETS N 44), 6 May 1963, and amended by Protocol No. 3 (ETS N 45), 6 May 1963, Protocol No. 5 (ETS N 55), 20 January 1966, Protocol No. 8 (ETS N 118) of 19 March 1985, and Protocol no. 11 (ETS N 155), 1 November 1998.

Section I – Rights and Freedoms

Article 2. Right to life

1. Everyone's right to life shall be protected by law. No one shall be deprived of his life intentionally save in the execution of a sentence of a court following his conviction of a crime for which this penalty is provided by law.
2. Deprivation of life shall not be regarded as inflicted in contravention of this article when it results from the use of force which is no more than absolutely necessary:
   a. in defence of any person from unlawful violence;
   b. in order to effect a lawful arrest or to prevent the escape of a person lawfully detained;
   c. in action lawfully taken for the purpose of quelling a riot or insurrection.

Article 3. Prohibition of torture

No one shall be subjected to torture or to inhuman or degrading treatment or punishment.

Article 4. Prohibition of slavery and forced labour

1. No one shall be held in slavery or servitude.
2. No one shall be required to perform forced or compulsory labour.
3. For the purpose of this article the term "forced or compulsory labour" shall not include:
   a. any work required to be done in the ordinary course of detention imposed according to the provisions of Article 5 of this Convention or during conditional release from such detention;
   b. any service of a military character or, in case of conscientious objectors in countries where they are recognised, service exacted instead of compulsory military service;
   c. any service exacted in case of an emergency or calamity threatening the life or well-being of the community;
   d. any work or service which forms part of normal civic obligations.

Article 5. Right to liberty and security

1. Everyone has the right to liberty and security of person. No one shall be deprived of his liberty save in the following cases and in accordance with a procedure prescribed by law:
   a. the lawful detention of a person after conviction by a competent court;
   b. the lawful arrest or detention of a person for non- compliance with the lawful order of a court or in order to secure the fulfilment of any obligation prescribed by law;
   c. the lawful arrest or detention of a person effected for the purpose of bringing him before the competent legal authority on reasonable suspicion of having committed an offence or when it is reasonably considered necessary to prevent his committing an offence or fleeing after having done so;
   d. the detention of a minor by lawful order for the purpose of educational supervision or his lawful detention for the purpose of bringing him before the competent legal authority;
   e. the lawful detention of persons for the prevention of the spreading of infectious

diseases, of persons of unsound mind, alcoholics or drug addicts or vagrants;

f. the lawful arrest or detention of a person to prevent his effecting an unauthorised entry into the country or of a person against whom action is being taken with a view to deportation or extradition.

2. Everyone who is arrested shall be informed promptly, in a language which he understands, of the reasons for his arrest and of any charge against him.

3. Everyone arrested or detained in accordance with the provisions of paragraph 1(c) of this article shall be brought promptly before a judge or other officer authorised by law to exercise judicial power and shall be entitled to trial within a reasonable time or to release pending trial. Release may be conditioned by guarantees to appear for trial.

4. Everyone who is deprived of his liberty by arrest or detention shall be entitled to take proceedings by which the lawfulness of his detention shall be decided speedily by a court and his release ordered if the detention is not lawful.

5. Everyone who has been the victim of arrest or detention in contravention of the provisions of this article shall have an enforceable right to compensation.

Article 6. Right to fair trial

1. In the determination of his civil rights and obligations or of any criminal charge against him, everyone is entitled to a fair and public hearing within a reasonable time by an independent and impartial tribunal established by law. Judgment shall be pronounced publicly but the press and public may be excluded from all or part of the trial in the interests of morals, public order or national security in a democratic society, where the interests of juveniles or the protection of the private life of the parties so require, or to the extent strictly necessary in the opinion of the court in special circumstances where publicity would prejudice the interests of justice.

2. Everyone charged with a criminal offence shall be presumed innocent until proved guilty according to law.

3. Everyone charged with a criminal offence has the following minimum rights:
   a. to be informed promptly, in a language which he understands and in detail, of the nature and cause of the accusation against him;
   b. to have adequate time and facilities for the preparation of his defence;
   c. to defend himself in person or through legal assistance of his own choosing or, if he has not sufficient means to pay for legal assistance, to be given it free when the interests of justice so require;
   d. to examine or have examined witnesses against him and to obtain the attendance and examination of witnesses on his behalf under the same conditions as witnesses against him;
   e. to have the free assistance of an interpreter if he cannot understand or speak the language used in court.

Article 7. No punishment without law

1. No one shall be held guilty of any criminal offence on account of any act or omission which did not constitute a criminal offence under national or international law at the time when it was committed. Nor shall a heavier penalty be imposed than the one that was applicable at the time the criminal offence was committed.

2. This article shall not prejudice the trial and punishment of any person for any act or omission which, at the time when it was committed, was criminal according to the general principles of law recognised by civilised nations.

Article 8. Right to respect for private and family life

1. Everyone has the right to respect for his private and family life, his home and his correspondence.
2. There shall be no interference by a public authority with the exercise of this right except such as is in accordance with the law and is necessary in a democratic society in the interests of national security, public safety or the economic well-being of the country, for the prevention of disorder or crime, for the protection of health or morals, or for the protection of the rights and freedoms of others.

Article 9. Freedom of thought, conscience and religion

1. Everyone has the right to freedom of thought, conscience and religion; this right includes freedom to change his religion or belief and freedom, either alone or in community with others and in public or private, to manifest his religion or belief, in worship, teaching, practice and observance.
2. Freedom to manifest one's religion or beliefs shall be subject only to such limitations as are prescribed by law and are necessary in a democratic society in the interests of public safety, for the protection of public order, health or morals, or for the protection of the rights and freedoms of others.

Article 10. Freedom of expression

1. Everyone has the right to freedom of expression. This right shall include freedom to hold opinions and to receive and impart information and ideas without interference by public authority and regardless of frontiers. This article shall not prevent States from requiring the licensing of broadcasting, television or cinema enterprises.
2. The exercise of these freedoms, since it carries with it duties and responsibilities, may be subject to such formalities, conditions, restrictions or penalties as are prescribed by law and are necessary in a democratic society, in the interests of national security, territorial integrity or public safety, for the prevention of disorder or crime, for the protection of health or morals, for the protection of the reputation or rights of others, for preventing the disclosure of information received in confidence, or for maintaining the authority and impartiality of the judiciary.

Article 11. Freedom of assembly and association

1. Everyone has the right to freedom of peaceful assembly and to freedom of association with others, including the right to form and to join trade unions for the protection of his interests.
2. No restrictions shall be placed on the exercise of these rights other than such as are prescribed by law and are necessary in a democratic society in the interests of national security or public safety, for the prevention of disorder or crime, for the protection of health or morals or for the protection of the rights and freedoms of others. This article shall not prevent the imposition of lawful restrictions on the exercise of these rights by members of the armed forces, of the police or of the administration of the State.

Article 12. Right to marry

Men and women of marriageable age have the right to marry and to found a family, according to the national laws governing the exercise of this right.

Article 13. Right to an effective remedy

Everyone whose rights and freedoms as set forth in this Convention are violated shall have an effective remedy before a national authority notwithstanding that the violation has been committed by persons acting in an official capacity.

Article 14. Prohibition of discrimination

The enjoyment of the rights and freedoms set forth in this Convention shall be secured without discrimination on any ground such as sex, race, colour, language, religion, political or other opinion, national or social origin, association with a national minority, property, birth or other status.

Article 15. Derogation in time of emergency

1. In time of war or other public emergency threatening the life of the nation any High Contracting Party may take measures derogating from its obligations under this Convention to the extent strictly required by the exigencies of the situation, provided that such measures are not inconsistent with its other obligations under international law.
2. No derogation from Article 2, except in respect of deaths resulting from lawful acts of war, or from Articles 3, 4 (paragraph 1) and 7 shall be made under this provision.
3. Any High Contracting Party availing itself of this right of derogation shall keep the Secretary General of the Council of Europe fully informed of the measures which it has taken and the reasons therefor. It shall also inform the Secretary General of the Council of Europe when such measures have ceased to operate and the provisions of the Convention are again being fully executed.

Article 16. Restrictions on political activity of aliens

Nothing in Articles 10, 11 and 14 shall be regarded as preventing the High Contracting Parties from imposing restrictions on the political activity of aliens.

Article 17. Prohibition of abuse of rights

Nothing in this Convention may be interpreted as implying for any State, group or person any right to engage in any activity or perform any act aimed at the destruction of any of the rights and freedoms set forth herein or at their limitation to a greater extent than is provided for in the Convention.

Article 18. Limitations on use of restrictions on rights

The restrictions permitted under this Convention to the said rights and freedoms shall not be applied for any purpose other than those for which they have been prescribed.

Section II – European Court of Human Rights

Article 19. Establishment of the Court

To ensure the observance of the engagements undertaken by the High Contracting Parties in the Convention and the protocols thereto, there shall be set up a European Court of Human Rights, hereinafter referred to as “the Court”. It shall function on a permanent basis.

Article 20. Number of judges

The Court shall consist of a number of judges equal to that of the High Contracting Parties.

Article 21. Criteria for office

1. The judges shall be of high moral character and must either possess the qualifications required for appointment to high judicial office or be jurisconsults of recognised competence.
2. The judges shall sit on the Court in their individual capacity.
3. During their term of office the judges shall not engage in any activity which is incompatible with their independence, impartiality or with the demands of a full-time office; all questions arising from the application of this paragraph shall be decided by the Court.

Article 22. Election of judges

1. The judges shall be elected by the Parliamentary Assembly with respect to each High Contracting Party by a majority of votes cast from a list of three candidates nominated by the High Contracting Party.
2. The same procedure shall be followed to complete the Court in the event of the accession of new High Contracting Parties and in filling casual vacancies.

Article 23. Terms of office

1. The judges shall be elected for a period of six years. They may be re-elected. However, the terms of office of one-half of the judges elected at the first election shall expire at the end of three years.
2. The judges whose terms of office are to expire at the end of the initial period of three years shall be chosen by lot by the Secretary General of the Council of Europe immediately after their election.
3. In order to ensure that, as far as possible, the terms of office of one-half of the judges are renewed every three years, the Parliamentary Assembly may decide, before proceeding to any subsequent election, that the term or terms of office of one or more judges to be elected shall be for a period other than six years but not more than nine and not less than three years.
4. In cases where more than one term of office is involved and where the Parliamentary Assembly applies the preceding paragraph, the allocation of the terms of office shall be effected by a drawing of lots by the Secretary General of the Council of Europe immediately after the election.
5. A judge elected to replace a judge whose term of office has not expired shall hold office for the remainder of his predecessor's term.
6. The terms of office of judges shall expire when they reach the age of 70.
7. The judges shall hold office until replaced. They shall, however, continue to deal with such cases as they already have under consideration.

Article 24. Dismissal

No judge may be dismissed from his office unless the other judges decide by a majority of two-thirds that he has ceased to fulfil the required conditions.

Article 25. Registry and legal secretaries

The Court shall have a registry, the functions and organisation of which shall be laid down in the rules of the Court. The Court shall be assisted by legal secretaries.

Article 26. Plenary Court

The plenary Court shall

a. elect its President and one or two Vice-Presidents for a period of three years; they may be re-elected;
b. set up Chambers, constituted for a fixed period of time;
c. elect the Presidents of the Chambers of the Court; they may be re-elected;
d. adopt the rules of the Court; and
e. elect the Registrar and one or more Deputy Registrars.

Article 27. Committees, Chambers and Grand Chamber

1. To consider cases brought before it, the Court shall sit in committees of three judges, in Chambers of seven judges and in a Grand Chamber of seventeen judges. The Court's Chambers shall set up committees for a fixed period of time.
2. There shall sit as an ex officio member of the Chamber and the Grand Chamber the judge elected in respect of the State Party concerned or, if there is none or if he is unable to sit, a person of its choice who shall sit in the capacity of judge.
3. The Grand Chamber shall also include the President of the Court, the Vice-Presidents, the Presidents of the Chambers and other judges chosen in accordance with the rules of the Court. When a case is referred to the Grand Chamber under Article 43, no judge from the Chamber which rendered the judgment shall sit in the Grand Chamber, with the exception of the President of the Chamber and the judge who sat in respect of the State Party concerned.

Article 28. Declarations of inadmissibility by committees

A committee may, by a unanimous vote, declare inadmissible or strike out of its list of cases an individual application submitted under Article 34 where such a decision can be taken without further examination. The decision shall be final.

Article 29. Decisions by Chambers on admissibility and merits

1. If no decision is taken under Article 28, a Chamber shall decide on the admissibility and merits of individual applications submitted under Article 34.
2. A Chamber shall decide on the admissibility and merits of inter-State applications submitted under Article 33.
3. The decision on admissibility shall be taken separately unless the Court, in exceptional cases, decides otherwise.

Article 30. Relinquishment of jurisdiction to the Grand Chamber

Where a case pending before a Chamber raises a serious question affecting the interpretation of the Convention or the protocols thereto, or where the resolution of a question before the Chamber might have a result inconsistent with a judgment previously delivered by the Court, the Chamber may, at any time before it has rendered its judgment, relinquish jurisdiction in favour of the Grand Chamber, unless one of the parties to the case objects.

Article 31. Powers of the Grand Chamber

The Grand Chamber shall

a. determine applications submitted either under Article 33 or Article 34 when a Chamber has relinquished jurisdiction under Article 30 or when the case has been referred to it under Article 43; and
b. consider requests for advisory opinions submitted under Article 47.

Article 32. Jurisdiction of the Court

1. The jurisdiction of the Court shall extend to all matters concerning the interpretation and application of the Convention and the protocols thereto which are referred to it as provided in Articles 33, 34 and 47.
2. In the event of dispute as to whether the Court has jurisdiction, the Court shall decide.

Article 33. Inter-State cases

Any High Contracting Party may refer to the Court any alleged breach of the provisions of the Convention and the protocols thereto by another High Contracting Party.

Article 34. Individual applications

The Court may receive applications from any person, non-governmental organisation or group of individuals claiming to be the victim of a violation by one of the High Contracting Parties of the rights set forth in the Convention or the protocols thereto. The High Contracting Parties undertake not to hinder in any way the effective exercise of this right.

Article 35. Admissibility criteria

1. The Court may only deal with the matter after all domestic remedies have been exhausted, according to the generally recognised rules of international law, and within a period of six months from the date on which the final decision was taken.
2. The Court shall not deal with any individual application submitted under Article 34 that
   a. is anonymous; or
   b. is substantially the same as a matter that has already been examined by the Court or has already been submitted to another procedure of international investigation or settlement and contains no relevant new information.
3. The Court shall declare inadmissible any individual application submitted under Article 34 which it considers incompatible with the provisions of the Convention or the protocols thereto, manifestly ill-founded, or an abuse of the right of application.
4. The Court shall reject any application which it considers inadmissible under this Article. It may do so at any stage of the proceedings.

Article 36. Third-party intervention

1. In all cases before a Chamber or the Grand Chamber, a High Contracting Party one of whose nationals is an applicant shall have the right to submit written comments and to take part in hearings.
2. The President of the Court may, in the interest of the proper administration of justice, invite any High Contracting Party which is not a party to the proceedings or any person concerned who is not the applicant to submit written comments or take part in hearings.

Article 37. Striking out applications

1. The Court may at any stage of the proceedings decide to strike an application out of its list of cases where the circumstances lead to the conclusion that
   a. the applicant does not intend to pursue his application; or
   b. the matter has been resolved; or
   c. for any other reason established by the Court, it is no longer justified to continue the examination of the application.

However, the Court shall continue the examination of the application if respect for human rights as defined in the Convention and the protocols thereto so requires.

2. The Court may decide to restore an application to its list of cases if it considers that the circumstances justify such a course.

Article 38. Examination of the case and friendly settlement proceedings

1. If the Court declares the application admissible, it shall
   a. pursue the examination of the case, together with the representatives of the parties, and if need be, undertake an investigation, for the effective conduct of which the States concerned shall furnish all necessary facilities;
   b. place itself at the disposal of the parties concerned with a view to securing a friendly settlement of the matter on the basis of respect for human rights as defined in the Convention and the protocols thereto.
2. Proceedings conducted under paragraph 1.b shall be confidential.

Article 39. Finding of a friendly settlement

If a friendly settlement is effected, the Court shall strike the case out of its list by means of a decision which shall be confined to a brief statement of the facts and of the solution reached.

Article 40. Public hearings and access to documents

1. Hearings shall be public unless the Court in exceptional circumstances decides otherwise.
2. Documents deposited with the Registrar shall be accessible to the public unless the President of the Court decides otherwise.

Article 41. Just satisfaction

If the Court finds that there has been a violation of the Convention or the protocols thereto, and if the internal law of the High Contracting Party concerned allows only partial reparation to be made, the Court shall, if necessary, afford just satisfaction to the injured party.

Article 42. Judgments of Chambers

Judgments of Chambers shall become final in accordance with the provisions of Article 44, paragraph 2.

Article 43. Referral to the Grand Chamber

1. Within a period of three months from the date of the judgment of the Chamber, any party to the case may, in exceptional cases, request that the case be referred to the Grand Chamber.

2. A panel of five judges of the Grand Chamber shall accept the request if the case raises a serious question affecting the interpretation or application of the Convention or the protocols thereto, or a serious issue of general importance. 3.If the panel accepts the request, the Grand Chamber shall decide the case by means of a judgment.

Article 44. Final judgments

1. The judgment of the Grand Chamber shall be final.
2. The judgment of a Chamber shall become final
   a. when the parties declare that they will not request that the case be referred to the Grand Chamber; or
   b. three months after the date of the judgment, if reference of the case to the Grand Chamber has not been requested; or
   c. when the panel of the Grand Chamber rejects the request to refer under Article 43.
3. The final judgment shall be published.

Article 45. Reasons for judgments and decisions

1. Reasons shall be given for judgments as well as for decisions declaring applications admissible or inadmissible.

2. If a judgment does not represent, in whole or in part, the unanimous opinion of the judges, any judge shall be entitled to deliver a separate opinion.

Article 46. Binding force and execution of judgments

1. The High Contracting Parties undertake to abide by the final judgment of the Court in any case to which they are parties.

2. The final judgment of the Court shall be transmitted to the Committee of Ministers, which shall supervise its execution.

Article 47. Advisory opinions

1. The Court may, at the request of the Committee of Ministers, give advisory opinions on legal questions concerning the interpretation of the Convention and the protocols thereto.

2. Such opinions shall not deal with any question relating to the content or scope of the rights or freedoms defined in Section I of the Convention and the protocols thereto, or with any other question which the Court or the Committee of Ministers might have to consider in consequence of any such proceedings as could be instituted in accordance with the Convention.

3. Decisions of the Committee of Ministers to request an advisory opinion of the Court shall require a majority vote of the representatives entitled to sit on the Committee.

Article 48. Advisory jurisdiction of the Court

The Court shall decide whether a request for an advisory opinion submitted by the Committee of Ministers is within its competence as defined in Article 47.

Article 49. Reasons for advisory opinions

1. Reasons shall be given for advisory opinions of the Court.

2. If the advisory opinion does not represent, in whole or in part, the unanimous opinion of the judges, any judge shall be entitled to deliver a separate opinion.

3. Advisory opinions of the Court shall be communicated to the Committee of Ministers.

Article 50. Expenditure on the Court

The expenditure on the Court shall be borne by the Council of Europe.

Article 51. Privileges and immunities of judges

The judges shall be entitled, during the exercise of their functions, to the privileges and immunities provided for in Article 40 of the Statute of the Council of Europe and in the agreements made thereunder.

Article 52. Enquiries by the Secretary General

On receipt of a request from the Secretary General of the Council of Europe any High Contracting Party shall furnish an explanation of the manner in which its internal law ensures the effective implementation of any of the provisions of the Convention.

Article 53. Safeguard for existing human rights

Nothing in this Convention shall be construed as limiting or derogating from any of the human rights and fundamental freedoms which may be ensured under the laws of any High Contracting Party or under any other agreement to which it is a Party.

Article 54. Powers of the Committee of Ministers

Nothing in this Convention shall prejudice the powers conferred on the Committee of Ministers by the Statute of the Council of Europe.

Article 55. Exclusion of other means of dispute settlement

The High Contracting Parties agree that, except by special agreement, they will not avail themselves of treaties, conventions or declarations in force between them for the purpose of submitting, by way of petition, a dispute arising out of the interpretation or application of this Convention to a means of settlement other than those provided for in this Convention.

Article 56. Territorial application

1. Any State may at the time of its ratification or at any time thereafter declare by notification addressed to the Secretary General of the Council of Europe that the present Convention shall, subject to paragraph 4 of this Article, extend to all or any of the territories for whose international relations it is responsible.
2. The Convention shall extend to the territory or territories named in the notification as from the thirtieth day after the receipt of this notification by the Secretary General of the Council of Europe.
3. The provisions of this Convention shall be applied in such territories with due regard, however, to local requirements.
4. Any State which has made a declaration in accordance with paragraph 1 of this article may at any time thereafter declare on behalf of one or more of the territories to which the declaration relates that it accepts the competence of the Court to receive applicationsfrom individuals, non-governmental organisations or groups of as provided in Article 34 of the present Convention.

Article 57. Reservations

1. Any State may, when signing this Convention or when depositing its instrument of ratification, make a reservation in respect of any particular provision of the Convention to the extent that any law then in force in its territory is not in conformity with the provision. Reservations of a general character shall not be permitted under this article.
2. Any reservation made under this article shall contain a brief statement of the law concerned.

Article 58. Denunciation

1. A High Contracting Party may denounce the present Convention only after the expiry of five years from the date on which it became a party to it and after six months' notice contained in a notification addressed to the Secretary General of the Council of Europe, who shall inform the other High Contracting Parties.
2. Such a denunciation shall not have the effect of releasing the High Contracting Party concerned from its obligations under this Convention in respect of any act which, being capable of constituting a violation of such obligations, may have been performed by it before the date at which the denunciation became effective.
3. Any High Contracting Party which shall cease to be a member of the Council of Europe shall cease to be a Party to this Convention under the same conditions.
4. The Convention may be denounced in accordance with the provisions of the preceding paragraphs in respect of any territory to which it has been declared to extend under the terms of Article 56.

Article 59. Signature and ratification

1. This Convention shall be open to the signature of the members of the Council of Europe. It shall be ratified. Ratifications shall be deposited with the Secretary General of the Council of Europe.
2. The present Convention shall come into force after the deposit of ten instruments of ratification. 3.As regards any signatory ratifying subsequently, the Convention shall come into force at the date of the deposit of its instrument of ratification.
4. The Secretary General of the Council of Europe shall notify all the members of the Council of Europe of the entry into force of the Convention, the names of the High Contracting Parties who have ratified it, and the deposit of all instruments of ratification which may be effected subsequently.

APPENDIX 5

American Convention on Human Rights[5]

Preamble

The American states signatory to the present Convention,

Reaffirming their intention to consolidate in this hemisphere, within the framework of democratic institutions, a system of personal liberty and social justice based on respect for the essential rights of man;

Recognizing that the essential rights of man are not derived from one's being a national of a certain state, but are based upon attributes of the human personality, and that they therefore justify international protection in the form of a convention reinforcing or complementing the protection provided by the domestic law of the American states;

Considering that these principles have been set forth in the Charter of the Organization of American States, in the American Declaration of the Rights and Duties of Man, and in the Universal Declaration of Human Rights, and that they have been reaffirmed and refined in other international instruments, worldwide as well as regional in scope;

Reiterating that, in accordance with the Universal Declaration of Human Rights, the ideal of free men enjoying freedom from fear and want can be achieved only if conditions are created whereby everyone may enjoy his economic, social, and cultural rights, as well as his civil and political rights; and

Considering that the Third Special Inter-American Conference (Buenos Aires, 1967) approved the incorporation into the Charter of the Organization itself of broader standards with respect to economic, social, and educational rights and resolved that an inter-American convention on human rights should determine the structure, competence, and procedure of the organs responsible for these matters,

Have agreed upon the following:

---

[5] O.A.S. Treaty Series No. 36, 1144 U.N.T.S. 123 entered into force July 18, 1978, reprinted in Basic Documents Pertaining to Human Rights in the Inter-American System, OEA/Ser.L.V/II.82 doc.6 rev.1 at 25 (1992).

PART I - STATE OBLIGATIONS AND RIGHTS PROTECTED

Chapter 1 – General Obligations

Article 1. Obligation to Respect Rights

1. The States Parties to this Convention undertake to respect the rights and freedoms recognized herein and to ensure to all persons subject to their jurisdiction the free and full exercise of those rights and freedoms, without any discrimination for reasons of race, color, sex, language, religion, political or other opinion, national or social origin, economic status, birth, or any other social condition.
2. For the purposes of this Convention, "person" means every human being.

Article 2. Domestic Legal Effects

Where the exercise of any of the rights or freedoms referred to in Article 1 is not already ensured by legislative or other provisions, the States Parties undertake to adopt, in accordance with their constitutional processes and the provisions of this Convention, such legislative or other measures as may be necessary to give effect to those rights or freedoms.

Chapter II – Civil and Political Rights

Article 3. Right to Juridical Personality

Every person has the right to recognition as a person before the law.

Article 4. Right to Life

1. Every person has the right to have his life respected. This right shall be protected by law and, in general, from the moment of conception. No one shall be arbitrarily deprived of his life.
2. In countries that have not abolished the death penalty, it may be imposed only for the most serious crimes and pursuant to a final judgment rendered by a competent court and in accordance with a law establishing such punishment, enacted prior to the commission of the crime. The application of such punishment shall not be extended to crimes to which it does not presently apply.
3. The death penalty shall not be reestablished in states that have abolished it.
4. In no case shall capital punishment be inflicted for political offenses or related common crimes.
5. Capital punishment shall not be imposed upon persons who, at the time the crime was committed, were under 18 years of age or over 70 years of age; nor shall it be applied to pregnant women.
6. Every person condemned to death shall have the right to apply for amnesty, pardon, or commutation of sentence, which may be granted in all cases. Capital punishment shall not be imposed while such a petition is pending decision by the competent authority.

Article 5. Right to Humane Treatment

1. Every person has the right to have his physical, mental, and moral integrity respected.
2. No one shall be subjected to torture or to cruel, inhuman, or degrading punishment or

treatment. All persons deprived of their liberty shall be treated with respect for the inherent dignity of the human person.
3. Punishment shall not be extended to any person other than the criminal.
4. Accused persons shall, save in exceptional circumstances, be segregated from convicted persons, and shall be subject to separate treatment appropriate to their status as unconvicted persons.
5. Minors while subject to criminal proceedings shall be separated from adults and brought before specialized tribunals, as speedily as possible, so that they may be treated in accordance with their status as minors.
6. Punishments consisting of deprivation of liberty shall have as an essential aim the reform and social readaptation of the prisoners.

Article 6. Freedom from Slavery

1. No one shall be subject to slavery or to involuntary servitude, which are prohibited in all their forms, as are the slave trade and traffic in women.
2. No one shall be required to perform forced or compulsory labor. This provision shall not be interpreted to mean that, in those countries in which the penalty established for certain crimes is deprivation of liberty at forced labor, the carrying out of such a sentence imposed by a competent court is prohibited. Forced labor shall not adversely affect the dignity or the physical or intellectual capacity of the prisoner.
3. For the purposes of this article, the following do not constitute forced or compulsory labor:
   a. work or service normally required of a person imprisoned in execution of a sentence or formal decision passed by the competent judicial authority. Such work or service shall be carried out under the supervision and control of public authorities, and any persons performing such work or service shall not be placed at the disposal of any private party, company, or juridical person;
   b. military service and, in countries in which conscientious objectors are recognized, national service that the law may provide for in lieu of military service;
   c. service exacted in time of danger or calamity that threatens the existence or the well-being of the community; or
   d. work or service that forms part of normal civic obligations.

Article 7. Right to Personal Liberty

1. Every person has the right to personal liberty and security.
2. No one shall be deprived of his physical liberty except for the reasons and under the conditions established beforehand by the constitution of the State Party concerned or by a law established pursuant thereto.
3. No one shall be subject to arbitrary arrest or imprisonment.
4. Anyone who is detained shall be informed of the reasons for his detention and shall be promptly notified of the charge or charges against him.
5. Any person detained shall be brought promptly before a judge or other officer authorized by law to exercise judicial power and shall be entitled to trial within a reasonable time or to be released without prejudice to the continuation of the proceedings. His release may be subject to guarantees to assure his appearance for trial.
6. Anyone who is deprived of his liberty shall be entitled to recourse to a competent court, in order that the court may decide without delay on the lawfulness of his arrest or detention and order his release if the arrest or detention is unlawful. In States Parties

whose laws provide that anyone who believes himself to be threatened with deprivation of his liberty is entitled to recourse to a competent court in order that it may decide on the lawfulness of such threat, this remedy may not be restricted or abolished. The interested party or another person in his behalf is entitled to seek these remedies.
7. No one shall be detained for debt. This principle shall not limit the orders of a competent judicial authority issued for non-fulfillment of duties of support.

Article 8. Right to a Fair Trial

1. Every person has the right to a hearing, with due guarantees and within a reasonable time, by a competent, independent, and impartial tribunal, previously established by law, in the substantiation of any accusation of a criminal nature made against him or for the determination of his rights and obligations of a civil, labor, fiscal, or any other nature.
2. Every person accused of a criminal offense has the right to be presumed innocent so long as his guilt has not been proven according to law. During the proceedings, every person is entitled, with full equality, to the following minimum guarantees:
   a. the right of the accused to be assisted without charge by a translator or interpreter, if he does not understand or does not speak the language of the tribunal or court;
   b. prior notification in detail to the accused of the charges against him;
   c. adequate time and means for the preparation of his defense;
   d. the right of the accused to defend himself personally or to be assisted by legal counsel of his own choosing, and to communicate freely and privately with his counsel;
   e. the inalienable right to be assisted by counsel provided by the state, paid or not as the domestic law provides, if the accused does not defend himself personally or engage his own counsel within the time period established by law;
   f. the right of the defense to examine witnesses present in the court and to obtain the appearance, as witnesses, of experts or other persons who may throw light on the facts;
   g. the right not to be compelled to be a witness against himself or to plead guilty; and
   h. the right to appeal the judgment to a higher court.
3. A confession of guilt by the accused shall be valid only if it is made without coercion of any kind.
4. An accused person acquitted by a nonappealable judgment shall not be subjected to a new trial for the same cause.
5. Criminal proceedings shall be public, except insofar as may be necessary to protect the interests of justice.

Article 9. Freedom from Ex Post Facto Laws

No one shall be convicted of any act or omission that did not constitute a criminal offense, under the applicable law, at the time it was committed. A heavier penalty shall not be imposed than the one that was applicable at the time the criminal offense was committed. If subsequent to the commission of the offense the law provides for the imposition of a lighter punishment, the guilty person shall benefit therefrom.

Article 10. Right to Compensation

Every person has the right to be compensated in accordance with the law in the event he has been sentenced by a final judgment through a miscarriage of justice.

Article 11. Right to Privacy

1. Everyone has the right to have his honor respected and his dignity recognized.
2. No one may be the object of arbitrary or abusive interference with his private life, his family, his home, or his correspondence, or of unlawful attacks on his honor or reputation.
3. Everyone has the right to the protection of the law against such interference or attacks.

Article 12. Freedom of Conscience and Religion

1. Everyone has the right to freedom of conscience and of religion. This right includes freedom to maintain or to change one's religion or beliefs, and freedom to profess or disseminate one's religion or beliefs, either individually or together with others, in public or in private.
2. No one shall be subject to restrictions that might impair his freedom to maintain or to change his religion or beliefs.
3. Freedom to manifest one's religion and beliefs may be subject only to the limitations prescribed by law that are necessary to protect public safety, order, health, or morals, or the rights or freedoms of others.
4. Parents or guardians, as the case may be, have the right to provide for the religious and moral education of their children or wards that is in accord with their own convictions.

Article 13. Freedom of Thought and Expression

1. Everyone has the right to freedom of thought and expression. This right includes freedom to seek, receive, and impart information and ideas of all kinds, regardless of frontiers, either orally, in writing, in print, in the form of art, or through any other medium of one's choice.
2. The exercise of the right provided for in the foregoing paragraph shall not be subject to prior censorship but shall be subject to subsequent imposition of liability, which shall be expressly established by law to the extent necessary to ensure:
    a. respect for the rights or reputations of others; or
    b. the protection of national security, public order, or public health or morals.
3. The right of expression may not be restricted by indirect methods or means, such as the abuse of government or private controls over newsprint, radio broadcasting frequencies, or equipment used in the dissemination of information, or by any other means tending to impede the communication and circulation of ideas and opinions.
4. Notwithstanding the provisions of paragraph 2 above, public entertainments may be subject by law to prior censorship for the sole purpose of regulating access to them for the moral protection of childhood and adolescence.
5. Any propaganda for war and any advocacy of national, racial, or religious hatred that constitute incitements to lawless violence or to any other similar action against any person or group of persons on any grounds including those of race, color, religion, language, or national origin shall be considered as offenses punishable by law.

Article 14. Right of Reply

1. Anyone injured by inaccurate or offensive statements or ideas disseminated to the public in general by a legally regulated medium of communication has the right to reply or to make a correction using the same communications outlet, under such conditions as the law may establish.

2. The correction or reply shall not in any case remit other legal liabilities that may have been incurred.
3. For the effective protection of honor and reputation, every publisher, and every newspaper, motion picture, radio, and television company, shall have a person responsible who is not protected by immunities or special privileges.

Article 15. Right of Assembly

The right of peaceful assembly, without arms, is recognized. No restrictions may be placed on the exercise of this right other than those imposed in conformity with the law and necessary in a democratic society in the interest of national security, public safety or public order, or to protect public health or morals or the rights or freedom of others.

Article 16. Freedom of Association

1. Everyone has the right to associate freely for ideological, religious, political, economic, labor, social, cultural, sports, or other purposes.
2. The exercise of this right shall be subject only to such restrictions established by law as may be necessary in a democratic society, in the interest of national security, public safety or public order, or to protect public health or morals or the rights and freedoms of others.
3. The provisions of this article do not bar the imposition of legal restrictions, including even deprivation of the exercise of the right of association, on members of the armed forces and the police.

Article 17. Rights of the Family

1. The family is the natural and fundamental group unit of society and is entitled to protection by society and the state.
2. The right of men and women of marriageable age to marry and to raise a family shall be recognized, if they meet the conditions required by domestic laws, insofar as such conditions do not affect the principle of nondiscrimination established in this Convention.
3. No marriage shall be entered into without the free and full consent of the intending spouses.
4. The States Parties shall take appropriate steps to ensure the equality of rights and the adequate balancing of responsibilities of the spouses as to marriage, during marriage, and in the event of its dissolution. In case of dissolution, provision shall be made for the necessary protection of any children solely on the basis of their own best interests.
5. The law shall recognize equal rights for children born out of wedlock and those born in wedlock.

Article 18. Right to a Name

Every person has the right to a given name and to the surnames of his parents or that of one of them. The law shall regulate the manner in which this right shall be ensured for all, by the use of assumed names if necessary.

Article 19. Rights of the Child

Every minor child has the right to the measures of protection required by his condition as a minor on the part of his family, society, and the state.

Article 20. Right to Nationality

1. Every person has the right to a nationality.
2. Every person has the right to the nationality of the state in whose territory he was born if he does not have the right to any other nationality.
3. No one shall be arbitrarily deprived of his nationality or of the right to change it.

Article 21. Right to Property

1. Everyone has the right to the use and enjoyment of his property. The law may subordinate such use and enjoyment to the interest of society.
2. No one shall be deprived of his property except upon payment of just compensation, for reasons of public utility or social interest, and in the cases and according to the forms established by law.
3. Usury and any other form of exploitation of man by man shall be prohibited by law.

Article 22. Freedom of Movement and Residence

1. Every person lawfully in the territory of a State Party has the right to move about in it, and to reside in it subject to the provisions of the law.
2. Every person has the right lo leave any country freely, including his own.
3. The exercise of the foregoing rights may be restricted only pursuant to a law to the extent necessary in a democratic society to prevent crime or to protect national security, public safety, public order, public morals, public health, or the rights or freedoms of others.
4. The exercise of the rights recognized in paragraph 1 may also be restricted by law in designated zones for reasons of public interest.
5. No one can be expelled from the territory of the state of which he is a national or be deprived of the right to enter it.
6. An alien lawfully in the territory of a State Party to this Convention may be expelled from it only pursuant to a decision reached in accordance with law.
7. Every person has the right to seek and be granted asylum in a foreign territory, in accordance with the legislation of the state and international conventions, in the event he is being pursued for political offenses or related common crimes.
8. In no case may an alien be deported or returned to a country, regardless of whether or not it is his country of origin, if in that country his right to life or personal freedom is in danger of being violated because of his race, nationality, religion, social status, or political opinions.
9. The collective expulsion of aliens is prohibited.

Article 23. Right to Participate in Government

1. Every citizen shall enjoy the following rights and opportunities:
   a. to take part in the conduct of public affairs, directly or through freely chosen representatives;
   b. to vote and to be elected in genuine periodic elections, which shall be by universal and equal suffrage and by secret ballot that guarantees the free expression of the will of the voters; and
   c. to have access, under general conditions of equality, to the public service of his country.

2. The law may regulate the exercise of the rights and opportunities referred to in the preceding paragraph only on the basis of age, nationality, residence, language, education, civil and mental capacity, or sentencing by a competent court in criminal proceedings.

Article 24. Right to Equal Protection

All persons are equal before the law. Consequently, they are entitled, without discrimination, to equal protection of the law.

Article 25. Right to Judicial Protection

1. Everyone has the right to simple and prompt recourse, or any other effective recourse, to a competent court or tribunal for protection against acts that violate his fundamental rights recognized by the constitution or laws of the state concerned or by this Convention, even though such violation may have been committed by persons acting in the course of their official duties.
2. The States Parties undertake:
   a. to ensure that any person claiming such remedy shall have his rights determined by the competent authority provided for by the legal system of the state;
   b. to develop the possibilities of judicial remedy; and
   c. to ensure that the competent authorities shall enforce such remedies when granted.

Chapter III – Economic, Social, and Cultural Rights

Article 26. Progressive Development

The States Parties undertake to adopt measures, both internally and through international cooperation, especially those of an economic and technical nature, with a view to achieving progressively, by legislation or other appropriate means, the full realization of the rights implicit in the economic, social, educational, scientific, and cultural standards set forth in the Charter of the Organization of American States as amended by the Protocol of Buenos Aires.

Chapter IV – Suspension of Guarantees, Interpretation, and Application

Article 27. Suspension of Guarantees

1. In time of war, public danger, or other emergency that threatens the independence or security of a State Party, it may take measures derogating from its obligations under the present Convention to the extent and for the period of time strictly required by the exigencies of the situation, provided that such measures are not inconsistent with its other obligations under international law and do not involve discrimination on the ground of race, color, sex, language, religion, or social origin.
2. The foregoing provision does not authorize any suspension of the following articles: Article 3 (Right to Juridical Personality), Article 4 (Right to Life), Article 5 (Right to Humane Treatment), Article 6 (Freedom from Slavery), Article 9 (Freedom from Ex Post Facto Laws), Article 12 (Freedom of Conscience and Religion), Article 17 (Rights of the Family), Article 18 (Right to a Name), Article 19 (Rights of the Child), Article 20 (Right

to Nationality), and Article 23 (Right to Participate in Government), or of the judicial guarantees essential for the protection of such rights.
3. Any State Party availing itself of the right of suspension shall immediately inform the other States Parties, through the Secretary General of the Organization of American States, of the provisions the application of which it has suspended, the reasons that gave rise to the suspension, and the date set for the termination of such suspension.

Article 28. Federal Clause

1. Where a State Party is constituted as a federal state, the national government of such State Party shall implement all the provisions of the Convention over whose subject matter it exercises legislative and judicial jurisdiction.
2. With respect to the provisions over whose subject matter the constituent units of the federal state have jurisdiction, the national government shall immediately take suitable measures, in accordance with its constitution and its laws, to the end that the competent authorities of the constituent units may adopt appropriate provisions for the fulfillment of this Convention.
3. Whenever two or more States Parties agree to form a federation or other type of association, they shall take care that the resulting federal or other compact contains the provisions necessary for continuing and rendering effective the standards of this Convention in the new state that is organized.

Article 29. Restrictions Regarding Interpretation

No provision of this Convention shall be interpreted as:

a. permitting any State Party, group, or person to suppress the enjoyment or exercise of the rights and freedoms recognized in this Convention or to restrict them to a greater extent than is provided for herein;
b. restricting the enjoyment or exercise of any right or freedom recognized by virtue of the laws of any State Party or by virtue of another convention to which one of the said states is a party;
c. precluding other rights or guarantees that are inherent in the human personality or derived from representative democracy as a form of government; or
d. excluding or limiting the effect that the American Declaration of the Rights and Duties of Man and other international acts of the same nature may have.

Article 30. Scope of Restrictions

The restrictions that, pursuant to this Convention, may be placed on the enjoyment or exercise of the rights or freedoms recognized herein may not be applied except in accordance with laws enacted for reasons of general interest and in accordance with the purpose for which such restrictions have been established.

Article 31. Recognition of Other Rights

Other rights and freedoms recognized in accordance with the procedures established in Articles 76 and 77 may be included in the system of protection of this Convention.

Chapter V – Personal Responsibilities

Article 32. Relationship between Duties and Rights

1. Every person has reponsibilities to his family, his community, and mankind.
2. The rights of each person are limited by the rights of others, by the security of all, and by the just demands of the general welfare, in a democratic society.

PART II - MEANS OF PROTECTION

Chapter VI – Competent Organs

Article 33

The following organs shall have competence with respect to matters relating to the fulfillment of the commitments made by the States Parties to this Convention:

a. the Inter-American Commission on Human Rights, referred to as "The Commission;" and
b. the Inter-American Court of Human Rights, referred to as "The Court."

Chapter VII – Inter-American Commission on Human Rights

Section 1. Organization

Article 34

The Inter-American Commission on Human Rights shall be composed of seven members, who shall be persons of high moral character and recognized competence in the field of human rights.

Article 35

The Commission shall represent all the member countries of the Organization of American States.

Article 36

1. The members of the Commission shall be elected in a personal capacity by the General Assembly of the Organization from a list of candidates proposed by the governments of the member states.
2. Each of those governments may propose up to three candidates, who may be nationals of the states proposing them or of any other member state of the Organization of American States. When a slate of three is proposed, at least one of the candidates shall be a national of a state other than the one proposing the slate.

Article 37

1. The members of the Commission shall be elected for a term of four years and may be reelected only once, but the terms of three of the members chosen in the first election shall expire at the end of two years. Immediately following that election the General Assembly shall determine the names of those three members by lot.

2. No two nationals of the same state may be members of the Commission.

Article 38

Vacancies that may occur on the Commission for reasons other than the normal expiration of a term shall be filled by the Permanent Council of the Organization in accordance with the provisions of the Statute of the Commission.

Article 39

The Commission shall prepare its Statute, which it shall submit to the General Assembly for approval. It shall establish its own Regulations.

Article 40

Secretariat services for the Commission shall be furnished by the appropriate specialized unit of the General Secretariat of the Organization. This unit shall be provided with the resources required to accomplish the tasks assigned to it by the Commission.

Section 2. Functions

Article 41

The main function of the Commission shall be to promote respect for and defense of human rights. In the exercise of its mandate, it shall have the following functions and powers:

a. to develop an awareness of human rights among the peoples of America;
b. to make recommendations to the governments of the member states, when it considers such action advisable, for the adoption of progressive measures in favor of human rights within the framework of their domestic law and constitutional provisions as well as appropriate measures to further the observance of those rights;
c. to prepare such studies or reports as it considers advisable in the performance of its duties;
d. to request the governments of the member states to supply it with information on the measures adopted by them in matters of human rights;
e. to respond, through the General Secretariat of the Organization of American States, to inquiries made by the member states on matters related to human rights and, within the limits of its possibilities, to provide those states with the advisory services they request;
f. to take action on petitions and other communications pursuant to its authority under the provisions of Articles 44 through 51 of this Convention; and
g. to submit an annual report to the General Assembly of the Organization of American States.

Article 42

The States Parties shall transmit to the Commission a copy of each of the reports and studies that they submit annually to the Executive Committees of the Inter-American Economic and Social Council and the Inter-American Council for Education, Science, and Culture, in their respective fields, so that the Commission may watch over the promotion of the rights implicit in the economic, social, educational, scientific, and cultural standards set forth in the Charter of the Organization of American States as amended by the Protocol of Buenos Aires.

Article 43

The States Parties undertake to provide the Commission with such information as it may request of them as to the manner in which their domestic law ensures the effective application of any provisions of this Convention.

Section 3. Competence

Article 44

Any person or group of persons, or any nongovernmental entity legally recognized in one or more member states of the Organization, may lodge petitions with the Commission containing denunciations or complaints of violation of this Convention by a State Party.

Article 45

1. Any State Party may, when it deposits its instrument of ratification of or adherence to this Convention, or at any later time, declare that it recognizes the competence of the Commission to receive and examine communications in which a State Party alleges that another State Party has committed a violation of a human right set forth in this Convention.
2. Communications presented by virtue of this article may be admitted and examined only if they are presented by a State Party that has made a declaration recognizing the aforementioned competence of the Commission. The Commission shall not admit any communication against a State Party that has not made such a declaration.
3. A declaration concerning recognition of competence may be made to be valid for an indefinite time, for a specified period, or for a specific case.
4. Declarations shall be deposited with the General Secretariat of the Organization of American States, which shall transmit copies thereof to the member states of that Organization.

Article 46

1. Admission by the Commission of a petition or communication lodged in accordance with Articles 44 or 45 shall be subject to the following requirements:
    a. that the remedies under domestic law have been pursued and exhausted in accordance with generally recognized principles of international law;
    b. that the petition or communication is lodged within a period of six months from the date on which the party alleging violation of his rights was notified of the final judgment;
    c. that the subject of the petition or communication is not pending in another international proceeding for settlement; and
    d. that, in the case of Article 44, the petition contains the name, nationality, profession, domicile, and signature of the person or persons or of the legal representative of the entity lodging the petition.

2. The provisions of paragraphs 1.a and 1.b of this article shall not be applicable when:
   a. the domestic legislation of the state concerned does not afford due process of law for the protection of the right or rights that have allegedly been violated;
   b. the party alleging violation of his rights has been denied access to the remedies under domestic law or has been prevented from exhausting them; or
   c. there has been unwarranted delay in rendering a final judgment under the aforementioned remedies.

Article 47

The Commission shall consider inadmissible any petition or communication submitted under Articles 44 or 45 if:
   a. any of the requirements indicated in Article 46 has not been met;
   b. the petition or communication does not state facts that tend to establish a violation of the rights guaranteed by this Convention;
   c. the statements of the petitioner or of the state indicate that the petition or communication is manifestly groundless or obviously out of order; or
   d. the petition or communication is substantially the same as one previously studied by the Commission or by another international organization.

Section 4. Procedure

Article 48

1. When the Commission receives a petition or communication alleging violation of any of the rights protected by this Convention, it shall proceed as follows:
   a. If it considers the petition or communication admissible, it shall request information from the government of the state indicated as being responsible for the alleged violations and shall furnish that government a transcript of the pertinent portions of the petition or communication. This information shall be submitted within a reasonable period to be determined by the Commission in accordance with the circumstances of each case.
   b. After the information has been received, or after the period established has elapsed and the information has not been received, the Commission shall ascertain whether the grounds for the petition or communication still exist. If they do not, the Commission shall order the record to be closed.
   c. The Commission may also declare the petition or communication inadmissible or out of order on the basis of information or evidence subsequently received.
   d. If the record has not been closed, the Commission shall, with the knowledge of the parties, examine the matter set forth in the petition or communication in order to verify the facts. If necessary and advisable, the Commission shall carry out an investigation, for the effective conduct of which it shall request, and the states concerned shall furnish to it, all necessary facilities.
   e. The Commission may request the states concerned to furnish any pertinent information and, if so requested, shall hear oral statements or receive written statements from the parties concerned.
   f. The Commission shall place itself at the disposal of the parties concerned with a view to reaching a friendly settlement of the matter on the basis of respect for the human rights recognized in this Convention.

2. However, in serious and urgent cases, only the presentation of a petition or communication that fulfills all the formal requirements of admissibility shall be necessary in order for the Commission to conduct an investigation with the prior consent of the state in whose territory a violation has allegedly been committed.

Article 49

If a friendly settlement has been reached in accordance with paragraph 1.f of Article 48, the Commission shall draw up a report, which shall be transmitted to the petitioner and to the States Parties to this Convention, and shall then be communicated to the Secretary General of the Organization of American States for publication. This report shall contain a brief statement of the facts and of the solution reached. If any party in the case so requests, the fullest possible information shall be provided to it.

Article 50

1. If a settlement is not reached, the Commission shall, within the time limit established by its Statute, draw up a report setting forth the facts and stating its conclusions. If the report, in whole or in part, does not represent the unanimous agreement of the members of the Commission, any member may attach to it a separate opinion. The written and oral statements made by the parties in accordance with paragraph 1.e of Article 48 shall also be attached to the report.
2. The report shall be transmitted to the states concerned, which shall not be at liberty to publish it.
3. In transmitting the report, the Commission may make such proposals and recommendations as it sees fit.

Article 51

1. If, within a period of three months from the date of the transmittal of the report of the Commission to the states concerned, the matter has not either been settled or submitted by the Commission or by the state concerned to the Court and its jurisdiction accepted, the Commission may, by the vote of an absolute majority of its members, set forth its opinion and conclusions concerning the question submitted for its consideration.
2. Where appropriate, the Commission shall make pertinent recommendations and shall prescribe a period within which the state is to take the measures that are incumbent upon it to remedy the situation examined.
3. When the prescribed period has expired, the Commission shall decide by the vote of an absolute majority of its members whether the state has taken adequate measures and whether to publish its report.

Chapter VII – Inter-American Court of Human Rights

Section 1. Organization

Article 52

1. The Court shall consist of seven judges, nationals of the member states of the Organization, elected in an individual capacity from among jurists of the highest moral authority and of recognized competence in the field of human rights, who possess the qualifications required for the exercise of the highest judicial functions in conformity with

the law of the state of which they are nationals or of the state that proposes them as candidates.
2. No two judges may be nationals of the same state.

Article 53

1. The judges of the Court shall be elected by secret ballot by an absolute majority vote of the States Parties to the Convention, in the General Assembly of the Organization, from a panel of candidates proposed by those states.
2. Each of the States Parties may propose up to three candidates, nationals of the state that proposes them or of any other member state of the Organization of American States. When a slate of three is proposed, at least one of the candidates shall be a national of a state other than the one proposing the slate.

Article 54

1. The judges of the Court shall be elected for a term of six years and may be reelected only once. The term of three of the judges chosen in the first election shall expire at the end of three years. Immediately after the election, the names of the three judges shall be determined by lot in the General Assembly.
2. A judge elected to replace a judge whose term has not expired shall complete the term of the latter.
3. The judges shall continue in office until the expiration of their term. However, they shall continue to serve with regard to cases that they have begun to hear and that are still pending, for which purposes they shall not be replaced by the newly elected judges.

Article 55

1. If a judge is a national of any of the States Parties to a case submitted to the Court, he shall retain his right to hear that case.
2. If one of the judges called upon to hear a case should be a national of one of the States Parties to the case, any other State Party in the case may appoint a person of its choice to serve on the Court as an ad hoc judge.
3. If among the judges called upon to hear a case none is a national of any of the States Parties to the case, each of the latter may appoint an ad hoc judge.
4. An ad hoc judge shall possess the qualifications indicated in Article 52.
5. If several States Parties to the Convention should have the same interest in a case, they shall be considered as a single party for purposes of the above provisions. In case of doubt, the Court shall decide.

Article 56

Five judges shall constitute a quorum for the transaction of business by the Court.

Article 57

The Commission shall appear in all cases before the Court. Article 58

1. The Court shall have its seat at the place determined by the States Parties to the Convention in the General Assembly of the Organization; however, it may convene in the territory of any member state of the Organization of American States when a majority of the Court considers it desirable, and with the prior consent of the state concerned. The seat of the Court may be changed by the States Parties to the Convention in the General Assembly by a two-thirds vote.

2. The Court shall appoint its own Secretary.
3. The Secretary shall have his office at the place where the Court has its seat and shall attend the meetings that the Court may hold away from its seat.

Article 59

The Court shall establish its Secretariat, which shall function under the direction of the Secretary of the Court, in accordance with the administrative standards of the General Secretariat of the Organization in all respects not incompatible with the independence of the Court. The staff of the Court's Secretariat shall be appointed by the Secretary General of the Organization, in consultation with the Secretary of the Court.

Article 60

The Court shall draw up its Statute which it shall submit to the General Assembly for approval. It shall adopt its own Rules of Procedure.

Section 2. Jurisdiction and Functions

Article 61

1. Only the States Parties and the Commission shall have the right to submit a case to the Court.
2. In order for the Court to hear a case, it is necessary that the procedures set forth in Articles 48 and 50 shall have been completed.

Article 62

1. A State Party may, upon depositing its instrument of ratification or adherence to this Convention, or at any subsequent time, declare that it recognizes as binding, ipso facto, and not requiring special agreement, the jurisdiction of the Court on all matters relating to the interpretation or application of this Convention.
2. Such declaration may be made unconditionally, on the condition of reciprocity, for a specified period, or for specific cases. It shall be presented to the Secretary General of the Organization, who shall transmit copies thereof to the other member states of the Organization and to the Secretary of the Court.
3. The jurisdiction of the Court shall comprise all cases concerning the interpretation and application of the provisions of this Convention that are submitted to it, provided that the States Parties to the case recognize or have recognized such jurisdiction, whether by special declaration pursuant to the preceding paragraphs, or by a special agreement.

Article 63

1. If the Court finds that there has been a violation of a right or freedom protected by this Convention, the Court shall rule that the injured party be ensured the enjoyment of his right or freedom that was violated. It shall also rule, if appropriate, that the consequences of the measure or situation that constituted the breach of such right or freedom be remedied and that fair compensation be paid to the injured party.
2. In cases of extreme gravity and urgency, and when necessary to avoid irreparable damage to persons, the Court shall adopt such provisional measures as it deems pertinent in matters it has under consideration. With respect to a case not yet submitted to the Court, it may act at the request of the Commission.

Article 64

1. The member states of the Organization may consult the Court regarding the interpretation of this Convention or of other treaties concerning the protection of human rights in the American states. Within their spheres of competence, the organs listed in Chapter X of the Charter of the Organization of American States, as amended by the Protocol of Buenos Aires, may in like manner consult the Court.
2. The Court, at the request of a member state of the Organization, may provide that state with opinions regarding the compatibility of any of its domestic laws with the aforesaid international instruments.

Article 65

To each regular session of the General Assembly of the Organization of American States the Court shall submit, for the Assembly's consideration, a report on its work during the previous year. It shall specify, in particular, the cases in which a state has not complied with its judgments, making any pertinent recommendations.

Section 3. Procedure

Article 66

1. Reasons shall be given for the judgment of the Court.
2. If the judgment does not represent in whole or in part the unanimous opinion of the judges, any judge shall be entitled to have his dissenting or separate opinion attached to the judgment.

Article 67

The judgment of the Court shall be final and not subject to appeal. In case of disagreement as to the meaning or scope of the judgment, the Court shall interpret it at the request of any of the parties, provided the request is made within ninety days from the date of notification of the judgment.

Article 68

1. The States Parties to the Convention undertake to comply with the judgment of the Court in any case to which they are parties.
2. That part of a judgment that stipulates compensatory damages may be executed in the country concerned in accordance with domestic procedure governing the execution of judgments against the state.

Article 69

The parties to the case shall be notified of the judgment of the Court and it shall be transmitted to the States Parties to the Convention.

Chapter IX – Common Provisions

Article 70

1. The judges of the Court and the members of the Commission shall enjoy, from the moment of their election and throughout their term of office, the immunities extended to

diplomatic agents in accordance with international law. During the exercise of their official function they shall, in addition, enjoy the diplomatic privileges necessary for the performance of their duties.
2. At no time shall the judges of the Court or the members of the Commission be held liable for any decisions or opinions issued in the excercise of their functions.

Article 71

The position of judge of the Court or member of the Commission is incompatible with any other activity that might affect the independence or impartiality of such judge or member, as determined in the respective statutes.

Article 72

The judges of the Court and the members of the Commission shall receive emoluments and travel allowances in the form and under the conditions set forth in their statutes, with due regard for the importance and independence of their office. Such emoluments and travel allowances shall be determined in the budget of the Organization of American States, which shall also include the expenses of the Court and its Secretariat. To this end, the Court shall draw up its own budget and submit it for approval to the General Assembly through the General Secretariat. The latter may not introduce any changes in it.

Article 73

The General Assembly may, only at the request of the Commission or the Court, as the case may be, determine sanctions to be applied against members of the Commission or judges of the Court when there are justifiable grounds for such action as set forth in the respective statutes. A vote of a two-thirds majority of the member states of the Organization shall be required for a decision in the case of members of the Commission and, in the case of judges of the Court, a two-thirds majority vote of the States Parties to the Convention shall also be required.

PART III - GENERAL AND TRANSITORY PROVISIONS

Chapter X – Signature, Ratification, Reservations, Amendments, Protocols, and Denuciations

Article 74

1. This Convention shall be open for signature and ratification by or adherence of any member state of the Organization of American States.
2. Ratification of or adherence to this Convention shall be made by the deposit of an instrument of ratification or adherence with the General Secretariat of the Organization of American States. As soon as eleven states have deposited their instruments of ratification or adherence, the Convention shall enter into force. With respect to any state that ratifies or adheres thereafter, the Convention shall enter into force on the date of the deposit of its instrument of ratification or adherence.
3. The Secretary General shall inform all member states of the Organization of the entry into force of the Convention.

Article 75

This Convention shall be subject to reservations only in conformity with the provisions of the Vienna Convention on the Law of Treaties signed on May 23, 1969.

Article 76

1. Proposals to amend this Convention may be submitted to the General Assembly for the action it deems appropriate by any State Party directly, and by the Commission or the Court through the Secretary General.
2. Amendments shall enter into force for the States ratifying them on the date when two-thirds of the States Parties to this Convention have deposited their respective instruments of ratification. With respect to the other States Parties, the amendments shall enter into force on the dates on which they deposit their respective instruments of ratification.

Article 77

1. In accordance with Article 31, any State Party and the Commission may submit proposed protocols to this Convention for consideration by the States Parties at the General Assembly with a view to gradually including other rights and freedoms within its system of protection.
2. Each protocol shall determine the manner of its entry into force and shall be applied only among the States Parties to it.

Article 78

1. The States Parties may denounce this Convention at the expiration of a five-year period from the date of its entry into force and by means of notice given one year in advance. Notice of the denunciation shall be addressed to the Secretary General of the Organization, who shall inform the other States Parties.
2. Such a denunciation shall not have the effect of releasing the State Party concerned from the obligations contained in this Convention with respect to any act that may constitute a violation of those obligations and that has been taken by that state prior to the effective date of denunciation.

Chapter XI – Transitory Provisions

Section 1. Inter-American Commission on Human Rights

Article 79

Upon the entry into force of this Convention, the Secretary General shall, in writing, request each member state of the Organization to present, within ninety days, its candidates for membership on the Inter-American Commission on Human Rights. The Secretary General shall prepare a list in alphabetical order of the candidates presented, and transmit it to the member states of the Organization at least thirty days prior to the next session of the General Assembly.

Article 80

The members of the Commission shall be elected by secret ballot of the General Assembly from the list of candidates referred to in Article 79. The candidates who obtain the largest number of votes and an absolute majority of the votes of the representatives of the member states shall be declared elected. Should it become necessary to have several ballots in order to elect all the members of the Commission, the candidates who receive the smallest number of votes shall be eliminated successively, in the manner determined by the General Assembly.

Section 2. Inter-American Court of Human Rights

Article 81

Upon the entry into force of this Convention, the Secretary General shall, in writing, request each State Party to present, within ninety days, its candidates for membership on the Inter-American Court of Human Rights. The Secretary General shall prepare a list in alphabetical order of the candidates presented and transmit it to the States Parties at least thirty days prior to the next session of the General Assembly.

Article 82

The judges of the Court shall be elected from the list of candidates referred to in Article 81, by secret ballot of the States Parties to the Convention in the General Assembly. The candidates who obtain the largest number of votes and an absolute majority of the votes of the representatives of the States Parties shall be declared elected. Should it become necessary to have several ballots in order to elect all the judges of the Court, the candidates who receive the smallest number of votes shall be eliminated successively, in the manner determined by the States Parties.

APPENDIX 6

Statute of the International Criminal Tribunal for the former Yugoslavia[6]

Having been established by the Security Council acting under Chapter VII of the Charter of the United Nations, the International Tribunal for the Prosecution of Persons Responsible for Serious Violations of International Humanitarian Law Committed in the Territory of the Former Yugoslavia since 1991 (hereinafter referred to as "the International Tribunal") shall function in accordance with the provisions of the present Statute.

Article 1 – Competence of the International Tribunal

The International Tribunal shall have the power to prosecute persons responsible for serious violations of international humanitarian law committed in the territory of the former Yugoslavia since 1991 in accordance with the provisions of the present Statute.

Article 2 – Grave breaches of the Geneva Conventions of 1949

The International Tribunal shall have the power to prosecute persons committing or ordering to be committed grave breaches of the Geneva Conventions of 12 August 1949, namely the following acts against persons or property protected under the provisions of the relevant Geneva Convention:

(a) wilful killing;
(b) torture or inhuman treatment, including biological experiments;
(c) wilfully causing great suffering or serious injury to body or health;
(d) extensive destruction and appropriation of property, not justified by military necessity and carried out unlawfully and wantonly;
(e) compelling a prisoner of war or a civilian to serve in the forces of a hostile power;
(f) wilfully depriving a prisoner of war or a civilian of the rights of fair and regular trial;
(g) unlawful deportation or transfer or unlawful confinement of a civilian;
(h) taking civilians as hostages.

Article 3 – Violations of the laws or customs of war

The International Tribunal shall have the power to prosecute persons violating the laws or customs of war. Such violations shall include, but not be limited to:

(a) employment of poisonous weapons or other weapons calculated to cause unnecessary suffering;
(b) wanton destruction of cities, towns or villages, or devastation not justified by military necessity;

---

[6] Adopted 25 May 1993 by the United Nations Security Council resolution 808, Amended 13 May 1998.

(c) attack, or bombardment, by whatever means, of undefended towns, villages, dwellings, or buildings;
(d) seizure of, destruction or wilful damage done to institutions dedicated to religion, charity and education, the arts and sciences, historic monuments and works of art and science;
(e) plunder of public or private property.

Article 4 – Genocide

1. The International Tribunal shall have the power to prosecute persons committing genocide as defined in paragraph 2 of this article or of committing any of the other acts enumerated in paragraph 3 of this article.
2. Genocide means any of the following acts committed with intent to destroy, in whole or in part, a national, ethnical, racial or religious group, as such:
   (a) killing members of the group;
   (b) causing serious bodily or mental harm to members of the group;
   (c) deliberately inflicting on the group conditions of life calculated to bring about its physical destruction in wholeor in part;
   (d) imposing measures intended to prevent births within the group;
   (e) forcibly transferring children of the group to another group.
3. The following acts shall be punishable:
   (a) genocide;
   (b) conspiracy to commit genocide;
   (c) direct and public incitement to commit genocide;
   (d) attempt to commit genocide;
   (e) complicity in genocide.

Article 5 – Crimes against humanity

The International Tribunal shall have the power to prosecute persons responsible for the following crimes when committed in armed conflict, whether international or internal in character, and directed against any civilian population:
(a) murder;
(b) extermination;
(c) enslavement;
(d) deportation;
(e) imprisonment;
(f) torture;
(g) rape;
(h) persecutions on political, racial and religious grounds;
(i) other inhumane acts.

Article 6 – Personal jurisdiction

The International Tribunal shall have jurisdiction over natural persons pursuant to the provisions of the present Statute.

Article 7 – Individual criminal responsibility

1. A person who planned, instigated, ordered, committed or otherwise aided and abetted in the planning, preparation or execution of a crime referred to in articles 2 to 5 of the present Statute, shall be individually responsible for the crime.

2. The official position of any accused person, whether as Head of State or Government or as a responsible Government official, shall not relieve such person of criminal responsibility nor mitigate punishment.
3. The fact that any of the acts referred to in articles 2 to 5 of the present Statute was committed by a subordinate does not relieve his superior of criminal responsibility if he knew or had reason to know that the subordinate was about to commit such acts or had done so and the superior failed to take the necessary and reasonable measures to prevent such acts or to punish the perpetrators thereof.
4. The fact that an accused person acted pursuant to an order of a Government or of a superior shall not relieve him of criminal responsibility, but may be considered in mitigation of punishment if the International Tribunal determines that justice so requires.

Article 8 – Territorial and temporal jurisdiction

The territorial jurisdiction of the International Tribunal shall extend to the territory of the former Socialist Federal Republic of Yugoslavia, including its land surface, airspace and territorial waters. The temporal jurisdiction of the International Tribunal shall extend to a period beginning on 1 January 1991.

Article 9 – Concurrent jurisdiction

1. The International Tribunal and national courts shall have concurrent jurisdiction to prosecute persons for serious violations of international humanitarian law committed in the territory of the former Yugoslavia since 1 January 1991.
2. The International Tribunal shall have primacy over national courts. At any stage of the procedure, the International Tribunal may formally request national courts to defer to the competence of the International Tribunal in accordance with the present Statute and the Rules of Procedure and Evidence of the International Tribunal.

Article 10 – Non-bis-in-idem

1. No person shall be tried before a national court for acts constituting serious violations of international humanitarian law under the present Statute, for which he or she has already been tried by the International Tribunal.
2. A person who has been tried by a national court for acts constituting serious violations of international humanitarian law may be subsequently tried by the International Tribunal only if:
   (a) the act for which he or she was tried was characterized as an ordinary crime; or
   (b) the national court proceedings were not impartial or independent, were designed to shield the accused frominternational criminal responsibility, or the case was not diligently prosecuted.
3. In considering the penalty to be imposed on a person convicted of a crime under the present Statute, the International Tribunal shall take into account the extent to which any penalty imposed by a national court on the same person for the same act has already been served.

Article 11 – Organization of the International Tribunal

The International Tribunal shall consist of the following organs:
(a) The Chambers, comprising three Trial Chambers and an Appeals Chamber;
(b) The Prosecutor, and
(c) A Registry, servicing both the Chambers and the Prosecutor.

Article 12 – Composition of the Chambers

The Chambers shall be composed of eleven independent judges, no two of whom may be nationals of the same State, who shall serve as follows:

(a) Three judges shall serve in each of the Trial Chambers;

(b) Five judges shall serve in the Appeals Chamber.

Article 13 – Qualifications and election of judges

1. The judges shall be persons of high moral character, impartiality and integrity who possess the qualifications required in their respective countries for appointment to the highest judicial offices. In the overall composition of the Chambers due account shall be taken of the experience of the judges in criminal law, international law, including international humanitarian law and human rights law.

2. The judges of the International Tribunal shall be elected by the General Assembly from a list submitted by the Security Council, in the following manner:

(a) The Secretary-General shall invite nominations for judges of the International Tribunal from States Members of the United Nations and non-member States maintaining permanent observer missions at United Nations Headquarters;

(b) Within sixty days of the date of the invitation of the Secretary-General, each State may nominate up to two candidates meeting the qualifications set out in paragraph 1 above, no two of whom shall be of the same nationality;

(c) The Secretary-General shall forward the nominations received to the Security Council. From the nominations received the Security Council shall establish a list of not less than twenty-two and not more than thirty-three candidates, taking due account of the adequate representation of the principal legal systems of the world;

(d) The President of the Security Council shall transmit the list of candidates to the President of the General Assembly. From that list the General Assembly shall elect the eleven judges of the International Tribunal. The candidates who receive an absolute majority of the votes of the States Members of the United Nations and of the non-Member States maintaining permanent observer missions at United Nations Headquarters, shall be declared elected. Should two candidates of the same nationality obtain the required majority vote, the one who received the higher number of votes shall be considered elected.

3. In the event of a vacancy in the Chambers, after consultation with the Presidents of the Security Council and of the General Assembly, the Secretary-General shall appoint a person meeting the qualifications of paragraph 1 above, for the remainder of the term of office concerned.

4. The judges shall be elected for a term of four years. The terms and conditions of service shall be those of the judges of the International Court of Justice. They shall be eligible for re-election.

Article 14 – Officers and members of the Chambers

1. The judges of the International Tribunal shall elect a President.

2. The President of the International Tribunal shall be a member of the Appeals Chamber and shall preside over its proceedings.

3. After consultation with the judges of the International Tribunal, the President shall assign the judges to the Appeals Chamber and to the Trial Chambers. A judge shall serve only in the Chamber to which he or she was assigned.

4. The judges of each Trial Chamber shall elect a Presiding Judge, who shall conduct all of the proceedings of the Trial Chamber as a whole.

Article 15 – Rules of procedure and evidence

The judges of the International Tribunal shall adopt rules of procedure and evidence for the conduct of the pre-trial phase of the proceedings, trials and appeals, the admission of evidence, the protection of victims and witnesses and other appropriate matters.

Article 16 – The Prosecutor

1. The Prosecutor shall be responsible for the investigation and prosecution of persons responsible for serious violations of international humanitarian law committed in the territory of the former Yugoslavia since 1 January 1991.
2. The Prosecutor shall act independently as a separate organ of the International Tribunal. He or she shall not seek or receive instructions from any Government or from any other source.
3. The Office of the Prosecutor shall be composed of a Prosecutor and such other qualified staff as may be required.
4. The Prosecutor shall be appointed by the Security Council on nomination by the Secretary-General. He or she shall be of high moral character and possess the highest level of competence and experience in the conduct of investigations and prosecutions of criminal cases. The Prosecutor shall serve for a four-year term and be eligible for reappointment. The terms and conditions of service of the Prosecutor shall be those of an Under-Secretary-General of the United Nations.
5. The staff of the Office of the Prosecutor shall be appointed by the Secretary-General on the recommendation of the Prosecutor.

Article 17 – The Registry

1. The Registry shall be responsible for the administration and servicing of the International Tribunal.
2. The Registry shall consist of a Registrar and such other staff as may be required.
3. The Registrar shall be appointed by the Secretary-General after consultation with the President of the International Tribunal. He or she shall serve for a four-year term and be eligible for reappointment. The terms and conditions of service of the Registrar shall be those of an Assistant Secretary-General of the United Nations.
4. The staff of the Registry shall be appointed by the Secretary-General on the recommendation of the Registrar.

Article 18 – Investigation and preparation of indictment

1. The Prosecutor shall initiate investigations ex-officio or on the basis of information obtained from any source, particularly from Governments, United Nations organs, intergovernmental and non-governmental organizations. The Prosecutor shall assess the information received or obtained and decide whether there is sufficient basis to proceed.
2. The Prosecutor shall have the power to question suspects, victims and witnesses, to collect evidence and to conduct on-site investigations. In carrying out these tasks, the Prosecutor may, as appropriate, seek the assistance of the State authorities concerned.
3. If questioned, the suspect shall be entitled to be assisted by counsel of his own choice, including the right to have legal assistance assigned to him without payment by

him in any such case if he does not have sufficient means to pay for it, as well as to necessary translation into and from a language he speaks and understands.

4. Upon a determination that a prima facie case exists, the Prosecutor shall prepare an indictment containing a concise statement of the facts and the crime or crimes with which the accused is charged under the Statute. The indictment shall be transmitted to a judge of the Trial Chamber.

Article 19 – Review of the indictment.

1. The judge of the Trial Chamber to whom the indictment has been transmitted shall review it. If satisfied that a prima facie case has been established by the Prosecutor, he shall confirm the indictment. If not so satisfied, the indictment shall be dismissed.

2. Upon confirmation of an indictment, the judge may, at the request of the Prosecutor, issue such orders and warrants for the arrest, detention, surrender or transfer of persons, and any other orders as may be required for the conduct of the trial.

Article 20 – Commencement and conduct of trial proceedings

1. The Trial Chambers shall ensure that a trial is fair and expeditious and that proceedings are conducted in accordance with the rules of procedure and evidence, with full respect for the rights of the accused and due regard for the protection of victims and witnesses.

2. A person against whom an indictment has been confirmed shall, pursuant to an order or an arrest warrant of the International Tribunal, be taken into custody, immediately informed of the charges against him and transferred to the International Tribunal.

3. The Trial Chamber shall read the indictment, satisfy itself that the rights of the accused are respected, confirm that the accused understands the indictment, and instruct that the accused enter a plea. The trial Chamber shall then set the date for trial.

4. The hearings shall be public unless the Trial Chamber decides to close the proceedings in accordance with its rules of procedure and evidence.

Article 21 – Rights of the accused

1. All persons shall be equal before the International Tribunal.

2. In the determination of charges against him, the accused shall be entitled to a fair and public hearing, subject to article 22 of the Statute.

3. The accused shall be presumed innocent until proved guilty according to the provisions of the present Statute.

4. In the determination of any charge against the accused pursuant to the present Statute, the accused shall be entitled to the following minimum guarantees, in full equality:

(a) to be informed promptly and in detail in a language which he understands of the nature and cause of the charge against him;

(b) to have adequate time and facilities for the preparation of his defence and to communicate with counsel of his own choosing;

(c) to be tried without undue delay;

(d) to be tried in his presence, and to defend himself in person or through legal assistance of his own choosing; to be informed, if he does not have legal assistance, of this right; and to have legal assistance assigned to him, in any case where the interests of justice so require, and without payment by him in any such case if he does not have sufficient means to pay for it;

(e) to examine, or have examined, the witnesses against him and to obtain the attendance and examination of witnesses on his behalf under the same conditions as witnesses against him;

(f) to have the free assistance of an interpreter if he cannot understand or speak the language used in the International Tribunal;

(g) not to be compelled to testify against himself or to confess guilt.

Article 22 – Protection of victims and witnesses

The International Tribunal shall provide in its rules of procedure and evidence for the protection of victims and witnesses. Such protection measures shall include, but shall not be limited to, the conduct of in camera proceedings and the protection of the victim's identity.

Article 23 – Judgement.

1. The Trial Chambers shall pronounce judgements and impose sentences and penalties on persons convicted of serious violations of international humanitarian law.
2. The judgement shall be rendered by a majority of the judges of the Trial Chamber, and shall be delivered by the Trial Chamber in public. It shall be accompanied by a reasoned opinion in writing, to which separate or dissenting opinions may be appended.

Article 24 – Penalties

1. The penalty imposed by the Trial Chamber shall be limited to imprisonment. In determining the terms of imprisonment, the Trial Chambers shall have recourse to the general practice regarding prison sentences in the courts of the former Yugoslavia.
2. In imposing the sentences, the Trial Chambers should take into account such factors as the gravity of the offence and the individual circumstances of the convicted person.
3. In addition to imprisonment, the Trial Chambers may order the return of any property and proceeds acquired by criminal conduct, including by means of duress, to their rightful owners.

Article 25 – Appellate proceedings

1. The Appeals Chamber shall hear appeals from persons convicted by the Trial Chambers or from the Prosecutor on the following grounds:
   (a) an error on a question of law invalidating the decision; or
   (b) an error of fact which has occasioned a miscarriage of justice.
2. The Appeals Chamber may affirm, reverse or revise the decisions taken by the Trial Chambers.

Article 26 – Review proceedings

Where a new fact has been discovered which was not known at the time of the proceedings before the Trial Chambers or the Appeals Chamber and which could have been a decisive factor in reaching the decision, the convicted person or the Prosecutor may submit to the International Tribunal an application for review of the judgement.

Article 27 – Enforcement of sentences

Imprisonment shall be served in a State designated by the International Tribunal from a list of States which have indicated to the Security Council their willingness to accept convicted persons. Such imprisonment shall be in accordance with the applicable law of the State concerned, subject to the supervision of the International Tribunal.

Article 28 – Pardon or commutation of sentences

If, pursuant to the applicable law of the State in which the convicted person is imprisoned, he or she is eligible for pardon or commutation of sentence, the State concerned shall notify the International Tribunal accordingly. The President of the International Tribunal, in consultation with the judges, shall decide the matter on the basis of the interests of justice and the general principles of law.

Article 29 – Cooperation and judicial assistance.

1. States shall cooperate with the International Tribunal in the investigation and prosecution of persons accused of committing serious violations of international humanitarian law.
2. States shall comply without undue delay with any request for assistance or an order issued by a Trial Chamber, including, but not limited to:
   (a) the identification and location of persons;
   (b) the taking of testimony and the production of evidence;
   (c) the service of documents;
   (d) the arrest or detention of persons;
   (e) the surrender or the transfer of the accused to the International Tribunal.

Article 30 – The status, privileges and immunities of the International Tribunal

1. The Convention on the Privileges and Immunities of the United Nations of 13 February 1946 shall apply to the International Tribunal, the judges, the Prosecutor and his staff, and the Registrar and his staff.
2. The judges, the Prosecutor and the Registrar shall enjoy the privileges and immunities, exemptions and facilities accorded to diplomatic envoys, in accordance with international law.
3. The staff of the Prosecutor and of the Registrar shall enjoy the privileges and immunities accorded to officials of the United Nations under articles V and VII of the Convention referred to in paragraph 1 of this article.
4. Other persons, including the accused, required at the seat of the International Tribunal shall be accorded such treatment as is necessary for the proper functioning of the International Tribunal.

Article 31 – Seat of the International Tribunal

The International Tribunal shall have its seat at The Hague.

Article 32 – Expenses of the International Tribunal

The expenses of the International Tribunal shall be borne by the regular budget of the United Nations in accordance with Article 17 of the Charter of the United Nations.

Article 33 – Working languages

The working languages of the International Tribunal shall be English and French.

Article 34 – Annual report

The President of the International Tribunal shall submit an annual report of the International Tribunal to the Security Council and to the General Assembly.

APPENDIX 7

The Treaty of Amsterdam amending the Treaty on European Union[7]

Article 35

1. The Court of Justice of the European Communities shall have jurisdiction, subject to the conditions laid down in this Article, to give preliminary rulings on the validity and interpretation of framework decisions and decisions, on the interpretation of conventions established under this Title and on the validity and interpretation of the measures implementing them.
2. By a declaration made at the time of signature of the Treaty of Amsterdam or at any time thereafter, any Member State shall be able to accept the jurisdiction of the Court of Justice to give preliminary rulings as specified in paragraph 1.
3. A Member State making a declaration pursuant to paragraph 2 shall specify that either:
   (a) any court or tribunal of that State against whose decisions there is no judicial remedy under national law may request the Court of Justice to give a preliminary ruling on a question raised in a case pending before it and concerning the validity or interpretation of an act referred to in paragraph 1 if that court or tribunal considers that a decision on the question is necessary to enable it to give judgment, or
   (b) any court or tribunal of that State may request the Court of Justice to give a preliminary ruling on a question raised in a case pending before it and concerning the validity or interpretation of an act referred to in paragraph 1 if that court or tribunal considers that a decision on the question is necessary to enable it to give judgment.
4. Any Member State, whether or not it has made a declaration pursuant to paragraph 2, shall be entitled to submit statements of case or written observations to the Court in cases which arise under paragraph 1.
5. The Court of Justice shall have no jurisdiction to review the validity or proportionality of operations carried out by the police or other law enforcement services of a Member State or the exercise of the responsibilities incumbent upon Member States with regard to the maintenance of law and order and the safeguarding of internal security.
6. The Court of Justice shall have jurisdiction to review the legality of framework decisions and decisions in actions brought by a Member State or the Commission on grounds of lack of competence, infringement of an essential procedural requirement, infringement of this Treaty or of any rule of law relating to its application, or misuse of powers. The proceedings provided for in this paragraph shall be instituted within two months of the publication of the measure.
7. The Court of Justice shall have jurisdiction to rule on any dispute between Member States regarding the interpretation or the application of acts adopted under Article 34(2) whenever such dispute cannot be settled by the Council within six months of its being referred to the Council by one of its members. The Court shall also have jurisdiction to rule on any dispute between Member States and the Commission regarding the interpretation or the application of conventions established under Article 34(2)(d).

---

[7] The Treaty of Amsterdam amending the Treaty on European Union, the Treaties establishing the European Communities and Certain Related Acts, 10 November 1997.

SELECTED BIBLIOGRAPHY

Treaties and Monographs

ABBÉ DE SAINT-PIERRE, *Project pour rendre la paix perpétuelle en Europe (1723)*, 1986.
ADEDE, A. O., *The System for Settlement of Disputes under the United Nations Convention on the Law of the Sea: A Drafting History and a Commentary*, 1987.
ANDRÉ, Alexandre, *De l'Arbitrage obligatoire dans les rapports internationaux*, 1903.
ALEXANDROV, Stanimir A., *Reservations in Unilateral Declarations Accepting the Compulsory Jurisdiction of the International Court of Justice*, 1995.
ANAND, Ram Prakash, *Compulsory Jurisdiction of the International Court of Justice*, 1961.
———, *Studies in International Adjudication*, 1974.
———, *International Courts and Contemporary Conflicts*, 1974.
BALDWIN, Simeon E., *The New Era of International Courts*, 1910.
BASSIOUNI, Cherif, *Commentaries on the International Law Commission's 1991 Draft Code of Crimes Against the Peace and Security of Mankind*, 1993.
BARBOSA, M. Ruy, *Dieuxième Conférence de la Paix: Actes et Discours*, 1907.
BEALES, A. C. F., *The History of Peace: A Short Account of the Organised Movements for International Peace*, 1931.
BOULERY, Catharine, *Bibliography of the Peaceful Settlement of International Disputes*, 1990.
BRACKMAN, Andrew, *The Other Nuremberg: The Untold Story of the Tokyo War Crimes Trials*, 1987.
BROWN, L. Neville and Tom Kennedy, *The Court of Justice of the European Communities* (4th ed.), 1994.
CECILLIA, Medina, *The Battle of Human Rights: Gross, Systematic Violations and the Inter-American System*, 1988.
CORY, Helen May, *Compulsory Arbitration of International Disputes*, 1932.
COT, Jean-Pierre and Alain Pellet, *La Charte des Nations unies*, 1989.
CRAIG, Paul and Cráinne De Búrca (eds.), *EU Law: Texts, Cases, and Materials* (2nd ed.), 1998.
———, *The Evolution of EU Law*, 1999.
DAVIDSON, Scott, *The Inter-American Court of Human Rights*, 1992.
DAMROSCH, Lori F. (ed.), *The International Court of Justice at the Crossroads*, 1987.
DARDY, W. Evans, *International Tribunals: A Collection of Various Schemes which have Propounded; and of Instances in the Nineteenth Century*, (4 ed.), 1904.
———, *Modern Pacific Settlements Involving the Application of the Principles of International Arbitration*, 1904.
DAVIS, Calvin D., *The United State and the First Hague Peace Conference*, 1962.
———, *The United State and the Second Hague Peace Conference*, 1975.
DAVIS, Hayne, *Among the World's Peacemakers*, 1907.
DE LAPRADELLE, A. and N. Politis, *Recueil des arbitrages internationaux*, (three volumes), 1905, 1923, and 1954.
DICEY, A.V., *Introduction to the Study of Law of the Constitution*, (10th ed.) 1960.
DOUMA, J., *Bibliography of the International Court Including the Permanent Court*, 1966.
EGGER, E., *Étude historique sur les traités publique chez les Grecs et chez les Romain*, 1866.
EVANS, Howard, *Sir Randal Cremer: His Life Work*, 1909.
EYMA, Jean, *La Cour de Justice Centre Américane*, 1928.
FALK, Richard, *Reviving the World Court*, 1986.
GULIERREZ, Carlos Jose, *La Corte de Justicia Centroamericana*, 1978.
HOYOSA, C., *el al.* (eds.), *The Tokyo War Crimes Trial: An International Symposium*, 1986.
HUDSON, Manley O., *Is the World Court Important?*, 1925.

HUDSON, Manley O., *The World Court, (1921-1931)*, 1931.
———, *The Permanent Court of International Justice: A Treatise*, 1934.
———, *The Permanent Court of International Justice 1920-1942: A Treatise*, 1943.
———, *International Tribunals: Past and Present*, 1944.
HULL, William, *The Two Hague Conferences and their Contributions to International Law*, 1908.
JAY, William, *War and Peace: The Evils of the First and a Plan for Preserving the Last*, J. B. Scott (ed.), 1919.
JANIS, Mark W. (ed.), *International Courts for the Twenty-First Century*, 1992.
JENKS, C. Wilfred, *The Prospects of International Adjudication*, 1964.
JENNINGS, Robert, *International Courts and International Politics*, 1986.
KATZ, Milton, *The Relevance of International Adjudication*, 1968.
KELSEN, Hans, *Law and Peace in International Relations*, 1949.
LADD, William, *An Essay on a Congress of Nations for the Adjustment of International Disputes without Resort to Arms, (1840)*, 1916.
LA FONTAINE, Henri, *International Judicature*, 1915.
———, *Pasicrisie Internationale: Histoire documentaire des arbitrages internationaux (1794-1900)*, 1902.
LANGE, Christian, *L'Arbitrage obligatoire entre nation en 1913*, 1914.
LANGLADE, Edouard, *De la clause compromissoire et des traités d'arbitrage permanent*, 1899.
LATANÉ, John H. and David W. Wainhouse, *A History of American Foreign Policy, 1776-1940*, 1941.
LAUTERPACHT, Hersch, *The Development of International Law by International Courts*, 1958.
LECOURT, Robert, *L'Europe des Judges*, 1976.
LODER, B. C. J., *The Permanent Court of International Justice*, 1920.
MALAUZAT, Auguste, *La Cour de justice arbitral*, 1914.
MANNING, William R., *Arbitration Treaties among the American Nations to the Close of the Year 1910*, 1924.
MINEAR, Richard, *Victor's Justice: The Tokyo War Crimes Trials*, 1971.
MERRILLS, John Graham, *International Judicial Settlement*, 1991.
MOSLER, Herman and Rudolf Bernhardt, *Judicial Settlement of International Disputes*, 1974.
MULLINS, Claude, *The Leipzig Trials: An Account of the War Criminals Trials and a Study of German Mentality*, 1921.
OELLERS-FRAHN, Karin and Norbert Wühler, *Dispute Settlement in Public International Law*, 1984.
POLITIS, Nicolas, *La justice internationale*, 1924.
RASMUSSEN, Hjalte, *On Law and Policy in the European Court of Justice*, 1986.
RHYNE, Charles S., *A Grand Design for World Peace: The Rule of Law*, 1961.
ROLIN, Albéric, *Les origines de l'Institut de droit international*, 1923.
RÖLING, B.V.A. and Antonio Cassese, *The Tokyo Trial and Beyond: Reflections of a Peacemonger*, 1993.
RÖLING, B.V.A. and Rüter (eds.), *The International Military Tribunal for the Far East*, 1997.
ROSENNE, Shabtai, *The Law and Practice of the International Court*, 1998.
SCHWARZENBERGER, Georg, *William Ladd: An Examination of an American Proposal for an International Equity Tribunal*, 1935.
SCOTT, James Brown, *The Project of a Permanent Court of International Justice and Resolutions of the Advisory Committee of Jurists: Report and Commentary*, 1920.
SOONS, A.H.A. (ed.), *International Arbitration: Past and Prospects*, 1989.
STUYT, A.M., *Survey of International Arbitration (1794-1989)*, 1990.
SYBESMA-KNOL, Neri (ed.), *The Compulsory Jurisdiction of International Court of Justice: A Turing Point?*, 1991.
SZAFARZ, Renata, *The Compulsory Jurisdiction of the International Court of Justice*, 1993.
THÉVENAZ, Henri, *Les compromis d'arbitrage devant la Cour permanente de justice internationale*, 1938.

VAN STAUFENBERG, B. Schenk, *Statut et Règlement de la Cour permanente de Justice international*, 1934.
VASAK, Karel, *La Commission interaméricanne des droits de l'homme*, 1968.
WARREN, Tully Evans, *The Projected Inter-American Court of Justice as a Part of the Inter-American Peace Machinery*, 1950.

Contributions to Periodicals and Other Collective Works

ALBORS-LLORENS, Albertina, "Changes in the Jurisdiction of the European Court of Justice under the Treaty of Amsterdam", *Common Market Law Review*, Vol. 35, 1998, pp. 1273-1294.
ALLAIN, Jean and John R.W.D. Jones, "A Patchwork of Norms: A Commentary on the 1996 Draft Code of Crimes against the Peace and Security of Mankind", *European Journal of International Law*, Vol. 8, 1997, pp. 100-117.
ALLAIN, Jean, "The Evolution of Dispute Settlement in Africa: From Pacifism to Militarism", *South African Yearbook of International Law*, Vol. 23, 1998, pp. 65-92.
———, "Judicial Independence in Practice: The Case of Judge Odio Benito, Vice-President of Costa Rica", *Revue de droit international de science diplomatiques et politiques (International Law Review)*, Vol. 77, 1999, pp. 1-22.
BASDEVANT, M., "Premier litige porté devant la Cour de justice permanente Centre-américaine", *Revue générale de droit international public*, Vol. 16, 1909, pp. 99-107.
BEDJAOUI, Mohammed, "The 'Manufacture' of Judgments at the International Court of Justice", *Pace Yearbook of International Law*, Vol. 3, 1991, pp. 29-61.
BILDER, Richard B., "Some Limitations of Adjudication as a International Settlement Technique", *Virginia Journal of International Law*, Vol. 23, 1983, pp. 1-12.
BOREL, E. and N. Politis (Rapporteurs), "L'Extension de l'arbitrage obligatoire et la compétence obligatoire de la Cour permanente de Justice internationale", *Annuaire de l'Institut de droit international*, Vol. 2, 1927, pp. 669-761; and Observations, pp. 762-834.
BOUKRIF, Hamid, "La Cour africaine des droit de l'homme et des peuples: un organe judiciaire au service droit de l'homme et des peuples en Afrique", *African Journal of International and Comparative Law*, Vol. 10, 1998, pp. 60-88.
BRIERLY, James L., "the Rule of Law in International Society", Hersch Lauterpacht, and C. Waldock (eds.), *The Basis of Obligation in International Law and Other Papers*, 1958, pp. 250-264.
BRIGGS, Herbert W., "Reservations to the Acceptance of Compulsory Jurisdiction of the International Court of Justice, *Collected Courses of The Hague Academy of International Law*, Vol. 93, 1958, pp. 229-363.
BROWNLIE, Ian, "The Peaceful Settlement of International Disputes, *Pace International Law Review*, Vol. 7, 1995, pp. 257-281.
BUERGENTHAL, Thomas, "Self-Executing and Non-Self-Executing Treaties in National and International Law", *Collected Courses of The Hague Academy of International Law*, Vol. 235, 1992, pp. 303-400.
CAFLISCH, Lucius, "L'avenir de l'arbitrage interétatique", *Annuaire français de droit international*, Vol. 25, 1979, pp. 9-45.
CAHIER, Phillip, "Cours général de droit international public", *Collected Courses of The Hague Academy of International Law*, Vol. 195, 1985, pp. 9-374.
CERNA, Christina, "The Structure and Functioning of the Inter-American Court of Human Rights (1979-1992)", *The British Yearbook of International Law*, Vol. 63, 1992, pp. 135-230.
CURTIN, Deirdre, "The Constitutional Structure of the Union: A Europe of Bits and Pieces", *Common Market Law Review*, Vol. 30, 1993, pp. 17-69.
DUE, Ole, "The Impact of the Amsterdam Treaty upon the Court of Justice", *Fordham International Law Journal*, Vol. 22, 1999, pp. S48-S71.
DE VISSCHER, Charles, "Reflections on the Present Prospects of International Adjudication", *American Journal of International Law*, Vol. 50, 1956, pp. 465-474.

DRZEMCZEWSKI, Andrew, "The Major Overhaul of the European Human Rights Convention Control Mechanism: Protocol No. 11", *Collected Courses of the Academy of European Law*, Vol. 6, 1995, pp. 121-245.

ESPIELL, Héctor Gros, "La Convention américaine et la Convention européenne des droits de l'homme", *Collected Courses of The Hague Academy of International Law*, Vol. 89, 1989, pp. 175-410.

FINCH, George A., "The Treaty with Nicaragua Granting Canal and Other Rights to The United States", *American Journal of International Law*, Vol. 10, 1916, pp. 344-351.

FITZMAURICE, Gerald, "The General Principles of International Law considered form the Standpoint of the Rule of Law", *Collected Courses of The Hague Academy of International Law*, Vol. 92 (II), 1957, pp. 5-222.

FRANÇOIS, M.J.P.A., "La Cour permanente d'arbitrage, son origine, sa jurisprudence, son avenir", *Collected Courses of The Hague Academy of International Law*, Vol. 87, 1955, pp. 460-551.

FROWEIN, Jochen A., "The European and The American Conventions on Human Rights – A Comparison", *Human Rights Law Journal*, Vol. 1, 1980, pp. 44-65.

GIUSTINI, Antony, "Compulsory Adjudication in International Law: The Past, The Present and Prospects for the Future", *Fordham International Law Journal*, Vol. 9, 1985-1986, pp. 213-256.

GREY, Christine and Benedict Kingsbury, "Inter-State Arbitration since 1945: Overview and Evaluation", M. W. Janis (ed.), *International Courts for the Twenty-First Century*, 1992, pp. 55-83.

GUGGENHEIM, Paul, "L'élaboration d'une clause modèle de compétence obligatoire de la Cour international de Justice", Annuire de l'Institut de droit international, Vol. 44, 1952, pp. 458-468.

GUILLAUME, Gilbert, "The Future of International Judicial Institutions", *International and Comparative Law Quarterly*, Vol. 44, 1995, pp. 848-862.

HELFER, Laurence R. and Anne-Marie Slaughter, "Towards a Theory of Effective Supranational Adjudication", *Yale Law Journal*, vol. 107, 1997, pp. 276-391.

HUDSON, Manley, "Central American Court of Justice", *The American Journal of International Law*, Vol. 26, 1932, pp. 759-786.

———, "The Permanent Court of Arbitration", *American Journal of International Law*, Vol. 27, 1933, pp. 440-460.

JACOT-GUILLARMOD, Oliver, "Protocol No. 11 to the European Convention on Human Rights: a response to some recent criticisms", *Yearbook of the European Convention on Human Rights*, Vol. 38A, 1995, pp. 172-188.

JANIS, Mark. W., "The International Court", M. W. Janis, (ed.), *International Courts for the Twenty-First Century*, 1992, pp. 13-41.

JENKS, C. Wilfred, "Regionalism in International Judicial Organizations", *American Journal of International Law*, Vol. 37, 1943, pp. 314-320.

JIMÉNEZ DE ARÉCHAGA, E., "The Compulsory Jurisdiction of the International Court of Justice under the Pact of Bogotá and the Optional Clause, *International Law at a Time of Perplexity: Essays in Honour of Shabtai Rosenne*, 1989, pp. 355-360.

KRIEGER, David, "A Permanent International Criminal Court and the United Nations System", N. Al-Nauimi and R. Meese (eds.), *International Legal Issues Arising under the United Nations Decade of International Law*, 1995, pp. 761-792.

KELSEN, Hans, "Compulsory Adjudication and International Disputes", *American Journal of International Law*, Vol. 37, 1943, pp. 397-406.

LACH, Manfred, "The Development and General Trends on International Law in our Time", *Collected Courses of The Hague Academy of International Law*, Vol. 169, 1980, pp. 9-377.

LANGE, Chritian L., "Histoire de la doctrine pacifique et de son influence sur le développement du droit international", *Collected Courses of The Hague Academy of International Law*, Vol. 13, 1926, pp.171-426.

LAUTERPACHT, Hersch, "The Absence of an International Legislature and the Compulsory

Jurisdiction of International Tribunals", *The British Yearbook of International Law*, 1930, pp. 134-157.

MARSHALL-BROWN, Ph. and N. Politis, "La classification des conflits comportant un reglement judiciaire", *Annuaire de l'Insitute de droit international*, 1922, pp. 23-58.

MATTLI, Walter and Anne-Marie Slaughter, "Revisiting the European Court of Justice", *International Organizations*, vol. 52, 1998, pp. 177-209.

MCWHINNEY, Edward, "International Arbitration and International Adjudication: the Different Contemporary Lots of the Two Hague Tribunals", *Canadian Yearbook of International Law*, Vol. 29, 1991, pp. 403-412.

MURDOCK, James Oliver, "The Organization of a Postwar International Judicial System", *World Affairs*, Vol. 107, 1944, p. 257-259.

PLENDER, Richard "The European Court as an International Tribunal", *Cambridge Law Journal*, Vol. 42, 1983, pp. 279-289.

QUIGLEY, John, "Prospects for the International Rule of Law", *Emory International Law Review*, Vol. 5, 1991, pp. 311-320.

QUINTANA, J.J., "The Hague Declaration and the Acceptance of the Compulsory Jurisdiction of the International Court of Justice: A Missed Opportunity?", M. Brus, S. Muller and S. Wiemers (eds.), *The United Nations Decade of International Law: Reflections on International Dispute Settlement*, 1991, pp. 43-49.

RASMUSSEN, Hjalte, "Between Self-Restraint and Activism: A Judicial Policy for the European Court", *European Law Review*, Vol. 13, 1988, pp. 28-38.

RUEGGER, Paul, "Des clauses arbitrales et de juridiction dans les conventions internationales récentes", *Recueil d'études de droit international en hommage à Paul Guggenheim*, 1968, pp. 687-701.

SAHOVIC, Milan, "The Concept of International Law at the End of the Twentieth Century", P.S. Pathak and R.P. Dhokalia (eds.), *International Law in Transition*, 1992, pp. 86-93.

SCHINDLER, Dietrich, "Les Progrès de l'arbitrage obligatoire depuis la création de la Société des nations", *Collected Courses of The Hague Academy of International Law*, Vol. 25, 1928, pp. 237-361.

SCHACHTER, Oscar, "Creativity and Objectivity in International Tribunals", *Völkerrecht als Rechtsordnung Internationale Gerichtsbarkeit Menschenrechte: Festschrift für Hermann Mosler*, 1983, pp. 813-821.

SCOTT, James Brown, "The Evolution of a Permanent International Judiciary", *American Journal of International Law*, Vol. 6, 1912, pp. 316-358.

———, "The Closing of the Central American Court of Justice", *American Journal of International Law*, Vol. 12, 1918, pp. 380-382.

SETTE-CAMARA, José, "Methods of Obligatory Settlement of Disputes", M. Bedjaoui (ed.) *International Law: Achievements and Prospects*, 1991, pp. 519-544.

SHELTON, Dinah, "The Jurisprudence of the Inter-American Court of Human Rights", *The American University Journal of International Law and Policy*, Vol. 10, 1994, pp. 333-373.

SHRAGA, Daphna and Ralph Zacklin, "The International Criminal Tribunal for the former Yugoslavia", *European Journal of International Law*, Vol. 5, 1994, pp. 360-380.

SOHN, Louis B., "The Function of International Arbitration Today", *Collected Courses of The Hague Academy of International Law*, Vol. 108, 1963, pp. 205-292.

———, "Settlement of Disputes Relating to the Interpretation and Application of Treaties", *Collected Courses of The Hague Academy of International Law*, Vol. 150, 1976, pp. 195-294.

———, "The Role of Arbitration in Recent International Multilateral Treaties", *Virginia Journal of International Law*, Vol. 23, 1983, pp. 171-189.

———, "The Future of Dispute Settlement", R. St. J. MacDonald and D.M. Johnston (eds.), *The Structure and Process of International Law*, 1983, pp. 1121-1146.

———, "Peaceful Settlement of Disputes", M. W. Janis, (ed.), *International Courts for the Twenty-First Century*, 1992, pp. 3-8.

TOMUSCHAT, Christian, "International Courts and Tribunals with Regionally Restricted and/or Specialized Jurisdiction", H. Mosler, and R. Bernhardt (eds.), *Judicial Settlement of International Disputes*, 1974, pp. 285-416.

TRIDIMAS, Takis, "The Court of Justice and Judicial Activism", *European Law Review*, Vol. 21, 1996, pp. 199-210.

WALP, P., "The Central American Court of Justice", *Revue de droit international*, Vol. 1, 1927, pp. 89-108.

WATTS, Arthur, "The International Rule of Law", *German Yearbook of International Law*, Vol. 36, 1993, pp. 15-45.

WEERAMANTRY, Christopher, "The Function of the International Court of Justice in the Development of International Law", *Leiden Journal of International Law*, vol. 10, 1997, pp. 309-340.

WEILER, Joseph, "The European Courts of Justice: Beyond 'Beyond Doctrine' or the Legitimacy Crisis of European Constitutionalism", Anne-Marie Slaughter, A.S. Sweet, and J.H.H. Weiler (eds.), *The European Courts and National Courts*, 1998, pp. 365-391.

WILSON, Robert R., "Clauses Relating to Reference of Disputes in Obligatory Arbitration Treaties", *American Journal of International Law*, Vol. 25, 1931, pp. 469-489.

———, "Reservation Clauses in Agreements for Obligatory Arbitration", *American Journal of International Law*, Vol. 23, 1929, pp. 68-93.